IN PARENTING, BALANCE IS THE KEY . . .

- Learn when to say "no," when to say "yes," and when to try "maybe."
- Decide for yourself if your child should sleep in his own room or in your bed—regardless of what the "sleep experts" say.
- Consider what you are really teaching your child when you are "matter-of-fact" about sex, body parts, and babies.
- Decide for yourself what your child should eat using common sense instead of a measuring cup.
- The best way to stop sibling rivalry is never to create it in the first place. Head this avoidable family problem off at the pass, even if the "sibling experts" have you all revved up to expect it.
- Think what we are really teaching about racism when we pretend race itself doesn't exist.
- Encourage ways that do not foster gender stereotypes—yet let them be boys and girls.

From day care, enrichment classes, and toddler chores to dealing with homeless people, from choosing a pediatrician to confronting death; for full-time moms trying to get your dawdler out of the house and working moms trying to make home time the best time, there's something here that just might help you if you have a baby, toddler, or preschooler.

BIG LESSONS
FOR LITTLE PEOPLE

*Teaching Our Kids Right from Wrong
While Keeping Them Healthy, Safe, and Happy*

Lois Nachamie

*Best wishes,
Lois Nachamie*

A DELL TRADE PAPERBACK

A DELL TRADE PAPERBACK

Published by
Dell Publishing
a division of
Bantam Doubleday Dell Publishing Group, Inc.
1540 Broadway
New York, New York 10036

Library of Congress Cataloging in Publication Data
Nachamie, Lois.
Big lessons for little people / Lois Nachamie.
p.   cm.
ISBN 0-440-50740-5 (pbk.)
1. Child rearing.   2. Parenting.   3. Moral education (Early childhood)
I. Title.
HQ769.N195   1997
649′.1—dc20   96-44877
CIP

Printed in the United States of America

Published simultaneously in Canada

August 1997

10   9   8   7   6   5   4   3   2   1

CONTENTS

Part II: AT HOME

Part III: OUT IN THE WORLD

Acknowledgments

To the 92nd Street Y, I owe deep thanks for allowing me to be part of such a vibrant institution.

To all my colleagues at The Parenting Center, with a special word for Gaby Greenberg, I owe thanks for being so wonderful to work with and wish there were a way to acknowledge each of their specific, rich ideas, so many of which are reflected in this book in one form or another.

To Fretta Reitzes, director of Family and Youth Services, I thank her for taking a chance on hiring me, even though the only teaching experience I had was at a college level.

To Beth Teitleman, director of The Parenting Center, I owe grateful thanks for being a good friend and the best boss I have ever had the luck to work for. If all institutions and organizations would model themselves after her caring style and crackerjack administrative skills, the world would be a better place.

To Barbara Katz, assistant director of The Parenting Center, who so ably leads the Toddler Seminars and is justifiably considered a guru by many moms, I cannot thank her enough for her friendship, generous time, and her invaluable input into this book. Besides a million little tips and hints, there were three parts of this book that were impoverished until she got her hands on them: her ideas on siblings, her championing boys every time I forgot them, and her insightful message to shift gears.

To the care givers, grandparents, dads, and especially the moms, full-time dads, and children who allow me to be a little part of their lives. They enrich my life tremendously. I owe deep thanks and love.

* * *

The help of many others made the book so much better than it was.

To Madeline Fisher, C.S.W., whose unfailing support is reflected on every page.

To Penny Donnenfeld, Ph.D., whose ideas and work with very sick children inspired some parts of the section on medicine.

To Mark Kaminsky, poet and scholar, who helped me reconnect with being a writer when ''all'' I'd become was a mommy.

To Donna Brodie and The Writer's Room for including me in a community of writers and giving me a chance for some peace and quiet so I could think.

To Kathy Lord, the copy editor who worked so hard on everything from commas to content.

To my wonderful, smart, caring editor, Mary Ellen O'Neill, who is also a terrific mom.

To the best agent in the world and another woman who makes motherhood a role to be proud of, Jane Dystel, who made this whole thing possible.

On a personal note of thanks, to all my friends, and especially to the following families for pitching in in so many ways and for sharing their family lives with ours: The Mota-Leshens, the Perez, the Nachmans, the Magazines, the Coleman-Sahagians, the Simon-Kleins, the Dorr-Pouschs, the Shulman-Papageorges, the Steier-Gravers, and the Sheimans.

To all my brothers and sisters by marriage and to my mother-in-law, who will be sure every time she sees the word *grandma* that I'm talking about her, even though I use the word generically. She is the best mother-in-law I could ask for.

To the loving memory of my father and grandmother, and to my mother, who gave me life, love, and taught me right from wrong.

And to my husband and daughter, who make every day a new adventure, who offer rich material to write about, and whom I love deeply.

From all these thanks, you might think this were the definitive book on the history of the world. It's just a nice little parenting book with hopefully one or two useful hints for each parent who reads it. But all the people who helped treated it as if it were a big deal. My undying gratitude and thanks.

The life of the individual only has meaning in so far as it aids in making the life of every living thing nobler and more beautiful.

—*Albert Einstein*

Letter of Greeting

Dear Fellow Mom,

Hello. My name is Lois Nachamie. Please feel free to think of me as Lois. That's what my friends call me. And so do the mothers, care givers, and children in the groups I lead at The Parenting Center at the 92nd Street Y in New York City. The children range in age from five months to three years. My experience has been with this group, but this book is for you.

Like you, I am a mom. Also like you, *I* have The Most Perfect Child in the World. I promise I will not blab about Annie. I will, however, share with you some problems I've encountered as a mother. Because of the nature of this book, the problems cover the hardest parts of my child's preschool years. Someday Annie may resent what I have revealed in public. If you and I ever meet, I may hang my head. You have seen us at our worst.

I have not bragged about the best. How loving, generous, sweet, pretty, and likable my child is. And how every once in a while my mothering skills aren't half bad.

Our family also includes my husband, Howard, and our dog, Blazer.

Big Lessons for Little People stems from my own concerns as a mother and answers questions mothers consistently raise. I have included many practical techniques to handle predictable situations. Hopefully, some of them will work for you when you are at your wit's end.

Besides the nuts-and-bolts parenting questions all of us share, there is a deeper concern resounding throughout our culture more and more urgently: How can we raise decent human beings in today's world?

I am not a philosopher, a political activist, or a psychologist. I am a teacher.

Above all, I am a mother.

Motherhood gives me, like you, the right and the responsibility to philosophize, interpret, make value judgments, and use my ability as best I can to do everything in my power to make the world a better place for my child—and to give my child the skills to make the world a better place for all.

I look forward to spending time with you. I hope to hear from you to know what you found useful and what you didn't like. Please feel free to write to me care of Dell Publishing, 1540 Broadway, New York, N.Y. 10036.

I wish you and your family all the health, happiness, and pleasure in the world.

Fondly,
Lois

P.S. Fathers are active participants in parenting. In my experience, however, the largest number of parents who *read* parenting books are moms. For any dads reading this, please don't take my lack of inclusion personally. Our concerns are the same: our children.

P.P.S. For general discussions, where it doesn't make a difference, I have alternated between ''he'' and ''she'' in each chapter.

Introduction

No book can give you a recipe for raising your child. There is no script that says, "If your child does this, you should do that," or "If you do this, your child will do that."

Even the most predictable event has no universal "correct" response.

Let's look at a common sight in any home with a child under the age of six: a spilled bowl of Cheerios.

A hint that we often encounter in parenting books is this: Clean up the bowl of Cheerios without recriminations. Say to your toddler, "No problem. Accidents happen." To your four- or five-year-old, "Here's a sponge. Let's clean up." No anger, no reproach. Everything fine and dandy.

This would seem to be advice worth following.

But if we pretend to be a movie camera and pull back from the innocuous spilled bowl of cereal on the tile floor in the kitchen, here are just some of the larger pictures we might see:

- ❖ You are late for work, the phone is ringing, the dog is barking, your husband is in the shower singing—because *he* can't function in the morning until he's jogged five miles and had his shower. *And* you have no more milk.
- ❖ It was his turn to buy milk, and he forgot.
- ❖ It was your turn. You forgot.
- ❖ You and your husband had a big fight that morning, which your child heard and saw.
- ❖ You and your husband have been working long hours, you really

miss him, and the only thing you really want to do is sit down out back with a cup of coffee, lean on his shoulder, and talk. Uninterrupted.

❖ Your husband comes into the kitchen, says cheerily, "Hey, Pal," lifts the baby out of the high chair, and carries him into the den. You can hear them laughing uproariously as you clean up the mess.

❖ You just brought a new baby home from the hospital.

❖ Your child—good-naturedly and unintentionally—spills everything, relentlessly, day in and day out, no matter what it is or where you are.

Pull back the camera a little farther.

The TV is on. Images flick by. A young black man, handcuffed, hooded sweatshirt covering most of his face, is led away by white cops. An eye-catching animated monkey croaks in a cute voice how yummy chocolate cereal is. An ad for sports clothing pans from the face of a beautiful, smiling woman down to her tight stomach muscles, belly button, and ends with a close-up of her crotch as she slips off her pants. Your child watches curiously.

Spilled Cheerios, Take two: out in the world.

❖ You're in a restaurant.

❖ You're at your mother's. No matter what your child does, including heaving the bowl of cereal against the dining room wall, she thinks it's the cutest thing she's ever seen.

❖ Alternative: Your mother laughs—spitefully, in your opinion— and says, "Boy, are *you* getting it all back in spades."

❖ Alternative: No matter how you respond, your mother gives you a "look" that fills you with self-doubt.

❖ Your grandmother suggests a good, swift swat.

❖ You're at your mother-in-law's. According to her, as she informs you at the moment and will repeat every half hour for the rest of the weekend, your husband *never* spilled anything when he was little. "Were *you* a spiller?" she asks. She says "spiller" the way she might say "murderous chicken-blood-drinker."

Bowls of Cheerios never spill in vacuums.

"We've spilled the Cheerios. Let's clean up" is a useful response in a calm moment where nothing is going on except you, your child, and his breakfast.

But we do not live in a never-never land where every home is well-ordered, where external pressures never intrude on a parent's response, where no mothers have short fuses or lives of their own, no couples ever disagree, and no cultural influences are at play.

Our children don't punch in like clockwork on developmental stages at the "right" time. Nor do they fall neatly into the most well-thought-out categories.

If I were to say to you, "Do this and your child will do that," and you were to follow that advice to the letter, we'd be living in a fantasy world.

I can offer you some things to think about while raising your own family.

I can pass along practical tips that have worked for others. That doesn't mean they will work for you. Moreover, what works one day with a child may not work another day. By "work," I mean any technique that helps you get your child to do what you want your child to do at that moment.

A Thought to Hold On To

No one statement, slipup, wrong turn, explosion of anger, or crying jag will permanently damage your child.

I will suggest ways you might handle a given moment in your child's life. I will suggest other ways to rehandle it if you're not happy with how things are going. Nevertheless, remember that the shaping of a personality comes from many, many moments.

In addition to the cumulative experience of a child's life, even past these important first five years, the personality type your child is born with will shape who your child becomes.

Over the long haul, if you are essentially a loving parent your love will have a profound effect. There is never any one moment when you should rend your clothes and strew ashes on your forehead, keening, "Now I've done it! Now I have really messed up my kid!"

The likelihood of your wanting to be a perfect parent is high. Otherwise, you wouldn't spend time reading about parenting.

If this is helpful, let me toss this idea your way: I give you permission not to be perfect all the time. Your child will not be picking off people from a bell tower twenty years from now because you said something stupid this morning.

We are advised in most parenting literature to present a united front with our husbands. While this makes sense in theory, it does not always reflect normal, happy homes. Hopefully, both parents agree on the fundamental values they want to instill in their children. But parental disagreements and different ways of handling the same situation, from the largest to the most mundane, might not be so terrible. They are real. You, your husband, and child are living real life, after all, not in a textbook. An important lesson for a child to learn about the real world is this: Different people have different ways of doing things. Children need to learn how to be flexible and adjust to these differences. They need to recognize that we can be different and still get along. They need to learn that we can be different and still be in love.

As we go along I will bring up other areas where I feel that maybe the pronouncements made in books ought to be questioned. I will write about some topics that I never see anywhere else, and I will write about some topics where I think the universal approach might not be so useful.

Although I, like any other writer and teacher, have very definite opinions, I will do the best I can to present them in ways that encourage you to figure out what you think makes sense, theoretically and practically. And even if I get up on my high horse and start pontificating, when all is said and done, your family is your family.

You are the ones who really know what's best for you.

GENERALIZATIONS ABOUT CHILD DEVELOPMENT

By *six months* your child understands almost everything you say to him about his world. Honest.

Until *fourteen to eighteen months* your child will be very eager to please you by following your instructions. Take advantage of the time you have.

From *eighteen months to three years*, depending on your child, new skills will be very important. Among those skills will be seeing how much he can control you.

Threes tend to be a very agreeable group, as happy as you are to have weathered their "twos."

Fours will give you a taste of the teen years. They will be interested in other people, how they fit in, and will listen to you—as long as what you say is interesting. Interesting is often a matter of personal taste.

Fives are a pleasant, competent lot, usually fascinated by "rules."

With each stage of increasing mobility and maturity, specific situations become more varied. Thus it's easier for me to predict scenes you may encounter with your infant than to project what your five-year-old may say. For the preschool years you will notice there are more generalizations by necessity than for the baby and toddler periods.

All children go through "stages." They begin as angels. You fall head over heels in love with them; their bank account of love is solid enough for you to draw on in order to bear the next stage. Each time you think that if they continue behaving like this you're going to do something drastic, *wham!* they revert to angelhood. Once they know they're treading on firm ground again, they will go as far as they can.

The periods of oscillation from angel to devil vary from child to child, ranging anywhere from six months to a year. Whenever they're delightful, enjoy, but don't think it's permanent. Whenever they're totally obnoxious, remember that this, too, shall pass.

Food for Thought: In our culture we make children grow up too fast in certain areas; we keep them babyish too long in others. We force them to confront divorce, death, and sex, but we take away their pacifiers and won't let them suck their thumbs. We applaud them when they know their alphabet and can use computers at two; we wipe their tushes, put on their socks, and pick up after them when they're four. Perhaps you and I might realign this imbalance.

My absolute promise to you: I do solemnly promise that, barring any medical problem, by the time our kids are in high school they will all walk, talk, feed themselves, and not need diapers, bottles, or "paccies." Relax. Marvel as they develop at their own pace.

THE UNDERLYING PRINCIPLES OF PARENTING

The basic elements of parenting as I see them are:

1. To love.
2. To teach your child how to get along in the world.
3. To teach your child how to choose.
4. To provide positive alternatives to unacceptable behavior.

1. Love

We can best love our child by accepting his inherent nature, including his strengths and limitations. By accurately assessing who he is and not by finding that person to be wanting. By not trying to make him what we want him to be or a miniature version of ourselves in an idealized form.

The world needs all kinds of people. Short, tall, pretty, ugly, stupid, smart, funny, serious, humdrum, and charismatic. Any good nursery school actively seeks not only the aggressive go-getters, but the shy hang-behinds as well, for the express purpose of creating a whole. We need leaders and followers equally.

Your specific child needs his parents to find him terrific, no matter what kind of child he is.

Further, your child needs you to show your love.

Just as we need different children, so do we need different adults. You may be huggy-feely or standoffish. A small smile from a reserved mother carries the same weight as a big hug and squeal of delight from a demonstrative type.

Showing love, however, is more than unilateral approval. Love requires teaching your child that there are limitations in the world. This is often harder than a hug at the appropriate moment.

2. Teaching How to Get Along in the World

We must arm our children with enough social skills so that every interaction with other people is not abrasive. This includes everything from simple manners to controlling our basic instincts. In order to do this we have to be firm sometimes and lenient others.

3. Teaching Our Children How to Choose

We must give our children enough leeway to learn how to pick themselves up and start over again when they make the wrong choice. This requires guidance when appropriate and getting out of their hair when we need to, even if we have to bite our tongues and sit on our hands.

4. Providing Positive Alternatives to Unacceptable Behavior

We must teach our children right from wrong.

Since all ''unacceptable behavior'' that a child manifests is normal and human, we must respect the impulse yet at the same time teach acceptable ways of behaving.

These are all very big lessons indeed.

Food for Thought: The Paradox of Parenting. In every other loving relationship we work hard to stay together. In parenting we strive to give our child enough independence to leave.

PSYCHOLOGY AND PARENTING

Our culture embraces psychology.

Many of us have had some kind of therapy, whether group, couple, or individual. Self-exploratory movements, smoke-ending groups, weight-loss groups, and twelve-step programs abound. We explore our childhoods. We believe in growth and change.

A therapeutic approach can be a very helpful tool—*perhaps* for people who are truly mentally ill (although I have my doubts), but *particularly* for those of us who are the garden-variety-type neurotic. These people genuinely profit from examining why they do something with an eye toward being able to change it, whether they have conversations with a therapist, a group with or without a leader, or a good friend. In short, you and me.

But if we're not careful the very strengths of the therapeutic model can generate a new set of problems in our children.

Useful Applications of Psychology in Parenting

❖ A working knowledge of each developmental stage of childhood. This helps us to understand what our child is going through and therefore to respond appropriately.

❖ Recognizing that sometimes behavior reflects a response to something else; moving to aid our children if we see they're in over their heads developmentally.

❖ Having a clear picture of our own shortcomings. It can help us not inflict our problems on our children.

Less Useful Applications of Therapeutic Techniques

❖ Approaching parenting as if it were therapy.

❖ Trying to analyze in the moment what's going on. "Are you feeling angry?" is not a useful statement from a mother when her child is pitched backward on the floor, screaming. A mother would do better to pick her child up and hold him if that's the kind of response that helps him, or to walk away if he is a child who needs to be left alone.

❖ "Exploring" behavior unjudgmentally. "Why did you mess up Jason's picture?" is not an appropriate question to ask a preschooler. With its implied lack of judgment so useful in therapy, "Why?" tacitly communicates to a child that it's okay. Your child needs you to teach what is and what is not okay. "It's not nice to mess up other people's pictures" is a value judgment. Mothers need to teach values to their children.

❖ Mistaking self-expression for thoughtlessness. "I don't want to play with you. I don't like you" is honest. But it is not nice. Not correcting by suggesting either that we all play together for a short time or else that we keep the "I don't like you" part to ourselves does not teach a child to articulate personal preferences. It teaches a child to be a thoughtless snothead.

All these kinds of approaches are useful in therapy, where we are trying to correct problems that have already occurred. But there is nothing wrong with your kid! Your kid is just a kid—a wonderful, perfect human being without one single psychological problem!

Sometimes, when exploring our own histories, we blame our parents. While I believe that we cannot move forward without being aware of what went wrong in our own history and taking steps to correct any problems, I also believe that true maturity comes when we stop blaming our parents for our faults.

As adults we are able to discard what didn't work, but keep what did.

Exercise: What did your parents do that you liked? What did they do that you want to do differently?

Food for Thought: Have you found, now that you're a parent, that you understand your own parents better? Have you found that your relationship has improved? If you were mad at them for some of the things they did, do you feel more kindly now?

More Food for Thought: Life is short. If you still have your parents, thank them for what they did that you value. Unless you think discussion may change your current relationship for the better, don't bring up old hurts. Find a more helpful ear to discuss the past.

PARENTING IN THE WORLD AROUND US

Without wishing to sound melodramatic, our society is tattered, if not downright shredded to pieces. As a nation we've lost our moral ballast. In an effort to enhance individual human potential, we've lost the perception that we are all part of a whole and that our actions affect other people. Further, we seem to feel that the ends justify the means and that we are beholden only to ourselves.

Sports heroes are drug addicts. Government officials are thieves. Teachers are child molesters. The list goes on.

Someone has to say "Stop." That someone is you.

Whether we like it or not, whether it's fair or not, it seems to me that mothers might be able to turn things around.

We need to instill our children with basic, nonnegotiable moral principles. At the same time that we encourage their self-esteem, we need to imbue them with a deep awareness of community, its privileges and obligations. It's an awesome responsibility, and I don't throw around the word *awesome* the way a surfer does.

For me, as a mother, what makes such a responsibility tenable is my daughter. When I see her sweet face and hear her laugh, I know that I have to teach her to the best of my ability how to say no to things that will harm her. Do I want to turn her into a repressed prude? Adamantly not. But just as adamantly I do not want her to take lessons from a culture that says that life and sex are cheap, that love is temporary, and that she should buy anything an ad tries to sell her. I want her to love learning for learning's sake. I want a pit of revulsion to rise up in her at the idea of cheating on a test. Only that way can she feel the profound pleasure of knowing that she did well. I want the idea of stealing to be so loathsome to my daughter that she'd rather go hungry. I want her to have good, strong friendships. And I want her someday to be lucky enough to fall in love with and marry a man as good as her father.

It is for my daughter, your sons and daughters, and their future together that I write in hopes of helping all of us help the next generation.

It is for you, a mom, doing the best you can, that I pass along any information I've gathered along the way.

PART I

THE INTERNAL CHARACTER OF YOUR CHILD

The types of personalities our children have are theirs from birth. But all children need their parents to help them develop a conscience, establish their relationship to the world around them, and help instill honorable qualities that money can't buy and adversity can't destroy.

Right from Wrong

I'm a nice woman. You're a nice woman. We could ask each other to watch our bags—and even our kids—at the airport and know that when we got back everything would be safe and sound.

What worries me is this: How come we nice women are letting all the goody-two-shoes and the holier-than-thous do all the talking about morals?

I want to talk about the biggies. Lying. Cheating. Stealing. Feeling entitled to everything just by virtue of being alive. Figuring better you than me; accepting extenuating circumstances; winning at all costs; worshiping money, fame, and power; ignoring the future; living only in the present. Everybody out for themselves. What's mine is mine, and what's yours is mine. Accepting—even expecting—that people do bad things. Minor bad things, and really bad things.

Sometimes in parenting we get so caught up in apple juice, socks, and clutter that we forget the big issues. The biggest lesson that we need to teach our children is to *choose right instead of wrong*.

1. Not hurting anybody is right; hurting somebody is wrong.
   This includes ourselves and others, physically and emotionally.
2. Honesty is right; dishonesty is wrong.
   This includes words and deeds.

Developmentally, a child under three has no real ethical ability. Psychologists have done some interesting studies. When they told toddlers to sit in a room alone but not peek at the toy behind them, they were not able *not* to peek. What I find really fascinating is this: When they asked each child, ''Did you peek?'' none of them was able to lie!

By five, however, most children would not admit they peeked. Now aware of the rules and the repercussions and knowing right from wrong, they often chose to do ''wrong'' and say they hadn't.

What does this mean to a parent? It means that building a conscience takes years. No child was ever civilized by one well-chosen phrase of correction. No child was ever civilized without many, many repetitions of both words and deeds by his parents, who set the tone and expectation of knowing right from wrong.

The single most important way a parent can raise a principled child is through example. In parenting we call this *modeling*. Although this sounds obvious, sometimes in practice it may be harder than we think.

Before we begin looking at specific lessons that I think we need to teach our children, I'd like to remind you of the most powerful tool you have at your disposal to teach your child right from wrong.

SECTION 1: THE POWER OF YOUR VOICE

Now that you're a mom, how many times have you heard a sentence come out of your mouth that makes you step back and say, ''Oh, my Lord! I sound just like my mother!''

If this hasn't happened to you, your baby is probably not crawling yet. There comes a moment, usually when your child is challenging you beyond your limits, when *bam!* out comes your mother's voice.

Sometimes we laugh. Sometimes we get upset. It depends on how we feel about our own mothers and their mothering skills. If we got along famously with our moms, we are less inclined to mind when we sound like them. But it is a rare child who has never vowed, ''When *I'm* a mom, I'll *never* say that to *my* child!'' It is a rarer parent who can keep this vow.

The mental echoes of our own childhood usually reflect the structure and style of the family we grew up in. If your mother was a worrywart, for example, it's likely that as an adult ''Be careful!'' resonates in your mind every time you encounter an imagined threat. A curb, an elevator, a stranger, an unfamiliar road. If your mother was courageous you may hear an echo: ''Go on. You can do it.''

We have other important voices that join us during our day. Our dads, grandparents, brothers, and sisters.

If your father was a disciplinarian his thundering threats of ''or else'' may resound when you feel put upon at work. You meet your deadline, nervously afraid not to even though you know the project is busywork designed to make your boss look good. If your father was a peacemaker, interceding when your mother was on a roll, in anxious moments you may hear his deep voice saying, "That's enough now," and you feel soothed and protected.

The power of the memory of these voices, which we all carry with us in adulthood, is the stuff that psychology—and poetry—are made of.

Rather than run from this, pretend it doesn't exist, or senselessly promise that we're going to do it all differently, why not use this extraordinary power wisely?

A. POSITIVE USE OF YOUR VOICE—MEMORABLE LESSONS

As old-fashioned as it may seem, some of those stupid homilies that mothers pepper their conversations with make sense. They teach. They reverberate.

"Haste makes waste," "A stitch in time saves nine," "All things come to he who waits" are the kinds of phrases a child remembers. As an adult we often laugh about them. If you have brothers and sisters, at an appropriate moment one of you will say to the other in a perfect imitation of your mother's voice, "Pretty is as pretty does," and you will howl with the laughter of a lifetime of memories. Remembering your mother's words can be cozy, comforting, and give you a strong sense of belonging. Even hardened criminals from violent homes whom you'd think would want to erase every trace of what they had to endure when they were small will chuckle fondly, "Like my ma always said . . ."

Don't be afraid to trot out those old tried-and-true adages. As sophisticated as you may be, sometimes the phrase that springs to your lips unbidden may be "just what the doctor ordered."

On the other hand, sometimes it may not.

B. NEGATIVE USE OF YOUR VOICE—NAME-CALLING

There are scads of studies about the effect of calling a child names. *Self-fulfilling prophecy* is the term sociologists and educators use.

Food for Thought: I know two sisters, both adults, near to one another in age. Feature by feature they could pass for twins. Both have interesting insights, are quick-witted and well-informed. One was cast as the family beauty, the other as the family brains. The "beauty" is a drop-dead-gorgeous woman whom men invariably turn to look at on the street. She has had a heck of a time with her career, floundering from one lousy job to the next. The "brains" has features that are strikingly similar to those of her sister, yet because of the way she carries herself and dresses, she is downright homely. She is a high-powered lawyer. I rest my case.

If you tell your child she is clumsy, sassy, nasty, or mean, don't be surprised if eventually other people begin to perceive her that way. She will act out your implied stage directions.

When I hear a mother in a baby class complain that her baby is "into *everything*" with a disapproving tone that implies being into everything is akin to being an ax murderer, I murmur, "How wonderful. He's curious," hoping she'll hear the difference. When a two-year-old grabs my hand to drag me over to a puzzle she's just finished and her mother announces loudly to the room at large, half-bragging, half-ashamed, "She's such a little show-off," I hope the mother hears me when I say to the child, "You must feel very proud of what you've just done."

Of course, in teaching you have to say things delicately enough that the mother won't feel threatened.

I can't baldly say, "Listen to yourself! You're eroding your baby's intellectual curiosity and love of life!" I can't say, "Call her 'show-off' enough and your child may well turn her developing sense of accomplishment into a pathetic bid for attention!"

But here with you, where I'd rather not pull any punches, I know you won't take it wrong if I come right out and say: Don't call your kid names! It's not nice. It will harm her in the long run.

By the same token, try not to label your child even when you mean it nicely. If your child has her head buried in your skirt and won't look up at a friendly neighbor, you may not help her as much as you think by explaining, "She's shy." Labels limit children and put pressure on them to live up to your expectations.

Now that you're not editing out any of the charming speech patterns of your family and you're carefully controlling the inclination you may have picked up from your own childhood to label behavior (self-awareness is exhausting, isn't it?), let's jump right in to some typical, distressing scenes of childhood to see when the power of Mommy's voice should ring with the chords of right and wrong.

C. GUILT AND REMORSE—WHEN "BAD" IS GOOD

Guilt, in the commonly accepted psychological meaning of the word, is a negative thing.

Guilt and sex are an unhealthy pair. Some people are unable to succeed for fear of surpassing their parents' worldly accomplishments; others may be driven to succeed out of the reverse sense of guilt—they're afraid to let their parents down.

We throw the word *guilt* around in our everyday conversation: *I feel so guilty; ever since the baby came, my dog's lucky if I feed him, let alone take him for a run.*

In all of this, guilt is a negative emotion, implying that something is not right, that we are not perfectly evolved *psychologically.* Guilt is something we try and get out of our lives.

I'd like to offer an old-fashioned meaning of the word and suggest that in certain circumstances guilt may not be so bad. It may even be good.

I think a person should feel deep, internal remorse and guilt if we do something bad. Even more important, we must be armed with a strong internal mechanism that warns us *before* we do something bad, thereby preventing us from doing that thing.

In the adult this mechanism is the conscience. For a child the conscience is his mother and father. Like Jiminy Cricket, our voices must ring in our children's ears. In most cases, over and over again.

Let's look at a classic.

It happens in the nicest families. You bring home a new infant. Your two-year-old hauls off and slams the baby in the head. Not an experimental poke or jab, but a real scary hit.

If "bad boy!" falls out of your mouth in a harsh tone with eyes flashing, that's fine.

This child is not peeved or distressed; this child is not annoyed. This child is having an elemental experience. His entire existence, *from his point of view,* is in jeopardy. Let's not put these feelings into bland, socially acceptable euphemisms. Your child is in a murderous rage.

What is it then, in this moment of deep, passionate, human emotion, that you want to teach?

You don't want to teach him not to feel rage. You want to allow him to feel whatever he feels. You do not, however, want him to do whatever he feels like doing.

There is nothing wrong with being angry.

There is everything wrong with being unable to control your anger.

The ability to control our behavior, no matter what we are feeling, is one of the main ways we distinguish between "good" people and "bad" people.

Should this happen in your home you would be a thoughtful, considerate mom if you found a quiet moment to draw your two-year-old onto your lap and say kindly and lovingly, ''I know it's hard. The new baby is taking up a lot of Mommy's time right now.'' This acknowledgment and acceptance of his feelings is very important to a small child.

But just as he deserves to have you accept his passion and still love him, so he deserves to hear a stern, uncompromising tone enter his mommy's voice that he will carry deep inside him all the days of his life: ''But no matter how you feel, you *may not* hit the baby.''

Should you not come down hard when it first happens, you are cheating him. Should you not let him out of the doghouse later and back into your arms, you are cheating him. Should you not let him know that if he ever does it again you'll be just as mad as the first time, you are cheating him. This is the process of teaching right from wrong.

Now, holding our toddler's hand in ours, let's see what happens when we venture out into the world, where right and wrong sometimes gets murky. Let's go to the playground.

Here are two three-year-olds. One is Jed. A nice boy, learning social skills. For Jed, a push sometimes comes into his hands as automatically as a smile comes over his face. The other child is Colin. He is a nudge. He oversteps physical boundaries often, getting too close to others. In addition, he is clumsy. The combination means that he frequently messes up what other children are doing. These two boys live near each other and go to the same nursery school. They see each other a lot.

Jed, busily digging an elaborate ditch in the sandbox, sees those annoying dinosaur sneakers appear and clumsily kick sand into the ditch. He looks up. There is Colin. ''Can I play with you?'' Colin says, moves closer, and completely destroys the ditch. Jed stands up and gives Colin a good, sound push. He knocks him down.

Jed's mother sees the whole thing. There are two responses that a thoughtful mother could have, depending on her style and values, both of which have validity to my way of thinking:

1. She could stay out of it, letting the boys work it out, and move in only if the shoving increased. Later, if she wanted, she could talk to their nursery-school teacher or even Colin's mother, if she feels generous and thinks Colin's mother might be receptive to a dialogue. She could ask for suggestions to help the boys interact in a different way. She doesn't think that Jed's response is off the wall, and she's caught between two issues: wanting to teach her child not to hit, and wanting to encourage her child to defend what he's worked hard on.

2. She could correct Jed in a calm voice, reminding him that if he doesn't like something that happened he can tell Colin, but he can't push.

Although these are different styles, in both cases Jed's justifiable feelings have been taken into account by his mother, and he has not been made to feel guilty for responding to someone violating his space and concentration. In both cases, the first by omission and the second by the mother's tone of voice, self-defense is recognized as a viable, if not mannerly, response.

Let's up the ante. Same two boys, the big-kids' sliding board, eight feet tall. Jed happily lets 'er rip down to the bottom, runs around to the back, and climbs up the ladder again. As he nears the top, who should appear? Colin. Right behind him. Crowding him. Right on the rung below Jed's, scaring Jed because Colin is so clumsy that Jed is afraid Colin may knock him off. Jed holds on to the rail with one hand and gives Colin a shove.

From Jed's point of view, motivationally and psychologically, this shove is exactly like the shove in the sandbox.

Colin falls. He needs stitches.

Many experts would advise: Get help for Colin. Reprimand Jed. Tell him in no uncertain terms that we do not use our hands. We use words. We do not hurt people.

In this case I am uncomfortable with words like *reprimand* and *no uncertain terms*.

If Jed were my kid I'd raise holy hell.

The moment help arrived for Colin I would face my child. If he were crying or drain-faced with fear, as most children would be, I would make sure I sounded good and mad. "You *should* feel bad. No matter how you ever feel, you may not hurt anyone else."

If he was not crying or showing some sign that he emotionally understood the enormity of what happened, I would grab my kid by the shoulder, kneel down right in his face, point my finger, and shout, "Don't you ever, ever, *ever* push another child from a sliding board. You hurt him! That is *bad!* I am very angry with you!"

I would want my child to feel that Attila the Hun had come down from the mountains. I would want him to feel small and bad. I would want my anger to be so big, so frightening, and so unexpected that it would scare the living daylights out of him. I would want him to feel so guilty that he *would never do it—or anything like it—again.*

That's the point.

An apology from Jed while Colin's mother was rushing him out of the playground would be a lot of hot air.

Later that afternoon or evening, however, I would find out how Colin was, apologize, and offer to cover any medical bills. Jed's apology to both Colin and Colin's mother would be appropriate and called for then, not in the heat of the moment.

I would also talk to my son. I would reinforce how angry I'd been and tell him that seriously hurting someone else is one of the things that will always make Mommy that angry. I would not keep him floundering on the hook indefinitely. I would acknowledge what went wrong. ''I know Colin crowds you.'' I would bring up the sandbox incident. ''Remember when you pushed Colin in the sandbox? That wasn't nice. You're learning not to push, but today was different. Because today you hurt him. You cannot *ever* hurt anybody.''

Why am I stressing this point and lingering here for so long? Because I have seen intelligent, well-informed mothers who don't believe in guilt, who believe in teaching through reason rather than fear, who ''reprimand'' in ''no uncertain terms.'' With the same tone of voice, word choice, and mood, they treat serious incidents the same as a sandbox tussle. They are not the same.

If you, the mother, don't make a distinction, how can your child? Although his feelings, motivations, and behavior may have been absolutely the same, there was a *difference in the real world*.

We do not live only in our heads. Our psychological state of mind and motivations are not the end-all and be-all. Other people count. Actions have consequences.

This is the basis for a decent, moral life.

D. SELF-REVULSION AND SHAME—WHEN "BAD" IS BAD

Bad is a small word that packs a big punch.

To teach right from wrong we have to make distinctions.

If your child does something that seriously jeopardizes his or someone else's real welfare, he should know that he's been bad.

But there are a couple of other ways we use *bad* that are not so hot.

I often hear moms laughingly—and sometimes not so laughingly—say, ''Oh, he's so bad,'' meaning he's intractable, difficult to be around, or makes really big messes.

It is not useful to make a child feel bad for being who he is. This includes his personality type and the fact that he is a child.

Here are some examples of times when you need to rethink what *bad* really means and become more conscious of what you say:

❖ Bad boy! You got your hands dirty!
❖ Bad boy! You ripped your pants!
❖ Bad boy! You're not paying attention!

You may be angry because you have to wash his hands even though you're all dressed up and late for a wedding. You may be weary of how clumsy he is, causing you to have to sew his pants yet again. You may be beside yourself because he inattentively put his glass down on the edge of the table for the umpteenth time and it has spilled yet again. But these things aren't bad. They are inconvenient, possibly annoying, and if they happen frequently enough they may even be enraging. But they are not morally bad. They are part of being a child.

By calling him bad when you really mean he has caused you inconvenience, you may unintentionally do one of two things that you probably wouldn't want to do if given the choice:

❖ You may erode his self-confidence to the point that he feels like a piece of doody most of the time, no matter what he does.
❖ You may overuse the word so much that it begins to roll off his back and become meaningless. He may not be able to distinguish between right and wrong and end up really being bad, meaning living outside the norms of decent society.

Another time we get a little hazy on how to use the word *bad* is when we're involved in the daily grind of teaching right from wrong.

Let's return to the sandbox, when Jed shoved Colin. Was Jed being bad? No. He was being a kid who is still learning right from wrong and who had been thwarted at play. *He* was not bad. His *behavior,* however, was bad. There is a big difference. Just as we must distinguish when he has done something terrible and give him a feeling deep in the pit of his stomach should he ever feel like doing something like that again, so must we be careful not to make him get that stomach-wrenching feeling for every correction we make. We don't want him to feel bad all the time. But we do want to make our child keenly aware that certain *kinds of behavior* are bad and that we will not tolerate them.

In this type of normal, everyday correction a kind mother uses a firm tone. In everyday situations, reprimands and no uncertain terms are sometimes called for when reminding our children that "We don't push. We use words." "Bad boy! You pushed" isn't really useful. He may feel shame and hang his head because he's been scolded. But he hasn't had his *behavior* corrected in a way that will help him the next time he feels like doing it.

Finger Pointing

In the same way that telling him he's bad when he makes a minor mistake along the road toward civilization may have a damaging effect over time, so will finger pointing every time he's less than perfect.

Finger in face: "You put those shoes on right now!" Finger in face: "Don't you ever dig in that spot in the garden again!"

This kind of finger pointing, during the normal course of a child learning what he can and cannot do, will ultimately have a degrading effect.

Eventually, a child who is made to squirm every time he steps out of line will feel yucky about making mistakes, yucky about learning, yucky about being a kid, and by inference, yucky about being himself.

Too Much Reading the Riot Act

If you yell at the slightest infraction, you have lost the power of your anger as a teaching tool and turned it into an unpleasant personality quirk that your child will learn to ignore at home and mimic when he's out.

Inappropriate Response to Accidents

In the event that your child accidentally injures another child, please make sure you don't make him feel guilty. He will feel badly enough. That is a justifiable moment to hold him, comfort him, and make sure he understands that accidents, as awful as they are, are mistakes.

Too Much Explanation

"Put the book back on the shelf so we can find it tomorrow." "Eat your carrots so you get enough vitamins." "Thank Mrs. Davis or she'll think you have no manners."

While cause and effect is valid, don't always suggest that he do one thing so that something else won't happen. Ultimately, this may translate to restraining from cheating, stealing, or lying only for fear of getting caught. "Put the book back on the shelf" is a fair request. It needs no more explanation.

E. MINOR INFRACTIONS OF RIGHT AND WRONG
Not Nice

Not sharing is not nice. Sassing a grown-up is not nice. These are forms of ungenerous behavior that are inconsiderate of others.

By using this phrase when you correct your child, you are teaching that you expect him to be "nice," meaning to take other people's feelings into account. Furthermore, you are implying that he can expect the people whom he chooses to be around later in life to be "nice" also.

Offer him suggestions about what he can do to be "nice." "Keeping all the crayons on your side of the table and not letting Bart have any is not nice. Next time it'd be better to share them without Mommy having to remind you.'' You've corrected him and given him an alternative.

Naughty

''Naughty'' is a useful word for describing behavior that is mischievous. Putting paint on the cat, crayons on the wall, or chalk on the front of the house is naughty. Any phrase that comes out of your mouth naturally that doesn't include ''bad boy!'' works.

F. DON'T FORGET "GOOD"

In the same way that we sometimes use *bad* to mean annoying, we often use *good* to mean no trouble or well-behaved. We hear new moms saying, ''Oh, she's such a good baby. She never cries.'' Does this mean that the colicky baby is bad? No. What it means is that the ''good'' child's presence doesn't give the adult any trouble.

But a good child does not necessarily mean a child who is *always* obedient. The worst-case scenario, of course, is the child who follows a stranger out of the park because the child has been taught always to obey his elders.

We often use the phrase ''Be good,'' when what we really mean is ''Do it my way.''

It's not useful to expect our child to be so good, in the sense of not causing trouble, that he follows that stranger out of the park. That is why we need to give our children leeway when they learn and not come down on them so hard that they are always afraid to question an adult.

What we should really mean by good is a child who is improving.

Sometimes we become so busy correcting, adjusting, and pointing out ''errors'' that we forget to tell our child when things have gone well. Your approval carries great weight.

For the willful child, good means not spending every waking moment being abrasive. At the end of a pleasant, stress-free experience, tell him what a good boy he was. Remind him that when it was time to go he didn't carry on. He said, ''Not ready,'' and you said, ''Let's leave the playground so we can go to the library.'' He thought that was a fun idea and left. That was very good.

For the compliant child, good may very well mean the opposite. ''I noticed how good you were today. You chose a book in the library that you liked. When the little boy wanted to go ahead of you on the sliding board, you told him, 'My turn.' You were so good.''

Little by little your child will learn right from wrong, and at the same time, little by little, you will learn the best way to teach him.

Tip: Reserve your frowns, angry tones, and angry language for the big ones. Make sure you pull out the artillery when needed, but keep your gun in the holster when all's quiet on the western front. Or just a little bit messy.

If you manage to maintain this balance most of the time, your child will eventually learn right from wrong.

Exercise: At the end of the day, when you're wondering whether you reacted appropriately or whether tomorrow maybe you'll try a different approach, run these ideas by to see where your child's behavior might have fallen on the "right and wrong" scale.

Naughty is behavior that someday you'll laugh about. "I remember the time you got into my makeup!" The image of your daughter with lipstick smeared all over her face and the furniture will be funny. Maybe not today. Or even tomorrow. But in twenty or thirty years it will be fondly remembered.

Not nice won't ever look cute, even with the passage of time. It's hard to imagine chuckling over the time your four-year-old became a completely intransigent brat about not wanting her cousin to borrow a pair of pants after they'd been out playing in the snow and came in all wet.

Bad behavior will make you smile as you stretch out on a lawn chair and watch your grown son, whom you're very proud of, mediate between his own son and a neighborhood boy. You'll be able to call out, "If I had a dollar for every time I had to remind *you* not to grab . . ."

Bad will still make your adrenaline flow and your mouth get dry as you watch yourself again in your mind's eye, in slow motion. You stand paralyzed, too far away to get there in time as that other kid falls way, way down before hitting the ground.

SECTION 2: HONESTY

Although a young child does not yet have what we call a conscience, he has the cognitive ability to take his cues from what he sees around him.

A. HONESTY IN COMMUNICATION—MOMS' LIES

In order to teach your child not to lie, as well as to maintain the basic trust each child is born with, you'd do best to be scrupulously honest in your dealings with him.

Yet sometimes I see moms tell their children lies, mistakenly thinking they'll make things better. Here are some common lies that moms tell to soften the truth. This is a parenting technique that backfires.

1. Lies of Commission

* The kid falls down and cries. The mother says, "That didn't hurt." It *did* hurt. Acknowledging that it hurt doesn't turn him into a crybaby. "I bet that really hurt" and a hug show that you understand what he feels. After you comfort him, direct his attention to something else. But don't try to get his "mind off it" by pretending it didn't happen or that he doesn't really feel what he feels.
* Going somewhere. Kid's getting cranky. Asks how much longer. Mom lies. "We're almost there." You're *not* almost there. You're a half hour away. Tell your child you're half a *Sesame Street* show away. Introduce a game or a song to keep him occupied. Don't lie.

2. Lies of Omission

* Sneaking out and leaving your baby with a baby-sitter because you're afraid the baby will miss you.
* Alternate excuse I've heard: "He won't know I'm gone." Of course, he'll know you're gone! From day one, tell your baby "good-bye" before you leave.
* Springing something unpleasant on your child, such as a doctor's appointment or that Grandma's got to go right this minute to catch her plane, but you didn't want to interrupt your child because he was playing. Prepare your child for things he might not like, even if he'll carry on when he knows.

These kinds of pacifying lies aren't whoppers. But they set a tone. Little by little you become less and less of a reliable person in your child's eyes. Your words carry less and less weight. By these small lies you erode what ought to be one of your most sacred possessions: your child's trust.

There is another kind of lying that I see moms do that I find even more serious in terms of eroding a child's trust.

3. Emotional Lies

I've seen quite a number of moms in class, in playgrounds, and in the neighborhood who don't respond to their children honestly.

There are often things that happen during the course of a day with a small child that can drive you up a wall.

If you say, "Honey, that's the sixth glass you spilled today," in the same tone of voice that you say, "Honey, I love you," it's confusing, at best. Constantly monitoring your tone of voice, being ever so careful to be calm and loving even when you don't feel "calm and loving," is a form of emotional dishonesty. It's a lie.

You wouldn't be human if you weren't angry, or distressed, or upset in your own style at a moment such as this. During moments of normal stress your child deserves honesty.

A Very Unpleasant True Tale from the Trenches: We had a two-and-a-half-year-old in class once who was, if you'll pardon the clichés, as cute as a button and as smart as a whip. But she seemed to do irritating things on purpose. While we were having a snack and listening to a story, Colleen would purposely dump her juice on the table. At first I thought her mother was a saint. She wouldn't turn a hair; instead, she would say in an almost cheerful voice, "Oops. Spilled juice," and clean it up without so much as a note of reproach. Colleen dumped a big box of stacking pegs. They clattered and skidded across the floor. "Oops. Pegs on the floor. Let's pick them up." This woman has nerves of steel, I thought to myself. But as the weeks went by I began to find myself wishing she would crack. The quasi-cheerful voice was relentless. I began to feel afraid. What rage was the mother covering that she found so frightening she couldn't let it out? If I, an acquaintance and an adult, found her response—or lack of response—chilling, what must Colleen have felt? A small child unable to get a response from her mother, *no matter what she did.* I often wonder what happened to that pretty child. Has she grown up to be increasingly more annoying? Has she become cowed and flattened? I wish her well. Perhaps she's fine. But I rather suspect she's not.

If your child has spilled the sixth glass of milk, calling him bad is not fair. Because he hasn't been bad. He's been a kid. But saying, "Oh, how I wish you hadn't done that!" or "Now what? We don't have any more milk!'' and letting whatever exasperation you feel show in your voice and face is honest.

Please don't take these suggestions as scripts. But if you find that you're worried about sounding ''unpleasant,'' don't worry.

* Admitting that you are angry will take the pressure off him.
* He won't be afraid that your anger will kill him if it ever comes out.
* Through your example you'll allow him later in life to admit that he did something that made you angry without fearing for his life, and he will also be able to admit to feeling angry himself.

4. Responses that May Encourage Your Child to Lie

Overreacting to minor events is not such a terrific parenting technique either.

One reason that both adults and children lie is to escape the untenable consequences of their acts. Therefore, parents would do well to control their responses to the minor mistakes their children make.

* If your wrath is so severe when he makes the normal mistakes of childhood, by the time he's in his threes a child may very well choose to lie in hopes of avoiding your rage.
* Hitting, screaming, or severe punishments—such as being sent to his room without supper—for small crimes such as spilling food may eventually turn some kids into liars. Other kids become sneaks. Some will wait until they're out of the house to ''do a little bad stuff,'' if their home is too strict and punitive.
* Flying into a white-lipped silent rage and glaring at your child as if you wish to murder him can make him unwilling to own up to having done something wrong.

5. Family Lies

Another habit some families get into that may not help a child learn honesty is doing something behind somebody else's back. Here's a typical example. ''Let's go get ice cream, but let's not tell Daddy.'' Because Daddy's on a diet and you feel unsupportive eating ice cream. Or Daddy always worries about money, but you know a couple of bucks won't send you to the poorhouse. Even though your motivation may be kind, ''Let's not tell Daddy'' sets up a duplicitous mood that in the long run will not make it a better home.

B. HONESTY IN COMMUNICATION—KIDS' LIES
1. Reality Check

The child under three can't lie. Not the way you and I might lie. The response to a straightforward question such as "Did you peek?" will receive a straightforward answer of yes or no.

But sometimes their reality is a little different from ours and needs gentle guidance from Mom. If a two-year-old sees a toy across the room, moves toward it, and another child picks it up before he can get there, he means it when he shouts, "Mine!" He does not perceive any difference between wanting it and having it.

He needs a reality check from Mommy. "You wanted it"—that's reality—"but Kimberly got there first." This is a piece of information he may need to consider. And perhaps have pointed out several, if not many, times hence.

By four and five we see two kinds of behavior that are in the reality-check area. The four-year-old who tells you that there were seven, no eight, no maybe nineteen hundred balloons at the party is not lying. He is not even exaggerating. He is accurately reporting on his experience: There were a lot of balloons at the party.

He will profit from a simple piece of information. "Was there a balloon for every kid?"

"Yes! Everybody got one!"

"I think Maggie invited everyone in your class to her party. That means there were probably twenty-five balloons."

"Her cousins were there too."

"Oh, so there were more than twenty-five. It must've been wonderful."

"It was."

This type of gentle introduction to numerical reality will help your child. Saying, "There couldn't have been that many balloons," or even laughing, "What an imagination! You made up so many balloons," will not necessarily help your child learn how to report honestly and accurately. It will, however, instill in him the feeling that he has said something wrong or bad.

On a trickier note, we start to see kids defend themselves by twisting the truth. If your child is in a store playing with something he's not supposed to and a stranger yells, "Hey! Get your hands off that!" your startled child may very well cry and say, "I wasn't touching it." Is he lying? Not like you or I would be if we said the same thing. What's the difference? He's young and hasn't been taught yet. Asking if the man frightened him when he yelled will help your child admit that something unpleasant happened. Suggesting that he didn't know he wasn't supposed to touch that will help him. Letting him know that it might have been better to say to the man, "I'm sorry," or "I didn't know," instead of "I wasn't touching it," will offer him alternatives to how he might've acted. Calling him a liar won't help him. It won't give him an alternative, and it will give him a label to live up to or live down.

What will help your child eventually learn the difference between truth and willful fabrication is your unflinching truth in your communications with him.

That leads us to an even trickier part of things, where "honesty" and "not hurting anyone" meet.

2. Little White Lies

By the preschool years of four and five we can begin to teach our children another big lesson: Honesty is important—and so are feelings.

Here's a typical example of when a little white lie is not a bad thing to teach your child. Grandma sends a toy that is in some way unsuitable.

One of those down-home phrases should kick right in. "It's the thought that counts." This is the truth.

Should your child utter an astute, resounding countertruth such as "Yeah, but Grandma *knows* I don't like Legos," offer something soothing such as "Grandma may have forgotten." Even if you secretly agree with your child, even if Grandma consistently gives all the grandchildren gifts they don't like, even if Grandma is a real piece of work.

Your child may very well not want to thank her or may even come right out and say he didn't like the gift. Then he needs you to remind him that telling someone you don't like their gift, while honest, is not nice. It's honest to thank Grandma for thinking of you. It's not nice to make her feel bad that she didn't make a good choice.

Here's another typical example. Your child is invited to a birthday party that he doesn't want to go to.

"I don't like Jesse. Do I have to go?"

"No. But it's not nice to say, 'I don't like you.' You can say, 'Thank you for inviting me, but I won't be able to come.' "

"What if he asks why not?"

"We'll make other plans. Then you can say I have other plans that day."

Lesson: *People's feelings count. We do not say hurtful things.*

C. HONESTY ABOUT POSSESSIONS

Whatever your personal choices in life may be, if you want to raise a child who by his teen years knows that it's wrong to steal, you have to pay attention when he's little to the kinds of things you do, which is your modeling, and to the kinds of things you let him do, which is your teaching. This is not always as easy as it sounds.

I. Kids and Things

A young child doesn't steal. He doesn't know the difference between mine and yours. Here are some ways to show him. They are not always the easiest or most convenient choices for you to make, but he will take all his cues from you.

Toys and Other Objects

- ❖ If your child leaves a store holding an object you didn't pay for, tell him we have to pay for things in stores. Go back and return it. If you go back and pay for it, don't be surprised if he expects you to pay for anything he filches when he's older.
- ❖ If you discover it when you get home, point out to your child that you didn't pay for it. Go back to the store the next day, *making sure your child hears,* and say, ''We mistakenly left the store with this book.'' Again, do not buy the book. A clever child may catch on to this as a way to get something you didn't agree to buy.
- ❖ If your child leaves someone's home holding something, return immediately. If you discover it when you get home, call the person *while your child is listening* and say he took whatever it was. Return it when your child is with you. Explain in kid-friendly terms that he wouldn't like it if Joey took home one of his toys.
- ❖ If you're the last ones leaving the playground and he sees a toy and wants to take it home, remind him that it's not his. He wouldn't want someone to take the toy he'd forgotten. He'd want them to leave it so he could come back and find it tomorrow.
- ❖ In these examples the word *stealing* never has to be uttered. It is the behavior you are trying to instill, not name-calling.

Lesson: *Something I pick up somewhere besides home, no matter how interesting, is not mine.*

Understandable, but Nevertheless Less-useful Responses

❖ You look down and see your child holding a pack of gum, realizing he must've picked it up three stores back. You figure, "No big deal. It only cost a quarter," and continue shopping.

❖ You find a freebie kid's-meal toy in his backpack and realize it must've come from his play date at Joey's. When you're on the phone that evening with Joey's mom, you mention, "By the way, we seem to have inherited Joey's Aladdin-on-a-skateboard." She answers, "Better your house than mine. I'm going to have to move soon just to get a bigger house to hold all these freebies." You both laugh, hang up, and that's that.

❖ Why shouldn't we take home this bucket? If that kid's mom didn't care enough about it to remember it, why shouldn't my kid have it?

> **Not-so-hot Lesson:** Anything I can get my hands on is fair game to claim.

Money

A penny lying on the sidewalk counts as "finders keepers." But not if you know whose money it is.

If he sees a penny lying in the candy rack at child's eye level in a store, explain that it's the store's money. Tell him to tell the cashier, "I found some of your money."

> **Lesson:** When I know whose money it is, I return it.

2. Moms and Things

Besides responding to your child's actions, the things he sees you do will sink in.

Useful Mom Models

❖ If you find a hat lying in the street, hang it on a gate, on top of a mailbox, or somewhere where the owner may be likeliest to find it. Tell your child somebody will be looking for this, and we'd want somebody to do this for us.

❖ If a restaurant doesn't charge you for something you ate, or a cashier makes a mistake in your favor, make sure your child hears you say, "You forgot to charge us for the ice cream" or "You gave me extra change."

Less Useful Mom Models

❖ You don't pay full fare on the bus, plane, or train. Mentioning that no one will ever know, you discuss it with your husband with your child in earshot.

❖ In order not to have to pay full fare, you teach your child to say he is younger than he is.

❖ You pinch silverware, napkins, etc., from restaurants and hotels.

> **Not-so-hot Lesson:** These are all petty crimes, small stuff. But they teach, by example, a very tricky lesson that someday you may wish you'd never taught: We do whatever we can get away with.

SECTION 3: GAMES: WINNING A MORAL VICTORY

Some fifty percent of our high school and college students report that they cheat. What's worse, *they don't find anything wrong with it.*

They have been taught to succeed at all costs. That the final score matters more than the satisfaction of legitimate accomplishment.

This troubling tendency is not a Sunday school discussion. What this means is that when you are sitting in an airplane or going under anesthesia or driving over a bridge or entrusting your life's savings to a money manager, you have a fifty-fifty shot that the person in charge knows what they're doing.

I do not believe that the moms who raised all these cheaters are not nice. I think they were asleep at the wheel.

How can we do differently with this next generation? First let's look at it developmentally. And then let's see what we should do.

Developmentally, they are not yet equipped to learn what it means to cheat.

Little kids peek at each other's cards, they put back a card they don't want, they turn the dice the way they want them.

To give you a time frame of what you can reasonably expect, by the time your child is in first or second grade he will understand what it means to cheat. If he cheats too much, the other kids will not want to play with him.

In the meantime, during this foundation-building period at home while they're still little, there are two major things that we mothers of young children should teach through games that will help build character and keep winning in perspective.

1. It's fun to play.
2. We do not always win.

A. USEFUL WAYS TO PLAY

If your four-year-old turns the die while playing Cootie until he gets the number he needs, don't call him a cheater. Instead, point out that picking the number you want isn't fair. Then suggest something playful.

Make It a Team Effort

❖ Root for each other. Try wishing, ''Oh, we need a one, we need a one, did we get a one? No! We got a three. My turn. We need a five, we need a five, did we get a five? Yes! We got lucky. Okay, your turn again. We need a one!''
❖ Don't allow him to move until his number comes up. (That encourages bending the rules to suit ourselves.) Even though it's tempting, because his number hasn't come up in twenty rolls. Focus on having fun together rather than his getting the specific number he needs, whether by fair means or not.
❖ Take turns rolling the dice for each other.
❖ Have as much fun laughing about the game as possible, so that he gets a feeling that playing is as important as winning.
❖ Make light of who wins.

Variation: Count how many times it takes to roll the dice to build two Cooties. Sometimes suggest, ''Let's not play to win, let's just play for fun.'' While you're busily taking turns and building Cooties together, mention how much fun this is.

Lesson: *Playing games is fun.*

B. LESS USEFUL BUT COMMON PARENTING TECHNIQUE
Always Let Your Child Win

While it might give you luxurious pleasure to see the big smile come over your two-and-a-half-year-old's face when you say, "You won!" it won't be so much fun in a couple of years when he's playing with friends and he's scowling, accusing everybody else of cheating, and throwing his cards down in a huff because he expects to always win. Make sure you give your child the opportunity to learn how to lose.

SUMMARY:

❖ In order to teach right from wrong, match your words, tone of voice, and expression to suit what he's done: when he's been bad, when he's exasperated you, when he's been mildly remiss, and when he's been good.

❖ In order to teach honesty, you must be honest yourself in all your dealings with your child.

❖ Focus on playing, not on winning, and don't always let your child win.

Discipline Is Not a Dirty Word

If from infancy you treat children as gods
they are liable in adulthood to act as devils.
—P. D. James

Whenever grandparents visit our classes I always ask them what they think the major difference is between how they raised their kids and how kids are being raised today.

Their answers are always a variation of the following: ''When you were kids we were in the driver's seat. But it seems to me that today the children rule the roost.''

Former generations of parents got into trouble because their idea of proper behavior came closer to the bone than was helpful. There were strict rules for everything, from when you could wear white shoes to what color your friends could be. In a classic backlash we are getting into problems because we are loath to impose any restraints on our children for fear of destroying their creativity, autonomy, and self-esteem.

If a parent is too strict the child has to either cave in or bust out. She will spend a lifetime nervously following rules or defiantly breaking them.

Conversely, if a parent is too permissive the kid doesn't know which end is up. Out in the world she often may be in trouble. Or she may make her life a constant quest to define rules; she may impose them on herself or, more likely, try and impose her rules on others.

Our job, as parents, is to find a happy medium. While teaching our child right from wrong we need to allow her enough personal space, in the common parlance, to flourish and grow as an individual.

SECTION 1: OVERVIEW

Definition

Discipline is the combination of techniques—including teaching, correcting, rewarding, and punishing—that molds a child's behavior.

The Purpose of Discipline

The world is full of rules. If your child does not learn how to respect and follow rules at home, she will be in big trouble out in the world.

General Advice

Start young, stay firm, and keep clear on who is responsible for what.

Meaningful Discipline

In order for discipline to be effective it must be predicated on two basic concepts:

1. The adult is in charge.
2. The adult is fair.

Successful Discipline

Our goal should be to teach our child how to determine, from within herself, what is acceptable. In order to achieve this end we have to establish areas that brook no nonsense while at the same time respecting other areas where there is leeway for the child to experiment, thereby learning.

Choose Your Battles

Your child, from birth onward, will be trying to do exactly what she wants. Who wouldn't? This natural attempt manifests itself in a million big and small ways, making some days feel like a series of unending power struggles. If you are clear from the git-go about which general areas of life she has a perfect right to be in charge of and which areas are not hers to discuss, both of you will feel better.

Parents are in charge of:

* Setting the rules.
* Running the household.
* Safety.
* Health.

Children are in charge of:

* All personal preferences, as long as they do not interfere with the areas above.

Setting the Rules

- ❖ Keep your rules broad and fair.
- ❖ Good rules accommodate human behavior, but establish parameters beyond which we cannot go, *under any circumstances.*
- ❖ Be prepared to alter some rules, such as kitchen safety, as your child matures.
- ❖ Accommodate your child's individual personality. Some children can function only with strict, specific limits; others catch on more quickly to the principles and can adjust their behavior accordingly.
- ❖ Rules in families with more than one child, by necessity, should not be across-the-board; we have different rules and expectations for different ages and personalities. This in itself is a valuable lesson about life.

The Rules Do Not Shift to Accommodate Your Convenience

- ❖ If you lay down the law when it's convenient for you, but let things slide when it's easier to ignore your child because something else is going on, you will teach your child that in life anything we can get away with is okay as long as the authority is busy elsewhere. It is not okay.

General Lessons Your Child Will Learn

- ❖ There is right and wrong.
- ❖ There is an order and hierarchy in human relationships.
- ❖ There are parameters of behavior beyond which we may not go.
- ❖ Children are expected to follow fair rules and instructions.
- ❖ Mommy and Daddy love me enough to stick to their guns even when I'm acting like a jerk.
- ❖ Mommy and Daddy love me enough to let me have complete control over my personal tastes, likes, and dislikes.

Personality Types Who Have Trouble with Discipline

- ❖ **The strong-willed child:** Some children's temperaments are such that the very idea of their not being in charge is enraging. They often grow up to be leaders. But you can't be a good leader until you've learned to be a good follower. These children need to know that the grown-up is in charge.

❖ **The tractable child:** Some children accept whatever you tell them. The challenge in parenting them is to foster their ability to make choices and show preferences.

❖ **The mom who is uncomfortable being in charge:** In spite of shifting roles and fathers' participation in parenting, women are essentially in charge of the children. Many women, for a number of reasons, have trouble being in charge. Children are not uncomfortable being a child. Nor are they uncomfortable with your being an adult. Even if you are. One of your child's real needs is for you to act like an adult—which means being in charge.

❖ **The mom who has trouble relinquishing control:** For some women the domestic arena is the only place where they reign supreme. Other women are bosses at work and continue at home. All children, however, regardless of their mother's lives, need to be given autonomy to choose their own way of doing some things, even when it doesn't fit their mother's prescribed notion of the "best way" to do something.

Situations Ripe for Too Much Leeway

❖ The "nicer" or more compliant you are, the harder staying in charge is.

❖ The less time you spend with your child, the more likely it is that you want to have every moment pleasant; therefore, you have trouble saying no.

❖ Only-children tend to be treated as adults, which means they are given too much power.

❖ Verbally precocious children tend to lull us into thinking that they're also ahead of themselves emotionally. They are not. In fact, some of the most verbal children can be very immature emotionally. We develop unevenly. Parents of a "talker" need to remind themselves frequently that they are dealing with a young child, not a small adult.

Situations Ripe for Too Little Leeway

❖ The more dictatorial you are, the harder it may be to let your child have a say over what should be her provenance.

❖ The less autonomy you have at work, the more likely you are to want to be completely in control at home.

❖ If you have a domineering husband you may be inclined to take it out on your kid.

❖ The more of a perfectionist you are, the harder it may be for you to allow your child the freedom to learn from mistakes.

Common Erroneous Assumptions about Discipline Moms Make

❖ "My child and I are peers." You are not peers. If the parent is not in charge, the child will be.

❖ "I'm my child's best friend." You are not your child's friend. You are a parent.

❖ "Children are just little grown-ups with the same powers of reason." They may have equal intellectual abilities, but they do not have as much knowledge. Reasoning is predicated on being able to follow an idea to its logical conclusion. A child does not have enough knowledge to predict, through reason, what may result. She needs to be told.

❖ "I respect my child. I treat her the same way I treat my friends." This inappropriate relationship with your child actually shows a lack of respect. It refuses to recognize her developmental needs.

Now that you're revved to take charge, I want you to back off—if you have an infant.

SECTION 2: THE FIRST SIX MONTHS: BABY IS BOSS AND BENIGN DESPOT

Infancy is rich, rare, and special. And it never comes again. It offers parents the chance to grow into our new roles in baby increments.

Babies' needs are basic. They are either sleeping or awake. When awake they are either happy or unhappy. When they are unhappy they cry. Their unhappiness, with the exception of colic, can be alleviated by physical contact, food, a new diaper, a change in temperature, or stimulation.

Because a baby is such an uncomplicated ball of raw emotion, the only one who should be subject to any discipline is you! Your baby is completely in charge. Forget your own schedules, forget anything resembling a normal life. You don't have a normal life. You have a baby.

Grab sleep when you can, grab food when you can, and grab a shower when you can.

In the first half year of life, meeting your *baby's* needs should be the determining factor in your own life, even if it means that *your* needs, at least temporarily, don't count.

CRYING

Infants cry as their only means of telling us that something's wrong. From a beginning whimper or fuss to a full-fledged wail, babies cry from hunger, sleepiness, gas pains, or loneliness. Any of these conditions need adult intervention.

Let's put ourselves in the place of an infant.

A few weeks or months ago you were inside your mommy. Complete with sloshing, warmth, and far-off comforting sounds.

You are now outside your mommy. Garbage truck brakes squeal, vacuum cleaners run, phones ring. You are on a flat, somewhat inhospitable surface instead of being completely surrounded by softness.

You feel hunger, which you certainly never felt in that nice, dark, warm place. Your mouth feels funny. You want to suck.

You are unhappy. You start to cry.

What should Mommy do?

Pick up your crying baby.

Lesson: If I cry, I will be comforted. If I am in need, my mommy will be there.

Will you teach your baby that every time she cries, someone's going to come running? You bet!

Frequent advice to new mothers, often from grandmothers, who paradoxically can be fonts of boundless love: ''Don't pick her up so much! You'll spoil her!''

Response: ''You can't spoil an infant.''

If you *don't* pick her up, you will teach your crying infant that human beings do not meet each other's elemental needs. That there is no one alive, including your own mother, who will hold you and comfort you when you need to be held. Life for that crying baby is emotional hell. Unhappiness is the established norm. Physical discomfort, fear, extreme existential loneliness, and emotional pain are the conditions of existence.

Now, you tell me, is that what you want to do to that darling lying in a room that you spent six months decorating? I think not.

Food for Thought: If you don't get held when you're a baby, when *do* you get held? Chances are you will spend the rest of your life trying to make up the loss.

Caution: If you're a mom who is reading this after the first half year of your child's life and you did listen to somebody who said, "Watch out, you'll spoil her," don't panic. It is never too late to hold your child. Never.

Question (frequently felt, rarely spoken): What about *my* needs?

Tough-love Answer: Obviously, you need to eat and sleep. But your real need, as a mother, is to be completely devoted to your child during this brief period. If you lay the groundwork now for your child's emotional well-being and security, you will avoid harder problems later. If you're lucky you've got a husband who will spell you. If you're even luckier you've got a husband who remembers that you like tuberoses and back rubs. But even if you have no backup, your baby's needs should take precedence over yours.

Question: That's all well and good, but I've got other children, a job, a sick mother, or any of the other normal events that occur in life.

Answer: None of these conditions takes away the infant's needs. Find a baby-sitter, a grandmother, or somebody who can pitch in to make sure that this infant doesn't get lost in the shuffle.

Food for Thought: You rarely see a baby in a Snugli crying. You frequently see a baby in a carriage or car seat crying. Most babies crave physical contact. Strap your baby next to your body in and out of the house as much as you can for the first three or four months. Carry your older baby next to your body outside of the house for as long as you can bear the weight. Once they become mobile, most prefer exploration on their own steam in the house and seem to enjoy being out in the world in a stroller.

Further Food for Thought: Crying babies in carriages are often offered a pacifier. By default, their crying stops. Who can cry with a mouthful?

Experiment: If your baby stops crying when you pick her up, then the need is to be held, not to suck. If that same baby gets plugged in every time she needs to be held, we have taught her that something in the mouth—whether you need something in your mouth or not—is a useful substitute for a different need. Later in life this may translate to eating disorders, smoking, nail biting, and any number of other ways to meet emotional needs orally.

Please don't misread this as antipacifier. If a baby needs to suck and a pacifier satisfies that need, it is useful. The trick is to determine what need your baby is expressing and meet it directly.

If your baby is crying from a minor accident—if she falls off your bed or the changing table—try not to scream, gasp, yell, or shout. You're the grown-up. She's the one who needs comforting. Stay calm. Your fear will frighten her; your calm will soothe.

Food for Thought: A new baby is like a new car. It's easier after the first scratch or dent. Hope that your baby has a minor tumble between the ages of three to six months, when no injury occurs! After that both of you can relax.

The goal is not to get them to stop crying.
The goal is to make them feel better.

SECTION 3: THE SECOND SIX MONTHS: SHIFTING THE BALANCE OF POWER

Most young children have trouble with transitions. So do most adults.

Often, we don't notice that she has developed sufficiently to begin being able to handle subtle shifts in the balance of power. Whereas crying in infancy has only one satisfactory response, an older baby's crying offers us a rich opportunity to respond with various alternatives, which begin teaching that there are rules in life and that Mommy is in the lead.

A. LETTING YOUR BABY CRY

There comes a time when your baby understands that if she cries, Mommy will appear. This is different from an infant crying, because she doesn't know what else to do. Crying now becomes a conscious decision that a baby makes. Six months is a ballpark figure, although depending on your child this may happen any time from five to eight months.

The best way to gauge when this shift occurs will be an unmistakable "knowing" look in her eye when she's crying.

Let's examine a typical domestic scene.

Your baby is in her bedroom sleeping. Suddenly, you hear a cry and go running. Grace lights up when she sees you. She stretches her arms up toward you. You pick her up out of the crib, dance around, and ask if she had a nice nap, while she twists your hair around her finger. You waltz into the living room.

So far, so pretty. You settle down on the couch for a nice snuggle. She nurses or has a bottle. Then you put her in her infant seat for a rousing game of "Where's Grace?" The dryer beeps. You say, "Oops! There's the dryer," hand her a rattle, and leave the living room.

Grace starts to wail.

You come dashing back.

Grace immediately stops crying. She grins and starts chatting. "Goo goo, blahzzz."

You say, "Mommy's going into the kitchen."

You turn to go and Grace starts to cry.

You look back and see:

1. Grace crying with her eyes wide open, a dead giveaway that you have a conscious creature on your hands. Depending on her temperament, she may have a mildly expectant look, a confused look, or an angry look.
2. Some babies don't even bother to cry. They go "Eh, eh, eh," in a perfect imitation of a cry! (If your baby is one of these, she will probably be a talker sooner than later.)

At this very moment you and your baby have entered the world of *discipline and setting limits.* This is a perfect time to begin to establish who's in charge and why.

You have a choice of what you communicate:

Choice 1: If she's in real need you're there for her, but if she wants to run the whole show it won't work.

Choice 2: You are available for emotional blackmail.

Choice 1 is clearly more attractive than Choice 2. But what's easy to think in the abstract is not always so easy to do. Therefore, let's look at how you can teach your baby that she follows Mommy's lead in many areas of life. (Please read the section that follows, "Not Letting Your Baby Cry," before you try any of these ideas. Thanks.)

Activity: Teaching Your Six-month-old that Life Isn't Over When She's Alone

Your baby needs to learn that there are times when being alone is part of life. She needs to learn how to amuse herself. Choose a moment when she's fed, rested, and has spent some time playing with you.

Step 1:

- ❖ Put your baby comfortably and safely in a baby seat with several interesting objects within reach.
- ❖ Say, "Mommy will be right back."
- ❖ Leave the room, wait a minute, stick your head in the door, and say, "Here I am!" Baby laughs.
- ❖ Do it again. And again. And again.

> **Lesson:** Mommy's face is such an interesting object. It keeps disappearing and reappearing. Those sounds she makes, "Mommy will be right back," mean that her face will reappear in a little while. How very, very interesting.

Question: How do I keep my baby from thinking this is a game?
Answer: You don't. That's the point. Babies live to play!

Step 2:

After your baby enjoys this game of hide-and-seek every once in a while for a week or so, move on.

- ❖ Same setup, baby safe, several toys at hand.
- ❖ Say, "Mommy's going into the kitchen to load the dishwasher [or some other ten-minute job]. You stay here and play. Mommy will be right back."
- ❖ Leave.
- ❖ If baby calls out, answer in kind, calling, "I'm in the kitchen. I'll be right back."
- ❖ If baby cries, still call out that you'll be right back. (Again, check section on "Not Letting Your Baby Cry.")
- ❖ Even if your baby is still fussing, don't return until you've loaded the dishwasher. This is for you as much as for her. *You've* got to start getting clear on what you're allowed to do as a parent just as *she* has to learn the ropes of childhood.

❖ Most babies will stop crying before ten minutes are up, so that you can return to a happily engaged baby.
❖ When you reenter the room, say, ''Hi! You see? I told you I'd be back, and here I am!''

Lesson: When Mommy says she'll be back, she comes back. Actually, these plastic keys are so interesting and tasty that once I stopped fussing, I had a pretty nice time. So if Mommy disappears and says she'll be right back, it won't be so bad. I'll just play a little. I can be alone and survive quite nicely, thank you very much.
Corollary Lessons: Language development: Now I know what the words "I'll be right back" mean. Basic trust: Mommy can be relied on to tell the truth.

Question: Isn't loneliness a legitimate baby discomfort that should be attended to?
Answer: Yes. Sticking a baby by herself in a playpen all day long in front of the tube is child abuse. Letting a well-cared-for baby experience ten minutes by herself, even if those ten minutes are unpleasant, is helpful.
Question: Remind me again. Why am I doing this?
Answer: Two reasons:

1. There are times when she can play by herself. If she never learns to amuse herself, she may find that as she grows she is completely at the mercy of external stimuli.
2. Her carrying on doesn't dictate your behavior.

Predictable Pitfall: At the outraged wail you run back, pick her up, hold her tight, and feel so guilty that *you* begin to cry.

Unfortunate Lesson: If I fuss even though nothing's really wrong, I can get Mommy to come running, to hold me, and to make that funny face where she wrinkles her skin and her face gets wet. That's kind of fun, even if I had to get all worked up to do it.

Question: What should I do if this happens?

Answer: Go get a cup of tea and listen. There, there, Mommy, you're doing fine. You're attached to your baby. There's nothing wrong with that. It's beautiful. It's loving and human.

Tomorrow I want you to take your baby to a playground. Watch a two-year-old in the middle of pitching a fit over a shovel. Now watch closely. Her mommy is leaning toward her, talking, trying to hold her. *The mom* looks very upset and sad. *The toddler* looks very angry. Now watch! The mom hands her the shovel. She stops crying immediately. Not a trace of being upset on her face. In fact, she looks quite pleased.

Then go to a schoolyard. Watch a five-year-old stamp her foot, scream, and slap her mother on the arm because her mother said she couldn't have an ice cream cone. Now watch. The mom looks pained and sad. The child screams, "You promised!" The mother shakes her head, as if she's not sure whether or not she did promise. The child's eyes are flashing. Now watch! The mommy gives in. She buys the ice cream. The child snatches the ice cream from the vendor's hand without so much as a "thank you" and turns from the mother as if she weren't there.

Now go home and try again. Tell yourself that you can do it. Your baby won't die and she won't hate you. She'll be glad to see you when you come back, just the way you said you would.

Question: If I lost this battle did I lose the war?

Answer: No. If you aren't happy with the way you handled something today, try a different approach tomorrow. Both you and your baby are learning. You will grow with the process of parenting. Expect mistakes. There is no formula.

B. NOT LETTING YOUR BABY CRY
I. Distress

There is crying and then there is crying. Fussing, and even fuming, are very different from real distress. If you're feeling unsure of your own judgment, consider these ideas.

❖ A truly distressed baby's eyes will be shut when she's crying.
❖ If your baby is gasping, shuddering, silently crying, unable to catch her breath, or any other major physical upheaval, your baby is very distressed.
❖ What dialogue would you provide for the expression you see? If it's something like "How dare you leave me here!" your baby is peeved, possibly angry. If it might be, "Oh, my gosh. I don't

think I like *this* very much,'' it's fussing. These are not cries of distress.

Any truly distressed baby should be attended to. Figure out what's wrong and adjust it.

2. Low Tolerance

Some babies have a low tolerance for being away from human contact. If your baby is really distressed whenever you leave the room, your baby will not benefit from enforced bits of time alone.

Here's a revised activity for teaching your baby with low tolerance for isolation how to begin to get along independently:

❖ Take the baby into the kitchen with you.
❖ Put her comfortably in an infant seat where she can see you.
❖ Give her some toys.
❖ Go about your business without paying too much attention to her.
❖ Turn your back as you work.
❖ If she fusses and throws her keys, hand them back. Tell her she's okay and you want to load the dishwasher.
❖ If she hollers, soothe her with words. Smile and talk, without picking her up.
❖ When you're done loading the dishwasher, pick her up. Say, ''We made it!'' Hug her. Hug yourself.

Lesson: *I may not love it, but I can engage in an activity of my own while Mommy does something grown-up.*

---

3. Separation Anxiety

Textbook separation anxiety occurs at eight months. This, like all other developmental stages, may span any age from four months to three years, or may never occur at all, depending on your child. Most clock in somewhere in the second half of their first year. Although we can speculate on the psychological reasons from now till doomsday, it is the behavior that you need to attend to.

You will know that your baby is experiencing this if she becomes intensely attached to you. Suddenly a baby-sitter she's had all her life becomes a terror. Her beloved grandmother's face sets her into fits, clutching at you for dear life.

In our classes approximately one out of every twelve babies has this response even to their dads. This one is particularly devastating. Please pass on to your husbands that this usually lasts no more than two weeks for most babies. Even though it feels like an eternity.

At this period in your baby's life, she needs you. I don't know why. I don't care why. She needs you. Keep her with you. Take her into the kitchen, into the laundry room, wherever you have to go. It won't last long, but while it lasts it's intense. This is a real need, not a manipulative one.

Food for Thought: To try and empathize with your baby, see if you remember how you felt at any of the following times in your own life: the first day of kindergarten, overnight camp, college, or on your own wedding day.

Remember the excitement and the fear all at once? But you had a million social skills by this time to deal with conflicting emotions. Your baby doesn't. She has no experience with the process of getting past the fear of something new and realizing that it's fun on the other side of the fear.

Question: I thought you just said that I have to teach her from the time she's little that she's not completely in control, and that a good place to start is around the house when she tries to get me to stay with her.

Answer: There are no hard and fast rules in parenting. People go through different things at different times. When your baby is in the throes of separation anxiety, it is not the time to be firm about staying away. It is the time to be firm about meeting her emotional needs.

Respond from the heart and the head, and hope that they are in accord. If you have to err in favor of one, go with the heart.

Separation Anxiety and the Working Mom

Some of us work because we have to, others because we want to. Both are valid life choices.

But the validity of your choice doesn't soften the blow on the day when you're dressed for work, your baby-sitter arrives or you go to day care, your baby starts screaming, and you have to make one of those god-awful transfers of clinging arms and adults crooning, ''There, there,'' as you extricate yourself and leave your baby. Here are some ideas that may soothe your baby's anxiety—and your own.

❖ Listen at the door. Don't go back in. You'll drive your kid nuts.
❖ The crying will stop within five to ten minutes. You'll feel better. Go to work and do a good job.
❖ If it doesn't stop within a half hour, find a new child-care arrangement. Period. What that tells you is that the care giver is incapable of engaging your child in an interesting activity.
❖ When you get home from work, no matter how exhausted you are, hold your baby. If you have to order out to keep her physically near you instead of cooking, eat pizza. If the phone rings, monitor with your answering machine and keep necessary conversations short. When your husband comes home, if your baby wants to be with him, terrific. If not, hold your baby.
❖ Many working families find letting their babies sleep in their beds during this period helps (please see Chapter 8).
❖ If the same thing happens tomorrow, go to work. But decide that on the following day you will call in sick. I know that sounds radical, but sometimes one full Mommy day does the trick. Your baby gets whatever reassurance she needs, and back you both go to your regular routines. In all honesty, sometimes this method backfires, making the next day harder. If it works, terrific. If it doesn't, you tried.
❖ Cancel any social plans that require leaving your baby, day by day, for the next few weeks, until this period has ended. There will be plenty of parties, dinners, and business meetings in the future.
❖ Pray that you don't have any crucial business events to attend at night during this short period. Juggle like you've never juggled. Reschedule. If you can't, at least shorten your participation in the event.
❖ Hold on to the fact that this particularly intense separation anxiety comes once and is usually short in duration.

All this is strictly during separation anxiety. If you feel that you *never* want to leave your baby with your baby-sitter or in day care, that is a whole different issue. You may need to figure out how to stop work and be a full-time mother. If your baby never wants you to go, there may be a problem with the care arrangements you've made. You will need to change them

Here's a tip for an occasional bout of your toddler suddenly not wanting you to go, which is different from separation anxiety. Sometimes, out of the blue, they just get that way.

❖ Say, "Mommy always comes back. Always. If you feel lonely, just say that out loud. Say it with me. 'Mommy always comes back. Always.'"

❖ When you come back, say, "See? I told you. Mommy always comes back."

Some day-care workers have reported that children come up to them during the day and seriously announce, "Mommy always comes back. Always," before toddling off to play. Clearly, their mommy's words comfort them. Ah, the power of your voice.

4. Out and About

Another time not to let your baby cry in order to encourage independence is out of the house. An untended baby crying in a stroller or car seat is an unhappy baby.

Things that Help

❖ Physical contact. Hold her hand as you push the stroller, or stick your hand into the backseat and stroke her leg (if you're not speeding along an expressway).

❖ Offer a new board book or rattle.

❖ Sing. I made up a silly, soothing song: "We're almost there, we're almost there, we're almost there, my girl, my little girl." It still does the job when my daughter gets bored at the end of a long trip. Now she sings along. Whether a made-up song or a song you know, after a few times most babies find a consistent song soothing and will settle down.

> **Lesson:** *Mommy doesn't just let me wail my head off as if she can't hear me out here. She gives me lots of different things to do. If we still have to be rolling along here, all strapped in, I think I'll just . . . zzzzzzzzz.*

C. TERRIFIC OPPORTUNITIES TO ESTABLISH HABITS OF DISCIPLINE

Besides letting your baby cry for short, safe periods at home, there are several other nifty things that almost all babies in the second half of their first year do that allow you—together—to dip your toes into the turbulent waters of *right and wrong, who's in charge, and setting limits.*

A smart mom takes advantage of these predictable events to gently begin the correcting process. A nice mom often has trouble recognizing that these seemingly innocuous, adorable pieces of behavior, unchecked, aren't so cute.

Since I know that you're both smart and nice and love your little baby to bits, I know you'll at least consider trying some of these tips.

Hair Pulling

How many Moms I have seen, their heads bent over sideways, strained smiles on their faces as their surprisingly strong babies yank on their hair!

❖ Don't grab your baby's wrist—the normal reflex—because then the hair is still being pulled. Babies often pull other babies' hair, so train yourself to respond carefully. Undo baby's fingers.

❖ Say, "We don't pull hair." Shake your head "no." Look serious.

❖ Don't make an enormous, angry frown, which will either scare your baby or make her laugh.

❖ Don't smile, which tells your baby the opposite from what you mean.

❖ Offer an alternative. Hand her something she can pull on, saying, "This is a good thing to put in your hand."

❖ Repeat all of this as many times as necessary until your baby catches on.

Caution: Don't space out and let her do it sometimes. For example, if you're talking to someone and don't want to be distracted, you kind of let the hair-pulling thing slide. This will teach your baby that hair pulling is acceptable as long as she can get away with it. She can do anything as long as you're distracted. As long as she doesn't get caught. Think about the long-term ramifications of this.

Biting

There are interesting theories about why babies bite. They are overcome with love; their mouths are their major source of expression. That is terrific, lovely, and primordial. In the meantime, we don't bite!

Nursing Mothers

❖ You are allowed to have a normal, human response.

❖ Look stern. Say, "No," in a firm voice.

❖ Remove your baby from the breast.

Usually, one or two bites on the breast is all they do, so please don't give up nursing just because your baby nips you.

General Biting

- ❖ Same as above, adding, "We don't bite people."
- ❖ Sometimes a gentle hand closing her mouth gets the idea across.
- ❖ Hand her something she can bite. "This is a good thing to bite."

Glasses

Show me a baby who doesn't want to pull glasses and I'll show you a stuffed toy. Dads, are you listening? In my experience, many dads find this cute. But is it cute when you're carrying your baby across a busy intersection and your glasses fly off your head? When your glasses get bent out of shape? Cute? Not!

- ❖ "Glasses are not a toy."
- ❖ Hand her a toy, saying, "This is a toy."

Earrings

Same as above.

Lesson: Humans have physical boundaries. We don't bite or yank on parts of people or things dangling from their faces. But nice Mommy showed me something I can bite or yank on. She understands what I need, but won't let me do what I shouldn't, even if she's busy doing something else.

SECTION 4: THE MOBILE BABY

The situations we've described so far take place in almost every home with a baby. They are small, predictable, and handy for beginning to teach your baby that some things are allowed—and some aren't.

Once your baby is mobile, the variety of situations where discipline can be successfully introduced to teach your child right from wrong—as well as the physical trouble your child can get into—increases dramatically. In the following chapters we'll look at specific situations.

Here are some generalizations about discipline to keep in mind.

A. USEFUL TECHNIQUES

- ❖ Help her with your visual cues. Look her in the eye when telling her not to do something.
- ❖ Don't look around at your spouse or some other adult as if you're sharing a joke.
- ❖ Don't laugh or smile as if you think she's the cutest thing in the world. (Even though she is!)
- ❖ Avoid overusing the word *no*. Reserve that for real danger.
- ❖ For all other corrections, provide her with alternatives. Example: "We don't put the cat's tail in our mouth. We put this teething ring in."

B. LESS USEFUL TECHNIQUES
The Fateful Gasp

If you gasp every time your kid goes near the edge of something or picks up something she shouldn't have, your child will learn to tune out your gasp. What happens then is if you gasp when your child is in real danger, she won't respond.

The Overreaction

If your sitting baby falls over or your toddler topples, don't scream, jump up, grab her to you, etc. Your overreaction will scare her more than the fall. Stay calm. Pick her up and comfort her—only if she needs it.

> **True Tale from the Trenches:** I can't tell you how many new walkers I've seen fall down, have absolutely no reaction, and look up to see what Mommy thinks. If she looks upset they immediately squall. If she smiles reassuringly and says, "You're okay," they pick themselves up and stagger off in the Frankenstein imitation new walkers are so good at.

SECTION 5: TODDLERHOOD UP

Beyond babyhood, the number of rules, expected behaviors, and potential conflicts increases dramatically. So do our children's responses. Sometimes the tenacity and sophistication of their responses catches us off guard.

A. USEFUL TECHNIQUES

- ❖ As we discussed in Chapter 1, respond honestly in tone and body language. Do the best you can to have your response match the level of "the crime."
- ❖ Be consistent. If you're unsure about consistency, look at some of the baby advice. Don't let some things slide sometimes because it's easier in the moment to ignore whatever it is.
- ❖ Provide positive alternatives to the best of your ability.
- ❖ Use verbal reminders ahead of time about the kind of behavior you expect, and have a conversation afterward about something that really wasn't good.
- ❖ Don't forget to praise when you notice that your child is catching on.

"Because I Said So"

If used judiciously this phrase will give your child a sense of security that the parent is in charge. What might such a time be? When the child is wielding too much power. How does "too much power" manifest? When you've spent the morning arguing about socks, shoes, cereal, and sweaters, and it's enough already.

Frequently a testy toddler—and even a considerably older child—will be relieved that the grown-up broke the pattern.

If, however, "because I said so" is the only answer you offer in the face of every confrontation, it will lose its effectiveness.

Quiet Moments

Throughout the book I suggest talking about difficult lessons "in a quiet moment." *Please* make sure you don't use *every* quiet moment to teach. *Please* make sure that most of your quiet moments are spent snuggling, giggling, discussing the day's events, planning something pleasurable, and having fun.

B. LESS USEFUL TECHNIQUES

Here are some approaches, many of which you may try in desperation once or twice, only to discover that they are completely ill-suited to teaching anything you really want to teach. If you use any of them as a major method of discipline, you should rethink how you spend your day with your child.

1. The Demon of Negotiation

Leave "Let's make a deal" to Monty Hall. "If you put on your coat without carrying on, we can go to the playground" is the wrong reason.

"If you put on your coat, you won't be cold" makes sense. A child should be expected to do something because it is good in and of itself, not because they will get something for good behavior.

Bribery usually backfires. By three and four, if you use bribery don't be surprised if you hear, "Mommy, if you don't make me take my medicine, I'll stop carrying on."

2. The Empty Threat

"If you hit Bobby again, I'm going to take away all your toys."

Get off it. You are *not* going to take away all her toys. Your words are just that—empty words.

On the other hand, if you *do* take away all her toys, your punishment is so extreme that it's cruel.

3. Let the Punishment Fit the Crime

When you pick a punishment, make sure it doesn't punish yourself. Let's say that you love connecting with other moms in the park and look forward all morning to getting there for adult contact. Saying to your recalcitrant two-year-old, "If you don't get dressed right now, we can't go to the park," punishes you more than your child. If you have more than one child, not getting to go to the park punishes the others as well. Instead, you might try, "If you don't get dressed right now, you can't go on the swings when we get to the playground." Then stick to it when you get there, reminding your child that tomorrow when you ask her to get dressed, she should remember how this feels.

4. Don't Bear Grudges

Children's moods shift dramatically and quickly. This is one place where we would do well to follow their lead. Don't hold on to your anger past its usefulness.

5. Time-out

The basic idea of a time-out is to give your child the time, when she loses control, to collect herself before reentering the fray. It is not seen as a punishment, but rather as a method to learn self-control.

The rules of the technique are:

❖ Find a neutral spot.
❖ Have your child sit there one minute for each year of life.
❖ Instruct her to think about why she's there.
❖ Tell her when she can come back.

I have seen this technique used effectively as a means of stopping disagreeable behavior. I have even used it myself. It didn't sit right with me when I did it. The more times I've watched it in action with other mothers and children, the less happy I am with it as a disciplinary technique when dealing with young children. Here's why.

You're not supposed to be punishing the child; you're supposed to be helping him collect himself. But what kid in his right mind doesn't experience being banished as a punishment? For a small child who is emotionally incapable of calm reflection on what went wrong, time-out *is* a punishment. There's an underlying dishonesty about this method for a preschooler.

A two-year-old in the midst of a tantrum is not being bad. He is being a two-year-old, albeit an unruly one. While a time-out for this child may stop the behavior, it doesn't teach how to gain self-control. Rather, it teaches the opposite: If you lose control, someone else will take over. Ultimately, you have taught the opposite from what you want.

You, the same as I, may at some point be desperate enough to try this technique on for size. If you do I ask you to consider the following:

❖ If you are so angry with your child's behavior that you feel like hitting, time-out is a viable alternative. As long as you keep in mind that it's for *your* self-control, not your child's.

❖ Don't give a time-out to a child younger than two, and try to wait until they're at least into their threes. Time-out is most effective from the ages of six through ten, way beyond the emotional capabilities of the children in this book.

❖ Don't use their crib or room. These places should be cozy havens, not places of banishment.

❖ If you find that you're using time-out regularly over more than a week or so, step back. Look at the "Problems" sections in Chapter 11 for suggestions about taking the pressure off your family.

6. Physical Force

Did your parents ever hit you when you were little? Try and remember the incident. In most cases adults remember *getting hit,* but usually *not the reason why.* Therefore, besides being mean, hitting is an ineffective means for teaching anything useful.

Most readers of this book probably don't have to worry about out-and-out physical abuse.

Some women are more gentle than others; some kids are more temperamental than others. But in almost every home there will come a moment—usually when your child is anywhere from eighteen months to three, during what we call the "terrible" twos—where she climbs up on the windowsill once too often. And you lose it. You grab her and yank her down.

What do you do? You take a deep breath, you step back, and you feel extremely upset. So does your kid. You would do both of you a favor by apologizing, saying how sorry you are that you lost your temper and that wasn't nice.

If you still feel rage, walk away.

Although I am most assuredly not suggesting that you lose your temper on purpose, there is one positive aspect. Your child has been testing limits. Now you both know what those limits are. Furthermore, when you have weathered this unpleasant experience, you both now know that people lose their tempers, get real mad at each other, but still love each other. This is not an insignificant lesson to learn.

However, should you physically lose it, either in intensity of your physical response or in the number of incidents occurring—more than "in one of those moments"—something else is going on. Either motherhood is putting too much pressure on you, something else is going on in your life that is stressful and your kid's behavior is more than you can bear, or you're not handling your child in a way that either of you is finding useful. In any of these situations you would do you and your child a big favor by getting some outside help.

TRUE TALE THAT I REVEAL ONLY BECAUSE IT LED ME TO SOMETHING POSITIVE

There was a nasty period in our home, just as there will probably be in yours. In this instance my then newly turned three-year-old decided bedtime was the perfect opportunity to act out.

The mention of getting ready for bed brought on clutching of hands and sobbing. Using the toilet was like climbing the stairs to be guillotined. Brushing teeth and washing face and hands was out of the question. Putting on pjs was preceded by many pounding barefoot runs up and down the hall. Backing against the bathroom wall, hiding behind the towels, at least ten minutes of meshing moods from many cultures: Italian opera, Spanish bullfighting, the anguish of the Russian steppes, some Apache howls of raging war, and a couple of kamikaze nosedives all rolled into one female preschooler. Talk about your fun-filled memories.

I resorted to some "less useful techniques."

Time-out worked for a couple of nights. Although I felt grateful that it "worked," meaning that she then ran and brushed her teeth, I felt extremely uneasy about the nasty, self-righteous feeling in the pit of my stomach as I stood there, glowering, timing her, and being *in power*.

Two nights later we were back in the game.

I then used this parenting ''technique.'' Tighten your entire body and through clenched teeth say, ''You brush those teeth or else.'' That ineffective, empty threat is good for a laugh—years later. We weren't laughing then.

Here's another parenting approach, which if used properly will make you want to die from remorse for the rest of your life. ''I'm bigger than you are, and if I have to I can make you brush those teeth.'' I grabbed her hand and shoved her toothbrush right up next to her face. This is not a high point in your mothering career.

After that ''method'' and the indescribably horrible feelings that followed, I was not looking forward to bedtime. Nor was my daughter.

Yet there we were, next night, standing in the bathroom, glaring at each other. She hadn't peed, her teeth weren't brushed, and I don't even want to talk about washing hands and face.

I don't know what came over me. Something deep inside me stopped being angry. I shook my head a little sadly and said in a quiet voice, ''Go to bed now.''

She was stunned. She went into her room.

My daughter, perhaps like your child, adores bedtime reading and snuggling. It is a ritual we both treasure, as does my husband when it's his turn.

I said simply, ''Get in bed.'' My voice was different. I wasn't yelling or threatening. She obeyed.

''Turn out the light.'' She did.

''I'm leaving the room now.'' I left.

After a minute of stunned silence a banshee-like wail came from her room. ''I don't want to go to bed without a story. I *can't* go to sleep without a story.''

I went back in. ''Tomorrow, when it's bedtime, remember this feeling. If you don't brush your teeth, wash your face, and pee, we'll do this again.'' I left.

She cried and screamed for a good twenty minutes. My husband came home and found me balled up in a chair, hugging myself, listening to her scream. He moved toward her room. I stopped him. ''If either of us goes in there, we're all goners.''

He understood, although he glared at me as if I were Judas. After all, she's his little girl and can do no wrong.

I peeked in her room a half hour later. She was asleep.

I crawled in bed and worried, afraid she'd hate me.

The next morning she woke up happier than I'd seen her in days. At breakfast she looked at me, beamed, and said, "Mommy, you're a terrific woman." (She had learned the word *terrific* from the movie *Charlotte's Web.*)

I have never had such a wonderful compliment in my life.

Why was my child so happy in the morning after such a rocky night? Because she went to bed secure. *There was a grown-up in charge.* Finally.

THE GROWN-UP IS IN CHARGE

This is really the underlying need for the whole family, children and adults. But it's not always so easy. Being a grown-up doesn't mean being bigger and older. It doesn't mean you can yell louder, physically overpower her, or punish her. That's basically just being a bigger baby.

Being a grown-up means that you do not take your child's boundary testing personally. You do not feel the same need to "win." You are not playing the same game that your child is playing. If there is a game at all, the grown-up must be the ump, the ref, the fair dispassionate observer who guides when things get out of line.

A child needs the grown-up to be in control emotionally. Although we all agree in theory to this, most mothers lose it, some with more frequency than others. But none of us is immune to the powerful urge to get in there and scrap.

My daughter and I have had other power struggles. I have sometimes forgotten myself in the heat of the moment. I have never grabbed her hand again. That was a mistake too loathsome to repeat. But I have gotten angry, unreasonably "laid down the law," and realized midstream that I am exacerbating the fight by being a willing participant. Whenever I disengage, we smoothly pass the storm. We both feel better.

I pass along this image I summon in case it helps you: the Chinese finger trap. Do you know those woven cylinders? You put your fingers in both ends and pull. When you pull, it tightens. You can't get out. The more you struggle, the tighter it gets. When you loosen up the pressure you are released. Now, whenever I feel I'm getting ready to lose it, I picture the finger trap. I let go. The trap no longer exists.

Happy Ending

At this writing my daughter is seven. The other night I said to her, "Time for bed, sweetheart."

"Okay, Mommy."

I heard her skip down the hall, the bathroom light click on, the water run, the water turn off, the toilet flush, the light click off. During all this was the sound of her humming.

Parenting, after all, is a series of interactions, some more successful than others.

Some days are better than others. You're a human being, with strengths and weaknesses. Your child is lucky. She landed in a home where all her basic human needs are met, with a mommy who loves her and is trying the best she can.

When you go to sleep tonight, thank your lucky stars and remind yourself that you did a wonderful job of parenting today. If you didn't, you'll do better tomorrow. We are all learning every day.

SUMMARY:

- ❖ General advice: Start young, stay firm, and keep clear on who is responsible for what.
- ❖ For the first six months, meeting your baby's every need should be your overriding concern.
- ❖ During the second six months shift the balance of power and begin establishing rules of acceptable behavior.
- ❖ Mobile babies do better with a calm response.
- ❖ From toddlerhood throughout the rest of childhood, children learn more from positive adult intervention and correction than from negative, punitive responses.
- ❖ The grown-up is in charge. The grown-up is mature.

Materialism and Greed: The Gimmies

America is a land of plenty.

Plenty of shopaholics. Plenty of people living beyond their means via credit cards. Plenty of teenagers killing each other for $150 sneakers. And plenty of sports administrators, businessmen, and elected officials caught with their hands in the till.

All these adults with serious moral and psychological problems were once adorable children whose lives spread before them filled with hope and promise. Just like your child.

Certainly, you don't croon in your infant's sweet-smelling ear, "Someday, when you grow up, I hope your obsession with material objects puts Imelda Marcos to shame."

Yet many of us are hard-pressed to know how to teach our children simple values such as: No one gets everything all the time. Getting love and getting things are not the same. People do not like us for what we have, but because of who we are. We should like other people for how they act, rather than for what they own. We should cherish things we really value and not need to acquire the rest.

What Makes Teaching These Lessons So Hard?

If we were all PC—psychologically correct—we would respond automatically and appropriately to our child's natural, indiscriminate desires. We would set limits clearly and consistently, thus helping our child learn self-control.

But "things" dredge up unresolved emotional baggage in many parents. As children some of us were given too much, some not enough; as parents we often try for the opposite of our own early experience. Some of us feel guilty for working so many hours; giving our kids things seems to make up for the time we can't spend with them. Some of us have trouble relinquishing control to others, and find our children's constant demands annoying, if not downright enraging; we say no on general principle. Others have trouble saying no to anyone, under any circumstances.

Besides whatever "developmental issues" each adult must contend with, there is another, more subtle element that contributes to this child-raising dilemma. A baby's joy is so unvarnished that it's fun to offer as many new sensations as possible. Many of the things that small children want are so cheap that we shrug and figure: "This makes ya happy, kid? Here, have it." Unthinkingly, we establish a habit of buying our way up and down the mall.

Often it isn't until this habit dovetails with typical two-year-old behavior that we realize we have a problem on our hands. Caught off guard by the intensity of our child's demands, we vacillate, we equivocate, or we lash out instead of saying no in a way our child can hear. Sometimes we moms are just too darn exhausted, physically and emotionally, to say no. By the time our children are five, many have developed pernicious expectations: Anything they want should be theirs.

Another factor that affects what we give our children is money. Some families can buy out the entire stock of Toys "R" Us and not blink. For others, a twenty-five-dollar Barbie doll eats up a large quantity of the weekly budget. Yet all of us, including those between the extremes, have to decide on a daily basis which and how many things our children can have. Our decisions, however, should not be predicated solely on how much we can afford.

Whatever our own psychological makeup and financial position, we owe it to our children to teach them how to be in control of things rather than have things be in control of them.

THE GIMMIES
Definition
The Gimmies is the condition where a child indiscriminately wants everything he sees and cannot take no for an answer.
General Advice
The best way to avoid the Gimmies is to teach a child that he does not have to buy or own everything he sees that he likes.

General Lessons Your Child Will Learn by Not Getting the Gimmies

- ❖ Restraint.
- ❖ Self-control.
- ❖ The ability to choose.
- ❖ Reality: No one gets everything they want, as a child or as an adult.

Hardest Developmental Stage

The "terrible twos," which, depending on the child, may begin as early as fourteen months and may end as late as three years old.

Normal Developmental Issues that Get Played Out in the Arena of the Gimmies

- ❖ Testing limits.
- ❖ Power struggles.
- ❖ Demands for immediate gratification.

Predictable Difficulties Parents Face

- ❖ Saying no.
- ❖ Being patient.
- ❖ Confusing giving things with giving love.
- ❖ Imposing parental needs and tastes on the child.

Situations Ripe for Showering a Child with Things

- ❖ Divorced parents.
- ❖ Newly successful parents.
- ❖ Older parents.
- ❖ Single parents.
- ❖ Families where both parents work long hours.

You might want to glance at the whole chapter, even if your child is not the age of a particular section. Some suggestions for younger children might give you ideas about how to handle your older child. Ideas for older children might give you help on where you're heading down the road.

Just about the only Americans who won't find this chapter relevant are the Amish. All the rest of us are inundated with things from the minute we wake up till the minute we flop down. Good luck!

SECTION I: PREVENTING THE GIMMIES

As in most of life, an ounce of prevention is worth a pound of cure. Here are some activities to begin when your baby is tiny that will save you—and your child—frustration and anger later on.

A. ESTABLISHING HABITS THAT DO NOT INCLUDE BUYING EVERYTHING THAT INTERESTS YOUR CHILD

In the first year of your child's life, *your* habits require more modification than your baby's—who doesn't have any habits yet!

Six Months to One Year

Activity for Grown-ups: The Cash Register Is Not Necessarily Our Friend

As an experiment, monitor a typical day with your baby. Pay attention to how many times you go to a cash register and then hand your baby something, whether it's a banana, a new book, or a rattle. Were you surprised by how many things you bought your baby?

- ❖ Spend an entire day without buying anything for your baby. This does not include necessities such as diapers.
- ❖ Did this feel impossible? If it did, skip to the part about two-year-olds while you still have an angel baby on your hands, and then try this exercise again, filled with new purpose!

Lesson for Grown-ups: We don't need to buy our way through the day.

One to Two Years

Activity for Grown-ups: Using the Supermarket to Help You Hone Your Resistance Skills

The idea is to teach your child by example and osmosis that we do not buy, buy, buy!

- ❖ Don't go during your child's meal or snack time.
- ❖ Pack a favorite snack and a drink. If your child should ask for something to eat, reach into your bag.
- ❖ Don't go up and down the aisles handing your child a bagel, then

a Baby Bel cheese, then a box of Cheerios, even if he asks for them.

Lesson for Child: *What we already have and like is enough. We do not have to have something else just because we see it.*

Food for Thought: If you always feed your baby on demand from the shelves of a food store, as if it were a smorgasbord, by the time he's a toddler he expects to get handed whatever he wants, which inevitably leads to supermarket tantrums. Further, teaching him that a store's stock is his for the taking may unknowingly set the stage for shoplifting at a later age.

Activity for Grown-ups: Using Errand-running to Help You Hone Your Resistance Skills

- ❖ Always carry several favorite books and toys.
- ❖ When your child becomes interested in something—for example, plastic animals near the checkout lane of the drugstore—let him handle them. Encourage his interest. Name them. "Here's a tiger and an elephant. Here are his ears and his tail."
- ❖ When it's time to go, do not succumb to the fifty-nine-cent price tag.
- ❖ Help him put them back. Even if he screams and hollers, don't budge!

Lesson for Child: *Although things we see are interesting and worthy of our attention, we do not have to acquire them.*

Tips: When Your Child Resists Relinquishing an Object

In ascending order of resistance, which will coincide with your child's developing sense of self:

Diversion: Whip out the favorite toy or book you brought. Happy toddler hands reach for the proffered object while you remove the tiger from his fingers.

Engage newfound skills: Wave and sing happily, "Say bye-bye, Tiger." The same child who won't let go of an object when asked to will proudly wave "bye-bye" as you gently remove it from his hand.

Introduce outside authority: ''The tiger lives here with this lady.'' If you're lucky the checkout lady will nod, and if she's a mother will probably hold out her hand. Your obedient toddler will give up the tiger. If you don't have backup support from the checkout lady, it's time to pull out the big guns.

Take charge, Mommy: Remove the tiger. Leave the store.

Common Mistakes

❖ If your child cries, *do not* relent and say, ''Gosh, I didn't know you wanted it so much. Here, sweetheart.''

❖ *Do not* continue talking about the darn tiger and how much he wanted it as you are leaving the store. Once out of the store, point out something interesting to divert the entire episode. ''Oh, look! There's a black and white doggie just like Blazer.'' The crying will stop.

❖ *Do not* kneel in front of the stroller, wipe your child's face, and croon how hard it is to grow up. If you do, the next time you are confronted by the same scene your child will cry even harder, hoping that Mommy will play that fun drama game that ends in solicitous attention.

Eighteen Months Through Five Years

Besides the guidance through modeling that you give your child, somewhere in early toddlerhood your child will be developmentally ready to tackle learning skills in his own right.

The earlier you start, the easier for your child to learn these skills, but even a much older child who has the Gimmies may profit from—and even enjoy!—the following. (I don't recommend any of these activities for a child at the peak of oppositional behavior called the ''terrible twos.'' Please see Section 3, ''A Full-blown Case of the Gimmies,'' if that's where your child is now or seems to be heading.)

Activity: Just Looking

Make an expedition to a hands-on toy store with the express purpose of *buying nothing*.

Appropriate places:

❖ F.A.O. Schwarz throughout the country.

❖ The Zany Brainy chain in the Philadelphia Valley.

❖ Any kid-friendly local toy shop that encourages children to play with display toys.

Inappropriate places:

Large discount stores, such as Toys "R" Us and Kiddie City. Kids can't play with toys in stores like this.

What to do:

❖ Explain in advance that today you are going to a store where you will be "just looking."

❖ Set aside enough time that you will not have to rush. For most toddlers an hour is sufficient. By five, your child may enjoy an entire morning or afternoon.

❖ Allow your child to play with anything that strikes his fancy.

❖ Keep in mind that what may strike *his* fancy may not be what strikes *yours*. He may not wish to visit all the departments. If you are dying to see everything, go back another time without your child!

❖ Let your child dictate the pace. Some will rush from toy to toy. Others will glom onto one thing and not want to move. Whatever choice they make in this instance is the perfect choice.

❖ At the end of an unhurried visit, wind up. "We spent this time just looking. Wasn't it fun? Now it's time to leave." And leave, *empty-handed*.

Lesson: We can play, explore, learn, have fun, and leave without owning a new object.

Predictable Behavioral Variations

You can apply these hints to any kind of situation where your child's temperament might alter how he responds. Since this is a "he" chapter, these are boys, but the exact same behavior will be typical of girls.

Budding Building Manager (Eighteen Months Through Five Years)

Legos and Duplos are sissy stuff. This child finds kid-height water fountains, escalators, and bathrooms fascinating. Besides obvious safety restraints, such as automatic doors, I urge you to let your child determine *what* he plays with and *for how long,* even if he never lays a finger on a display toy.

Timmy the Stacker and Knocker (Toddler Behavior, as Late as Two and a Half)

His idea of a hot time is to pull boxes off shelves. Although tricky for the adult to handle, this experience does not have to end in disaster.

❖ When he pulls the first box off a shelf, make your voice enticing. "Come! Let Mommy show Timmy toys the store wants you to play with!" Offer your hand.

❖ If Timmy doesn't take your hand, don't grab his. Simply move away, saying, "Ooh, look at those blocks they have out. We can stack them and knock them over!" Chances are, Timmy will toddle along like a duck in your wake and soon be engaged with the blocks.

❖ If our boy Timmy only wants to pull boxes off the shelf, it requires extreme patience in order to fulfill our need to get the darn boxes back on the shelf and Timmy's need to knock things down.

❖ Sit down on the floor. "Let's play a game. Get the boxes back on the shelf. Look! Mommy can put a box back on the shelf. Can Timmy?" Offer him a box. Don't push his hands. See if with a bit of encouragement he can do it himself. "Good!" Pick up the pace. "Now let's see how many boxes we can replace as quickly as possible." Make it playful, handing him one for every five or six you put on. When all the boxes are back on the shelf, congratulate him.

❖ If your child is Timmy the Stacker, cut the visit short.

❖ Try not to sound irritated. Remember: He's not bad. He's learning.

Victor, the Velcro Boy Wonder (Toddler Behavior, as Late as Three, even Four)

This child doesn't want to play with the toys. He wants to sit in your lap.

❖ Find a chair, or the floor if necessary, and draw your child onto the safety of his mother's lap where he can comfortably watch the goings-on around him.

❖ There is nothing wrong with this child. He doesn't need to be asked, "Don't you want to play, like the rest of the kids?"

❖ Give him enough time to get used to his surroundings. He may slide off your lap and make tentative forays into the action.

❖ If not, try this: "Mommy would like to play with this puzzle before we leave." Mentioning leaving reassures a tentative child. Still holding him, move to the puzzle and start playing. From this humble beginning you may find that your lap-sitter willingly plays, as long as he is in physical contact with you.

❖ He may sit in your lap the entire time, happily watching. Although difficult for many adults to understand, some children are active observers who take as much pleasure from watching as other children take from participating.

❖ For the child who often seems overwhelmed in new situations, arrange your expedition for an off hour. Crowded times such as right after school, weekends, or holidays are bad choices for this child. If these are the only times your schedule permits, shoot for a gorgeous day when everyone else is outside.

Caution: Do not undertake "just looking" under the following conditions:

❖ If it's nap time, feeding time, or you are coming from a stimulating experience, such as a toddler class, a visit to Grandma, or the playground. This goes for you as well as your child, because the "just looking" game requires patience and no agenda on the parent's part other than to spend pleasurable free time.

❖ If your child is a full-fledged *fleer*. A fleer lives for the purpose of running away from you as fast as he can. Tip: If you lose your child in a department store, drop to your knees. You will be able to see little sneakers running along the floor, even though you can't see cute heads above the clothes racks. Fleers need to be given as much time as possible in playgrounds or other places where they can run without your having to be hot on their trail. Serious fleeing usually stops by the end of the threes. Until then wear sneakers, avoid big places without another adult along as backup, and pass on this year's crowded fairs and chaotic circuses, where a fleer can get far enough fast enough to get in real trouble. If you absolutely must go to a crowded place, such as an airport during the Christmas season, a harness might not be such a bad idea. As a habitual piece of equipment for daily use, however, a harness is like a leash. We use them for dogs. Not for children.

Caution for grown-ups: "Just looking" will backfire badly if you decide that during this expedition *you* simply have to buy something. Then you blew it!

Good-citizen tip: If you play "just looking" in a hands-on store, buy something at that store when you're shopping without your child in tow.

Activity: Apply "Just Looking"

In any other store, when your child starts whining or shouting that he wants something, say, "Remember the fun we had at Dollies and Dump Trucks? Well, you're just looking here too, while Mommy buys something that we need for the whole family."

Activity: Just Reading

Do the same thing in a bookstore or library. Leave empty-handed after having spent a long, enjoyable time simply reading, not acquiring.

B. TEACHING THE ART OF CHOICE

An often-overlooked element of why children get the Gimmies is the inability to choose. We even have the indulgent phrase, "Like a kid in a candy shop."

Once learned, the skill of making a choice will stand both of you in good stead as your child gets older and you are confronted more and more with "I want this, I want that."

Although it's possible that a younger child just might have the capacity to choose the kinds of objects I'm going to talk about, for the vast majority of one-year-olds choice should be limited to areas of home life. Orange juice or milk to drink, for example, is familiar territory where a one-year-old will feel competent enough to make a choice. By the time they're eighteen months most children have developed enough that you can begin introducing choice in terms of acquiring possessions. If you feel your own child will find these activities overwhelming or confusing, wait. Certainly by the time your child is three you owe them the chance to learn how to choose selected things from many.

Eighteen Months Through Five (and Probably into Maturity!)

Activity: Learning How to Choose in the Bookstore

Make an expedition to a bookstore with the express purpose of allowing your child to choose *one* book.

Appropriate places:

❖ Barnes & Noble superstores and junior stores.
❖ Any local children's bookstore that encourages children to read books there.

What to do:

❖ Explain in advance that today you are going to a bookstore where your child may choose any *one* book that he wants.

- ❖ If budget is an issue, limit the choice to paperback, a certain rack, or a sale table.
- ❖ For any child having difficulty selecting, sit down and read several books with him.
- ❖ Let your child carry his prize to the cashier.
- ❖ At home, when you read the book together, mention how proud he must feel that he's learning how to choose.

Lesson: *We can successfully choose one thing from among many.*

Common Pitfalls

- ❖ If your child absolutely cannot make up his mind, tell him you see he's not having fun. Ask if he'd rather try one, two, or three books. Sometimes, for beginning choosers, just hearing that the choice is not so strictly "one" frees them enough to be able to choose one. Or two or three, once you've made the offer. If broadening the choice doesn't help, reassure him that choosing is hard and try it again a month or two later. For the child who cannot choose at that point, drop the whole experience and try six months later.
- ❖ Some toddlers are drawn to a book they already have precisely because it's familiar. Mention that maybe he'd like a different one. But don't insist. At home later, when he understands that now he has two copies, suggest that he may want to choose a different book next time. Don't nag. If the next time he wants to do the same thing, you now have information available that he can use. "Remember the last time you chose one you had, and we got home and there we were with two? Why don't we look for a new one this time?"
- ❖ If it's a book he knows from preschool, don't suggest he get a different one. Congratulate his choice; he is instinctively teaching himself how to read through repetition.

Recommendation: In addition to regular visits to the library or bookstore when you understandably get a big pile of books, make a special time to *pick out only one* book once a month or so. He will begin to notice which books give him the most pleasure; slowly his powers of discernment will grow. For the preschooler, a dialogue might be fun.

"This is the very first book you ever chose." "Do you like the one you chose this month more or less than the last one?" Most preschoolers won't be able to articulate *why* they like it more. But they profit from a small amount of guidance suggesting that they can evaluate and have preferences.

Activity: Learning How to Choose in the Toy Store

Several weeks later do the same thing with *one* toy in a toy store.

❖ Limit your child's choice to a specific type of toy, such as a doll or car.

❖ For the child who is overwhelmed, offer two specific toys to choose from.

❖ If at home your child does not play with the toy, use this as a learning experience. On your next one-toy outing, remind him that the toy he chose wasn't much fun to play with. Explain why: It had only one way to play with it; it didn't really look the way the package made it look; or it was too grown-up. Suggest that this time he try to find something he will play with more often.

Money Tips

❖ Clever merchandisers put expensive toys at adult-eye level, figuring we're all too stupid and lazy to bend down. Thus, cute, inexpensive toys are on the bottom toddler-level shelves. The likelihood of your having to mention budget to your toddler is low. Relax. Enjoy.

❖ By the time a child is four or five, however, money becomes an issue, both for you and for them. For the child who's not yet interested in the written word, tell him ahead of time that you have a budget and you will let him know if what he wants is "fine" or "too much." For a preschooler who is interested in numbers and reading, see Chapter 5, "The Love of Learning," for a number recognition game.

Activity: The Pleasure of Choosing for Another

Go to another store on another day with the express purpose of *buying something for someone else.*

❖ Arrange this activity for a day when you have no other shopping to do. (You can do it, as hard as it seems!)

❖ Tell your child that today he's going to choose something for

Daddy. Make it simple, such as a pair of socks. Let him choose the color.

❖ On the way home pass by *anything* David wants to buy, even a banana, saying, ''Today is Daddy's day for getting something. Not Mommy's day, not David's.''

❖ Tell your husband before he gets home that David picked the color (to preempt a tired husband who hates green and has 175 pairs of socks).

❖ Daddy: Thank him profusely and genuinely for thinking of you while you were at work.

Lesson: *Thinking of others is a rewarding experience.*

The activities to learn how to choose can be fun to begin with many eighteen-month-olds, some two-year-olds, most two-and-a-half-year-olds, and certainly any preschooler.

Once most children hit three their abilities to reason improve dramatically. A typical nursery-school classroom full of threes and fours or a kindergarten room is an exciting place intellectually. They learn to evaluate, to discern, to become familiar with past, present, and future, and generally to leave babyhood behind as they begin their steady progress into childhood. These wonderful, exciting abilities to reason can be used by the wise mom to encourage her kid to learn how to control the Gimmies.

Here are some ideas to encourage your child to use her brain instead of her desire to acquire!

Threes, Fours, and Fives
Activity: Making Decisions Ahead of Time

❖ At the beginning of an expedition to the playground, say, ''I've noticed that you're not a baby anymore. And so today is a special day. I'm going to let you decide *before we go out* if you'd rather have a treat when the ice cream truck comes to the playground or from the store on our way home.'' (Notice that privilege is implied in your language.)

❖ If Andrew chooses the store, he may have trouble when the ice cream truck arrives.

❖ Keep in mind that children at this age are fuzzy about the future. Suggest that if he'd rather have an ice cream now and not later, that's fine. Since this is such a hard lesson to learn, it's appropriate to cut your kid a little slack and let him change his mind.

❖ When you pass the store on the way home, however, stick to your guns.

❖ With no regret in your voice say that he chose the ice cream truck today. Maybe tomorrow he will choose the store when the ice cream truck arrives.

❖ Keep pushing that stroller or accelerator. You may be pleasantly surprised by how quickly the whining stops.

❖ The next time you go to the playground, offer a choice again in advance.

❖ Remind him that he chose the truck on his last visit. Maybe he'd like to wait today.

❖ When the ice cream truck arrives, remind him again that if he wants something from the store later, he can't have anything now.

❖ If—oh, miracle of miracles!—he chooses to wait, praise him highly. Tell him he must be proud of how well he's learning to choose.

❖ When he chooses the truck and doesn't raise Cain when passing the store on the way home, reinforce how proud he must be of himself.

Lesson: *The abilities to choose, to delay gratification, and to handle my emotions makes me feel grown-up and proud.*

Caution: For the child who becomes enraged after making a choice, the less said during the moment, the better. Later, at a cozy time such as bedtime or bath, mention that you noticed that it was hard. Try this: In a fond, dreamy voice say, "I remember when you were a baby"—right away, they're all ears—"and you were learning how to walk. You would take a few steps and then fall down. Oh! you would carry on. But then one day you didn't fall down. And you smiled at me as you walked toward me. You were very, very proud of learning something new. And that's just what you're doing now. I bet tomorrow, or maybe the next day, when we drive past the store you won't carry on. And won't we both smile!" Putting your child's behavior in the context of learning and supplying him ahead of time with a behavioral goal helps tremendously.

Activity: Choosing Ahead of Time for Outings

Use choice for outings such as crafts fairs, parks, zoos, and the like.

❖ On the way to the beach mention that you will be seeing lots of toys for sale. Which toy does your child think he'll want: a new shovel-and-bucket set or a sieve?

❖ If he doesn't know the kind of toys he'll see, try, "You can have one new toy when we get there." Stick to it.

Activity: Choosing Toys Ahead of Time

❖ Refrain from buying toys immediately if your child asks, "Can I have that?"

❖ Discuss which toy as much as your child wants to.

❖ Make a special date to buy the toy.

Corollary Activity: Choosing Gifts Ahead of Time

At this age most children start in on, "I want this for my birthday; I want that for Christmas; Hanukkah's coming, and I want this."

❖ Respond to these seemingly endless requests with the benign "Okay. Add it to your list."

❖ Pay attention. Some things will be repeated, and some will be mentioned only once. Buy the toys that reappear on the list consistently. This tells your child that you listen and also over several years teaches the lesson that we don't respond to whims, we respond to consistent desires.

Lessons: I can learn how to plan for the future. I can learn how to discriminate between a passing fancy and a genuine desire. Anticipation is almost as delicious as actually getting something. When I do get something it's meaningful and not just a ho-hum, empty acquisition of another piece of plastic.

Typical four- and five-year-old dialogue: "Can I have that truck? Jack has that truck. I want the same truck Jack has. All the kids have that truck except me."

The sensible parent's response: "Jack can play with your truck when he's here, and you can play with his at his house. It would be boring if we all had the same things.''

"Learning how to choose" activities can be repeated as often as you both enjoy them. Keep in mind, however, to limit the scope of the choices you offer. Although you want to foster your child's ability to choose, it's not useful for your preschooler to feel that within his hands rests the selection of which house the family will buy.

SECTION 2: SIDESTEPPING THE GIMMIES

Here are typical well-meaning, even loving acts many parents do that inadvertently may teach children to equate the acquisition of things with success and love. And while it's indisputable that our culture rewards success with money and things, the adult who excels because of love of the subject has a more rewarding experience than the adult who strives only to amass things.

A. WELL-INTENTIONED ADULT MISTAKES
Rewarding Good Behavior with Things
"If you don't hit in the playground today, Mommy will buy you a truck or a treat." No good.
More Useful

- ❖ Hug him.
- ❖ Say how proud he must feel, and how proud you are of him.
- ❖ Call Daddy or Grandma and let your child tell them he didn't hit.
- ❖ Read a favorite book.

The Rob Petrie Syndrome
Remember *The Dick Van Dyke Show?* Whenever Rob Petrie came home, his son Ritchie said, ''Whadja bring me?'' Everybody laughed. I bet you didn't laugh the last time you crawled into the house after a long, hard day and got a snotty ''Whadja bring me?''
Don't bring home a present every day. Don't bring home a toy every time you return from a business trip.
More Useful

- ❖ Tell an interesting story about your day.
- ❖ Relate an ongoing story, which you make up new installments of on your way home from work.

❖ Begin a daily ritual: fifteen minutes down on the floor playing before doing anything else.
❖ Give your child a hug.
❖ Pull out a map and show where you were; show pictures describing something you saw there.

> *Lesson:* I get affection, praise, support from my extended family, and intellectual stimulation as rewards and pleasures from my parents.

B. PLACES WE CAN GO, SEE, ENJOY, OR PASS WITHOUT BUYING
Libraries

Libraries are wonderful places. Use them to teach that we do not have to own everything we enjoy. Make sure you take your child with you to return the books.

Museum Gift Shops

❖ Tell your toddler, "This is part of the museum. We just look."
❖ From three years and up, explain in advance that you are going to the museum to see the exhibits and that your family chooses not to buy anything today.

Candy Counters, Toys in Shop Windows

Your child points or says, "I want that."

❖ You respond, "Not now. Maybe tomorrow." For mysterious reasons children are satisfied by the possibility as much as by the actuality.
❖ Please, however, do not use the word "maybe" to really mean "no."
❖ If, for example, your child is pointing to a toy he's been hankering after and you know he's getting it for his birthday, "maybe" is true.
❖ If you have no intention of ever getting that toy, it's time to say no.

> *Lesson:* Buying is not the major or expected part of every outing.

C. TOYS

Playing is the major provenance of childhood. Through play children learn, have fun, mature, and acquire lifelong habits. Toys, then, are not really a luxury. In some part they are a necessity. Because we recognize their importance we sometimes lose perspective. Here are some ideas that may help you supply your child with what he needs, including understanding that the acquisition of large numbers is not the goal of the game.

Quality

❖ The more open-ended a toy, the better. Toys that foster imaginary play and creative thinking are better than plastic flower-making kits with a finite number of designs.

❖ Toys that do all the work, such as battery-powered Barbie cars, do not develop muscles or balance the way bikes, skates, and scooters do.

❖ Found household objects inspire a child to play creatively with what's around.

Quantity

❖ Too few: If you're reading this book the likelihood that your child has too few toys is the same mathematically as your child being six feet tall. The truth is, a child who has a cardboard box, a pack of white paper, a box of crayons, and freedom to play for most of his waking hours with anything in the house that isn't breakable has plenty of toys. In the typical or even atypical American home this wholesome, utopian scenario is extremely unlikely.

❖ ''Too many'' is when the child has no idea what toys he owns.

❖ ''Too many'' is when a child plays with something once and then loses it in a sea of other unexplored toys.

Keeping Toys from Becoming Overwhelming

Rotate Toys

Toddlers:

❖ Make ten or so toys available at a time.

❖ Put the others out of reach.

❖ Every week or so take away the ones not played with and put other ones out.

Preschoolers:

❖ Threes are developing and most four- and five-year-olds have better selection processes.
❖ Make their toys easily available to them on shelves that they can reach so they can choose and also put away.

Trade Toys
With a like-minded mother, encourage trading toys on loan. After a week the children return each toy to its rightful home.

Winnow Toys
Before holidays and birthdays, help your child choose which toys he still plays with and which should move on. Let him designate a younger child to give certain toys to. Take toys in good condition to a hospital or hospice, as long as you check in advance that they accept donations. Put away a treasured toy from each stage of development that your child can then pass on to his child.

Lesson: *I choose some from among many; I share with my friends; anything I do not use, I do not have to own.*

Handling Lots of Toys that Arrive for Special Occasions

Birthday Presents
Birthdays are appropriate times for kids to get a lot of things. But the quantity all at once can be overwhelming—except for one-year-olds. Surrounded by thousands of dollars worth of stuff, they like the wrapping and boxes. To avoid dazed, glazed, and sometimes bored toddlers and preschoolers overwhelmed by too much:

❖ Open the presents after the guests have gone home. This keeps a toddler from being overwhelmed, and for preschoolers it shifts the emphasis of the party from ''Whadja get?'' to ''Isn't this fun?''
❖ For ones and twos, put the gifts on a shelf out of reach. Offer your toddler a new toy occasionally, making sure he knows it's a gift from whomever. A preschooler may have more fun opening them all at once when the house is not filled with friends and it's not at the end of a party. Even so, tuck them away. Let your child choose one at a time to play with over the course of several weeks

or even months. Please make sure your preschooler participates in the thank-yous, even if it's just a scribble on a note you send.

Appropriate Times to Throw Restraint Out the Back Door

Unlike a daily flood of things that will drown your child, indulgence in small doses can be a good thing:

❖ Christmas, Hanukkah, or any other traditional family time of gift-giving. *Everyone* is together, surrounded by wrapping paper and hugging. These moments often become favorite childhood memories.

❖ When you buy a special, longed-for item. Example: a bike. Go whole hog. Besides a necessary helmet, let your child pick out a basket, a horn, handlebar streamers—which are good solely because they're frivolous—or any other extras he's hankering for.

❖ Extended family. If your child is lucky enough to have grandparents, aunts, uncles, or a special family friend who loves to spoil him, back off. Let your child have a doting relationship. It's nice. It's downright divine. Only a parent can really spoil a child. Others make them feel special.

SECTION 3: DEALING WITH A FULL-BLOWN CASE OF THE GIMMIES

A baby is developmentally not yet a candidate for a good case of the Gimmies. Yes, a baby wants what he wants when he wants it. But diversion works with a baby in ninety-nine cases out of a hundred. When diversion, removing the object of desire, and most other tricks known to moms fail to head off an emotional melodrama, you have entered the developmental stage of the terrible twos. Your child may hit this stage earlier, or later than two, or not at all. For the sake of discussion, however, I'm going to talk about twos first and then move on to preschoolers.

A. TERRIBLE TWOS AND THE GIMMIES

The Gimmies and a two-year-old are a match made in hell. A two-year-old wants everything in sight, he wants it now, he wants to be in control, he wants to win every fight, and every interaction is ripe for a fight.

When your child reaches this stage forget teaching him quality over quantity, how to choose, or any other value. Your goal is to help him control his emotional responses. From a practical point of view, do everything in your power to avoid situations that provoke tantrums.

General Tips

- ❖ Avoid long shopping expeditions to stores, malls, or any other busy public places during this brief developmental stage.
- ❖ Have sugar-free snacks available. If you happen to be out and about and you see that lunch is going to be a bit late, don't wait until your child is ravenous. Feed him a healthy snack before he melts down.
- ❖ End activities way before disintegration time.
- ❖ Open-ended questions such as "What do you want to play with?" invite disaster. Instead, offer your child a choice between two things. "Do you want to play with bubbles or a ball?" is a manageable choice for a two-year-old.
- ❖ Limit your use of the word *no*.
- ❖ Provide your child with interesting alternatives.

Activity: Heading a Tantrum Off at the Pass

Although you planned your supermarket shopping to coincide with Allen's nap, everything took longer than you figured. He woke up in the last aisle. Now, in the checkout line, he's starting to squirm. He reaches for a box of nerdy-gummy junk. "I want dat. I want dat! I want DAT!"

- ❖ Do not say no.
- ❖ Let him handle the box.
- ❖ Look at it with interest. Point out the colors. Look at the drawings.
- ❖ Then say, "Oh, look at this box." Pick up another box and hand it to your child.
- ❖ Gently remove the nerdy box as your child gets interested in the next one.
- ❖ Keep this up until you are ready to unload your cart.
- ❖ Then say, "Help Mommy put these things on the conveyor belt."
- ❖ Hand your child something light and engage him in helping.

Lesson: *Mommy is an agreeable sort of person who is filled with interesting activities.*

Now, I know this hasn't happened to you. But let's say you have a neighbor—a very civilized, polite, decent woman—who, when her child first started exhibiting "willful" behavior, was a little nonplussed. She handed her two-year-old whatever he asked for. Until her child pitched an enormous fit in a store when told, "No, you can't have those beads." Now, several weeks and an alarming number of tantrums later, our neighbor wishes she'd responded differently in the first place.

Activity for Mom: Choosing One Thing to Master

This activity is for moms who need to backpedal in their limit-setting skills.

❖ In your own mind choose an object of contention that you have unsuccessfully dealt with so far—a lollipop, for example.

❖ Tell *yourself* that you can say no to this one thing, even if for the last two weeks you have given in and gotten the lollipop.

❖ Tell your child that today you're going to do lots of fun things. "Mommy's taking Brian to the playground; then we're seeing Grandma; then Brian can spend the afternoon out back on the swings with Spot and the twins from next door. But today Brian is not getting a lollipop." (This reiteration of planned, nice things is a reminder for you as much as for Brian!)

❖ When you pass the lollipop store and your child points, say, "Not today." *Move on.* Don't talk anymore. There is nothing else to say. No matter how extreme Brian's response.

❖ If Brian is in a stroller or car it will be easier. Push that stroller; step on that accelerator.

❖ If Brian is on foot you may have to pick him up bodily and remove him from the scene.

❖ If you can stick to your guns about one thing for one day, eventually you can get back in the driver's seat with your child.

Lesson for Mommy: I can say no, I can say no, I can say no. When my child needs me to be firm, I can!

Pick Up Your Child and Remove Him from the Scene

We encounter this blithe piece of advice frequently in parenting books. Although it sounds so simple it is one of the most difficult actions to pull off. Here are some helpful thoughts.

❖ Think of your child as an unwieldy, emotion-free bag of groceries, not as an attacker who is trying to hurt you.

❖ Your child wants the tantrum to end as much as you do; he just doesn't know how. By holding him with strong but loving arms, you are telling him that he has a parent he can rely on.

❖ Do not yank, grab, squeeze, or in any other way physically transmit whatever anger you may be feeling. There is a difference between physical restraint and violent overpowering.

❖ Do not scream or holler. This will only prolong the episode.

❖ Do not wheedle, cajole, ask why, ask what he wants, ask what's the matter. Verbal communication is not only wasted during a tantrum, but often exacerbates it.

❖ You did not do anything wrong. Your child's behavior is developmentally appropriate.

❖ Your child is not throwing a tantrum to embarrass you.

❖ That frowning man in the suit over there has never spent an entire day with a two-year-old.

B. PRESCHOOLERS WITH OCCASIONAL BOUTS OF THE GIMMIES

It is the rare preschooler, even the most cooperative and reasonable, who does not from time to time get an attack of the Gimmies. As their language becomes more and more sophisticated, so does their ability to dicker, turning many interactions with a preschooler into negotiations worthy of Henry Kissinger.

Helpful Dialogue Tidbits

❖ "End of discussion." Mean it!

❖ "You can have one new thing, as we discussed before we came, or none. Your choice." Mean it!

A glorious aspect of the preschool years is that most children have fabulous senses of humor. You can turn what looks like an incipient attack of the Gimmies into fun for both of you.

Activity: Fight Drama with Drama

You're in the mall. Your child whines, "Mommy, can I have that Nellie Belch Bride Baby with the jeweled hair? Oh, please, oh pleeease. I really want it!"

You're cool. You answer, "Maybe."

Twenty paces later: "Mommy, can I have that turbojet robot-eating dinosaur knock-'em-dead destroy-o machine? Oh, please, oh pleeease. I really want it!''

You answer, ''Not now.''

Twenty paces later: ''Mommy! There's the ice cream shop. You *said* I could have an ice cream! You did! I heard you!'' Which you did not, except in your child's imagination.

- ❖ Do not snap, ''No!''
- ❖ Say in an equally dramatic tone, ''Oh, I want that too. And I'd like to have a chocolate bar! And some cotton candy!''
- ❖ Your startled child turns to see who has inhabited Mommy's body.
- ❖ Crank it up. Appeal to your child's sense of silliness. Make a dramatic crying face. Keep up your litany of things you wish you had. (Here, I invite you to indulge. Get in touch with what your child feels. Provide your own dialogue. The sky's the limit.) ''I want an Armani jacket! A Paloma Picasso ring! A cleaning lady!''
- ❖ Your kid will be amazed. You will be far away from the source of the initial indiscriminate desire. And you will both be laughing like loons, having a good time together.

> **Lesson:** *Mommy's a very silly lady (the highest compliment a pre-schooler can pay) who feels the same way I feel.*

Try the book *The Berenstain Bears Get the Gimmies* as a fun way to reinforce the fact that the Gimmies is a problem we all work on.

Every once in a while every child loses it. Most children lose self-control when they're overstimulated, tired, and/or hungry. In the event that your child can no longer be reasonable, the less said on your part, the better.

Activity: Dealing with an Occasional Tantrum in an Older Child

It's five o'clock in a crowded, noisy store. Your child points imperiously. ''I want this.'' You answer in the negative. He begins to shout, cry, kick the counter, or any other acting out.

- ❖ Say calmly and without malice, ''It's not nice to act that way.''
- ❖ Don't bother to address the object of desire.

❖ Keep walking. And—oh, is this scary—don't look back.
❖ He may scream. He may stomp his foot. He may cry. But I promise, he will catch up with you, screaming and sobbing.
❖ If he seems willing, put your arm around him as you walk and don't mention what just happened. This is a time to let him save face.

Lesson: *Mommy can't be roped into giving in, no matter how bratty I get. What a relief!*

Four- and five-year-olds are prime candidates for the movie *Willy Wonka and the Chocolate Factory*. Verruca Salt is the embodiment of a spoiled brat. Rent the movie. Let your child enjoy it without any moralizing. After an episode where your child has been particularly obnoxious, say, "Usually you're a dream kid, but when you act the way you acted this afternoon, you reminded me of Verruca Salt."

The poor little rich kid is a sad image. It depicts a child getting everything but what he really needs. Learning not to make things a substitute for other more complicated needs is a lesson that will make your child's life richer in the long run. The only real deprivation most of our children are at risk for is being denied the chance to learn self-control and choice. Teaching these lessons to your child is one of the most rewarding tasks of parenthood.

SUMMARY:

❖ Base limits on your child's emotional needs, not on what you can afford.
❖ Establish habits for yourself and your child that discourage constant buying.
❖ As your child matures, provide the opportunity to learn how to choose.
❖ Don't reward good behavior with things.

4

Sex and Gender; Gender and Sex

Men and women are different.

Although this simple observation seems obvious, contemporary society at large is struggling with shifting roles and expectations for men and women. We are operating in uncharted waters.

Parents walk a tightrope, trying to tease out which strands of behavior our children exhibit that are gender-based and which are simply cultural expectations. While it may be harmful—and probably impossible—to try and change gender-based behavior, it is equally harmful to promote behavior based on stereotypes that our culture is discarding. We don't want to leave our children in the dust.

Some people theorize that men and women behave differently because we are treated differently from day one. From the moment of birth (and even earlier for parents who know their baby's gender through amniocentesis) we make a distinction. We say "he," "she," slap pink bracelets and lace booties on girls, and blue ID's and miniature sneakers on boys.

Although it is indisputable that we immediately identify a baby's gender, I don't think identification alone determines behavior.

There is the argument that we handle boys and girls differently from birth, therefore engendering different behavior. We see distinct differences.

Mothers often cuddle their baby girls gently, but toss their baby boys up into the air. They tell little boys, "Don't cry," when they're hurt; little girls are comforted, "There, there, sweetie, yes, Mommy's baby," when they cry from the same slight injury.

Fathers model different behavior. Men tend to play rougher, have larger movements and deeper voices. A girl is often "Daddy's little girl," a boy, "Sport," "Champ," and "Buddy."

I frequently hear parents call their boys "Son." I *never* hear anybody directly address their girl as "Daughter." This might suggest that on a subtle level having a son is a proud accomplishment that we publicly proclaim. Daughter, however, is not a relationship we even directly acknowledge, as we do "Mom," "Dad," "Grandma," "Uncle So-and-so," "Sis," and "Bro." What does this lack of direct address say about having a daughter?

On the other hand, let me ask if you had the same experience when you were pregnant that I did. Other women—old, young, across cultural lines—whispered conspiratorially, "I hope you have a girl. They're so delicious." Then they added loudly, as if we live in Albania and have to say what the authorities want to hear, "Of course, whatever you have, as long as it's healthy, right?"

Does this mean that we have two overlapping societies? Public and private realities that do not match? I don't know. I just offer the observation.

When I first started working with young children I was firmly in the "nurture, not nature" camp. Raise a gender-free child, and you will rid the world of sexism. Quite unwillingly, I have had to alter my opinion.

I have been blessed with the privilege of working with children who have all of their basic needs met. They are human beings at our purest. Because there is no adversity (such as hunger or isolation) affecting these babies, they are as close to a scientific control group as you can get in terms of observing natural, unimpeded human behavior unfold.

My own belief, after observing many young children, is: We treat boys and girls differently because they behave differently, not the other way around.

In order to try and help our children by acknowledging their gender-based behavior while discouraging cultural sexual stereotypes, I'd like to present some ideas to you. First we'll look at gender and how it affects parenting. Then we'll move on to sex.

GENDER

Boys will be boys and girls will be girls . . .

SECTION I: OBSERVATIONS

As with any generalization there are always individuals who do not fall neatly into their "category." We will get to them in a minute. What follows is behavior typical of some eighty to ninety percent of the children I've seen.

A. BABIES—FROM FIVE MONTHS TO ABOUT A YEAR
I. Gender-free Characteristics

Well-tended babies like yours are all curious, responsive, and intelligent. Personality types cross gender lines. Boys and girls are equally fussy, placid, or lively.

A phenomenon that all we leaders marvel at is how the littlest babies catch on to the fact that there's a leader in the room. They seem to take the same nonverbal cues as grown-ups. When we sing in a circle the babies watch the leader, not necessarily the person with the loudest voice. If a leader enters the room at the same time as the other adults, the babies pick us out of the group: They greet us, smiling, babbling, saying baby hellos. It's wild.

Both sexes seem to have equal senses of justice. Babies often inadvertently bop each other on the heads. They are actually trying to touch the other baby, but because their muscles aren't controlled, the touch often turns into a smack. Time and again I see a baby, gender insignificant, turn with shock to Mom after having been hit for verification that this has happened. Then, eyes wide open, the baby wails with indignation. It is a different cry from when they fall over. The mature fury at the injustice that we see on their faces would be funny—if it weren't so heartfelt and real.

This instinctive outrage at "man's inhumanity to man" gives me hope for the human race. Repeatedly, I see that we are born with a profound sense of justice. How we get corrupted is a long discussion.

There are other behaviors, however, that I witness over and over again in group after group, beginning with five-month-olds, that I have to conclude are absolutely gender-based. After all, how much culture can a five-month-old have absorbed?
2. Gender Differences: Sitting Babies

Boys knock things down. Girls put things in piles. Girls, in general, are more interested in face-to-face direct conversation; a six-month-old girl will mimic my expressions, smile, and make fabulous baby babble back and forth. Most of the boy babies take several weeks to "warm up" before they'll engage; initially, they are more likely to bury their heads in their mommies' shoulders.

3. Gender Differences: Crawling Babies

The moment mobility enters their lives, the boys head for the hills, ranging around the edge of the room, while the girls frequently crawl around until they end up congregating in a group in the middle of the room.

The only time boys seem interested in joining a group is if there is a round, moving object to pursue. Girls often lean companionably against one another, pushing buttons on pop-up toys, touching other babies' faces, and glancing at the crawling team. They do not seem to have a genetic instinct to form a pack for the purpose of chasing a moving object.

Go figure.

B. TODDLERS—FROM THIRTEEN MONTHS TO LATE TWOS

1. Gender-free Behavior

As with babies, and on into adulthood, certain personality types are gender-free. Boys and girls are equally gregarious, temperamental, hot-blooded, or passive.

Independence from their care giver is gender-free. Some children need physical proximity or actual contact, whereas others couldn't care less if their moms or baby-sitters left for an hour and a half.

Both boys and girls are equally as passionate about possessions. They will assume ownership of a classroom toy and Lord help the toddler who attempts to touch that toy! Fortunately, in our classes not only do we have the Lord, but we have mommies, care givers, and group leaders to point out the splendors of the "sharing activity"!

A just-along-for-the-ride approach to a group experience is gender-free. They will not become "married" to a toy. If you hold their hand they will agreeably try another toy. They allow their grown-up to lead the way in art projects.

"The observer" is also gender-free. These children listen to a story riveted. Some have wonderfully expressive faces. Before lifting a flap of a book I ask, "Who is it?" "Who's behind here?" "Who's hiding in the grass?" Their eyebrows raise higher and higher. Sometimes their mouths even open in expectation. But they never shout out, *"Cat!"* the way some children do. Their mothers invariably say to me, "I don't understand it. He's like a different child when he's here. At home he talks, he laughs, he does the whole Wheels on the Bus, with all the hand motions. But here he doesn't do anything.'' If you should happen to have a child like this, try not to mistake quietness for ''not doing anything.'' Your boy or girl is participating with all four feet in the experience. It just so happens that that's the way he or she approaches a group.

Anger seems definitely gender-free. Both boys and girls are perfectly matched in their ability to pitch full-blown tantrums. Humor is also keen with both groups.

Toddler boys and girls seem equally drawn to both toy and real animals and to movement toys such as sliding boards and rocking toys.

2. Gender Differences

In general, boys tend to develop their gross motor skills first, while girls seem to develop their small motor skills. This striking difference manifests in many small ways.

By the time children in our classes reach toddlerhood, more girls enjoy table activities than boys. These include simple art projects, snacks, stories, and songs. All of these activities require good small motor skills, attention spans, the ability to sit in one spot, and the desire to be *near other people.*

I have some boys who so dislike both sitting down and being in a group that they can only listen to a story if they stand all the way at the other end of our forty-foot classroom. How do I know they're listening and not off in toddler dream world?

Showing a picture of a cow, I ask a searching, mind-ripping toddler question, such as ''What does the cow say?'' From forty feet away our pipsqueak shouts out, ''Moo!'' before he hurls himself down the sliding board, gets up, makes a run, bangs with both hands into the back wall, picks up a toy carrot, and waves it around like a phallic symbol. Whoops! Did I say that? Like a sword. Meanwhile, most of our girls are sitting at the table, eating their snack, answering questions, often (since they know my routines) shouting out the answers ahead of time.

More girls are verbally precocious than boys. Thus, in a roomful of kids ranging in age from thirteen to eighteen months, we frequently have at least one if not several girls who are able to string a coherent sentence together and have a vocabulary of a hundred words or so. Which, I might add, they *really* like to use. By their twos many girls are able to express complicated thoughts using a rich vocabulary. Less frequently, we see very verbal boys.

I do see many boys who have enormous passive vocabularies. They can follow complicated instructions using lots of words. They don't, however, seem interested in saying much. I've had many boys whose voices I've rarely heard and whose moms tell me that even at home they don't talk much. Yet I can say to them, "I need your help. Can you please close the doors of the cabinet where we keep the sand?" Off they go, across the room, and close not the art cabinet but the sand cabinet. Sometimes they look across the room at me to get my affirmation. Other times they simply carry out the instruction and then head off for greener pastures. The girls, however, quite frequently not only close the cabinet, but come to *tell* me they did. They are even likely to take me by the hand to show me, and often they do me one better! They tell me, "and I close da odder door too!" They have very carefully closed every open door in the room. My interpretation of this is that the girls seem to desire verbal *communication* back and forth more than the boys; further, they often seem to take pleasure in broadening an idea and going as far with it as they can.

When presented with a roomful of toys, girls are more apt to choose puzzles, shape sorters, dolls, and kitchen stuff, while boys are more inclined to choose cars, trucks, and tools. If boys are drawn to table toys, many of them prefer stacking and construction toys.

One out of every hundred or so two-year-old boys in my classes can accurately identify makes, models, and years of cars, both real cars on the street and toy replicas in the classroom. Ask your local two-year-old if he knows the name of that car. I'd like to know the results. So far I haven't met any girls with this interest.

Experiment: Take a Richard Scarry book, such as *Best First Book Ever*. Sit down and read it a few times with a toddler. At first reading the child looks objectively at every page. After their initial acquaintance with the book, however, girls impatiently flip past the truck, train, and bulldozer pages, while boys are disinterested in the room descriptions. Please let me know if your child does this too.

Boys brandish toys such as paint brushes, ladles, and wooden spoons, whereas girls are more likely to attempt to mimic adult use of these objects.

A toddler boy who is finished with a toy is apt to hurl it behind him, whereas a toddler girl more often puts it down right side up when she's through playing.

When presented with an unappealing limitation (example: "You can leave the table and go play, but your cracker must stay at the table,") boys will more often either drop the cracker and rush off, or rush off holding the cracker, *as if they haven't heard you*. Girls, on the other hand, are more likely to stand there, scream and cry, or look you in the eye *knowing full well that they're disagreeing* before they run off holding the forbidden cracker.

By age two for many and certainly by three, most girls are into clothes. Most boys couldn't care less.

C. PRESCHOOLERS—THREES, FOURS, AND FIVES
1. Gender-free Behavior
Intellectually, we see equal amounts of interest in nature and the world around us. Extraordinary aptitude in areas such as math, reading, music, and art stem from innate talent rather than gender.

But the older a child gets, the more we start to see a different approach to the world.
2. Gender Differences
Since most girls acquire small motor skills more readily, which are involved in reading, writing, and speech, this gender-based proclivity gives them a leg up when adjusting to nursery school and kindergarten (which are the provenance of the children in this book. Later, girls' self-confidence plummets. You and I will tackle that issue when our children are older.) See ''In Group Settings,'' page 88, for some help with your active boy in preschool.

Most children still show preferences for gender-based toys. One of the biggest changes for the better has been the encouragement of block-playing for girls, an activity that used to be relegated only to boys. Yet even here we often see differences in the *way* children play with the same toy. Boys build massive structures and often take as much delight in knocking them down as in building them. Girls create structures for imaginary play: ''Here's the kitchen, here's the living room.'' Some girls show distress, if not downright horror, at knocking these structures over. On the other hand, some girls, once *shown* how to knock things down, enjoy doing it.

As a group girls are more inclined to follow instructions in school settings (don't get excited, moms—*your* instructions are a horse of another color!). Is this because they are malleable? Although that's a possible interpretation, I think it's because girls find group activity more interesting than boys do. In order for a group to work there has to be a common articulated goal and cooperation.

Until the end of their threes most children play with both boys and girls, although many of them begin to show a same-sex preference for friendship.

By four and definitely by five you see distinct gender preference when they choose their friends, even though in these early years they willingly cooperate with partners of the opposite sex when their teachers assign them to work with one another.

During the preschool years we see common human impulses that manifest differently. For example, the desire to be in physical contact with someone we like comes out differently in boys and girls. A typical nursery-school scenario is this: At lunch boy best friends have to be separated so that they can eat, because they're punching each other, whereas girls are separated because they're hugging. Same desire, different technique.

D. CHILDREN WHO DON'T FIT THE PICTURE

By this time many of you are bristling: What a bunch of old-fashioned, sexist stereotyping. *My* little girl isn't like that, *I* wasn't like that. That's got nothing to do with *my* little boy.

I know, I know, I know. These are the broad strokes. Observable generalizations that, frankly, I have had to accept unwillingly. Yet human behavior is rich with diversity. And gender is only an *indicator* of behavior.

Let's take a look at what happens to one of the many children who fall on the ''other'' side of whichever gender scale we're looking at.

Perhaps one out of every twenty of my girls actively dislikes group activities. Like many toddler boys, she prefers to range around the outskirts of the room on her own. She often likes to bang, knock, and throw.

I find this child as attractive as the little girl who sits at the table churning out beautiful artwork and chatting gregariously. Yet what's interesting to me is that most adults, both mommies and sitters, are more distressed by a little girl who behaves this way than by a little boy who does. Her care giver will try much more assiduously than that of a boy to get her to come to the table, to settle down, to be ''nice,'' to ''behave.'' They are more upset if she throws, hits, and bangs.

True Tale from the Trenches: A mother, whose opinion about child-raising I admire immensely when it comes to her own children, drew me aside and suggested that our "hooligan" girl of the semester needed to be tested for ADD: Attention Deficit Disorder. Several months after class had ended I ran into the child with her baby-sitter, a lovely woman with a big heart and excellent skills. She proudly announced that the child was "better" and had settled down some. Had this child been a boy, neither of these women would ever have thought something was "wrong." Our gender-based expectations of behavior are deeply embedded.

By the same token, when we have a little boy who sits nicely at the table doing stickers for twenty minutes, plays with dolls and kitchen toys, talks in complete sentences, and cries (this is the big one, the crying), their care givers have a tendency to try and "toughen them up." I notice that the other adults in the room raise eyebrows. They wonder . . .

Homosexual. There. Now I've said it. Is the girl who heaves blocks or the boy who likes dolls going to grow up to be homosexual? Probably not. Many heterosexuals report that when they were small they were "tomboys" or "wusses." Most adult homosexuals report that they knew from the time they were very small that that's what they were. Attempts to "soften unruly girls" or "toughen sensitive boys" will not change who they are. What it may do, however, is make them feel *bad* for being who they are.

Do your child a favor. Allow the choice of activities he or she enjoys to be free from censure. Rather than trying to make your child someone he or she is not, use these observations to get to know your child and to accommodate his or her own individual tastes.

SECTION 2: PARENTING TIPS

With quite young children gender difference is not a particularly pressing issue. You won't be doing much that requires careful social guidance. A group of mothers of eleven-month-olds will all be concerned primarily with safety and hygiene. "Sockets are dangerous!" "Dust balls are not food. Would you like a bagel?" "Shoes are dirty. Why don't you chew on this toy?" "That isn't your bottle. Here's yours."

But as the children leave babyhood, with each ensuing developmental stage, mothers of boys and girls may have different challenges requiring distinct approaches.

A. RESPECTING GENDER-BASED BEHAVIOR
I. General Behavior
Boys

Boys like weapons. Create a weapon-free home and your boy will shoot you with his finger. Some mothers get upset by this. If you react negatively you are doing the opposite of what you wish. You are creating an *emotional* battle that you cannot win. Like any other behavior, when forbidden it may pop up somewhere else with less-pleasant ramifications. Better ways to deal with weaponry:

❖ Accept this common behavior. Make it a game. Shoot back with your own finger.

❖ Point out from time to time that toy guns may be fun, but real guns hurt people. And we don't hurt other people.

❖ If you or your husband have guns, start early on (by one year) teaching respect for guns and basic safety. Teach, over and over, that we never point a real gun at someone, even when the safety's on and it's not loaded. Never have a loaded gun *anywhere* a child is able to find it.

❖ Limit carrying toy weapons and shooting games in inappropriate places. Houses of worship, ceremonies, or homes of formal older people, just to name a few, are not good places to play bang-bang.

Most boys are into throwing. But saying "Don't throw" to a boy, or to any girl who enjoys it a lot, is as useful as saying, "Don't grow!" Instead, offer socially acceptable ways for them to do what they like to do.

❖ "We throw balls and kisses" is a helpful way to allow throwing without allowing him to throw anything he wants. Try to have a ball handy so that the minute he lets a block fly, for instance, you can quickly substitute a ball. If you don't have a ball, see if you can divert with the fun game of "throwing kisses." That tactic should work for at least thirty seconds with a real thrower!

❖ Limit *where* he can throw. "You can throw in the backyard or family room. You can't throw in the living room, dining room, or kitchen. There are too many things there that can break." "You can't throw in the restaurant [doctor's waiting room, or any other public place]. Do you want to go outside and throw while we wait, or would you rather take a look at this book?" Although some moms try to limit throwing by not carrying a ball, an inveterate thrower will be happy with a sugar pack or any other hand-sized object. By three—often much earlier—many boys are miserable if they don't have a ball with them at all times. Try those soft, spongy ones so his tossing it around won't break a window or smash into someone going in the door.

❖ "I see that you feel like throwing. Let's see if you can toss all your trucks into this bin." Help him to learn aim. Engage his desire to improve his aim rather than try to stop him from throwing.

Boys like banging. The more noise, the better.

❖ "If you need to hammer, here's a hammering toy. We don't hammer on the dining room table."
❖ A door slammer (one who has managed to weaken the hinges on your kitchen cabinets) might profit from a play kitchen or any other toy made for banging doors. "If you feel like slamming, go slam your play kitchen."

Girls

Many girls are interested in clothes and hair stuff. Is this because they see us as role models? I don't think so. I have seen countless "girly-girls" whose mothers don't wear makeup and are visibly disinterested in their own looks or clothes.

❖ Please avoid focusing on how she looks, no matter how interested she seems in it. There are creative ways to channel this interest. In many ways art is the same aesthetic urge. Pattern recognizing is involved with sorting, categorizing, and math. "Don't you look pretty?" is not the predominant theme a girl should hear throughout her day.
❖ Please see the sections in Chapter 9 on "Kids and Clothes," if you find her interest hard to deal with.

Many girls play with dolls. They hold them, feed them, take care of them, talk to them, become attached to them. If you find that this interest annoys you, please see the section on page 92, "Inappropriate Attempts to Rid Your Child of Stereotyping."

Because clothes and dolls are more socially acceptable than throwing and banging, girls often have less restrictions than boys about their choice of activities.

2. Outside Play

Most boys outside will be more rambunctious than most girls. A yard or playground, of course, is the perfect place for any child with a lot of energy. But even outside we moms are dealing with predictable differences in behavior for most of our girls and boys.

Boys

On hot days water play can be fun. But it's not fun for someone who doesn't want to play. We frequently see girls screaming, crying, or furious at being unwilling participants in water war games.

❖ Teach your child to aim where it's not annoying. "It's never nice to squirt water in someone's face."

❖ "If someone asks you not to shoot them with the water pistol, that means they don't want to play that game. If you shoot her again I will take away your water pistol." Should your child "not remember" this advice, take away the pistol.

❖ The same goes for buckets full of water, cups, water balloons, or any other bomb, weapon, or creative dousing creation. They can play a game that suits them, but they may not force someone else—boy, girl, or adult—to "play" who doesn't want to.

Snow is beautiful. Each flake is different. It is fun for sledding, eating, and making angels. Yet some boys, when they see snow, see only a handy-dandy ready-made weapon.

❖ Snowballs are fun. Ice balls are not. Snow shoved down somebody's back is only fun if they're laughing. If they're crying they do not want to play.

❖ Throwing snowballs at moving objects such as toddlers, dogs, and cars with open windows, although alluring, is not acceptable.

Girls

Many girls are active tumblers, creative crawlers, fearless gymnasts, bikers, and skaters. But often girls use the playground as an extension of how they play at home. Sometimes, moms think they're missing out. They're not.

❖ Many girls' idea of a hot time in the playground is coloring with chalk on the ground. Bring chalk. Leave them alone about how there are so many things to do out here and all they want to do is draw. These are probably children whose small motor skills are much more highly developed than their gross motor skills. Making them feel incompetent and forced into activities they don't like won't make them more athletic. It will either make them dread going outside, mad, or ashamed of who they are.

❖ Some girls like to sit on a bench, eat a snack, and watch the other kids.

❖ By four and five many girls are coordinated enough to like jumping rope. They may not like hurling themselves off the top of the jungle gym.

3. In Group Settings

Whereas many boys seem to use the playground to better advantage, girls are more likely to shine in group settings.

Whether it's day care, a toddler class, nursery school, or kindergarten, most collective enterprises require cooperation, following instructions, and group activities including eating, singing, sharing, art, and listening to stories together.

For most boys, as well as particularly active girls, these activities are sometimes too much of a reach. These children should not be made to feel "bad" because they have ants in their pants. A competent leader or teacher will figure out a way to incorporate their need to move. An incompetent leader will punish the active child for being unruly. But there is a difference between disruptive and unruly.

If you are attending a toddler class where the leader insists that your child do what everybody else is doing, and you find your arms wrapped around your screaming child as you suggest he paint like the other kids are doing, this is not a good class for you or your child.

In day care or nursery school, if your child is being given a lot of time-outs (more than two or three a week for more than one week is a lot), you might want to explore under what conditions. Has your active child been made to sit too long, to listen too long, to follow too many complicated rules? If this is the case, the day-care center or nursery school is not equipped to meet your child's needs. If, on the other hand, frequent time-outs are because your child is so aggressive during free play that he is hurting lots of other kids on purpose, please see the sections in Chapter 11 on "Problems with All Kids and/or All Situations."

Most girls, in any group that is adequate and certainly in a creative group setting, will thrive. They will be able to handle a strict setup better than boys, meaning they will not get in "trouble." I'm not sure, however, that too "strict" an environment, which includes lining up, no talking, sit on this bench, cover the whole page with paint not just this corner, don't put the blue bears with the pink ones, is an early-childhood environment that will foster critical thinking skills for any child.

If you have the opportunity to choose age placement in any of these groups, including kindergarten, I would suggest having your child be the oldest, rather than the youngest. This is *particularly relevant for boys,* whose ability to function in a group usually lags behind that of girls.

Self-esteem, or the lack of it, is pretty much a done deal by five, although we all continue to get strokes and knockdowns throughout life.

Yet in these vital early years much of how we feel about ourselves in relation to the world is being put into place.

I am always surprised by the number of parents who are inclined to push their kids ahead. I understand their thinking. They figure, if my squirt is the littlest he'll learn more from the older kids. And while it is true that a younger sibling picks up some things earlier than a firstborn, in a group setting of nonsiblings the likelihood of your child becoming more advanced is lower than the probability that your child will feel incompetent and not as good as the other kids.

B. INEQUITIES TO ADDRESS
What's Good for the Goose Is Good for the Gander

Accommodating gender-differentiated behavior is one thing. Sexual stereotyping is another. It's too easy to slide from observing that boys are active loners to allowing them to grow up to be spitting, belching, unfeeling boors; it is just as easy to confuse girls' seeming interest in others with expecting every girl to be Mother Teresa, fulfilled only when she nurtures others, never thinking of her own needs.

Exercise: When you find a correction or the words "Good girl" or "Good boy" springing to your lips, see if you can imagine saying the same thing to a child of the opposite sex for the same behavior. If you can't, maybe it's not such good advice.

May the Best Person Win

I often see disputes about toys settled by the adults in inequitable ways. One child is playing with a toy. Another walks up and takes it.

Boys are more frequently allowed to ''win'' the toy through dominance—in this case, through holding on. Mothers of two boys are much more likely than mothers of two girls to allow a tug of war where the strongest wins. Mothers of girls who have had a toy taken from them are more often inclined to say, ''Oh, that's okay,'' and suggest that their girl find some other toy to play with—in other words, back down. Mothers of girls who have taken the toy are much quicker to move in and say, ''It's not nice to grab,'' and move their daughter to another toy.

Now, I ask you. Is that fair?

The same kind of inequity shows up around whose turn it is. Mothers of girls seem more attuned to letting the other child go first if they both get there at the same time. Mothers of boys more often accept that their son shouldered ahead in line because he's quicker.

Exercise: Imagine your child as a teenager on a date. What kind of behavior would make you feel you'd done a competent job of parenting? What you think may be different, but what I think is this: Girls need to be taught to say no. Boys need to be taught to ask.

Cleanup Is Not an Estrogen-driven Activity

Boys as well as girls need to be taught to clean up after themselves.

I am always stunned by the difference in the treatment of boys and girls during the cleanup part of our snack.

The majority of girls enjoy following instructions, the silly garbage-can song, and willingly bring their cups to the garbage and drop them in. The few who would rather run from the table to play are almost invariably pulled back. Both mommies and baby-sitters put the garbage in the girls' hands and then *physically guide* the girls by the shoulder to the garbage can. Then and only then are they encouraged to go play.

Boys are less inclined to follow the directions in the first place. I have no problem with this predictable gender-based behavior. But I do take issue with the adult response. It is shocking how many adults shrug as their boys run off to play. The adults drop the garbage into the can as if this were not a real part of the class for the boys.

I try "jokes": "*Your* mommy taught you to clean up. Why aren't you teaching Jason?" Or "Someday some wonderful daughter-in-law is going to be mighty mad that you didn't teach Jason to clean up after himself." We laugh. Ha-ha-ha! Next week, same thing.

Please don't let your boy off the hook. He will have to "get it." Mutual responsibility for domestic chores is a major area where gender expectations are changing. Cleanup is where it begins.

Sugar, Spice, and Everything Out of Kilter

Encourage her generosity. But encourage his too.

Often, children hand things to other children. But I see a curious disparity in how this simple act of kindness is responded to. The girls are encouraged resoundingly. We hear loud, long praise. "Isn't that nice? Lindsey gave the dolly to Alexandra! What a good girl!" Mothers of boys, on the other hand, often don't respond or simply say, "That was nice."

It would seem to me that both acts of generosity should be equally affirmed. In this case I would ask the moms of boys to respond more, rather than the moms of girls to respond less. Any act of kindness in our modern world should be praised to the hilt.

C. ENCOURAGING CHILDREN TO EXPLORE "OPPOSITE-GENDER" TOYS

Why? Because women have to pump gas and men have to load dishwashers. The child who is not encouraged to slide the scale of "boy" and "girl" toys is the grown-up who will have trouble living in the modern world.

How? Understand how a child instinctively plays. Although all children use their imaginations they are more inclined to "play" at adult behavior with toys that they're more comfortable with.

Activity: Boys and Dolls

Boys often play with dolls when there is a new sibling in the house. Yet their play seems to differ from that of girls. Rather than feeding, changing the diaper, and talking to the doll, as girls usually do, boys often line them up.

A fun way to encourage boys to play with dolls is a game of Wash the Baby. Girls also love this activity, by the way.

* ❖ Get a waterproof doll and a pan of water.
* ❖ Put the doll in.
* ❖ Say, "Shall we put soap in?" (Add some bubbles.)
* ❖ Say, "Now let's wash the baby."
* ❖ "Find the head, wash the neck, wash the arms," etc.

> **Lesson:** *Mommy's terrific. She understands that if she takes me step by step in an active game I might actually enjoy playing with this dolly. I might even pick one up the next time I see one.*

Activity: Girls and Cars

In the same way that boys don't seem to "mother" dolls, girls frequently don't "get" how to play with cars. If you are like many of the moms in my classes, you yourself may not know just what your boy finds so exciting about that garage!

* ❖ Pick up a toy car.
* ❖ Rev it and roll it along.
* ❖ Put the car at the top of the garage ramp and then, using accompanying *Whee!* sounds, let the car roll down.
* ❖ Most boys don't include dialogue, although they make crashing and *whee* sounds. Girls seem to like narrative. "Here comes the

car, now it's going up the ramp, *chug-a-chug-a*. Now it's about to drive down the ramp.''

Lesson: Mommy's neat. She knows how to play with cars. And the stories that go along with them are so interesting, it almost makes me want to play with these cars myself. Maybe next time I see a toy car I'll pick it up myself.

Anytime you can think of an idea or way to play that may not readily spring to your child's mind, try it.

Here's a beautiful alternative a mom did in class. She and her son were stacking cardboard bricks. Instead of knocking them, she was blowing them down.

D. INAPPROPRIATE ATTEMPTS TO RID YOUR CHILD OF STEREOTYPING

In the same way that we women are ''getting'' to do two—sometimes three—jobs these days, in my experience some girls are ''benefiting'' more from ''nonstereotype training'' than boys.

Their mothers are usually women I find extremely engaging. They are smart, well-read, and often very witty. They and their husbands do not divide the work of running a household and family along traditional lines. These women are usually very successful in their careers. They approach motherhood with the same intelligence and vigor that they approach all other aspects of their lives.

Yet here are some things I've noticed that some of these mothers do that unfortunately may backfire:

❖ Tossing a girl baby too vigorously. If a particular boy baby were to cry and show distress at being thrown around, the mother would stop. Yet I have seen a number of mothers so intent on making sure their girls aren't softies that they refuse to read their own babies' cues.

❖ Forcing physical activity when it's clear the toddler herself is not interested. How many times can you smile a forced smile and make your kid climb back up that sliding-board ladder when it's obvious she's not having any fun? If a boy wanted to go play with something else, most mothers would follow his lead.

❖ Gender-free naming and dressing: I have observed this fascinating phenomenon. I am presented with a baby dressed in beige, yellow, or black, with a neutral name such as Lee. As I make introductory small talk I avoid saying "he" or "she," because most mothers become surprisingly offended if you assign the wrong sex to their child, *whichever* gender their child is. The "neutral" Lee invariably turns out to be a girl. *No* mothers of boys—including the lesbian mothers I have met—attempt to conceal the gender of their sons. This same phenomenon often continues into toddlerhood. There is a wide range between lace, pink ruffles, and bows, and a black turtleneck and jeans. But if a toddler girl doesn't have hair and is wearing overalls and a turtleneck, everybody's going to call her "him." Although I agree with a mother wanting to prevent her daughter from having to conform to unpleasant sexual stereotyping and to exempt her adult daughter from the glass ceiling that exists in the workplace, I wonder whether this attempt to downplay her girlhood will later translate to self-confidence or to shame and self-revulsion about being female.

❖ Refusing to mention her looks, her clothes, or to ever call her pretty. There is nothing wrong with being pretty. If you base your entire existence only on your looks, your life ultimately may be empty and superficial. But if you happen to be pretty—and more importantly, feel pretty—as well as competent, smart, and empathetic, you have a full, rich life.

❖ Not stopping inappropriate physical aggression. Your girl is not going to be the president of a big corporation because she was allowed to hit when she was two. She's going to be a hitter. Although there are times when a physical response may be appropriate, girls, like boys, must be socialized.

❖ Substituting a truck or tool every time your child is drawn to a doll.

In all these instances, which I have seen repeatedly, the mothers are falling into a natural trap. You want to do the best for your child. But just because you resent how much your family focused on your looks and made it hard for you to achieve, ignoring your own child's natural inclinations is no different from how your parents ignored yours. It's not fair to hope your child will become what you couldn't be. We must try as best we can not to identify with our child, nor to assume that their tastes, desires, and wants are ours.

Now that we've looked at differences and similarities between boys and girls, it's time to move toward the topic that ultimately will be the most relevant to those differences.

<u>SEX</u>

Before tackling this delicate subject, I would like to say that I have some major disagreements, or at least questions, about the commonly accepted way we handle some aspects of introducing our children to sex. I will let you know the places where my ideas may be maverick.

Most parents hope that when their children are adults, they will have the experience of sharing happy, unself-conscious sexual pleasure and satisfaction with a person they love.

No matter how wild your own personal choices, it is a rare parent who looks down on their sleeping baby and daydreams, "Honey, I hope you nail anything that moves when you're big enough."

On the other end of the spectrum, I can't imagine hoping that your offspring will grow up to detest being touched, cringe at the thought of another person's body, and ultimately endure whatever it takes to make a baby, just for the sake of procreation.

As in all of parenting, we strive for balance.

Here is a clothesline I'd like to suggest to hang your attitudes from: When all is said and done, your child's sex life is none of your beeswax. It is private. If all goes well, by adulthood you and the memory of you will fade into the faraway distance. Where you belong.

Have you heard this one? One lover says to the other, "Whew, it's crowded in this bed. There are six of us: you, me, and both sets of our parents."

Some joke.

SECTION 1: IN THE HOME

Although you will be the first woman your son ever loves and your husband will be your daughter's first love, which is right and as it should be, there are ways you can help your child develop healthy sexual attitudes without intruding on their privacy.

A. ADULT BEHAVIOR

Some parents are self-conscious about their bodies; others are not. Nevertheless, certain behavior around the house will respect your own personal style while still meeting the needs of your child.

I. Nudity: Beyond One Year

❖ Don't keep your body covered constantly so that it becomes a mystery.

❖ If your same-sex child sees you without any clothes on, don't jump, gasp, and cover yourself as if you're ashamed. This will teach unpleasant things such as self-revulsion, revulsion for other people's naked bodies, shame, and other negative emotions that do not accompany healthy sexual development.

❖ If your opposite-sex child happens to come across you without clothes, again, don't freak. But put on a robe, wrap a towel around yourself, or whatever it takes to cover yourself—without hasty shame.

❖ Once a child is two, the opposite-sex parent shouldn't parade around in front of them without clothes. This may be alarming to a child, who is curious about other people's bodies. A preschooler may in fact become aroused.

> *Lesson: Bodies are different. These differences are interesting. I notice that we keep our differences covered.*

2. Adult Sexuality

In the same way that your child's mature sexuality ultimately will become none of your business, so your sexuality is no business of your child's.

❖ Don't make love when they're in bed with you.

❖ If your baby sleeps in your room, make love in another room even when they're sound asleep.

❖ If you happen to be a noisy couple, which is your privilege, try using a room as far away from theirs as possible or figure out a way to make love with abandon when they're out of the house.

❖ If they should walk in on you when you're in the middle of making love, stop, roll over, get yourself covered, ask them what they need, and get them back to bed. You don't need to look or feel guilty.

❖ If they ask you what you were doing, tell them something like grown-up cuddling. Someday, when they fall in love, they'll have grown-up cuddling too. Connecting love with physical contact is important in laying a foundation that we chose our partners carefully, not indiscriminately.

❖ Don't say, "Doing? We weren't doing anything." That's like, "Honest, Mom, I didn't have my hand in the cookie jar." Don't deny the experience, but put it properly in the arena of grown-up activity.

❖ Some advise locking the door. This is a choice that may appeal to you. I feel, however, that this creates a mood of both illicitness and having the parents off-limits, which may not be so healthy. If you are particularly active and you have a child who is consistently walking in on you, there are other alternatives besides a locked door. Lunch dates. Hiring a baby-sitter to take your child out for a couple of hours. Cutting back a bit for the short time when your child is going through his stage of wanting to walk in on you.

❖ A child who sees affection, both verbal and physical, pass between his parents is a secure child who is learning about love. Don't refrain from kissing and hand-holding because your child is around.

❖ *But,* if your kisses turn to passion, if one of you slips a hand somewhere "interesting," if you find your own feelings changing from affection to lust, you have entered a private place that your child should not be privy to. Get a grip! Cut it out. That's why they made bedroom doors!

Here's a subject that is often ignored in general parenting books and relegated to "specialty" books. It is an issue, however, that affects many homes in America.

If you are not part of a couple and are dating one or many, that is your privilege. It is your young child's privilege, however, to have his needs taken into account as well. Although who sleeps in your house and when is a personal choice that you are entitled to make, your child is entitled to be exempt from seeing any traces of your adult activities. This includes major things, such as closing doors and not showering together when your child is at home, as well as minor things, such as everybody being as dressed at breakfast and behaving as they would in a restaurant or any other public space. After all, the common areas of a home, outside of the bedroom and bathroom, are public places. Your child is entitled to respect.

B. CHILDREN'S BEHAVIOR—PERSONAL EXPLORATION

Some children begin exploring their bodies well before the age of two, others not until much later.

- ❖ When they touch themselves, don't push their hands away. They are getting in touch with what their body feels like. If you shove their hand away with revulsion, remonstrance, or any other negative emotion, without having said one word you will have set them on the long, unpleasant road toward guilt in connection with sex.
- ❖ Little boys often find their genitals when they are babies. By toddlerhood, many get in the habit of playing with themselves constantly. Teach your toddler or preschooler that this is something we do in private. In some cases this may bear a fair amount of repetition. Try to keep your mood the same as it is around the long haul we face in teaching a child not to climb on furniture, throw things at the bird, or dump computer disks down the toilet.
- ❖ Limit the places where either gender child does it—for example, the bedroom or bathroom.
- ❖ Limit the times. For example, when company is over it is not nice to slip off into your room for a quickie.

> **Lesson:** These good feelings in and of themselves are okay. But I do not act on these feelings indiscriminately wherever and whenever.

C. YOU AND YOUR CHILD
1. Your Physical Relationship

There is no more intimate relationship in the world, in some ways, than that between a parent and a child. For those of us who are biological mothers who nursed our babies, it just doesn't get more physically intimate than that—sorry, hubby!

Whether biological or adoptive, mother or father, however, if you are not head over heels in love with your child, something's amiss. We feel an intense physical warmth toward our children, which they return. While we hope that the complete physical ease with one another we felt when they were babies in our arms continues, as they mature we have to make sure our intimacy doesn't slip over into the wrong place. By the same token we don't want to create an uncomfortable nervousness about each other's bodies. This is a delicate balance to achieve.

Here are some common places where your child needs you to show him the ropes of acceptable behavior without making him feel like he's done something wrong.

* Sometimes children straddle their parents' legs and rub. It's a natural activity, which your child does because it feels good. They are as innocent as can be. You and your husband are not.
* Don't shriek, yank them away, or in any other way indicate revulsion or horror. Your child will not understand the taboo, but will merely interpret your response as a personal revulsion toward him. Rather, simply readjust his or her body away from yours and continue reading, talking, or whatever you were doing.
* If your child's foot or hand inadvertently touches your breast (once weaning is a memory) or your or your husband's crotch while you're playing, again simply move his limb as you go on with your activity. Nothing needs to be said verbally; your body language has been eloquent.
* If your child actively reaches for any of these places, as you readjust your body mention that that's a private part of your body just as he has private parts, and go on with whatever you were doing. Do not respond as if he's offended you or committed a sin. He hasn't. He's a child. Furthermore, if you react too strongly you risk having your child become fascinated by how large a reaction such a simple gesture inspires in you. Then you've entered a gray area where you're trying to teach him to respect other people's physical, sexual boundaries and he's trying to win a power struggle.

Lesson: *Mommy's and Daddy's bodies are havens to me. Places I can go for comfort and warmth. But their private parts, just like mine, are private.*

---

2. Language

The commonly accepted terms among educated people are the words *penis* and *vagina*. These are simply body parts, the thinking goes, just as hand and foot are body parts. Nicknames often carry negative connotations of mystery, smut, or the unmentionable, which become mixed up with our feelings about these body parts. We would be better off without so much "baggage."

While I think it is a very good idea to keep negative associations as far from our concept of our own bodies as possible, I have some serious reservations about the particular words of choice.

The penis and vagina are *not* the same as hand and foot. Please forgive me if the following analogy makes you uncomfortable. It's supposed to. A shoe salesman, after shoehorning you into a pair of shoes, may make a friendly tap on your foot. A lingerie saleslady, after helping you adjust the straps of a teddy to wear under a formal gown, may not give you a friendly tap on your vagina.

Penis and *vagina* are clinical terms, appropriate in a clinical setting. They have no sexual overtones.

If we teach our children through the compelling subtext of language that all parts of the body are equal—hand, foot, penis, vagina—why shouldn't we expect them later in life to regard these parts—and what we do with them—as nonchalant, everyday, and "what's-the-big-deal"?

Furthermore, there is a forced innocence about the use of these words. We don't say buttocks, for example. We say user-friendly words like bottom and tush. Most unaffected families are comfortable with sissies, pees, and poops in favor of urination and defecation.

And yet suddenly, on the biggies we become a nation of Niles Cranes, Frasier's passionate, brilliant, fussbudgety, neurotically uptight brother! Penis and vagina, indeed.

Part of the problem, of course, is that there *is* no commonly acceptable language for these body parts on a par with tush or bottom. These parts truly were unmentionable in polite society for so long, relegating vocabulary for them to smutty words or inane family words, that we are in a modern abyss.

I think this topic warrants discussion in the community at large, not because we should be splitting linguistic hairs, but because our children's attitudes are profoundly shaped by the way we adults choose to describe things.

It seems to me we should follow our children's lead.

Children the world over delight in baby talk. Rather than exempting sexual body parts from normal linguistic development, we might consider adopting our children's words to suit the needs of our whole family.

Here are some suggestions that I think might be useful in terms of language and vocabulary. You may or may not agree.

❖ Many children naturally come up with pee-pee, or a derivative, and gine-gine, because they cannot pronounce penis and vagina. Don't insist, as I have heard so many mothers do, that they must say penis and vagina, any more than you insist that they say pacifier rather than paccy or any other word of their creation. Furthermore, just as so many families comfortably do with a word like paccy, *adopt their derivative as your own family word.* Use them yourself, rather than always using the clinical terms penis and vagina.

❖ I offer to you mothers whose babies are so small that you haven't even thought of what to call these things those two child-coined terms: pee-pee and gine-gine. Kind of a pleasant ring, don't you think? Not dirty, not nervous, and not clinical.

❖ If your child makes up baby-talk words for other parts of the body, use them. Many nursing babies come up with a word like nummies for breasts.

❖ These words become your family's personal language, an important part of developing a sense that there is a privacy and intimacy to this whole area that is different from other things and to be shared only with those to whom we feel close.

❖ If the words you grew up with were disparaging and implied something dirty, such as "down there," or your "eh-eh," get rid of them. Create a new relationship to those parts for your child— and for you.

❖ If you grew up in a home where those parts were completely unmentionable, consider mentioning them. Your child will not be able to get past day care, let alone kindergarten, in mainstream America without confronting these words. It will be better for all of you if he associates these words, and ideas, with home and intimacy rather than thinking they're acceptable only on the outside.

Lesson: *Certain parts of my body are different from the rest of my body. They deserve their own special language and, by extension, their own special treatment.*

SECTION 2: IN THE NEIGHBORHOOD: OTHER CHILDREN

As soon as your child begins to hang out with other people, sexuality becomes a reality. But there's "good clean fun," and then there's the other side of things that we all worry about quietly. Many of us don't like to mention the worry because of embarrassment, or a superstitious fear that as long as we don't say it, nothing will "happen," or because we're afraid we're being overprotective and paranoid. And yet, unfortunately, we have to guide our child through some rather rocky stuff. See if these simple ideas help.

A. DON'T WORRY

Most small children notice physical gender difference in the same way that they notice the difference between hair color and size. These are value-free observations that a mom can simply affirm. "Yes, Andrew and Daddy have pee-pees, and you and I have gine-gines."

Somewhere between three and five, kids start playing Doctor. You should know what they're playing, but not intrude. However, if your child is uncomfortable with it, please move to stop it with the same mood that you would discourage two children from melting crayons on the radiator. How will you know your child is uncomfortable? If he calls you, if he keeps coming out to get you, or if after his playmate has left he tells you they played something he didn't like. Most children, however, will choose one or two close friends with whom to begin basic, healthy exploration.

If you discover, either through your child's conversation or an adult telling you, that your child is playing Doctor in an institutional setting, such as the rare instances of day care or nursery school or the more likely instance of kindergarten, you need to work with the adults in charge. Children should not be playing with so little supervision. Explain to your child that these are activities we do in the privacy of our own home, not at school.

B. WORRY

A child who makes you uneasy in ways you cannot quite articulate or who has a precociously seductive style is a child who has been exposed to things a little child shouldn't. Discontinue any private time your child spends with that child. Some parents choose to discontinue the relationship completely. If you think you can help, by all means talk to a religious leader, your doctor, or someone who may be able to intervene in this child's behalf. But first, worry about your own.

❖ If you find out inadvertently or your child tells you directly that "my friend put something inside him or herself," discontinue that relationship.
❖ If the "something" went into your child, do not flip out in your

child's presence, no matter how distressed you feel. Call your doctor immediately. Consider arranging for counseling for yourself and your child. Your family needs someone with experience who is not emotionally involved to help you with your own emotions so that you can help your child.

SECTION 3: THE OUTSIDE WORLD

A. OTHER ADULTS
Strangers

There are a lot of creeps in the world. Are there more creeps now than there used to be? This may be an academic argument. But they, and their creepiness, are definitely more "in your face" than they used to be.

Chapter 13, "The Media," offers suggestions on how to handle a lot of junk we see around us. Chapter 12, "Public Places," has a section on street smarts called "Teaching Kids," which I hope you'll find useful for teaching your child how to deal with strangers, and who can pick him up, take him home, etc.

A useful rule to mention to your child in passing, without making it a big deal: "No one [besides Mom, Dad, and baby-sitter when they change your diaper, for the younger child] is allowed to touch you on any of your private parts. If anybody ever wants to, you tell Mom."

"Megan's Law" is a very attractive name to a child, since there are so many Megan's around. Should your four- or five-year-old ask you what Megan's Law is, you can explain that not touching on your privates is not just a rule in our house. It's a law in our country. Nobody is allowed to touch you there, except your doctor when Mommy or Daddy is in the room, or Mommy and Daddy if you hurt on your privates.

When choosing adults to be with your child, if you have the least, slightest, most minuscule "feeling" of uncomfortableness about the person—whether it's a vague apprehension about them sexually or any other discomfort—do not hire them. Do not push the feeling away or chalk it up to whatever "unkindness" you suspect on your part. This is one instance where you're better paranoid than polite. Never hire anyone to be with your child that you do not have profound basic trust in. This has nothing to do with style or class; it has to do with mood.

Adults You Know

We have to assume that the adults our child comes in contact with are on the up and up. If for any reason you wonder about something your small child says or does and can rule out your own overprotectiveness, first try some uninflected question. "That's interesting. Who taught you that?'' If you get any answer that makes you wonder, please get professional help. It's too hard to go it alone on that kind of thing.

B. "WHERE DO BABIES COME FROM?"

Here is another topic, closely related to my reservations about language, that I feel warrants discussion.

The accepted answer among educated people is a variation of this: ''A sperm and an egg meet, life forms, and a baby grows in a mommy's womb until it is big enough to be born.'' Only if pressed are we advised to introduce the idea that Mommy and Daddy get together with love. It is suggested that we keep our response matter-of-fact. We don't introduce the topic, but rather wait and address the issue at whatever age our child decides to ask.

If you offer this answer to your young child, you will be in the very good company of most respected early-childhood specialists, educators, psychologists, psychiatrists, and thinking people of our times.

This answer, their thinking goes, does several things:

1. It follows the child's lead in terms of timing.
2. It does not mention sexual intercourse.
3. It uses the word *womb* rather than *tummy*.
4. It sidesteps all the permutations of conception currently possible.
5. From a philosophical, psychological point of view, it satisfies certain requirements. It does not include any unverifiable, mythic information. Making up myths to obscure the truth is tantamount to lying. Lying to your child will engender distrust when they do find out the truth, perhaps making them unwilling to discuss this topic with you further. It satisfies a young child by its concreteness. It demystifies the topic. It informs.

I'd like to go point by point, because I think some parts of this answer are useful. There are other aspects of this commonly accepted answer, however, that I think deserve to be looked at again.

1. Follow Their Lead in Terms of Time

I agree with conventional wisdom that when they are ready is the best time to begin discussing it. Some children may begin asking as soon as they can string a couple of words together; others may very well wait till they're four or five. Most ask when they see a pregnant lady.

2. Sexual Intercourse

I agree wholeheartedly that this is not a useful piece of information for a toddler or preschooler. I have heard parents introduce the penis/

vagina aspects of reproduction to their three- and four-year-olds matter-of-factly, in an attempt to banish squeamish self-consciousness about sex. But a small child is not able to accommodate this information in a meaningful way.

In the worst-case scenario your young child may suggest to a play-mate that they "Make a baby! Mommy says you put your penis into my vagina! Let's try!"

3. Womb or Uterus Instead of Tummy

This makes sense to me. You avoid having an imaginative child think we somehow eat whatever makes a baby. Some experts advise, I think quite thoughtfully, that if your child asks later, as many of them do, "How does the baby come out?" tell them it comes from "a special part of the gine-gine that is different from where siss comes from."

4. Sidestepping Modern Technology

The number of possibilities of how one specific child is actually conceived are numerous. A toddler or preschooler doesn't need to know about petri dishes, sperm banks, and turkey basters, any more than he needs to know about intercourse. He also doesn't need to know about a cesarean birth unless his mom is recuperating from surgery, at which time it's enough to offer an age-appropriate explanation, leaving out the surgical procedure and focusing on the baby needing the doctor to help it be born.

5. It Does Not Include any Unverifiable Information: It Demystifies; It Is Not a Myth

Here is the part I want to disagree with.

The argument that the egg/sperm/birth answer is concrete, demysti-fies, and informs seems erroneous to me. I think, rather, it sets up a whole new series of mythical possibilities, all dressed up in white lab coats, that are equally as ripe for distortion as the cabbage patch and the stork. Your guess is as good as mine as to what flights of fancy an imaginative child may take. Does a toddler picture the egg as drawn by Dr. Seuss? Do we buy it in the dairy department next to the butter and cottage cheese? If I eat this scrambled egg am I eating somebody's baby sister? What is sperm? Well . . . you stall, thinking. It's a little part of Daddy. Does that mean Daddy has to go to the doctor to get the little part out? Do we use the nail clippers? Or does the barber take the little part at the same time that he cuts Daddy's hair?

Although later in life your child will find that you have accurately described part of the physical process, in terms of truth I think this answer misses the mark. While technically precise it is a narrow answer, in its way equally as naive as believing that if you want a baby you should go out in a field and spread ground chicken bones by the light of a new moon. It is our modern, scientific, technologically correct myth that we offer children. But myth it is nevertheless.

The truth is that *we do not know where babies come from.*

The head fertility doctor at Johns Hopkins doesn't know any more than the head fertility shaman of a caveman clan about the spark of life.

Our voluminous scientific knowledge of the *mechanics* of biological reproduction cannot explain why the same couple can copulate month after month, using the most sophisticated means to measure ovulation and sperm count, yet still be sterile for years. Nor can it account for their inexplicable ability to suddenly conceive. How many scientifically determined "sterile" couples do you know who adopt a baby and then conceive? How many teenagers "do it" once and conceive?

We understand the *mechanics* of conception at a microscopic, measurable level that is prodigious and obviously far more informed than our more primitive predecessors. Nevertheless, we, like they, must come face to face with what to us seems an unpalatable fact. We do not know. There is a force beyond our ken. Something happens that we cannot explain. There is a mystery.

The explicit desire to demystify this process concerns me. Why at our child's first sign of curiosity are we so loath to link babies with men and women, love, and something beyond our knowledge and control?

Love itself is a mystery. We can pick and poke at it, trying to discover its source from now till doomsday. But there is a moment, if we are very, very lucky, when we find our mate. If we are lucky enough to find someone we love, when the two of us physically come together we enter a state that is different from all others, a moment in time when everything else shuts down and the two of us become as one in a heightened, mystical realm unlike any other. Even if during the course of our lifetime we have other rich experiences, there is a quality to the experience with our chosen life and soul mate and the father of our child that resonates with meaning far beyond the physiological act itself.

If somehow in these formative years our children are not guided by us to expect something powerful and mythic, something distinctly *not* humdrum, ho-hum, and matter-of-fact, why will we then be surprised when they "nail anything that moves"? If we introduce babies as a mechanical event, why when they're older will they not view sex—which they will discover quite soon to be connected to babies—also simply an insignificant, mechanical event?

On the other hand, if they do not follow our lead and approach love and sex as matter-of-fact, but rather feel the pull of passion in all its intensity, won't we have betrayed them in the very way we wanted to avoid? Won't we have set up the very distance, the very off-limits aspect of sex, love, and passion that we thought we were so cleverly getting around? Won't our teenagers, throbbing with hormonal waves of glandular grandeur, one day look across the breakfast table at us and legitimately view us as the sexless, prissy, cut-off couple that we're trying so hard not to be?

Oh, Mom. You thought it was all about eggs and sperm. You just do not understand.

Let's say that our child is truly asking a concrete question. He sees his mommy or another lady with a big belly. He hears "baby." He wants to know. We're the grown-ups. We have a choice of what information to give.

If we take our children to Disneyland and they focus on the backpack the kid in front of them in line has, as children do, don't we suggest they lift their eyes? Look! There's Mickey! Don't we direct our child to look up past the peanut vendor to the castle's turrets? Even then, don't we look beyond? Don't we point out a dazzling sunset, a black rolling storm cloud, a rainbow? Don't we try and lift our children's vision beyond where their young eyes fall?

Why, then, on this fundamental question do we shove their heads down? Don't look! Here. Focus on this! The most insignificant detail.

Myths such as the cabbage patch and stork reflect a culture's deep-seated discomfort with sex. These distortions are created for the purpose of keeping the truth from children. I believe that our egg-and-sperm myth reflects our own form of discomfort. We are a scientific culture. We have a deep craving to have the answers. We suffer from hubris. We believe that we are in control. We cannot bear to say, "I do not know." We are so deeply rooted in the here and now, the verifiable and concrete, that we miss the forest for the trees.

"Where do babies come from?" is a profound, spiritual question that has challenged the deepest thinkers of all times. To my way of thinking, whether adopted or your biological offspring, your child deserves an explanation that includes the *miracle of life*.

Here are some answers to try on for size.

❖ "You need a mommy, a daddy, lots of love, and a baby blessing [from God, or nature—if these are the values you want to instill]."

❖ "A man and a woman fall in love [and get married—if this is a value you want to instill]. If they want to be parents, they'll find a baby blessing and have a little boy or girl just like you.''

Question: That leaves our family out. We're gay, or I'm a single parent who adopted.

Answer: In these cases, the man/woman/love part might not be what you want to stress. Here's the kind of answer to think about that introduces the idea of the miracle of life.

"You need a man and a woman to start a baby. Then the baby picks the home with the most love to grow up in. We were (I was) blessed when you picked us (me).''

This answer circumvents "We chose you," an idea that may be burdensome in the later, often trying teen years.

Question: We're divorced.

Answer: "Before Mommy and Daddy stopped living together we were in love. And that's when we were blessed with you.''

Question: What if my child doesn't "fall in love and get married"? Have I messed up his mind by that kind of answer?

Answer: Your child may grow up to take a different path. He may choose to be a single parent, may decide that love and marriage don't necessarily go together, he or she may be gay. These are *adult* choices that do not have to be factored in to your answer to a young child any more than you need to introduce artificial insemination. If you do not erode other elements of his self-esteem, he will have the capacity to make an *adult choice* when he is an adult himself that does not necessarily conform to your life-style choices.

Lesson: *Birth is a miracle. Me and my family are blessed to be together.*

These kinds of responses may not appeal to you.

As I said, the egg/sperm/baby answer has its merits. It is certainly much better than crossing your legs tight, having the color drain from your face, saying ask your father, ask your mother, talking about the birds and bees, saying when you're older you'll understand, or any of the more traditional evasive answers indicating shame and discomfort about sex and birth.

But perhaps in our worthy effort to correct this inappropriate mood we have sidestepped the issue rather than stepped up. To my way of thinking, the ''matter-of-fact, scientific'' approach is equally as prudish.

It does not address—in fact explicitly aims to ignore—the mystery, majesty, and special quality surrounding the experience of sex and birth.

I think that's a shame.

I'm suggesting that we reverse the order. We offer mystery first. Then, if pressed, we talk about technology.

Predictable Questions

Question: How does the baby get in your tummy?

Answer: It's a special place called the womb. It's the best place for babies to grow.

Question: (Persistent child) But how does it *get* there?

Answer: It was there already, just waiting for the right stuff to grow. Daddy (if there is one), love, a good home, and good nutrition.

Question: What's a daddy got to do with it?

Answer: You can't have a baby without a daddy.

If you're pregnant, when the baby starts to show you can introduce the idea that it's growing. You can show pictures of when you were pregnant with your child. There are scads of lovely books for children about babies and birth. Some people like to show books that include pictures of babies *in utero*. Others show their children sonogram pictures of themselves, but some of those pictures can look sort of spooky, so use your judgment. Families that are open about their bodies often let their children see the mother's pregnant body; others keep it covered; but all children enjoy feeling the movement if your new baby is an *in utero* kicker. (Please see Chapter 14, ''In Sickness and in Health,'' for other thoughts about pregnancy and birth.)

For the child who becomes keenly interested, grow some seeds, showing what they need and how they develop into baby plants. Predictably, some won't sprout. If you count how many seeds you plant and how many sprout, you may have an unexpected marvelous lesson from nature. There is a blessing in life and growth.

Children's questions are always profound; if we're lucky we can rise to their heights with our answers.

SUMMARY:

❖ Some behavior is gender-based and some a matter of temperament.
❖ We must respect each child for exactly who he or she is and try not to fit them into any kind of gender mold, whether traditional or nontraditional.
❖ Sexuality is a powerful force; we must be intimate with our children while maintaining boundaries.
❖ At the same time we must try and create a mood where one day they can take their place as adults with full ease in their own bodies and an expectation that they will have rich, satisfying experiences in life.

The Love of Learning

Let early education be a form of amusement; you will then be better able to discover the natural bent.
—Plato, *The Republic*

Living in your house right now is a young child who is very much involved in learning for learning's sake. She wants to know just to know. She doesn't think that knowing will make her look good, nor does she think she has to cover up if she doesn't know. She's a self-starter, completely equipped to do what only the best students in the finest colleges can: She is perfectly capable of designing her own independent studies. If something interests her she'll chase it into the ground. If it's boring she'll walk away. To a young child, learning is a hoot. If we follow her lead she will keep on loving to learn.

In later years this will have an immeasurably positive effect on her day-to-day life. Given a merely competent teacher, a child who loves to learn will like school. Given a terrific teacher, she will have a ball. Since our children all have to go to school for a minimum of twelve years, we might as well equip them with the wherewithal to enjoy themselves.

Learning, however, is more far-reaching than only in school. Love of learning gives you the drive to master a hobby, do well at your job, be an informed consumer and a better mom. When acquiring information is fun, the smallest to the largest decisions we must make in life become challenges rather than burdens.

SECTION I: LEARNING AND TEACHING

A. LEARNING

Learning is the primary activity of all children. From the moment they wake to the moment they collapse—or are forced—into bed, they learn. They learn through play; they learn from example; they learn by doing and by watching.

Definition

Learning is the acquisition of various bits of information. *Intelligence* is the ability to link these isolated bits to form a coherent pattern. *Creativity* is the ability to link information in novel ways or to discover something new.

General Advice

Interest in these early years should be worshiped. Follow your child's lead. She will be learning whatever she wants to learn. All learning should be fun. Anything that is not allowed to be fun will be harder, if not impossible, for a child to learn.

Rate of Learning

Different people have different rates of learning. Some require much repetition; others glom on after the first couple of go-rounds. Furthermore, some people catch on quickly to some things and more slowly to others. There is nothing inherently good or bad about this. It just is.

Innate Talent and Ability

Most children are predisposed to some kinds of activities more than others. Recognizing innate talent helps a child; trying to make a child what she isn't is a useless and often harmful activity.

Integration

There is a process in the human mind that takes in new information, chews it, swishes it around, swallows it, and then digests it. During the process we often see funny things happen. In the adult, for example, when we start a new job where we are learning many new things, we often forget to pick up milk on the way home. Our mind is "elsewhere." In the child this manifests a bit differently. When language really kicks in, for example, we sometimes see a toddler begin to physically stumble and fall. She is paying attention to something else. For many children, when major new bodies of information are being learned, such as walking, we see sleep disruptions. Sometimes toilet training gets lost in the shuffle of starting nursery school. Understanding and being sympathetic to this process will help you help your child.

Repetition

Most learning takes place through repetition. An eager learner will engage in an activity repeatedly until she masters it or finds it so difficult that she walks away to try it another time. If she walks away, let her. If she is engaged in repeating the same activity, leave her alone. She is mastering many skills that you may not even be able to identify. Furthermore, TV, with its quick-cut editing, is already so profoundly influencing this generation to think in disjointed bits that if you see your child engaged in protracted thought about *anything,* leave her alone. Please.

> **True Tale from the Trenches:** I overheard a mother say to her twenty-two-month-old daughter, "You've already done that puzzle. Let's try another." I suggested that maybe her daughter had a reason for wanting to try it again. The mom let her little girl retackle the puzzle in question. This child's work habits were impressive. First, using trial and error, she slowly went about getting all five pieces where they belonged. Then she practiced getting each piece in the right place without having to turn and twist it, sort of eyeballing it from far away and zooming in to the right position. Once she got placement down pat, she methodically took the pieces out and lined them up around the edges so that she didn't have to search around for where each piece went. Then, starting at the top and working clockwise, she zapped those pieces into the puzzle, lickety-split, pushed the puzzle away with a satisfied grunt like an old fat man leaving a real good dinner table, and went off to find new worlds to conquer.
>
> This was learning at its purest: repeating until mastery had been reached because it was so much fun!

B. TEACHING

As we are often reminded, we are our babies' first teachers. So here I'd like to run through some basic ideas about teaching itself.

1. Not-so-hot Teaching

I have never seen an unimpaired baby who was not curious.

Certainly by five, however, and sadly sometimes earlier, we see children who are slow to take in new information. We notice their inability. We rarely say it out loud, because it seems impolite. But privately we think, "Boy, is that kid dumb!"

I think that child started off smart. She was an apt pupil. She learned quickly from the people around her.

She's eighteen months old, in her stroller in a mall. She sees a picture of Big Bird. She points excitedly, maybe even says, "Big Burr." Mommy can affirm her perception. "Yes. Big Bird."

By this simple reply the mother has acknowledged that:

1. She heard her child.
2. The child was clear.
3. She understood the child.
4. The information was correct.

Instead, Mommy ignores her. Her stroller is pushed along as if she hadn't communicated a thing.

Message? "We don't make connections. We don't identify. We don't value communication." The child will continue pointing out things for a while; she will then stop pointing them out, but continue to notice; eventually, she will stop noticing. She has learned her lesson well.

At the opposite end of the spectrum we see a different type of glazed expression. This sometimes shows up during the school years. "Does not live up to potential" is now often fashionably labeled a "learning disability." (There are children who have physiological processing problems that manifest as learning disabilities. These are a different group.) But for some seemingly slow, inattentive children, the groundwork may have been laid during early childhood. This child shuts down from overload. Here's how it happens.

A two-and-a-half-year-old points to an object and says, "Blue." Mommy can affirm her perception. "Yes. Blue."

Instead, Mommy assaults her with too much advanced information. "Well, it's a *kind* of blue, but we really call it aqua. You see, the printer added green. It's not a true blue. This is the color we often associate with water, particularly Mediterranean water, and interestingly enough, in Italian *aqua* means water, whereas in Spanish *agua* is water. Blah, blah, blah . . ."

Message? "I do not understand your attempt to communicate to tell me that you can identify and name something. I do not value your perception. It is lacking."

A bright child, in self-defense against such an onslaught of verbiage, will most likely refrain from sharing perceptions, considering them inadequate. She may even stop having them altogether eventually in an attempt to establish personal territory that cannot be intruded upon.

The likelihood is higher that you, a reader, will fall closer to the second category than the first.

As in all of parenting, balance is the trick.

2. Master Teaching

I was once privy to a classic teacher-pupil interaction.

My daughter was eight months old; my friend's daughter, Rebecca, was thirteen months. All four of us were on the floor. Rebecca toddled away and returned with a pop-up toy. She pushed a button. Big Bird popped up. Annie was ecstatic. Rebecca shut the door. Big Bird disappeared. Annie looked shocked. Here comes the teaching.

Rebecca looked right in Annie's eyes. She held up her tiny forefinger. She looked at her finger and back at Annie. Then she slowly lowered her finger and pushed the button. She looked back at Annie, who was amazed. Rebecca then shut the lid fast, held up her forefinger again, pushed the button again, and looked back at Annie. She pushed the toy toward Annie and nodded with encouragement. Annie reached out and touched the button. Nothing happened. Rebecca gently touched Annie's hand and then withdrew. Annie pushed harder, and *pop!*

The girls laughed hysterically and busily set about repeating the miracle. Being a new mother with hormones still coursing through my veins, I wept at the brilliance of the interaction.

Let us all take a lesson from Rebecca's innate teaching skills.

❖ Focus your child's attention through eye contact.
❖ Show by example.
❖ Pay attention to your child's individual attempt to learn.
❖ Give gentle direction when needed, but do not do the task for the child.
❖ Reinforce by sheer delight.

3. Encouragement

Applauding, which comes instinctively to most mothers, is a wonderful encouragement for preverbal children. (Don't you just love to see a one-year-old accomplish something and applaud herself?)

As your child matures, use "good" and other verbal praise judiciously.

Your thirteen-month-old struggles her way up the three steps of the baby sliding board. As you hold her hands to steady her wobbling body and you see her foot finally connect to the next rung of the steps, you say, "Good girl! That's it! Up we go! Very good." You're proud. She's proud. Everybody's justifiably proud.

We have to be cautious, however, not to overuse this praise.

For as many attempts, or days, or weeks, as it takes her to accomplish the task of actually getting her uncoordinated body up those steps, she *should* be praised. But once she has mastered the skill and her feet no longer stumble, it is no longer useful for Mommy to continue to habitually say "Good girl!" every time she goes up the steps.

Accept her newfound skill silently. Allow her to integrate her accomplishment internally, without needing constant feedback from the outside world. Too much praise can set up a false expectation in your child. She will seek praise for each and every step along the way of life. And life will not praise her constantly. Nor should it.

Furthermore, as she gets older, certainly by her threes, she will know when something she has done has not been particularly "good." If you see a picture that she drew halfheartedly and you pick it up and rave, "Oh, I *love* this picture!" she will begin either to not value your opinion or to doubt everything she does. Because if you're calling that good, which she knows very well is not her best, then what does good mean?

> **Exception: Grandparents!** The Lord put grandparents on the face of the earth to provide many things. Among them is to have someone who dotes on you and thinks everything you do is better than anyone else in the whole wide world. A grandparent can't praise a child too much. Only a parent can!

4. Correction

Parents provide enormous amounts of information to their children. Since learning takes place not only from acquiring facts and ideas, but also from revising or learning from mistakes, parents need to find ways to correct that encourage rather than squash. Particularly during the early years, when the attitude about learning is as important as the actual data, if not more so, think twice before saying no.

- ❖ If your child is learning to identify colors, for example, and says "blue" instead of "yellow," don't automatically say no. She has gotten the *concept:* color. She has just not nailed down the specifics yet.
- ❖ Try, "Yes, it's a color. It's the color yellow."
- ❖ After the *concept* is firmly in place, which might take a week or several months depending on the child, you can point out differences. "This cup is blue, this shirt is blue. But look! This ball is yellow. See the difference?"

These are some of the common generalizations that young children make before learning to discriminate among the specific differences:

- ❖ The name of one color to stand for the concept color.
- ❖ One specific letter to stand for all letters.
- ❖ One specific shape for all.
- ❖ One number for all.
- ❖ One animal for all.
- ❖ One vehicle (car, for example) for all.
- ❖ The words *Mommy* and *Daddy* to mean all women and men.
- ❖ Baby for all children.

In each instance affirm that she is accurately noticing a major category; correct by simply adding the right specific without putting a negative in and implying that she was wrong.

> **Lesson:** *Mommy understands what I am saying or trying to do and encourages me to learn.*

5. Image: You as Teacher

During all your teaching, which you do from day one, think of your child as a marathon runner and yourself as a smiling volunteer on the side of the road, holding out a water bottle as she runs by. If she needs it and asks for it, have it handy and give it to her promptly. Don't shove it in her face. Don't run ahead of her, yelling, "Want this water? Here's the water! Want it?" Don't trail behind her, incessantly muttering, "What's the matter? You're slowing down. You can go faster than this. Hurry up." If she dashes ahead, don't caution her to slow down and save her strength for later. It is her race. Not yours. She will go at the clip that she's able to maintain. Help her. Don't push her or hold her back.

In learning, there is no finish line. There is only the long-distance run.

SECTION 2: "CORE CURRICULUM"

A. LANGUAGE
1. Preverbal

To paraphrase linguist Noam Chomsky: You can't think anything you don't have words for. Your child's passive language—what she understands—will develop much more quickly than her ability to say things out loud. Day one is a good time to start talking to your child!

a. Talking to Your Baby

❖ Introduce her to as many wonderful words and ideas as early as you want. A baby will happily listen to a detailed description of how to make the best vinaigrette; fanciful flights of imagination; political analyses; your hopes, wishes, and dreams for her; or any other ideas, stories, or thoughts you may have. Although we can only speculate, it seems that from this early listening they actually learn the meaning of many words, as well as the basic structure of the language, intonations, accents, and perhaps abstract ideas that we have no way of documenting.

❖ If you tend to be a "talker," try to spend some time with your baby when you're not talking. A comfortable silence can be as important a form of communication as language.

❖ Make up silly rhymes, songs, and stories.

❖ Describe activities as you're going about your business.

❖ Use nouns like "Mommy" and "Janie" instead of pronouns like "me" and "you."

❖ Identify each object in her world.

True Tale from the Trenches: One mother in my baby classes has two daughters. She noticed how much her first daughter seemed to know at a tender age. With her second child she decided to prove what she suspected about the first. She identified everything she handed her daughter. By the time Zoe was three months old she could easily reach for a bear when offered a choice between a bear and a rattle. Is this child brilliant? Only time will tell. I know her mother is! (If you should try this and your baby looks at you blankly, please back off! Remember your marathon job!)

b. Responding to Your Baby
When she babbles, repeat her sounds.

Teaching Tip: In addition to the fabulous, methodical mastery of each sound such as da-da and ba-ba, *many* babies by eight months will begin to repeat a particular babble at a particular moment. Listen. If you hear "blth, blth" every time Betty walks in the door, your baby is saying "Betty"! (Often this very early naming is of pets, siblings, and favorite baby-sitters.) Congratulate your child. Congratulate yourself too. You've done well. Many, many babies are trying to talk. But some of them don't have anybody listening.

Respond with words to her nonverbal language. For example, if she points to her bottle, supply words. "You want your bottle? Here."

> **Lesson:** *All these interesting sounds have meaning. It's fun to move my lips. I say something or point to something and Mommy hears me. She says something. I hear her. This is fun. I can get into this.*

c. Playing Games to Connect Words with Movements

At around six to eight months babies begin that terrific two-handed smacking on flat surfaces. Most of them are extremely pleased by this. I think they like the noise, the feel, the sensation of being able to repeat a motion volitionally. Two-handed smacking is generally considered a lot of very good fun in baby land. Once they begin doing this on their own, you can play a game that we do in our baby classes.

Activity: Tap-tap

You can use pat-pat, smack-smack, or whatever word you like as long as you're consistent.

❖ First use your own hand, demonstrating as you say, "Mommy's going tap-tap-tap! Now you go tap-tap-tap!"
❖ Your baby will probably look at you with a mixture of interest and confusion.
❖ Take your baby's hand gently, and as you tap it down say, "Go tap-tap-tap!"
❖ Different babies have different ways of responding to this. Some of them concentrate hard—you can see it in their faces—and then they tap. Others seem to tap almost by accident, as if their muscles rather than their brains did it, and they look fairly surprised.
❖ However your child taps, if she taps congratulate her.

Lesson: *I can connect a word with a movement. I can follow an instruction. I am an active participant in my world! Wowie!*

Teaching Tip: Some ten out of every twelve babies in our classes do this after the third week or so. The first time I tried it and I saw all those little babies with utter delight on their faces as they all tapped on beach balls, I got very teary-eyed. It's extraordinary to see how young babies can catch on to things when given the opportunity. But what about the two who *aren't* tapping? What does it mean? Nothing. Nada. Zero. Zip. It means they are looking at a bird flying outside the window, looking at another mommy's dangling earring, thinking about infinity, wondering where their bottle is. In other words, it doesn't mean they aren't as "smart" as the other babies. All it means is that they are interested in some other activity. I am always happy when their mommy lets them crawl after the rolling ball, if that's what they want to do instead of tapping. I am always willing to give gentle guidance to the mommy whose baby seems disinterested yet she continues to grab her unwilling hand and try to get her to tap. The mom is a good student and wants her child to participate in a class activity. For that I admire her. But for all of us it takes concentration on the mother's part to follow the child's lead.

There are many other classic games like this to play. Among them are:

❖ How big is baby? Sooooo big.
❖ Wave bye-bye.
❖ Give me high five.
❖ Blow a kiss.

If your child seems to enjoy them, have fun. Make up your own, based on some hand motion your child does.

Teaching Tip: However, please remember not to constantly ask your child to show off for other people. Some children will play these games only with their parents; others with extended family; others with the man in the street. Try to gauge your child's willingness. If you happen to go overboard and your child goes on strike, use this productively. On the next big round of learning maybe you won't want to go public with it, but rather savor it in the privacy of your own home.

d. Activities for Preverbal Crawlers or Walkers

At this young age many children are eager to please, thrilled to be able to follow instructions and show how much they know.

❖ Give almost any simple instruction you can think of that involves part of their daily routine, such as ''Please bring me your bottle,'' ''Find Piggy,'' or ''Want to take a bath?'' Thrill along with them as they bring you what you asked for or make a beeline for the bathroom.
❖ Many children can surprise you even further. Try this: As you read a book, consistently name it, using the title—*Good Night, Moon*—or a descriptive word—the bunny book. After you've named it often enough, one day ask your child to please find *Good Night, Moon.* Don't say I didn't tell you so if your preverbal

walker, or even crawler, can go pick one book out of a pile of many. They are amazing little creatures, these babies of ours!

If your child chooses not to follow your instructions, *all it means is that she's doing something else that is more important to her.*

2. Beginning Talkers

For your preverbal child, any kind of talking you choose to do is good talking. Once your child begins talking herself, however, you would do well to shift the focus. More and more of your conversation should be responsive to hers.

a. Baby Talk

Baby talk is good. The reason they use baby talk is because there's an enormous amount of muscular control required to form words. When their minds think ''bottle,'' their mouths say ''ba-ba.''

> **Teaching Tip:** Correct through example. When they say "Ba-ba," respond "Here's your bottle." If your child says, "No!" offer words. "You don't want your bottle?"

b. Introduce Vocabulary

Names of animals and the sounds they make are favorites and can accompany so many wonderful toddler books. Any word for any object in their immediate sphere is appropriate. Most mothers naturally introduce appropriate vocabulary during this exciting time. But sometimes we become just a little too excited.

Teaching Tips:

❖ Don't constantly ask, ''What does the cow say?'' Let them decide when they're ready to offer a response. Once they name things, don't ask them to do it on cue all the time. Allow them to progress at their own pace.

❖ Try not to *always* translate for them if they're talking to someone else. But if you see your mother-in-law squinting and repeating, ''What? What? What?'' you might want to step in with the word in question.

❖ Try not to repeat, only louder, every question another adult asks your child.

3. Emerging Talkers

Once a child has begun talking, after those first five or ten words the rate of development varies tremendously. One one-and-a-half-year-old may have exactly the same number of words and complexity of sentence structure as another two-and-a-half-year-old. Because their rates of language acquisition vary so vastly, only the most generalized statements are useful.

In general, the kinds of vocabulary you can introduce will pretty much follow the individual child's development. What that means is that the kid who says, "Cracker" and points will probably have a better shot at sticking to concrete words and naming things. She will be happy with "doll," "ball," and the names of the people around her. Once she starts in on stuff like "Jennie want cracker," she may be ready for abstracts.

Colors and shapes, for example, start to be interesting. Happy and sad start to enter her realm. All a sensible mother can do is to continue *talking* and *listening;* in other words, match your conversation to your child's.

Some toddlers begin stuttering when they're excited or trying to form a sentence. This is not the same as stuttering in an older child whose language is completely intact. Please don't rush any stutterers, lispers, "wascially wabbits," or any other baby talkers off to a speech therapist. They are babies. That's why we have the phrase baby talk.

By the same token, if your child is completely responsive in every other way, has an active/passive language, follows instructions and makes her feelings and wishes known with appropriate body language, but has noticeably less words than "the other kids," and has not reached the end of her twos, stop worrying, if you are, and leave the specialists' appointment books free for older children who really do need intervention. Your quiet child is a late talker. Somebody has to be the latest, or all the specialists wouldn't be able to make statistics!

Here's a little joke.

Alexandra was three. A lovely child, well-behaved, sensible, and agreeable, she drew, played, rode her trike and dressed her dollies. But she never said a word. Her mother and father worried.

One day Alexandra was sitting at the table having lunch. She put her napkin in her lap and said in clearly modulated tones, "Mother, may I please have a glass of milk?"

Her mother almost fell down dead. When she recovered, she said, "Alexandra, why haven't you ever talked before?"

Alexandra shrugged. "I didn't have anything to say."

Teaching Tip: No matter how excited you are by their language acquisition, try and contain yourself. Don't constantly ask, "What's this color?" Don't repeatedly ask them to tell people their name. Resist making them perform.

4. Talkers

Sometimes by three, often by four, and certainly by five, a child has a complex, highly competent working knowledge of her native tongue. She can begin to make jokes. Certain words will strike her funny. She has an extensive vocabulary, usually is able to name anything in her own personal sphere, and often is able to identify enormous numbers of things that she's seen in books and on TV. But she's still a kid, and sometimes her grammar gets a little shaky.

Teaching Tip: Grammar Mistakes. In the same way that when she was younger, you echoed "Bottle" when she said "Ba-ba," continue to correct through example. "Rachel brang her doll." Instead of "We don't say 'brang,' " simply correct in your version. "Rachel brought her doll?"

By this age your child may very well enjoy hearing all about aqua as a kind of blue. She might enjoy mixing colors together to get aqua. At this point, now that she has completely mastered color identification, new information becomes exciting rather than overwhelming.

As your child matures physically, emotionally, and developmentally, her intellect is also growing. Besides all the regular, everyday learning that goes on, you can encourage your child to love words, play with words, and play with ideas. These kinds of games are fun when you're in the car, waiting in line, at the dinner table, or any time when you're together with no pressing practical task.

Word Games

❖ Word problems: "I'm thinking of a white animal with four legs who purrs."
❖ Alliteration: Say whole sentences starting every word with the letter *B*. "Bome bere, bease. Bank bou bery buch."
❖ Word-association games: Say, "Sofa." Your husband answers, "Chair." Ask your child if she can think of another piece of furniture. If she seems disinterested, drop it without sounding disappointed.
❖ Go around the dinner table taking turns saying colors, animals,

pieces of clothing. When the child is older, play the same game, only each word has to start with the same sound.

❖ Stop when your child is bored. Restrain yourself from using words you know your child cannot know. Nobody likes a show-off.

Lesson: *Mommy and Daddy laugh a lot when they play with words and ideas. It's fun to learn new words.*

Question: I'm not good at stuff like that.

Answer: Try to find someone who is, either your husband, a baby-sitter, or a family member who will be around your child regularly.

Question: Will my child loathe me if I'm not creative in these ways?

Answer: Absolutely not. Your child adores you. You are her mother. You will teach your child as much about the world if you accept your own talents, strengths, and shortcomings as if you make rhymes till the cows come home.

B. ART

Once a young child has a long-enough attention span, art becomes fun. Art offers a child a chance for expression. It encourages manual dexterity. In many ways a precursor to science, art for the young child is a *tactile* experience. She explores feelings, textures, and colors.

There are many terrific books on the market filled with age-appropriate art projects. I want to concentrate not on the projects themselves, but rather on the underlying guidance a parent can give to foster not only art appreciation, but fun, which will ultimately encourage competency and self-esteem.

Important things to keep in mind:

❖ Never give a kid an art supply that will kill her if she eats it or blind her if she gets it in her eye.

❖ Regardless of innate talent, all young children should be involved with *process,* not *product.*

❖ If you have the interest, do as many art projects at home as you have time, money, and space for, as long as the projects are your child's, not yours. This means that most projects for toddlers should not have themes, preordained uses, or finished results. A picture from your child is a lovely gift for a grandparent. If you want to frame it, terrific. A picture frame, however—trimmed, polished, with stickers lined up in shape and size order—is a lovely gift from you! By preschool it might be fun to suggest making a picture frame for Grandma and supplying materials. But make sure you allow your child to use the materials *as she wishes,* not as you think she should.

❖ Conversely, nowhere is it written that your home has to be an art studio. If you can't stand paint in the house and have no room a kid can slop up without your becoming hysterical, find any of the scads of places where children can do art in groups. Museums, toddler centers, street fairs, and church bazaars are just some of the places where art tables and age-appropriate materials are readily found. Once there, please allow your child to make as big a mess as she wants. If the grown-up is preoccupied with cleanliness, the child cannot possibly attend to the fun at hand.

With those simple suggestions in mind, here are some thoughts on art by age.

1. Toddlers

This group ranges from about fourteen months and up, depending on your child—as soon as your child has a long-enough attention span and doesn't eat the supplies!

❖ Provide simple art supplies: fat crayons, plain paper, Play-Doh.
❖ Give one thing at a time. While we may be dazzled by a collage of myriad materials, including glue, paint, paper, pom-poms, and feathers, your child will be overwhelmed by the variety and not necessarily "feel" any of it. A simple project, even with one paint color, will be more thoroughly experienced than something that "looks better," because the materials themselves are jazzy. If you do a lot of art projects, where your child has had ample opportunity to explore one thing at a time, then it becomes fun to try wild, multimedia collages.
❖ Do not force a child to draw silly faces, houses, flowers, or trees. Representational art is too advanced for a toddler; the suggestion to do what she can't may make her feel incompetent. Furthermore, it will stifle her creativity. Wait to see what she wants to draw.
❖ Get excited over scribble-scrabble and dots.
❖ If your child sets about pulling apart something she's just made, leave her alone. This is part of the creative process.

❖ Do not require a child to use the art medium the way you use it. Some children, for example, will turn a paintbrush upside down and use the handle to bang or make lines and dots. This is fun and creative. Any inspired use of any material should be valued, not discouraged at this young age.

> **Lesson:** *I have fun when Mommy lets me try out art any way I want.*

2. Threes

They begin representational drawing (some children begin younger). Continue to exercise restraint, noticing what they do without making suggestions of how they might do it "better." Throughout all the preschool years bear in mind: *process, not product.* A picture is done when the child is through, not when all the white is covered.

3. Fours

Many of the best art teachers suggest giving a preschooler only plain paper and crayons in order to foster creativity and to help a child learn how to control her hands. This is a very valid point. In most homes, however, it is just a question of time before Magic Markers, which require less muscle control, and coloring books, which inhibit creativity, enter our sphere. If your child is carefully learning how to draw within the lines—meaning how to control the crayon or marker—these materials might be useful and fun. But if your child scribbles any which way and doesn't use the structure constructively to work on either eye-hand coordination, or color, have the coloring books take a long vacation. They are inhibiting rather than promoting growth.

4. Fives

By the time they're five and have naturally moved toward representational art, you can start winging out. By this age, if you haven't been too controlling early on, they will enjoy having you show them how you drew something—*if* they ask you to show them.

C. MUSIC

Any music you expose your child to is good music. Children love to sing, dance, clap, and sway.

Traditional nursery rhymes and hand songs are beloved in all cultures, first because young children enjoy them and second because they learn so much from them. Although on the surface it would appear that they're simply learning "Bah Bah, Black Sheep" through both the spoken poem and the song they are also learning the cadence of the language, rhythm, rhyming, coordination, and cooperation when they sing in a group or along with a tape or video. No matter how gifted your child may be musically, she needs traditional children's songs. They are fun, which is the major domain and right of every young child, and they are very important developmentally.

Just as art is the beginning of science, music is the beginning of math. I don't remember all the technical brain development stuff that documents how closely music and math are correlated. I don't have to. Neither do you. All we have to do is sing. Sing like a bird. Sing all kinds of songs, from classic children's songs to any other kind of music you enjoy. Sing!

D. TIME

Time is relative.

I watched a mother and child of five or six walk down the street yesterday. She was a good twenty paces ahead of him.

"Come on, Nicky," she called over her shoulder. "We're late."

He followed, his booted feet flopping sideways like the Scarecrow in *The Wizard of Oz*. He bounced his head. He flung his arms.

He stopped dead in his tracks and fished something from his pocket. "Mom, look at this!" He held up a card.

"I looked, I looked!" she shouted over her shoulder. "Come on! We're late."

He splashed in a puddle. He fell down. He laughed. He got up and did a little dance.

"Come *on!*" the voice urged.

She sped ahead. Nicky trailed behind.

One of the differences between adults and children is that adults are always trying to get somewhere. Kids are already there.

The way we experience time in the moment accounts for many disagreements. For children time stretches limitlessly before them. For us it goes by too fast.

Parents must accept children's time frame and also teach ways to ration time in order to exist in the real world.

Rushing hysterically is not fun. Nor is going so slowly that whenever you arrive somewhere you've either missed the best part or everybody's mad at you for making them wait.

So let us take a look at some handy ways to teach your little one that perhaps in outer space we aren't bound by the petty parameters of twenty-four hours, seven days, and twelve months, but here on earth clocks and calendars are mighty taskmasters with whom we must comply or spend our lives like the Mad Hatter.

1. Adult Decisions about a Child's Time

a. Scheduling

A child needs time to be a child. Time to develop her imagination, to daydream, to sit for hours watching an ant colony. Time to integrate what she's learned and discover new ideas.

Don't overschedule your child.

- ❖ Make sure your child has free time to do whatever she wants each day.
- ❖ Although many caring mothers arrange a variety of rich activities for their toddlers, for most children younger than three it's rough on their developing social skills to require that they be nice, share, and pay attention in a formal class setting more than three times a week. Ballet, gym, swimming, cooking, tae kwon do, music, and art are all fabulous. Choose two, maybe three.
- ❖ On a day when a formal activity is planned, spend the rest of the day hanging out, rather than arranging a play date where she will be expected to use social skills that are still challenging.
- ❖ If a child is in day care, where the day is paced to suit the needs of little ones, she doesn't need toddler classes. She's getting all the socialization she needs during the day.
- ❖ A nursery-school child may enjoy an afternoon ballet or tumbling class, but it would be kind to hold off registering them for an additional activity until they've gotten their sea legs the first year of nursery school. Many preschool enrichment classes have semesters. Wait until January or February if your child started nursery school in September.
- ❖ For a kindergartner, the same applies. If she has been going to a music class since she was three or four, continue what she's familiar with. But don't add new experiences. She's got enough to adjust to in kindergarten.

Don't underschedule your child. The flip side of the coin is the child who has never had a regularly planned activity until kindergarten. What a rude awakening that will be.

Arrange at least one activity a week that is regular. A play date, a play group, a class, once-a-week attendance at story time at the library or bookstore, a regularly scheduled visit to Grandma all fit the bill.

> **Lesson:** My life has a rhythm, just like Mommy's and Daddy's. I look forward to things I do with regularity.

b. Family Transition for Daily Attendance

One of the hardest transitions for most families is the relentless quality of having to be somewhere in the morning every morning, whether it's day care, preschool, or kindergarten.

Here are some tips:

- ❖ Pack her lunch and backpack the night before.
- ❖ If you work, have your clothes organized the night before.
- ❖ Whether you or your child picks them out, get her clothes ready the night before. (I recommend involving her in the choice to teach her independence.)
- ❖ Refuse to play the "I don't want to wear that" game in the morning.
- ❖ Get yourself up at least a half hour, if not an hour, before your child to give yourself time to do what you need to do (which, by the way, might include doing nothing!).
- ❖ Get your child up at least ten minutes, if not a half hour, before you think you need to.
- ❖ Most children like to play when they get up. Build playtime into their morning.
- ❖ Most children respond very badly to "Hurry up! Wake up! We're late!"
- ❖ If your morning can be spent getting your child into her clothes at a leisurely pace, your day will start off much more pleasantly than if you're screaming and hurrying.
- ❖ Should you find yourself screaming and hurrying, apologize once you're out the door. If your child is four or five, ask what she thinks you could've done to make the morning go more smoothly. Sometimes when you involve the child in solving the problem, the problem goes away.

c. Arriving On Time for Children's Planned Activities

I have had some mothers and baby-sitters who always arrive ten minutes to a half hour early; others, consistently very late.

If you fall into either of these categories, here are some tips:

❖ A young child should not have to sit in a stroller staring at the wall, feeling waves of relief that she's not late (which is what most early birds feel). If you are a consistent early arriver, please pack books, toys, be prepared to take your child out of the stroller and walk around, or find some other creative way to coordinate your need to not be late with your child's need to be happily occupied in the present.

❖ A young child should not have to dash frantically into the tail end of an activity set up for her. If you are chronically late, incorporate any number of mind games (such as setting your watch fifteen minutes ahead, pretending the class starts a half hour earlier than it does, or any other method) to get your child where she belongs when she belongs there.

That advice certainly sounds sensible. So how come it's so hard for so many moms? Here are some tips:

❖ When living with a child, suspend all logical, mathematical time calculations.

❖ It takes twice as long to accomplish any given task with a child as without one.

❖ For every child you add, the amount of time any task takes increases exponentially, not mathematically. Thus, if you have more than four kids you might as well not even bother trying to leave home!

❖ No matter how organized and prepared ahead of time for a day's outing you are, your child will mess up your schedule. Therefore, build in enormous amounts of lag time and view schedules as suggestions rather than plans.

❖ Never forget the Poop-in-the-Snowsuit Phenomenon, which defies all known statistical laws of probability. No matter when you begin bundling yourself and your child, not until the final zipper has been zipped, mitten mitted, hat tied, and front door opened does any child under the age of three poop. An unexplainable footnote is that these are invariably squoosh-out-the-side-of-the-diaper poops.

❖ Once your child passes diapers, you will enter the next stage. ''Mom? Did you remember to bring my . . . [choose the tiniest plastic toy you can imagine, which you haven't seen since Kelly's birthday party last August]. I can't leave without it!''

The preceding tips were brought to you courtesy of tongue-in-cheek to remind you that a sense of humor will stand you in very good stead when trying to integrate a child's sense of time into any planned activity or errand.

2. Strategies to Deal with "Child Time"

In order to deal with "child time" it is useful to repeat a basic generalization.

Your child is living in the moment. The future is essentially meaningless.

You will always have an easier time if you devise games. It's an exercise in futility to say to a three-, four-, and most five-year-olds, "Get dressed while I shower." It is not silly, however, to have a race to see who can get dressed first.

a. Dawdling

The time-honored child tradition of dawdling occurs for one of two reasons.

The first may be that your child is not necessarily dawdling, but simply living in kid time. The puzzle in front of her is real and fun; the *concept* of going somewhere else, either for fun or chores, is meaningless. Therefore, she continues to do what she's doing.

Another reason children dawdle is to drive you crazy. It becomes a power issue. They test boundaries, see how far they can push, and generally find dawdling an extremely satisfactory way of setting off fascinating emotional fireworks in the home. But although psychology is interesting, from a practical parenting point of view it doesn't matter *why* they're dawdling. What matters is to get 'em up and out!

For the child who drags her heels, play games that put her in charge.

Since different children discover the thrill of dawdling at different ages, here are some strategies, by age, that may help. There are as many games like this as there are mothers' imaginations. These are just to get your creative juices flowing. Adjust these ideas to suit dawdlers in bathrooms, coming down the stairs, getting in the car, or during any moment when your child turns into molasses.

Twos

Plan 1: Make a picture

❖ Cut out or draw pictures of the items of clothing she has to put on before you can leave.
❖ Let her point to each piece of clothing and then put it on.
❖ If she wants to put things on in a different order from how you would, let her.

Plan 2: Races

❖ See if she can beat the kitchen timer.
❖ See if she can get dressed before you do.
❖ See if she can get dressed before a song plays from beginning to end.

Threes
Plan 1: Pictures and charts

❖ As an art project on a day when you're not trying to get out of the house, have her cut out pictures of what she wears.
❖ Let her paste them on a piece of paper.
❖ Let her use stars, stickers, markers, or any other device to check her "list" as she puts on each thing.

Plan 2: Incorporate new learning
Once letters become fascinating, this is fun.

❖ Make a list using the first letter of each piece of clothes. Example: *P* for pants, *S* for shoes and socks.
❖ Ask if she wants to put her shoes on first and then her socks. Guaranteed giggle from a three-year-old.
❖ Have her check off each letter that stands for each item of clothing as you go.

Fours and Fives
They are more sophisticated, and therefore their methods of dawdling are more inspired. But are we not the grown-ups? Are we not as sophisticated as a preschooler? Ha-ha!
They are now ready to begin thinking about time, the clock, and its effect on leaving the house.

Plan 1:

❖ Suggest that you time how long it takes to get dressed so that tomorrow you can begin planning in advance.
❖ Break it down into parts. Two minutes to find pants, one minute to put them on, etc.
❖ You may be surprised at how long it actually does take.

❖ Write down each item, including things like getting her lunch box from the counter.
❖ The next day you have a clear chart at your disposal, plus a way to have fun.
❖ Say, "Okay. On your mark. Get set! Go!"
❖ Make it a game where she tries to beat her time from yesterday!

Plan 2:

❖ Give her the list of things to be done.
❖ "You can do them in any order you want."
❖ "Here's the chart and a Magic Marker. Go!"
❖ Off she goes to prove she's competent.

Lesson: *It's a lot more fun when I'm playing than when I'm fighting with Mommy about leaving the house.*

---

b. Anticipation

You may be excited about an upcoming event, a holiday, a new school, or a new house. Your child doesn't understand the future.

❖ A toddler who has heard that you are moving doesn't need to know when the truck is coming until a few days before.
❖ A preschooler will profit from looking at a calendar and checking off the weeks for the month preceding the move.
❖ If she's starting nursery school in the fall, don't talk about it all summer. Labor Day, at most a week before, is enough time to introduce specifics about what she may expect.
❖ Even a kindergartner who is excited about starting school like the big kids should not be constantly reminded of the future all summer long.

Lesson: *Mommy gives me enough time to chew on a new idea. She doesn't spring things on me; neither does she talk about it for so long that I can't remember what it was we were talking about in the first place.*

---

c. Transitions

Some children—and some adults for that matter—make transitions more easily than others. Many children profit from being apprised of an impending transition.

❖ "In ten minutes it will be time to stop playing and start getting our coats on." "Five minutes have passed. Soon we will start getting ready to go."

❖ Some advise setting the kitchen timer to end events. "When the timer goes off it's time to get out of the tub." The flavor is too institutional for my tastes, but I pass it along since so many people swear by it.

3. Teaching the Specifics of Time

a. Minutes and Hours

Make TV a learning tool. Mention that *Barney* is a half-hour show. One day try getting dressed while *Barney* is on. You can say, "It takes you a whole *Barney* show to put on your clothes. That means it takes you a half hour to get dressed."

When you are waiting and your child asks, "How much longer?" you can then say, a *Barney* show, two *Barney* shows, or whatever. As they reach their fours and fives you can introduce time words: "Half a show; that's fifteen minutes."

b. One Day

❖ "Good morning, this is the beginning of one day! Mommy's going to tell you tomorrow when it's the beginning of another day."

❖ The next morning say, "Good morning. Remember Mommy said yesterday I was going to show you what a day is? Well, remember how we got up yesterday, had Cheerios for breakfast, played puzzles, Mommy cleaned up the kitchen while Emmy dumped clothespins into the basket, then we got in the car and went to the grocery store, came home, had lunch, Emmy took a nap, then we got up, went to the playground, played on the seesaw, came home, had a bath, Daddy came home, we had chicken and corn for dinner out back, then we read a story, and Emmy went to sleep? That was one day. This is another day."

❖ Some children enjoy learning to say the days of the week the same as they learn their ABCs. They can recite them from rote way before they have any concept of what they mean. It is useful, however, to introduce the days of the week early. They will catch on to the concept of the progression of days much more easily if they have a name for them. By nursery school and often earlier, many children understand the progression of the days of the week, including weekends.

c. Establishing Memory and Time Sense

❖ Try to remember something a few days ago. Go through all the events backward so that your child can remember with you when you did something.
❖ At dinner, recount your day in chronological order. This is a wonderful ritual, not just for aiding memory and chronological order, but for sharing. You can get your child's point of view and give your impression.

d. Perseverance

Take on a project that requires waiting for completion. For example, make a necklace out of clay.

❖ Make the beads one day. Let them dry.
❖ The next day paint them. Let them dry.
❖ The next day string them.
❖ Mention the days of the week. "We made the beads on Sunday, painted them on Monday, and strung them on Tuesday. That was a big project!"

Lesson: *Not everything happens instantly. Some things take time.*

E. PROBLEM SOLVING

Puzzles encourage creative thinking, but *only* if your child likes them. Otherwise, they're frustrating. If your child likes puzzles:

❖ Start with easy ones, and work your way up.
❖ Often children's museums, libraries, and hands-on toy stores have a good selection.
❖ Don't grab the piece and stick it in the right place.
❖ Suggest things such as, "Why don't we find the border pieces first?" or "Let's look for all the blue pieces."

❖ Take an easy puzzle and turn it upside down so that the colors aren't showing.

Categorizing encourages logical thinking and is a precursor to many forms of mental prowess. If handled as a game, the whole feeling of "thinking about something" becomes fun.

Toddlers and Preschoolers

Examples:

❖ Put all the farm animals together.
❖ Find all the socks.
❖ Point to everything in your room that's red.
❖ Point out all the white cars.

Fours and Fives

Widen the categories to incorporate their increasing knowledge. Examples:

❖ Find all the four-legged things in the house. (A child with a sense of humor may notice animals and tables and laugh. If your child doesn't see something like this you might jokingly point it out. The point is to have fun with all these thinking games.)
❖ Let's look for all the wooden things.
❖ Find all the see-through things in the kitchen.

Teaching Tip: Don't be rigid about the "answers." Your child may be thinking of a category that you hadn't noticed.

SECTION 3: "EXTRA CREDIT"

I have called this section "Extra Credit" because I want to introduce numbers, prereading, and reading itself. In the past, and even today in some school systems, some basic concepts, including the alphabet, counting to ten, even colors and shapes, were considered inappropriate before kindergarten. Reading traditionally is begun in first grade. Yet because of the wonderful show *Sesame Street,* we have clearly seen that many toddlers and preschoolers enjoy learning to identify letters and numbers and can readily grasp the underlying concepts.

Child educators still vary widely on their philosophies about when to introduce certain ideas. This is another area, as in all of child-raising, where I think sweeping generalizations are helpful, but should be calibrated to suit the individual child.

One generalization that I think is essential to hold on to, no matter what your child is like, is this: *The basic provenance of a young child's life is to play.*

Any concept, idea, or information that is offered to them in a rigorous way is not fun. If a young child is encouraged to focus on "academics" at the expense of the socialization skills so necessary for development, two unpleasant things may occur: The child won't know how to get along with people, which negatively impacts on a lifetime. Furthermore, the child who is "pushed academically" too young will not have incorporated the fundamentals of real learning and will therefore be behind, rather than ahead, when she gets to real school. To put this bluntly, flash cards for preschoolers are stupid.

If any of the following stuff is not interesting or fun for your kid at whatever age she happens to be when you try it, let it go, leave it alone, move on. Play some other valuable, fun game.

Food for Thought: According to research, aerobic activities increase the density of the brain's blood vessels; sports that require skill increase the brain's synapses, improving the physical way the brain processes information. Therefore, if your kid wants to go outside, run around, and throw a ball, this is as valid an activity in terms of pure brain development as saying her ABCs.

With that said, let us move on to some activities that may be fun for you and your child.

A. NUMBERS
Starting from Birth Up

Sing number-related hand songs, using the motions to reinforce. (For children under three, use the number three. As they grow, increase the number to match their age.) Examples:

- Three little ducks.
- Three little monkeys.
- Three little spotted frogs.
- Ten little Indians, or babies.
- Johnny works with one hammer.

One Year and Up

- Teach your child how to hold up one finger for her first birthday, two for her second.
- If a number comes up in conversation, use your finger to reinforce the word. Example, "You can go down the slide one more time." Hold up one finger.
- When a child is having trouble leaving the playground, say, "How many more swings do you want to take before we leave?" Then count, "One, two, three, four, five! We're done!"
- Use the nursery rhyme One, Two, Buckle My Shoe.
- When you put some crackers on her plate, say, here are three crackers.

Eighteen Months and Up

Teach your child how to count, using her fingers and toes. Begin with one, two, three. When that's integrated, go up to five. After she has that, go on up to ten.

Twos and Threes

Many two-year-olds and most threes have the facility to eyeball numbers. That means that when you look at three crackers you don't have to count. You *know* there are three. This is a fundamental mathematical skill, but if you teach it young enough it is so much fun and gives them such a feeling of competence that you can forget long-term goals and just enjoy.

- Say, "Here are two crackers. One, two." Show her as you count.
- The next day put two out. Ask how many there are.
- She may not know what you mean.
- Say, "Look. Like yesterday, there are two crackers. One, two."
- The next day ask how many.
- If she catches on to the idea, but not the right number—for example, if she says, "One!" or "Three!"—enjoy it. She has the concept. Now she just has to learn the number crunching! Try, "I fooled you! There are only two! Here, let's count together. One, two."
- If she doesn't catch on after two days, this game is boring for her. Leave it alone. If this should happen it doesn't "mean" anything such as, oh, no, she'll flunk math. It means she's learning about something else!

Most twos and threes can eyeball up to three things. Older children, sometimes not until first grade, begin to eyeball more than that. Please don't push!

Fours and Fives

Mention numbers in your everyday conversation.

- ❖ We have three more miles to go. We're two blocks away.
- ❖ Help yourself to some cookies. Let me see if you can take three.
- ❖ Please go pick out five books from the shelf.
- ❖ I need ten crayons.
- ❖ Make sure that if the wrong number comes back, you don't sound reproving. Compare this potentially upsetting correction: "No! You didn't pay attention. I said five, not six," with the kind of answer that is a lot more encouraging to a young learner, such as "Uh-oh, we needed five and we have six! Try again!"

Activity for Fours and Fives Who Can Recognize Numbers

On a trip to the toy store:

- ❖ Ask if your child wants to play a number game. If she looks interested, explain that you have a budget, say, $10.00.
- ❖ Write "$10.00" on a piece of paper.
- ❖ Count the digits, including the decimal places, together.
- ❖ Explain that if the tag has any three numbers—$9.95, for example—she can have it.
- ❖ If there are four numbers, the first must be a 1 and the rest 0's.
- ❖ If the first number is not a 1, it's too much.
- ❖ Take the piece of paper with you as an aid.

You may be surprised how quickly your child catches on and how much fun your nascent number recognizer will have.

If your child is annoyed and not having fun, get her gently off the hook. "This doesn't seem to be as much fun as I thought it would be. Would you rather I tell you if it's too much?" That way you didn't make your child feel bad for not wanting to play the game.

B. PREREADING
From Birth On

Sing the ABC song.

One Year and Up

As you read a picture book, point to words the same way you point to other parts of the picture.

For example, take a photo book with a little girl, a doll, and the word *doll* printed. Point to each thing, identifying it: "Here's the little girl, here are her socks, here is her dress, here's her nose, here's the word *doll,* here is her foot."

This way you have identified a *printed word* exactly as you've identified her *sock*.

Lesson: *Those squiggles make Mommy say the word* doll.

Teaching Tip: When looking at a book together, let your child dictate the pace. If she flips through the pages, fine. If she wants to stay on one page for ten minutes, fine. Follow her lead. You have no idea what she's looking at or learning. You do have an idea, however, of how to help her enjoy the experience of looking in a book, rather than feeling as if she's "not doing it right," i.e., going too fast or too slow.

A Common Worry: "My child doesn't like books." Many children do not engage with books until their second or third year. If your child is one of them, leave her alone. If you try and force an interest in books—or anything for that matter—it will be counterproductive. If books matter to you, read in your child's presence. Stack books on your night table. Let your child see that when you have a free moment you read. If it's something you do naturally, discuss books with your spouse and your friends in your child's presence. Valuing books will rub off. Let your child come to each part of life at her own pace.

Eighteen Months and Up

❖ Make use of *Sesame Street,* which teaches letters and numbers through play.
❖ Write your child's name, singsonging the letters as you write *M-E-*. The last *G* is said with great enthusiasm and higher in pitch than the rest of the letters. Then point to the word as you say "Meg."
❖ When your child draws a picture (yes, that's right, those scribbles

are a picture!) add your child's name, singing the letters as you write, and then saying the whole name.

❖ Write the words *Mommy, Daddy,* and any siblings or animals in the house, singing the letters as you write and adding the whole name.

❖ "Today Mommy wants to show you magic. We can get Daddy to say your name." Write the letters, singing as you write. Then show the paper to Daddy. "What does this say?" Daddy says, "Meg!" Then you tell Meg, "See? It's magic. Daddy looks at this and says 'Meg'!"

> ***Lesson:*** *Letters and words are fun.*

When You're Waiting Somewhere

Interspersed with all the other activities of waiting, throw in a couple of minutes of looking at letters. For example, in the pediatrician's office:

❖ Look at the fish tank.

❖ Play with some of the toys (if you can keep from screaming, "Don't touch that germ-laden disease carrier! That kid's got strep!").

❖ Look at a poster of babies.

❖ Look at a notice about inoculations.

❖ Point to several letters. "Here's an *A,* and look, here's another *A,* and here's an *M.* That's the first letter of Meg's name and the first letter of Mommy. Oh, now we're ready to go see the doctor."

> ***Lesson:*** *Words and letters are part of the wonderful world around us. We notice them with interest.*

Logos

I have never understood why breaking down a word into letters and then sounds—phonetics—is taught to beginning readers. It seems bass-ackward to me.

Speed reading is taught by ignoring individual letters and words and focusing your eye on the whole line, paragraph, and then page if you're fast enough. A good speed-reader doesn't "see" individual letters in a word, but rather sees an entity that has all its lines in the right place. Dyslexia is when your eye sees something, but it's scrambled by the time it reaches your brain. The complete picture becomes fragmented.

Many of the two-and-a-half-year-olds I have are able to recognize their own names, as a consistent combination of squiggly lines in a particular order. Like a picture.

The visual ability to identify a certain shape as standing for a sound we utter that has meaning is the precursor, and foundation, of reading.

With this in mind you can have fun encouraging an activity that many young children catch on to quickly, often on their own.

All those logos that dot our highways and byways and rob us of our regionality so you don't know whether you're in Richmond, San Jose, or Albany might as well serve some use: Let them help lay the groundwork for our kids to learn to read! They are marvelous tools for helping your child recognize *symbols* that stand for *words!*

Identifying Logos

- ❖ Fast-food chains, supermarket chains, whichever gas company chain you frequent, clothing chains, bookstore chains, toy-store chains, or any other recognizable logo is a bonanza for a pre-reader.
- ❖ At whatever age your child begins excitedly pointing out the window at that big Toys "R" Us sign, you have hit pay dirt!
- ❖ Encourage. You might consider widening her view. Once she recognizes one, she can begin to recognize more. Point out a new one. If she takes the bait you're off and running. If she's disinterested, forget about it until she seems to notice again.

C. READING

> **Caution:** There is conclusive research that shows that forcing a child to read too early can be done, but is dysfunctional. Many children can learn to sound out words before they can connect a meaning. If you rush it, you may have serious problems on your hands by second grade. *Always follow your child's lead.* All of these activities should be engaged in only if your child exhibits interest in and enjoys them.

Late Twos and Up

(If your child should not come to reading until elementary school, you might want to glance again at all this. Whenever your particular child is interested in reading, there are little tips in here that will probably help you and your child.)

I'd like to share with you how I arrived at some of the following material.

In our house we cannot say the word *park* out loud unless we have a leash in our hand and an extra half hour. When the word *park* is uttered, our dog, Blazer, begins to dance. She chases her tail. She runs to the door, cocks her head like the RCA Victor dog, and wags her tail. She sits down by the door. She looks eager. She pants. She gets up and follows whoever said *park* around the house. Her nails clack on the floor. She sits back by the door and wags her tail. She looks hopeful, then hurt, and finally pitiful. She puts her head and tail down, walks sadly into the living room, and flops down. She puts her head down on her front paws and sighs. A deep, shuddering sigh.

She goes through this heartbreaking ten- or fifteen-minute ritual every single time she hears the word *park*. Can you blame us for never saying *park* unless we mean to take her?

From before the time Annie was born, we have spelled *park* if Blazer isn't going to get to go. By two Annie understood that the sounds *P-A-R-K* were used to mean *park*. What's the difference to a two-year-old if you say *park* or *P-A-R-K?* All words are new, all sounds are new. This child learned to say the sounds *P-A-R-K* to mean *park*.

By two-and-a-half she understood that we could say *park* when Blazer wasn't around. But when Blazer was in earshot we said *P-A-R-K,* which meant the same thing.

One day we were walking down the street. She stopped dead in her tracks and looked up the block.

She pointed and said very quietly and thoughtfully, almost to herself, *"P-A-R-K. Park. Park! Park!* Mommy, look! *P-A-R-K, park!"*

"That's right, sugar. *P-A-R-K, park."*

Bless the wonderful parking lot with its big neon sign. Bless my needy dog. She helped me stumble onto a fun way to introduce a child to the idea that letters combine to form words. We call it reading.

Since then, in every class I've had of two-and-a-half-year-olds and up, there are between one and three moms who will draw me aside with the same look of half-belief that I had the day Annie recognized a word. They will look nervous and say something like this: "Is Harry really recognizing his name or is it my imagination?'' ''Was it just a coincidence when Emma turned to me the other day and said, '*E-M-M-A, Emma,*' and pointed to the letters one by one on her footstool?'' ''Henry keeps pointing to words in books, on signs, on store doors, and he keeps asking, 'What does this say? What does that say? Tell me what that says.' Did you ever hear of a kid doing anything like that?''

If your child seems to be interested in words and letters, she may enjoy the following.

If she doesn't exhibit the slightest interest in letters at all or in letters in combination, leave her alone. She's learning something else!

Word Recognition

❖ **The Pizza Game:** Write the word *pizza,* spelling it as you write. When you talk about pizza, do what we did with *park.* Say, ''Want a piece of *P-I-Z-Z-A*?'' Then, when you're out and about, see if she can find the word *pizza.* (You can't go more than a city block or a suburban mile without it! The *Z*'s make it instantly recognizable. In terms of word recognition, *pizza* is a loaded deck!)

❖ **The Exit Game:** Same as above.

❖ **The Taxi Game:** For city dwellers. Same as above.

Hop on Pop

Dr. Seuss has given many parents and children countless hours of happiness. For a beginning or prereader, the book *Hop on Pop* is a bonanza. As you read it simply point to the letter that changes. Don't mention that the letters change, just point it out with your finger. *H*-op on *P*-op. Your child's eye will follow your finger. At her own pace she will have a light-bulb moment where she sees the similarities and differences in the words.

Writing

Usually at the same time that children become inspired to break the code of reading, they also become fascinated by writing. Most of them begin with trying to write the alphabet. Many get very, very engrossed in trying to write their own name. You don't have to second-guess them on this. You just have to follow. They will say, point-blank, ''How do you write *Meg?*'' If your child doesn't ask you to teach her how to write her name, don't bring it up yourself.

If she brings it up here are some tips:

❖ Magic Markers are the easiest to work with.

❖ Unlined paper is best. The lines drive them crazy; they require more dexterity than kids have.

❖ Leave out all suggestions about making the letters the same size or trying to write in a straight line. They don't have the physical coordination. If they should say, "Mine doesn't look like yours!" tell them that's okay, they're learning. Kids like this need a lot of reinforcement that things don't have to be perfect and exactly right from the beginning.

❖ Write their name in big letters, all caps. Skip any additional fancy stuff. For example, a capital *I* doesn't need the top and bottom seriphs. One straight line will do.

❖ Let them trace what you've written. Then let them try it on their own or repeat what you just did. They will tell you which they prefer.

❖ Another activity they enjoy is writing with you. Although most of us instinctively put our hand over theirs while they hold the marker, they might do better if you hold the marker and let them put their hand on top of yours. They seem to experience that as a more independent way to go. Write her name as many times as she wants you to, with her holding your hand.

❖ Sit side by side, each of you with a piece of paper and a marker. Draw the first line to form the letter *M*. (Make sure it's big. They don't have the muscle control yet for making tiny lines.) Let her draw a line like yours. Then draw the next single line to form the letter, and continue line by line. Use the plainest, simplest form of writing you can. Do this as many times as she wants.

❖ Write her name in nice, big plain letters at the top of a piece of unlined paper. Let her sit with it, by herself, and try it as many times as she wants.

Most of the children I've seen who get into stuff like this will stick with it until they can do it to their satisfaction. Some then drop writing and move on to something else; others move on, wanting to learn how to write *Mommy, Daddy,* animals' names, etc. Follow whatever your child wants to do. Remember your marathon job.

Three or Four and Up

Many very bright children who excel in school as well as other areas of their lives do not enjoy these kinds of activities until they are five, six, and even seven. Please keep that in mind.

❖ In a favorite book, find all the letter *T*'s. Find all the words that start with *S*.

❖ Find the word *the*. Find the word *a*. Find the word *I*.

The first few times you do it, point out the word. After that, try, "I see the word *the* somewhere. Can you find it?"

Teaching Tips:

❖ Although we all say, "Let's read a book," meaning "I'll read and you look," if your child begins to recognize words at a very early age, avoid using the word *reading* in relation to their activities. It's a word they associate with a grown-up activity and therefore may be counterproductive at such a young age. Let them go through the process without labeling it, in case the label itself may be misconstrued and make them feel as if they're in over their heads. Once they can pick up a book and read it, don't worry if you call it reading. It's just in those early-learning stages.

❖ Ignore phonetics. Do not try and sound out the word. Simply point out that this series of lines, like a pictograph, represents a certain sound.

❖ Do not play these games in order to create a supersmarty-pants. Only play these games if your child is interested and the two of you are having fun.

Fours and Fives
Turn the Idiot Box into a Teaching Tool: TV Listings as Primer

TV listings in the newspaper are easier to read than those in *TV Guide,* which has a hard layout for little eyes. Some newspapers even put children's programming in a certain color.

❖ Find the station (PBS) and corresponding number in the listing.

❖ Pick up the remote control and find the right number.

❖ Use the remote control.

Lesson: *I can get information from a source made of letters and numbers. And it's fun.*

By second grade all of our children will be reading. I can tell you from experience that it is a great thrill to see your child suddenly comprehend the connection between letters and words. You will have this thrill if you leave your kid alone. Let her "get it" when she "gets it."

Annie put the whole thing in the proper perspective when she was four and able to read almost anything she picked up.

A close friend of hers showed mild interest in academics, sometimes saying what a letter was, sometimes not interested. But her friend was already "hip." I don't know how else to explain it, but you just know that this child will be popular, with it, and on the cutting edge of social events. She has that certain something.

One day Annie turned to me and said out of the blue, "Well, *I* might be able to read. But Rachel *knows* everything."

Out of the mouths of babes.

SUMMARY:

❖ All children are curious.
❖ Children have different interests and different rates of learning.
❖ If you follow your own child's interests and positively reinforce whatever she chooses to learn, you will aid her in maintaining the love of learning that all people are born with.

A Sense of Belonging

Everyone has a place in the world.

Each individual is part of an immediate family. Our immediate family is part of an extended family. Our extended family is part of an ethnic group. (Some adopted children have a different background from their families, which both complicates and enriches their lives.) Our family is part of a socioeconomic class. Many families align themselves with groups held together by shared beliefs, such as religion and politics.

We are part of our neighborhood, city, state, our country, and continent. We are all citizens of the world.

Being a member of each group connects us with others. We are not isolated individuals whose personal survival is the only thing that matters.

The child with a firm sense of belonging in many groups, beginning with the family, is a secure child.

Let us drop a little pebble into the pond of life by starting with your baby's place in your family and following the ever-widening circles of connection from your family out into the world.

SECTION 1: YOUR FAMILY

From the time your baby is tiny he has the capacity to absorb information that will resonate long past babyhood. In the time-honored tradition of lullabies, you can begin introducing your baby to a who's who of your world.

Activity: Make Up Songs that Spell Out Baby's Immediate World

Any song you make up will do. A baby is *the* best audience in the world.

A mom in one of our classes used the tune of "Mama's Little Baby Loves Shortnin' Bread." She sang, "Mommy's little Evan loves Mommy and Daddy and Mommy's little Evan loves Evan, too." She didn't worry about fitting the syllables to the song exactly. She had fun making up free-form verses for grandparents, aunts, uncles, and cousins, and she added new relatives as they were born or married into the family. Depending on her mood, she crooned or gave her baby a good gospel rendition. As Evan grew, he continued to love "his" song.

Try making up a sentimental song for your baby to introduce him to his immediate and extended family, to baby-sitters, pets, and everybody he loves.

> *Lesson:* I have a family including brothers, sisters, aunts, uncles, grandparents, and pets, who I love and who love me. Nice. Cozy. Secure.

Activity: Point Out Similarities and Connections with Your Family

Whether your family is a unit formed by biology or adoption, your child needs to feel connected.

- ❖ Tell stories of when you and your husband were little and did the same things he does.
- ❖ Point out character traits that remind you of you, your husband, or other members of the family.
- ❖ For a biological child, show baby pictures of any family member he resembles.

Special Note for a Divorced or Separated Home: How hard it must be when it's gotten so bad that you can no longer bear to live with him. Yet for your child's peace of mind I urge you to say, "You look just like your dad when you sit like that." Use a tone that is friendly. Avoid spitting out venomously, "Oh, you're just like your father." Even if a gesture reminiscent of your former husband makes your skin crawl.

Lesson: *I am part of my family. I am like them, connected to them, and similar to them.*
For Biological Children: *I am connected by body to the generations of my family.*

Weave Your Extended Family into Your Child's Everyday Life

In "the old days" people lived among their extended family. Grandmothers, aunts, uncles, and cousins constituted the mainstay of people's social life as well as being part of their families. In America at present we are a nomad group, following jobs, life-styles, and weather. Yet a child still needs to know that he is part of an extended family. Whether you live next door to your sister and her family or across the continent, here are some ideas of ways to include your extended family into your child's sphere on a day-to-day basis.

❖ Speak kindly of your and your husband's relatives.
❖ Even if your mother-in-law drives you crazy, never let your child know.
❖ Look at pictures from the past and identify who everybody is.
❖ Tell stories of your family history.
❖ Look at pictures of cousins who live nearby and those far away.
❖ Make your child his own special photo album with a picture of each relative. Let him sit on your lap, point, name them, and kiss each one. This is wonderful particularly when you live at a distance.
❖ If appropriate, point out how your child resembles this aunt or that cousin.
❖ If you have any heirlooms (not just fancy antiques, but also the odd salad bowl from Aunt Martha) tell your child whose it was.
❖ Tell your child stories about what your grandmother cooked.
❖ Tell your child stories about your favorite aunt or uncle.
❖ Tell your child about any relatives you have or had that accomplished anything out of the ordinary.
❖ If possible, show your child where you and your husband grew up.
❖ If it's too far away, show pictures of where you grew up.
❖ Surround your child with the lore of your extended family.

Lesson: *I am part of a larger group of people of whom we are proud.*

SECTION 2: PERSONAL CULTURE

History is rich with the traditions of many cultures and the individuals who have sprung from each group. Here are some simple child-appropriate ways to begin introducing your toddler and preschooler to his own cultural heritage.

* ❖ Hang out with people who share your heritage.
* ❖ If there's a second language involved, help your child learn it.
* ❖ Cook meals that are part of the heritage.
* ❖ Learn about clothing.
* ❖ Go to museums.
* ❖ Read books (there are many lovely toddler and preschool books out now about different groups).
* ❖ Listen to the music of your culture.
* ❖ Look at a map.
* ❖ Teach how your people got to this country.

Lesson: *I belong to a fascinating larger group.*

Since many families are now made up of a mommy and daddy who come from different backgrounds, introduction to a child's own cultural heritage becomes more complicated.

It sounds obvious to suggest that each parent should be very careful not to indicate that his or her own culture is ''better.'' Yet competition and one-upmanship seem part of human nature. Even in a family where both sides come from exactly the same religious, ethnic, and socioeconomic pool, there are often subtle rivalries that children pick up. The simple phrase, ''That's how Daddy's mother sets the table, not how we do it,'' packs an enormous wallop over the long haul. There is the ''them-us'' tendency in us all. But a child of a mixed marriage, if subjected to subtle racism or religious prejudice, will come away with internal conflict.

Some simple ideas to keep in mind might be these:

❖ Do not pretend that there are no differences. This essential hypocrisy will confuse a small child and either hurt or enrage an older child. Acknowledge, identify, even point out the differences, as long as they are pointed out with respect.

❖ Make sure that both cultures get equal billing. It may be very valuable, and fun, to have Mommy and the child along as Daddy introduces the family to some element of his culture, and then on another weekend have Dad go along as Mom leads the way.

❖ Sometimes the partners of a mixed marriage distance themselves from both cultures or religions. This is one of those pre-baby decisions that you might reconsider for the sake of your child. While leaving your birth culture behind may be more comfortable for you as a couple, you deny your child a right to his heritage. As he matures he may begin to feel that there is something "wrong" with him or lacking in his life. He will not feel connected to a larger group that he has a right to feel part of.

Lesson: *I belong to two fascinating groups that Mommy and Daddy like.*

In addition to different backgrounds of the biological parents, we also have large numbers of adopted children whose ethnic background is different from their parents'. There are groups in most large cities that it would be useful to hook up with, even if you have to travel to get there. These groups usually have different days to immerse themselves in different cultures and introduce all kinds of fun kid activities. Perhaps most meaningful is the visual impact for your child. In a group like this he will see many families where the children do not physically resemble their parents. Although each family must decide individually how they will address this issue with their own children, from a child's point of view by about three and certainly four they notice the physical differences.

It is reassuring for them to see other families "like theirs." If they never see another family where the children don't resemble the parents, it's possible that they may worry about why they are different. It is important for all children to feel comfortable and part of a larger community where they fit in.

Lesson: *I belong to a group comprised of families who chose one another.*

SECTION 3: PEOPLE WHO ARE DIFFERENT

As soon as we identify our own culture, by definition we identify that we are different from other people in some ways. Keeping those differences value-free is an important part of parenting.

A. OTHER CULTURES AND RELIGIONS

Racism, jingoism, and sexism are all examples of the inability to see good in people who are different. Teaching a young child respect for other cultures and religions promotes constructive participation in the world around us and gives a child an expansive sense of belonging in the whole world. If other groups are peers rather than potential enemies, we can move through the world more smoothly.

Here are some simple child-appropriate activities:

- ❖ Go to museums when they have exhibits from other countries or cultures.
- ❖ Point out how different their art and traditional clothes are from ours. Point out what you find beautiful.
- ❖ Go to ethnic street fairs. Point out what's fun about that culture's food, music, and dance.
- ❖ Christmas, Hanukkah, and Kwanzaa are obvious times to respectfully point out religious and cultural differences.
- ❖ If you have friends who are active in an organized religion different from yours, take both sets of kids to fairs and bazaars. Expose them to social gatherings that are fun.

Lesson: *Other cultures and religions are interesting, just as mine is. I like some things about mine better and some things about theirs better.*

The ideas above give you suggestions to broaden your child's horizons by learning about cultures from all over the world that we see here in the United States. They do not directly address a pressing problem that we have: racism. This is an area we ignore in parenting in the early years, but talk about interminably in the teen and adult arenas, when it's too late. The lessons have already been deeply ingrained.

I believe in my bones two things: Racism exists, and racism is bad. How to raise a new generation that is not racist, however, is less clearcut.

I know many middle-class white families who, in their determination to raise nonracist children, completely avoid ever identifying anyone by race. But children are not blind. They can see that people have different-color faces. We identify a child as "the blonde," "the redhead," "the one with freckles." Yet suddenly, we're silent about skin color. God only knows what their imaginations do with that omission. If obliged, adults use "black" or "white," neither of which makes any sense to a small child. Equally as nondescriptive, and therefore confusing, to a preschooler, are the terms Afro-American and Hispanic. Many children, free from the political implications of terminology, unlike we adults, come up with "dark skin" and "light skin" as value-free descriptions on their own. We parents of young children might do well to follow their sensible, nonracist lead and identify and describe skin tone in the same way we mention eye color or height.

Here are some suggestions of choices a white family can make to discourage racism from developing in their young child:

- ❖ If you pass a group of dark-skinned kids who are menacing, introduce the concept of "rough." This, or any word you're comfortable with, will give your child a label that will not include race. Do not pretend that you pass by this group of kids with the same feeling that you pass by a group of geezers sitting at a bus stop. You don't.
- ❖ By the same token, identify nice teens. "He was a nice kid," you can mention in passing. Identifying *all* nice kids, black, white, Latin, and Asian, begins to form a pattern in your child's mind of judging by behavior rather than race.
- ❖ Watch the TV show *Family Matters,* particularly the early reruns before dating has entered the scene, for a positive image of an Afro-American family.
- ❖ Local news stations constantly broadcast pictures of young black men, handcuffed, being led away. Frequently, a child who has never heard anyone identified by race may zap you with a zinger such as: "Are all people with dark faces bad?" Explain to your child that newspeople like to show bad guys, not good guys. Mention someone you know who has dark skin and is nice. Point out that some dark people are nasty and some are nice, and some light people are nasty and some nice. Repeat that we judge people by how they act.

For families of all races, here are some suggestions to keep racism out of your home, to teach respect for other races, to bolster the self-esteem of your individual child no matter what race your family is, and to counteract the increasingly virulent name-calling that we and our children are hearing more and more frequently among all the races:

❖ Whatever race you are, commit yourself to teaching your child to judge people by their behavior, and not by their race.

❖ Avoid the use of any racist terms to describe a particular individual's behavior.

❖ If you hear someone use a derogatory name, tell your child we don't use ugly words like that.

❖ If you hear someone on the news or in the street shouting ugly names, tell your child we judge people by their behavior, not by their group.

❖ Avoid watching athletics such as boxing on TV, as well as rap videos. They foster the perception that black people are violent. This is not a healthy image nor role model for any child of any race to see.

❖ Have normal, friendly, civil conversations with other-race people in stores or wherever you take your child. Choose wisely. Learn to judge from body language which person will be pleasant and which will only serve to teach your child the opposite of what you want.

❖ Try not to have all people of authority in your lives be white, such as doctors and teachers, nor all people in serving positions, such as household help, be people of color.

❖ If you have a choice of nursery schools, choose one where the children are mixed racially, *as long as you like the school.* Do not force your child to go to a school that is not suited to him solely to expose him to different kinds of people.

❖ If you have a choice of two good schools and one has a racially mixed teaching staff, choose it. *Do not,* however, choose an inferior school solely based on the race of its teachers. This will ultimately foster racism.

❖ Make friends with a family of a different race. There is a caveat to this: Make sure that you have more in common than simply a desire to have a friend of a different race. There is nothing more phony or forced, and guaranteed to backfire from the child's point of view, than a friendship forged in "politically correct heaven." Try to choose a family that has more or less the same socioeconomic background as yours and the same level of education. It also helps to have your children be the same sex or temperament. With these similarities in mind, you have a fighting chance at having a positive experience.

Lesson: We do not pretend that race does not exist, nor do we use it as the sole means to evaluate someone. Color is simply one aspect of who we are, no more, no less.

B. PHYSICAL DIFFERENCES

In the same way that we want our children to notice and respect cultural differences, so should we try and help them recognize that some people are different physically or mentally.

❖ A young child, still using a stroller or fresh from the stroller experience, can understand a wheelchair very easily if it is put in simple, value-free terms. "Her legs need help. She uses a wheelchair."

❖ A child with cerebral palsy who uses leg braces, crutches, or any other aid to movement can be explained easily. "Those crutches help the little girl walk."

❖ If your child asks loudly, "Why is that person [or child] sitting in that chair?" don't hush your child up as if she's asked something unutterable. The person in the wheelchair knows they're in a wheelchair. Particularly for a child who needs help walking, as well as for yours, if the whole issue is kept matter-of-fact the negative spin has been removed. You can even say to your child, "Why don't you ask her?" The two children can begin talking. The wheelchair then becomes as normal and value-free as the color of her hair, or glasses, or any other element that makes that person unique.

❖ Help the person if it's needed. "Can I get that door for you?" is not an insult to a person in a wheelchair. It is a sensible aid.

Lesson: People are different. This difference is not bad or good. Just different.

C. AGE DIFFERENCES

One problem in our society is worshiping youth. But it engenders so many problems, when in fact there's a much richer way of looking at things. Each period of life is glorious.

❖ Allow your child to feel how wonderful it is to be a little child.
❖ Allow yourself to feel how wonderful it is to be an adult.
❖ Refrain from saying things such as ''I wish I were a kid again'' or ''I'm getting old.'' This puts a negative spin on adulthood.
❖ Honor the elderly. An act of kindness to an old person is a blessing. It makes the world a better place.

Here are some things you can do when you're with your child that will teach respect for older people.

❖ Give old people seats when they need them.
❖ Give old people a hand with their bags.
❖ Help old people when it's raining, snowing, sleeting, or any other weather that makes it hard to walk outside.
❖ If your elderly neighbor is so needy that you find yourself angry because you're the only one helping, call an agency in. This person obviously needs help, and you can't do it all.
❖ Ask them about their past.
❖ Don't expect all old people to be fonts of wisdom and kindness. Some nasty people manage to hang on well into their eighties and nineties. If they were lousy SOBs all the rest of those years, don't expect them suddenly to become saints in their dotage.
❖ If your small child is afraid of a particular old person, cut your contact down. Neither the old crone nor your child needs to upset the other.

SECTION 4: CITIZENSHIP

A. A SENSE OF NATIONAL PRIDE

Throughout this book I pick on America. We're messed up. We cheat. We lie. We're selfish. We're amoral and immoral. But the United States of America is the finest nation in recorded history.

Here's a little story.

I was in a taxi. The driver, from somewhere in the Middle East, told me he had lived before this in Saudi Arabia. In Saudi Arabia they cut off your hand if you steal.

He said, "You have very nice laws here."

I agreed.

He looked at me through the rearview mirror. I could see the wisdom of an ancient culture in his eyes. He laughed.

"Nice laws are for nice people. They only work when everybody's nice." We *do* have nice laws. Teach your child how lucky we are to live in a free land.

❖ Take him to vote with you! This may be the most important community lesson of all. Explain that we live in a democracy, that each grown-up gets a say in how we do things.

❖ Take your child to parades for American holidays such as the Fourth of July, Thanksgiving Day, etc.

❖ Show him the American flag.

B. CITIZENSHIP IN THE WORLD

❖ Show him maps of your city, your state, the United States, and the world.

❖ Play with an inflatable globe.

❖ If you see a world-map shower curtain, point out where you live and where your ancestors came from.

❖ If the Olympics or any other international sport is on TV, show our flag, then other people's flags.

SUMMARY:

❖ Help your child feel a part of the world.

❖ Help your child respect and appreciate differences.

PART II

AT HOME

Our children's characters are now well in hand. They know who is in charge and who they can depend on to teach them right from wrong. They're having fun learning, she enjoys being a girl, he's all boy, and nobody has too many toys. They feel secure in the warm embrace of their family and are members of a larger community.

Let's tackle some everyday stuff. Like food. Sleep. Baths. Clothes. And putting away our toys.

7

Food: The Staff of Life

One out of every three adult Americans is overweight. The diet industry rakes in billions annually. Ninth-graders suffer from anorexia and bulimia. We are overweight. We are underweight. We are obsessed with weight.

More than one out of every four of us are so clinically clogged that at any moment we may clutch our chests and either fall down never to get up again or get up seriously impaired. One out of every 180 of us will have some of our cells go so wildly out of kilter that they will eat us up alive or have to be sliced, exterminated, or nuked out of our bodies.

While there are environmental and genetic factors that contribute to many of our life-threatening diseases, the major reasons so many of us are fat and sick is because we have crummy diets that we shovel down our gullets while lying on the couch.

If you attend a Weight Watchers meeting, a recovering-cardiology-patients group, or any other gathering where people come together to support one another in reshaping their lives in order to be healthier, two themes consistently emerge:

1. Unhealthy eating habits, which include the ''wrong'' foods and way too much of them coupled with a sedentary lifestyle.
2. Food is not associated with hunger, but is used as a substitute for an emotional lack.

There is more. If these people trying so hard to relearn their entire approach to food succeed in altering their habits, either because they are sick of what they look like or are scared of dying, only one out of ten, at best, will change permanently. The rest will go back to their old habits. In the case of dieters, many will not only regain the weight they worked so hard to lose, they will put on more. In the case of many cardiology patients, they will die.

While it is indisputable that people have different genetic makeups and metabolisms, which should be accepted and respected, bad habits that lead to bad health begin very young and are reinforced all the way through the first couple of decades of a person's life. After that an adult must either change, which is incredibly arduous if not impossible, or ignore bad habits and suffer the medical, and sometimes social, consequences.

The knowledge of what so many adults are up against throws the ball into our court, Moms.

Before we get to ways that you can help your child establish healthy eating habits (please see Chapter 13, "The Media," for some lifestyle suggestions), I would like to introduce you to the healthy little person living in your home.

Up until the age of at least two, every child has a very accurate appestat, the internal control that connects food with hunger and bodily needs.

Research has revealed that over a period of time ranging from a week to a month, young children provided with variety will naturally select the amounts and kinds of foods they need to maintain good health.

Unlike adults, babies and toddlers do not eat out of boredom, loneliness, or existential emptiness. They do not eat because it's a sin to waste food or because they saw a picture of a starving child and feel so guilty that they shovel whatever is on their plate into their mouths. They do not eat because they had a fight with their spouse or because they didn't get the promotion they wanted at work.

Babies and toddlers eat because they are hungry. And they are only hungry when their bodies need fuel.

True Tale from the Trenches: In one of our classes was a seven-month-old. Tommy was chunky. Every once in a while, when one of the other babies cried, "Feed me," and his mother fed him, Tommy would get an eyeful of that bottle and wail. I asked Tommy's mother gently if Tommy was hungry. She looked self-conscious. She said their pediatrician felt that Tommy was gaining weight too fast. He should be getting only 32 ounces of formula a day. Since she didn't want to go over that amount, she was rationing when and how much he ate.

Not liking to buck medical advice, I let it go.

The next week the same thing happened. The other mothers in the room looked uncomfortable. It seemed so clear that Tommy was hungry.

I asked the mother if she was willing to try an experiment. Would she feed him, just for one week, as much as he asked for at a time? Had her child not been in such obvious distress, I never would've suggested it; she never would've agreed.

The first day Tommy gobbled 46 ounces. The next day Tommy took 40 ounces. By the following day Tommy cut himself down to 34. The next day he dropped to 30. He went back up to 35 and then down again to 30.

By the end of the week he had *regulated himself* to 32 ounces a day on an average.

From a mathematical point of view the pediatrician was correct. Tommy needed 32 ounces a day, *on an average.*

But healthy eating is not a daily mathematical formulation. Healthy eating is based on hunger; hunger is based on the body's need on a given day.

The pediatrician probably didn't express himself well. It's even possible he didn't take into account that appetite varies from day to day.

Tommy taught us that a baby knows *how much* he needs *when* he needs it.

Lessons for Moms: *Your baby or young toddler knows what she needs. Any blanket mathematical advice—even from your pediatrician—about amounts of food on a daily basis may need to be adjusted.*

SECTION 1: KIDS AND FOOD

Let's go back to the people with health problems so that we can avoid the mistakes their moms made. If you remember, their discussion began with **Problem Number 1:** Unhealthy eating habits, which include the ''wrong'' foods and way too much of them.

In order to know what the ''wrong'' foods are, we have to know what the ''right'' foods are.

A. WHAT KIDS NEED

Here is the best practical distillation I can give you of thousands of pages about health, nutrition, and diet-linked disease, both its cause and prevention.

1. Babies

Your pediatrician will give you *general sensible guidelines* about what kinds of foods to introduce when.

However, if you have an active seven-month-old who is crawling and has a couple of teeth, she will be hankering for solid foods much earlier than will your friend's nonmobile, toothless seven-month-old. So please use any time guideline that you get from any reputable source judiciously, accommodating the needs of your particular child rather than following a calendar.

An even-better source are Arlene Eisenberg, Heidi Murkoff, and Sandee Hathaway, who do the best job in town in *What to Expect the First Year.* They answer the nitty-gritty, month-by-month questions a mom has about when, how, and what kinds of food to introduce. Furthermore, their Best Odds Diet in *What to Expect in the Toddler Years* is top-notch and thorough.

In my experience, however, once past the introduction of food during the first year, when we are concerned with every single bite, most moms become so engrossed in other issues of child raising and family life that we are sometimes hard-pressed to pay attention to the details of food. Therefore, I would like to give you some broad strokes to supplement more-detailed food discussions.

2. One Year and Up

Use the basic food pyramid printed on the side of any cereal box for the general proportion of foods you are aiming to get your child to eat. Don't take these amounts literally or become rigid about what your child should eat every day. Try to think about these proportions during the course of a week, two weeks, even a month, rather than being a stickler for daily consumption.

If while young your child develops a taste for the following foods, by the time she's our age she will probably be in very good health and not have a weight problem.

1. Whole grains, vegetables, and fruit as the major portion of her diet.
2. About half that amount of protein and dairy, combined.
3. A little bit of fat.

4. An occasional sweet.

5. Water as her beverage of choice.

If you can pull off this ideal living in mainstream America, you are a better man than I, Gunga Din. These are the *ideals* toward which we are heading. Later I will suggest ways to reach these ideals.

In any detailed writing about food and nutrition, by necessity you will encounter the word *serving*.

As soon as you see that word, with its accompanying ½ cups, 8 ounces, 2″ slices, and 5 grams, it is likely that your eyes will glaze over.

Here is the very best generalization I found. It is from *Jane Brody's Nutrition Book. She* got it from Eva May Hamilton and Eleanor Whitney in *Nutrition: Concepts and Controversies.* I don't know where they got it, but bless their hearts and may their own children live to be a hundred!

A Child's Serving: Figure 1 tablespoon for each year. That means that a two-year-old's serving of mashed potatoes is only two table-spoonsful! A four-year-old's portion is only four tablespoons, which equals a mere ¼ of a measuring cup. We are talking about a teeny, tiny amount of food compared with what we all habitually heap on our plates every meal!

Tip: Just for fun, measure 1 tablespoon of rice, hamburger, Cheerios, banana, cottage cheese, or any food of your choice. Put it in the middle of an empty plate. Look at it. Marvel at its tininess. Then never measure your child's food again nor worry about how little she's eating!

Calories

If your child weighs in properly at regular pediatric visits, don't think about calories. If she doesn't, her doctor will help you.

Nutrition

Children need more nutrition than adults because they're growing. Therefore, every mouthful should have as many nutrients as possible.

Nutrients include vitamins, minerals, carbohydrates, protein, fats, and water. Nutrients abound in all fresh foods. All fresh food also contains fiber, plus stuff that even scientists have not yet discovered or named.

Grains

I hate talking about servings, but I know you think you need some guide! Your child should eat between 6–10 servings a day. Just remember not to get crazy if she eats a lot more or less on any given day. Think proportion. Whole grains have more nutrition than processed ones. Whole-wheat bread is better for you than white bread, which has had the natural nutrients stripped and replaced chemically.

Fruits and Vegetables

In the neighborhood of 6–10 servings. The more color, the more nutrition. The fresher the food, the more nutrition.

Dairy and Protein

In the neighborhood of 4–6 servings. Experts vary widely on what a ''serving'' of milk is, so just pour her a cup of milk—not a measuring cup, a cup cup.

Too much dairy and protein is as unhealthy as not enough. *Not enough* dairy and protein results in the serious malnutrition we see in underdeveloped countries. We very rarely see these deficiencies here. The diseases we suffer from are the ravages of *too much* dairy and protein. A child who is encouraged to drink three big glasses of milk, plus eat cereal with milk for breakfast, a grilled cheese sandwich for lunch, and a piece of chicken for dinner—with a piece of fruit and a couple of bites of carrots thrown in as an afterthought—every day, day in and day out, will probably have a very intimate, long-term relationship with her cardiologist in the years to come.

Tip: Our tendency is to concentrate on protein and dairy. Although I will talk about how not to overencourage your child to eat beyond hunger, I cannot say it enough. If you find that, even after reading Section 2, "Moms and Food," you simply cannot help yourself from urging your child to eat more at any given meal, force yourself *not* to say, "Finish your milk," or "One more bite of turkey." If you must stuff your child, stuff her with broccoli and cantaloupe.

Fat

A little. A little is a thin spread of cream cheese, not a half-inch slab. Your child is getting most necessary fat from all the other foods she's eating. Fat has become a big bugaboo in our society. We have lost all common sense about this topic. Try this: *A little fat* is necessary to stay alive. *A lot of fat* will kill you.

Point of Information: Do not give a child under two years old low-fat or skim dairy products. They need fat for their brains to develop! After two, switch them to 2% milk or even skim if you cook with a lot of fat. Make the switch in increments. Add 1 cup of skim, 1% or 2% to a quart of whole milk.

After several days to a week, increase the amount of the lower-fat milk until you've acclimated your child's taste buds to a lower-fat amount.

Thems is the basics of the "right" kinds of food.

B. WHAT KIDS DON'T NEED

Now let's go back to our people sitting in a room, trying to shed ten to fifty pounds or to keep their hearts from pooping out permanently.

Okay. What are the "wrong" kinds of food those people are eating way too much of?

Because I am at heart a silly person, I like to think of the "wrong" kinds of food as:

Evil Beasties that Lurk on Supermarket Shelves

Sugar Is an Evil Beastie

In nutrition circles sugar is called an empty calorie. This means that it does nothing positive for developing organs, bones, or muscles. Furthermore, it rots teeth and there is some evidence that it is addictive. The more you eat, the more you want. The data is mixed on the influence of sugar on children's behavior. It is not in the least mixed on its nutritional flaws.

Do not be fooled by unrefined sugar, honey, or fructose. They are all as nutritionally devoid as refined sugar, corn syrup, and confectioner's sugar. If you eat an apple, which contains fructose, you received a lot of nutrition from the fruit itself. If you add fructose to a cake, it's more or less the same as adding refined sugar.

If your preschooler has any *one* of the following several times a week, although not great, it's not a nutritional disaster: a piece of cake, three or four cookies, a junky Popsicle. If your child is under two and a half and eating any of these kinds of foods on a regular basis, I urge you to rethink how you are feeding your baby.

The "Wrong" Kind of Fat Is an Evil Beastie

The kind of fat (called saturated) found in junk food and a great deal of processed foods that pretend to be dinner is yummy. "Bet you can't eat just one!" is one of the few truth-in-advertising slogans. Enough of this kind of fat promotes being overweight, if not downright obese, with all the potentially harmful side effects of making your body haul around excess cargo. Eating a lot of it promotes high cholesterol; "hardening of the arteries"; heart disease; long-term, serious overall health problems; and death.

Too Much of Any Fat Is an Evil Beastie

If your child has any ONE of these a day, it is no nutritional disaster. A pat of butter, which is free from the chemicals in margarine, a splash of olive oil, or a little cream cheese. If every one of your child's meals includes lots of these added fats, in addition to nutritious, toddler-pleasing peanut butter, avocado, and cottage cheese, make that appointment with the heart specialist now. They book up early.

Chemicals Are Evil Beasties

Chemicals are in our air, water, the earth, and every bite all of us put in our mouths.

No one has any data on the long-term effects of all these chemicals. When they set numerical figures for "safe" amounts, scientists are shooting ducks by moonlight, as my high-school chemistry teacher used to put it. It is just plain dumb to think that all these chemicals won't have a cumulative, negative effect on our children's growing bodies.

Chemicals in our air, water, and food are one of the "environmental" factors contributing to cancer. Fresh fruits and vegetables contain identifiable vitamins, called antioxidants, as well as yet unidentified stuff that seem to counteract, or possibly protect, the body against the invasion of chemicals.

If your child has a minuscule amount of chemicals during a day, it may be no nutritional disaster. We are not sure.

Processed Foods and Junk Foods Are the Most Evil of Evil Beasties

They contain sugar, bad fat, and chemicals. What "nutrition" they contain is often chemically added, thereby discounting whatever nutrition claims they may make.

Not only that, but they are very clever, very sly evil beasties. They come in pretty packaging, kid-pleasing fun shapes, and fabulous colors. They beckon with gnarled fingers and cackling voices: "Come here, my pretty. Don't you want to taste this? Oh, yes. Cackle, cackle. That's fun, isn't it? Cackle, cackle. And it tastes good too, my pretty, doesn't it? Oh, yes!" These pernicious evil beasties are very hard to refuse!

If your child eats one processed food a day, such as a helping of a kid-favorite boxed mix of macaroni and cheese, with its stripped and chemically subsidized carbohydrates, processed cheese "food," preservatives, food coloring, salt, sugar, and a couple of grams of protein struggling up through the sewer to give your kid a little real food, it is no nutritional disaster. Ditto for such crowd pleasers as hot dogs, fish sticks, canned soup, American cheese slices, most jarred spaghetti sauces, pancake mixes, pop-tarts, and bologna.

Please. Don't even get me started talking about potato chips, wholesome yogurt tarted up with sprinkles, sugar, and artificial flavor, or those little kid-lunch packs of mystery meat, cheese "foods," and fatty crackers.

If your child eats all of this stuff—sugar, bad fat or too much good fat, and a lot of chemicals—day in and day out as the predominant part of her diet and does not eat a lot of fresh fruits, vegetables, and whole grains, it is a nutritional disaster. She is being set up to be fat, at best, and dead before her time.

For the sake of your child's future health, you should make it your business to limit evil beasties.

I. Shopping Choices

1. Cook as much as you possibly can from scratch.
2. Read labels when you shop. From the simplest can of beans to spaghetti sauce to quarts of milk that are unnecessarily fortified with protein and vitamin C, evil beasties can lurk.
3. If you have a choice between a product with no additives and one with additives, choose the one without.
4. Any organic food you buy is one less chemical cocktail you serve your family. Given the choice, go organic. If you have a good source of fresh organic produce and can afford it, it's definitely worth buying. If it's not fresh it's not worth it.
5. If you have access to an organic food co-op that sends you a weekly box of fresh kale, kohlrabi, acorn squash, Swiss chard, millet, groats and "unadulterated" peanut butter, and you are like most of the moms I know, you will eat it all yourself the first week or two and by week three you will end up dumping all those vitamin-packed fresh vegetables right down the disposal. Suggest your food co-op try a different selection.
6. If you have access to a local organic farmer, you hit the jackpot. The food will be fresh, and buying direct will keep the farmer in business. Win-win situation.
7. If you have a choice between a product with one or two additives and another with a long list of words you cannot pronounce, you get the idea.
8. If your child eats at McDonald's one day, make sure that the rest of that day's foods are as evil-beastie-free as is humanly possible.
9. Any cereal that is pink and purple is an evil beastie. Any cereal that does not contain raisins and has more than five or six grams of sugar per serving is an evil beastie. Find other cereals your child likes for breakfast, and either don't buy the evil beasties or

consider them snack food. Remember, one of any of these evil beasties won't kill your kid. A lot of them will.

10. When your child asks for a treat, give her a Frozfruit or home-made Popsicle made from frozen fruit juice. Suggest strawberries. Ask with real, not phony, eagerness, "Would you like some cantaloupe?" This way she develops a taste for healthy snacks when she's young.

11. When you do indulge in a sweet, such as an ice cream cone, have fun! Have a *real* ice cream cone, not chemicals whipped together to mimic ice cream. A little real cream, real sugar, and real flavor every once in a while tastes terrific and won't kill you. A lot of chemicals that coat the tongue and add to the cumulative amount ingested over a lifetime are not worth being eaten, let alone called a treat.

There is a question from the mom in the back row. Yes?

"Well, given all you've just said, wouldn't it be wise for us to never let our children eat any of these evil beasties?"

Ah! What an excellent question.

True Tale from the Trenches: My friend's nine-year-old invited a new boy at school over to play. (Our children will be nine sooner than you know it, so pay attention!) Before the date the new mom called with some "ground rules," as she put it. "My son doesn't eat refined sugar, refined wheat, or chemicals. If you are going to give him snacks, please make sure they're heathy and wholesome, such as whole-wheat pretzels and raisins." My friend felt mildly put off by the other mother's tone, but, nice woman that she is who respects other mothers' wishes, she went out and stocked up on "healthy" snacks. The moment the child walked through their front door after school, he said, "Do you have any cookies? Do you have any soda? Do you have any candy?" His mother had created her worst nightmare.

As in all of parenting, let moderation be our friend. It is almost impossible to live in mainstream America and raise a child who never puts one drop of evil beasties into her mouth.

2. Practical Strategies

Under Two

Monitor what your small child eats. Keep her as sugar and chemical free as you humanly can. There is no reason a child should eat real junk food at this tender age. They are so amenable to accepting whatever you offer them that it's easy once you make up your mind.

Do as much purification as you can while they're young and their cells are growing rapidly. There are many good organic baby food companies. Their prices aren't astronomical. It's a sensible choice.

Hit a health food store. But read the ingredients. Just because it's in a health food store doesn't mean it's healthy. Organic granola that is loaded with coconut, dates, raisins, canola oil, sesame seeds, and unrefined sugar is very high in calories and fat. The only advantage it has over a high-fat, high-calorie mainstream cereal is that it is chemical-free.

There are other foods, however, that are excellent choices. During these early years young children will gladly eat Oat-I-Ohs, for example, the health food brand of Cheerios, minus the sugar and additives.

Toddlers

Once you enter the world at large, your job is to *limit* the amount of junk. Here are the kinds of strategies to think about that may lessen the amount of evil beasties while not creating "food fights."

❖ Agree to the request in the moment. Example: "Sure, you can have a cupcake if you're still hungry after dinner," said in a nonchalant tone. Compare this with a tight-lipped "You may only have a cupcake if you eat all your dinner." The first suggestion is easy and doesn't make an issue of the cupcake. She may even forget she asked for it, preferring the asking and acceptance over the actual eating. The second way of saying it, however, sets up a big fight. Then she wants to win. But what did she win? The right to put stuff in her mouth that she may not even want and that's not good for her.

❖ "I want sweet potatoes the way Grandma makes them!" "Grandma puts marshmallows on her sweet potatoes. You can eat them like that at her house. We like them baked plain, here at home."

❖ "Sure, you can drink Hawaiian Punch at Billy's. But I don't buy it. Here we drink juice."

Preschoolers

❖ "Sure, you can have some soda. It's a party. But one glass is enough for a kid."

❖ "I know Daddy drinks soda with dinner. But his bones aren't growing like yours are. You need something to drink with dinner that gives you something good. What would you like? Water? Milk? Juice? Good choice.''

Lesson: *No food is completely off-limits all the time or makes my mom uptight. We have certain things we eat in certain places. Here at home we eat these yummy foods that Mommy makes and serves.*

For a preschooler pitching junk food fits, try reading the Berenstain Bears book called *Too Much Junk Food.*

Okay. Let's return to our friends sitting around a room, trying to get a handle on good health. Here are some of the tips the group leader is passing along about ''healthy eating habits.'' You would be a wise mom to establish these habits in your child's life at an early age so she doesn't have to sit around in a circle later in life talking about what she has to relearn.

C. HEALTHY EATING HABITS
1. Food Feeds the Body

- ❖ Small children need to eat every couple of hours. That means they need healthy snacks in between regular mealtimes.
- ❖ Eat breakfast, lunch, and dinner regularly. This does not have to be a schedule to make Mussolini proud. Try to have each mealtime fall within a half-hour range, every day, weekends included.
- ❖ Some children don't think much of certain meals. If your child is not a big lunch eater, be prepared to provide a nutritious midafternoon snack, such as a peach, apple, or piece of watermelon and a whole-wheat bagel, so that when she is genuinely hungry she's getting more than pizza-flavored Goldfish (cute little evil beasties frequently found in the backs of strollers!).
- ❖ Put out a nice variety at every meal.
- ❖ Be prepared to take away uneaten food.
- ❖ Model. If you eat Fritos, Cheez Whiz, and a Coke for breakfast, don't expect your child to chow down on Oat-I-Ohs, fresh strawberries, whole-wheat toast, and milk!

2. Meals Feed the Soul

Food for Thought: A recent study found that the only thing all National Merit scholars had in common was that *they ate dinner with their families.*

Further Food for Thought: In nutrition research there is an odd blip in statistics, dubbed "The French Paradox." French people smoke like fiends, guzzle wine, and eat enough croissants, snails drenched in butter, and similar high-fat, high-cholesterol foods that you'd think they'd all be clutching their hearts and keeling headfirst into big slabs of Brie.

Instead, they have thirty percent less heart disease than we Americans do. Researchers postulate that one reason might be because meals are such an affable, social, extended-family group affair in France that the good mood, laughter, and general *savoir-faire* offset the health hazards that our fast-paced, solitary, shove-it-in-on-the-run way of eating gives us.

- ❖ Children should not eat alone. They should always have an adult eating with them—not puttering around the kitchen when they eat, but sitting down with them.
- ❖ A parent should eat at least one meal a day with a child. If you work late and your child eats early dinner with a baby-sitter, wake up early and make breakfast your meal together.
- ❖ Children should not eat every meal in front of the tube. Although if I ran the world no one would ever eat in front of the TV, that does not seem to be a realistic expectation in many homes. But please make sure the number of meals with the TV as the major focus are limited.
- ❖ Although most of us live hectic lives, plan at least one dinner a week that's really a family get-together. This means everyone sits down at the same time, the TV is off, and you're paying attention to each other. If your family will stand it, turn on the answering machine. Try to make these meals fun and pleasant rather than a setting to introduce ''heavy'' topics. If you can do this at least once a week—or even better every night—you may have a happier, healthier home. You may even find yourselves suddenly speaking French to your Merit scholar! Barring that, you may find that family meals make up some of your and your children's fondest memories.

SECTION 2: MOMS AND FOOD

Let's go once again to our group meeting. The dieters or heart patients know each other pretty well by this time. The women have kicked off their shoes. Any men wearing ties have loosened them. They've talked about what kinds of foods they ought to be eating and which ones they ought to either avoid altogether or, more realistically, limit severely.

And now they're ready to let down their hair and really talk. How did their moms teach them to eat way too much, and how did food become a substitute to meet other emotional needs?

A. COMMON THINGS LOVING MOMS DO UNTHINKINGLY

If any of these hit home, do your child a favor: Rethink some of the things you may say or do.

1. Food as a Substitute for Emotions

Eating is not an emotional issue for your child—unless you make it one. Here are some common ways moms have of getting the two confused:

- ❖ Sticking a pacifier, bottle, or breast into a baby's mouth *every* time she cries. Figure out what's bothering her. Sometimes she might want to suck. Not all the time.
- ❖ Sticking a cookie or cracker into a toddler's mouth *every* time she falls down or cries for any other reason. Hugs do a lot better than cookies. Interesting distractions move us along. Cookies might be a reasonable choice every once in a while.
- ❖ Being emotionally involved with your cooking. How do you know if you're emotionally involved? See if this fits: You have spent several hours making fresh, homemade carrot-squash-zucchini bread, using only the finest ingredients and every kitchen implement known to Williams and Sonoma. Your child takes a bite, makes a face, throws it down, and asks for a bagel. If you feel angry, sad, hurt, upset, or any other possible *emotional* response, take a deep breath. Go out and buy bagels. Remind yourself that your entire existence and self-esteem are not sitting on a bread board.
- ❖ Thinking that food is equal to love. Making your child's favorite foods is a loving act. Making sure that there is nutritious food she

likes available when she's hungry is a loving act. Food itself is not love.

❖ Saying any variation on this theme: "What a crummy day. Let's go out and get some ice cream." Instead, try, "What a crummy day. Let's go out and have some fun." If the "fun" includes ice cream, terrific! Ice cream *is* fun. But focus on the fun rather than the food itself.

❖ Making mealtime a struggle. Eating together should be fun and social.

2. Food as a Reward

The only real reason anyone should eat anything is if they are hungry. And yet sometimes we get mixed up and think that a treat is a good bribe or eating is a virtue in and of itself.

Instead of "If you behave I'll give you a cookie," try any of these: "If you behave we'll read another story, go to the zoo, go to the playground and stay till dusk, stay in the pool longer than usual, go pick up Daddy at work."

3. Not Paying Attention to Hunger

If you encourage a child to eat more than she wants sometimes and less than she wants other times, you are teaching her to ignore her internal appestat—to eat too much for the wrong reasons.

❖ Shoveling spoonful after spoonful into a baby's mouth while you space out, look around, or remain unaware of the fact that she's turning her face. Try to remember how we eat: We take a bite, we talk, we look around, we think about what we want to put in our mouths next. If, that is, we have healthy eating habits.

❖ Putting extra food in front of her to buy yourself time to do something else.

❖ Any variation of "cute" baby-stuffing games such as "Let's see if we can find the bunny at the bottom of this bowl," or "Here comes the airplane! Open the hangar wide!"

❖ "Come on, sweetie. One more bite for Mommy." If Mommy wants another bite she can go help herself. Baby is full.

❖ "Clean your plate." Dishwashers clean plates, not eaters who are full.

❖ "Eat now. You'll be hungry later."

❖ "Don't eat now. You'll spoil your dinner."

B. DEALING WITH OUR OWN "FOOD ISSUES"

Now I have one for you. You happen to be one of the people in the room, trying to change your own eating habits!

1. Dieting

Many of us are on a diet right now. For a young child taking her cues from your modeling, if you focus on choice rather than deprivation it will help her tremendously in forming not only healthy eating habits, but healthy attitudes.

- ❖ Try not to use the word *dieting* with your child. Dieting, like sex, is a grown-up topic that a young child has no way of integrating and can only misinterpret and distort.
- ❖ Instead of saying, "Oh, no, Mommy can't have that cookie, she's on a diet," and looking yearningly at the cookie, try, "No, thanks, not now."
- ❖ Whenever you choose a "diet" choice over something else, such as melon instead of cake, use words that imply choice. For example, "Today I don't want any cake. Today I think I'd prefer some melon." Offer her some.
- ❖ When you leave half the food on your plate in a restaurant, rather than saying you're dieting, say, "I've had enough. I'm full." These are very valuable words for a child to hear coming from Mommy's mouth.
- ❖ Limit the amount of time your child hears you obsessing about dieting, counting calories, or yakking on the phone about this fabulous new liquid diet, that fabulous new no-fat diet, etc.
- ❖ If you're using something like a Weight Watchers chart or any other written diary of your food intake, let your child see it. It may even help her. But rather than saying "I'm dieting," try something like, "I feel better when I'm healthier. This is a way I use to help myself feel better."
- ❖ Stress *feeling better* and *being healthier* rather than *looking better*. This means that when you do lose your weight (and I know you will), instead of crowing about how much better you look, say how much better you feel. This is *particularly important for girls*. By the time they are five most girls in this culture know about fat. They have already been introduced to the idea that fat is ugly, that they should worry about fat, and that they don't want to be fat. Their mother will do them an enormous favor if she is clear about health, rather than fat.

Lesson: Mommy pays attention to what she eats, just as she pays attention to what I eat. She makes choices. She seems happy about those choices, rather than miserable.

2. Keeping Your Problems Out of Her Hair

❖ Don't limit what your child eats because you have to limit what you eat.

❖ Don't approach your child's food portions the same way you now have to approach yours. Don't weigh, measure, or in any other way become obsessional about her food.

❖ If your child is sitting with a group of children and each of them has several crackers, don't snatch the last cracker out of your child's hand, shrieking or gritting your teeth, "Oh, no, no, no! You've had enough! They'll make you fat!" Children often eat more in the presence of other children. It's a moment of companionable sociability. Leave her alone. Let her have fun and make friends.

❖ If you're at a party and your child wants another scoop of ice cream, don't refuse, voicing your concern that she'll get fat or she's had enough. A party is an appropriate time to eat cake and ice cream. Your four-year-old doesn't sneak into the kitchen late at night and eat all the Häagen-Dazs while standing in front of the open freezer door!

❖ Don't watch every bite she puts in her mouth as if it were poisoning her.

3. Overcompensating

Here are some ways I've seen moms overcompensate for the rigidity they grew up with. If any variation of these seems familiar, you might consider *not* doing them:

❖ Allowing your child to eat anywhere she wants to in the house. It's not sanitary, for one thing. You will have food, crumbs, and bugs all over the place. Furthermore, eating for your child then becomes something she does half-consciously. It encourages her to space out, no longer connecting food to hunger.

❖ Not giving your child a sense of mealtime. Feeding on demand is a very sensible way to deal with an infant's hunger. Past baby-hood, however, it becomes counterproductive. Establish an or-derly progression of the day, marked in part by meals.

❖ Allowing your child to wander around holding food she's no longer eating. If your child needs to hold something, which many toddlers do, find something more appropriate than food as a to-tem.

4. Handling Children's Weight

Because we put so much emphasis on our own weight, we sometimes get messed up about our child's weight.

❖ If your child is in the low-weight percentiles, do not try and "fatten her up."
❖ If she is medically underweight your doctor will help you.
❖ If your child is in the ninety-ninth percentile of weight and your doctor feels she's healthy, she is a big kid. Somebody's gotta be the biggest.
❖ Try not to call a bigger kid "fat," as in, "You're such a little fattie! Look at that tum-tum!"
❖ If your child is overweight because of a physiological imbalance, your doctor will help you.
❖ If your child is not overweight because of a medical reason, you need to readjust your family's eating and exercise habits, for your own health as well as for your child's.

SECTION 3: COMMON QUESTIONS

A reminder: During the first two years babies have no "issues" with food. Playing games about food with a child this age is inappropriate and introduces "issues."

AROUND SIX MONTHS

Question: My baby seems to want to eat what I eat. What should I do?

Answer: Unless you're eating something the wrong size that could choke her, such as whole grapes, hot dogs, mozzarella sticks, or peanut butter, or you're drinking coffee, soda, or alcohol, offer her a taste. Have you met any babies from China? They arrive in this country at six months eating noodle and rice dishes that we think are way too sophisticated for a baby's palette. Don't assume that your baby can eat only pureed carrots from a jar. If you're eating something inappropriate, find something else on the table to hand her. She's ready to explore and join you. This has layers attached: The first and foremost is food; the secondary layer is social. She wants to do what you do. Follow her lead.

Question: My baby makes the most-horrified faces when she tries new foods. Did I poison her?

Answer: No. Most babies look as if they just ate tar every time they get a new taste. Some specialists say a baby has to try a new food about ten times before the taste is palatable. Just keep offering it every once in a while till she gets used to it.

Question: My baby wants to drink my water. Should I give it to her?

Answer: Yes! Offer a sip from the very glass you're using, unless it's delicate crystal that might break. Many babies, particularly nursing babies, skip sippy cups, bottles, and in-between nipples and go directly to a cup when given the opportunity. Water is the healthiest drink around. Encourage your child to develop a taste for it.

Question: My doctor hasn't given me the okay about solid foods, but my baby is reaching out for them.

Answer: Give her some. Your baby's pediatric visits are regulated by schedule. Her growth is not.

Question: My baby slams her mouth shut and turns her face from the spoon.

Answer: She's done. Clean up.

Question: Sometimes I can't get the food into my baby's mouth fast enough. She acts as if she's starving. She finishes one bowl and opens her mouth for more!

Answer: Feed her. She eats only when she's hungry, and when she's hungry she wants to eat!

Food for Thought: Babies can grow one-half inch overnight! Think what that must feel like and how hungry you'd be on that particular day!

SECOND HALF OF THE FIRST YEAR

Question: My baby wants to hold the spoon herself.

Answer: Let her. If she's not getting any food, give her a spoon to hold while you do the actual feeding with another. Some babies have independent natures. These babies appreciate finger foods. Don't discourage independence.

Question: My baby refuses to take finger food and/or hold her own bottle.

Answer: Some babies are like that. When she's older she will feed herself. Right now she wants her mommy to do it. Life doesn't let you be a baby for too long. Please let her be a baby while she is, in fact, a baby.

TODDLERS

Question: My toddler threw her food off her high-chair tray.

Answer: She just told you she's done eating. Clear the food away, saying, "I see you're finished." Don't make it a big deal and she won't. However, if you *do* make it a deal by saying "No! No!" be prepared to live in the food-fight scene from *National Lampoon's Animal House*. Your toddler will enjoy watching your eyes bug every time she throws her food.

Question: My toddler insists on holding food in both hands.

Answer: Some toddlers are two-fisted food-holders. This quirky little habit usually disappears after several months. But if you insist that she not hold food in both hands, then you, not your child, have created an unpleasant emotional issue around food that doesn't have to exist.

Question: My toddler's a cheese freak (bread freak, pasta freak, or the particular food fondness of your child). This means that at almost any given moment this is the food of choice.

Answer: Rather than trying to curtail the preference, try making up for it in other ways. A cheese freak, for example, is getting lots of protein and fat. Back off on other dairy foods, but see if you can get broccoli and other high-calcium foods in her tum-tum. Buy unprocessed cheeses, to avoid additives. For bread and pasta freaks, try whole-wheat versions. If they won't accept whole-wheat ones, choose brands that have the least amount of additives. If you're ambitious and have the time, bake breads. You can throw in vegetables and soy flour, and if they don't drink milk add some powdered milk. The point is to compensate the best you can nutritionally without setting up "forbidden foods" while they're young.

BABIES, TODDLERS, AND PRESCHOOLERS

Question: My child seems to be a binge eater, wanting nothing but fruit one week and then nothing but bread the following.

Answer: This is not binge eating as it would be in an adult. This is a normal manifestation of your child instinctively eating what and how much of certain kinds of foods her body needs. Over the course of several weeks or a month, she will take in everything, if you don't make it an issue.

Question: Sometimes my child refuses to eat for days at a time.

Answer: She's not hungry. She will eat when she's hungry.

Question: Sometimes my child eats like there's no tomorrow.

Answer: Children have growth spurts as well as particularly active days. If you notice that your child is really packing it away, just for fun see if in the next week or two you start thinking her clothes must've shrunk in the dryer. If everything suddenly seems too small, she had a growth spurt.

Question: My children always wants to eat another kid's lunch!

Answer: Eating is a very social experience. Children naturally understand this. If you have a particular friend you go to the playground with, you can even plan in advance. If you want your child to have extra vitamin C, ask her to pack some red peppers. She may want her child to eat whole-wheat bread, which he won't do at home, so you pack that. After a bit of Mom drama ("Oh, this is Matthew's lunch, and this is George's. Well, okay, if you really want to . . ."), trade lunch boxes and you're all set!

PRESCHOOLERS

By this age, no matter how beautifully and nonemotionally you have handled food during her first few years, "stuff" starts to happen. In the same way that we adults set a pretty table, sometimes crave ambience, and have other ways of eating besides just slopping it in, so might you remember that your child has age-appropriate cravings and desires about food and its presentation. Furthermore, sometimes a good-natured game is not out of line during this period of life, whereas earlier it is dysfunctional.

Question: My child used to love vegetables. Now, even if I stand on my head, she won't eat them.

Answer: I don't know whether it's external forces or a change in their taste buds, but many children go off vegetables around this age. Make sure they get plenty of fresh fruit, particularly red and orange ones, which pack a lot of nutrition. Here are some suggestions for the kind of playful approach that will get a few bites in without making sweets the objects of desire and vegetables the "bad guys," à la "No cookies until you've finished your carrots."

❖ Said with high drama: "Don't—whatever you do, under any circumstances—eat anything that's *green*. Please, oh, please." Laughter, and down goes the string bean. You can also "not let them eat" anything crunchy, anything that got pulled out of the garden, anything red or orange (fruits and veggies, not Froot-Loop orange!).

❖ Build a forest out of mashed potatoes and broccoli. See if your child can eat the forest.
❖ Make a game of eating first one color, then another: There's some green, there's some orange, there's some green, there's some orange. Avoid stuffing your child; a few bites are plenty!

Question: My child goes ballistic if her mashed potatoes touch her chicken on the plate.
Answer: Make sure her foods don't touch.
Question: My kid can't stand foods that are "jumbled and yucky."
Answer: Don't offer your child stews, etc. Keep the foods separate for a child who wants them that way.
Question: My child is a picky eater. If it weren't for peanut butter and jelly she'd be dead from starvation.
Answer: Thank your lucky stars there's peanut butter and jelly. Many nursery schoolers, and on into elementary school for that matter, are creatures of habit. Only one lunch will do. It's comforting and predictable for them. Don't make a big deal out of it. *Let* them eat what they *will* eat. Exception: Tuna fish should not be their daily diet for months on end. The mercury levels are high enough in tuna to cause concern for a growing body. In the last couple of decades several people have gotten mercury poisoning from tuna. It has not been widely publicized, because they were "weirdos"—adults who ate tuna, and only tuna, every day for years at a time. But a weirdo adult eats exactly like a typical preschooler!

Once upon a time and long ago, food was scarce for most people. In order to eat a piece of chicken you had to raise it, feed it, kill it, and build a fire (and chop the wood) to cook it so you could share it with your family of seven. All this work for one little chicken wing, because you gave your husband and kids the other parts. Today you sit on your tush in the car, push a shopping cart fifty feet, and do a great big stretch to the back of the meat case. You throw it in a pan that you don't even have to scrub and knock off an easy half a chicken all by your lonesome.

We suffer from overabundance. And yet all of our attitudes about food, especially when raising children, hearken back to a time when a mother should have encouraged her child to eat, eat, eat. A lot of them didn't know where their next meal was coming from. We do. And if we all keep eating and teach our children to keep eating with the inappropriate fear of famine lurking over our shoulders, we will encourage two equally unpleasant scenarios: Either our children will overeat themselves right into the hospital, or they will overeat themselves right into not enough food to go around. Neither is a particularly pretty legacy to leave our children.

SUMMARY:

- ❖ Food is for nutrition.
- ❖ Eating together is social.
- ❖ Food is not a substitute for emotional needs.
- ❖ In order to teach our children healthy eating habits, many of us must rethink our own.
- ❖ Once unhealthy eating habits are established they are extremely difficult to change.

Sweet Dreams

There is a reason why sleep is perhaps the largest challenge we face in parenting. Like all developmental growth, learning to sleep all night long in your own bed is a complicated, long-term affair involving physical and psychological maturation. But unlike other areas of development, with all the normal fits and starts of integrating a major life lesson, this learning takes place in the middle of the night. Our defenses are down, we're not thinking clearly, and everybody's discombobulated.

During a baby's early infancy most mothers drift through seamless days and nights, grabbing bits of sleep here and there, perhaps hormonally programmed to accommodate baby time.

After a month or two some babies begin to self-regulate, learning the difference between night and day, extending their hours of sleep, slipping into their cribs easily. Some of these children remain "good sleepers" throughout their childhoods.

Most, however, are not like this. Some babies never "take" to sleep from early on. Others throw their families curveballs. They lull them into thinking they're "sleepers," and then *bam,* the mother who demurely announced in class how sleep was a nonissue with her one-year-old shows up bleary-eyed and frantic because her now-two-year-old hasn't slept longer than five hours at a clip for the last three months.

Whether we have a baby who doesn't seem to be the least interested in this "night and day, sleep and play" idea or a toddler who has begun challenging us at night as well as all day, at some point most of us look around, bags under our eyes, and say, "Hold 'er, Newt! Something's gotta give!"

Many of us, sooner or later, turn to the experts.

I'd like to give my opinion right up front: *No* expert can—or should—give general, across-the-board prescriptions for sleep.

Each child has his own sleep needs. As with food, there are *mathematical averages* of what a child needs at a given age. But your particular child may fall at either extreme used to calculate the average. Furthermore, just as with food, sleep needs and habits change according to activity and development.

However, since I know that for most of you it's just a question of time before you call in the big guns or at least hear them out, I, too, am going to turn to the experts first. Then I'll pass along some ideas from we mere mortals!

SECTION 1: THE EXPERTS: OPPOSITE ENDS OF THE SPECTRUM

Food for Thought: If most babies and children went to bed and stayed there until morning without so much as a toss, a turn, or a peep, if sleeping through the night was learned as easily as walking, we wouldn't have so many "sleep experts," would we?

The two most famous experts you are likely to consult are Ferber and the husband-and-wife team of Sears and Sears. They are diametrically opposed.

Ferber's book, *Solve Your Child's Sleep Problems,* complete with pages of precise charts and incremental schedules, makes a persuasive case for the baby version of tough love: Let 'em cry. Teaching them to go to sleep alone is for their own good.

Nighttime Parenting by Sears and Sears presents an equally compelling opposite view: Keep 'em in bed with you and in your room till they're ready to go it alone.

I have seen enough families who swear by the Ferber method to know that it *works.* The child goes to bed and stays there all night long. Indisputably, after enough crying any child will eventually quiet down. But I am far from convinced that teaching a child that he must deal with fear alone in the night is a useful lesson.

The Sears, whose comfortable family includes six kids, share with us that they find marital intimacy in other parts of the house. They have to. Their bedroom is crawling with kids! Without a doubt their hearts are in the right place. I'm not so sure, however, that their children are.

For my taste, Ferber leans way too far in one direction: Run a household in a well-regimented, shipshape way, with a distinct chain of command from the top down—come hell or high water. The *parents' needs* supersede those of the children's. The Sears, on the other hand, seem to list a bit to the port side: *Children's needs* dominate the house.

For all you moms out there to whom Ferber or the Sears make complete sense, if you decide to follow their leads I ask you simply to consider the following ideas.

A. IF FERBER RINGS TRUE TO YOU

If you like the sound of his approach—and I must admit that he makes some salient points—I ask you to do the following:

❖ Read the book. This way you will understand *what* you are doing and *why*. This will give you the insight necessary to accommodate your particular child.

❖ Do not ask your friend to photocopy the page on the amount of time you should let your baby cry and follow it blindly without understanding what you are doing.

❖ Do not pay any attention to your pediatrician's revised one-page chart, which is exactly like Ferber's except the amounts of time have been fiddled with.

❖ Both parents should not only *read* the book, but *agree* both in principle and practice. A genuine family nightmare is when the baby is screaming his head off and the parents are arguing about what to do—in the dark, in the middle of the night, in your robes. That is mental cruelty to all of you.

❖ He makes a valuable point: If we, as adults, were to wake up in a place that was different from where we went to sleep, we would freak out; therefore we're asking a lot of a baby to have him go to sleep in our arms only to wake up in his crib. It is useful for your child to learn how to go to sleep on his own. *How* you teach him this valuable lesson, however, is another story. Ferber's *method* may or may not appeal to your family.

❖ Do some soul-searching. Make sure you are not seizing on an expert's advice to get you off an emotional hook. If you find yourself at 3:00 A.M. thinking, "I cannot bear this one more moment. If I don't get a break, at least at night, I'm going to lose it," that may mean that motherhood's relentless meeting of somebody else's needs and its attendant irregularities are stressing you out. You are certainly not the first woman to ever feel this. Even the most nurturing people in the world can take only so much. Sleep deprivation, in fact, is a method of torture in prison camps. You sound as if you need a break and somebody to take care of you a little bit during this understandably stressful time. If you can arrange for baby coverage during the day, do so. Grab some sleep, go to a movie, see a friend who has no kids and talk about anything not related to babies. Talk to your husband, a friend, your mother, or another mother with older children about how you're feeling, as long as it's someone you can trust to be sympathetic and not tell you to stop complaining and buck up. Find some way to take care of and refresh yourself enough during the day to face the night. But please do not use Ferber to legitimize shutting the door on your crying baby at night because you have put out emotionally as much as you are able to all day long.

❖ Please *do not* "Ferberize" a baby younger than six months old.

❖ If your baby is sleeping through the night after two or three nights of five minutes' worth of halfhearted whimpering, thank your lucky stars. You have a baby who takes easily to sleeping on his own.

❖ If you have spent a week with everyone in your family an emotional wreck, if your baby has cried so hard he has thrown up or has finally fallen asleep, exhausted, over the bars of his crib, rethink what you are doing. This might not be the most caring way to introduce your child to the pleasures of independent sleep.

❖ If you find yourself in the middle of the night rocking back and forth on the edge of your bed, religiously rereading the section about how you are not damaging your child, while your baby wails in the other room, perhaps this method is not such a good choice for your family.

❖ If you hear yourself saying more than once during the first eighteen months of your child's life, "Oh, yeah, we had to Ferberize him *again,*" step back. Listen to your child. He's a good little boy. He's trying so hard to please you and to learn. But he's also trying to tell you something about his emotional, developmental needs, which in some way are not being met. Pay attention.

B: IF THE SEARS RING TRUE TO YOU

The Sears make many points that are right on the mark for my money. I really recommend reading their work. They offer many valuable insights and practical tips. They are the biggest proponents of the family bed, an idea that is catching on around the country, I think deservedly, in the wake of the rigorous Ferber method. If sharing your bed and your room with your growing child as a regular nightly routine is appealing, keep in mind several things:

❖ Some people will think you're crazy. They will let you know their feelings in no uncertain terms. They will tell you you're spoiling your baby. Murmur noncommittally and change the subject. It's none of their darn business.

❖ It is an interesting comment on our society that "Ferberites" tend to look down their noses at "Searsites," whom they consider spineless, whereas "Searsites" tend to feel either secretive and guilty or morally superior and self-righteous for enjoying sleeping with their babies. Both attitudes regard sleep as a political or religious issue. Sleep is a developmental issue. Every human being born on the face of the earth must grow into it in his own way.

❖ The Sears's point is true: We are one of the few cultures that banish their children to another room and make them sleep in "cages." Many other cultures permit their young to sleep with them. Many other cultures also insert plates into their lips, hack off the hands of pickpockets, and eat cats.

❖ If you and your husband are not in agreement about having your baby sleep in bed with you, something's got to give. Either your husband is feeling displaced, which is not good for your marriage, or you are feeling that you can't follow your own mothering instincts, which is also a strain on a union. One compromise, although it, too, creates its own set of discordant reverberations, is this: Sleep with your baby at nap time. Make his nighttime crib as comfy-cozy as possible. Sometimes this works, sometimes it doesn't. Somehow you and your husband have to come to a mutually comfortable agreement in order for your family to flourish.

❖ Do some soul-searching. Are you meeting your baby's need or yours? In the first few months, particularly for a nursing family, having an infant in bed *feels* right. Hands down, no questions. I think nature built it that way. But sometimes, with an older baby, *he* may acclimate to sleeping alone quite happily. It is *you* who feels a profound physical loss, a lack of wholeness without him near you. There are many ways to keep that strong bond alive. But even if you want to cling to him forever, parenting is a constant, often difficult process of letting go. If it is you, and not your baby, feeling as if something is missing in bed while you sleep, face your fears. Get a teddy bear. Hold your husband. Let your baby take baby steps. His first, safe step along the glorious path of life may very well be his own snug crib.

❖ Do some more soul-searching. Some people get all bent out of shape about the family bed because of its "impropriety," suggesting that there are underlying sexual implications. That's nonsense. There's no difference between feeling close to your child while cuddling on the couch and letting them feel the comfort of your body when they sleep. But there is a danger of establishing an imbalance in the home that may not be useful for anybody. During the first half year or so of having a baby, we actively engage in learning our mommy and daddy roles. Husband and wife go down the tubes. As they should. After that, however, everybody needs to regroup. If your child has his own space in your room and his own bedtime, that's reasonable. However, if you find that somehow you have slipped into a pattern where Mommy goes to bed with baby or growing child and stays there all night, Daddy falls asleep on the couch because he isn't ready to go to bed at eight, and by the time he's ready for bed he goes into the bedroom, realizes there's not enough room for him, and goes back to the living room so he can get a good night's sleep, you no longer have a family bed. You have a major imbalance that needs to be corrected for every member of your family.

❖ What starts out in infancy as incredibly sensitive to your baby's needs and your own physical need to be near your offspring sometimes makes less and less sense the older they get. Put more graphically, the tender, gentle newborn who smells so wonderful you could cry turns into a sweating, thrashing two-year-old who sleeps perpendicular with his foot jammed into your jugular vein and his head shoved into your husband's kidney. *And* he steals the covers. *And* he makes little burbling sounds that are almost as annoying as your husband's snores. This doesn't mean you shouldn't let him sleep with you during babyhood. It means you should be prepared to make a transition at some point that may be rocky. Show me a transition that isn't rocky and I'll show you something that isn't a transition.

IN SUMMATION

As much as enormous amounts of the practical techniques that the Sears have to offer are extremely useful and definitely worth your while to look at, I am concerned that their basic philosophical position leaves too much room for imbalance in too many homes.

On the other side of the spectrum we find Ferber.

We don't expect a baby to be able to feed himself, control his own excrement, or spend longer than fifteen minutes in a room untended. We don't call over our shoulder to our kindergartner, "Mom's going to run to the supermarket. I'll be back in a couple of hours. Stay in the den."

And yet Ferber advises that in the dark of night when the winds blow, the house creaks, sirens shriek, and dogs bark warnings in the distance, we should expect, require, and insist that our young child who suddenly awakens lie there, with a stuffed rabbit for company if he's lucky and a piece of plastic stuck in his mouth, till daylight dawns. Because grown-ups need their sleep. And children need to learn their place. Night in and night out, no matter what's going on outside or in.

Your child will learn to sleep. In his bed. All night long. Alone. I promise.

This complicated piece of human behavior, however, may very well take him several years, if not a whole decade. Once parents come to terms with that, often things go more smoothly.

I believe he will learn this lesson happily and securely if he knows that he has loving adults right down the hall, sleeping soundly, who will wake in an instant, available to him—on a night-to-night basis, whenever he needs them.

SECTION 2: ON A GIVEN NIGHT

With sleep, as in all of parenting, balance is the key. I feel it is useful for you, your child, and your family to be able to discriminate *on a given night* what your child needs and how to give it to him.

Sleep, and everything it represents, is a complicated issue.

Developmentally, sleep is a separation issue.

The first painful separation of birth resulting in exquisite joy is a metaphor for the rest of our days and nights together. At night, in the dark, in our sleep, both for the parent and the child, we relive that separation over and over, sleep a nightly birth, not a death as some call it. Some nights for our child the path is clear, speedy, free; he whizzes along it alone. Other nights, if he could he'd crawl back inside the warm, protected place.

Frequently in families an adult's need and a child's need may be in direct conflict. Nowhere do we see this more dramatically than with sleep.

You need a good night's sleep.

But here's the clinker: When you have a young child you may not always be able to get a good night's sleep.

In the first year, and often all the way through elementary school, your child's emotional need for comfort and security may have to supersede your need for sleep on a given night, however urgent and real your need for sleep may be.

An adult has many options available during the course of a night. Let's say you're worried about something. You can't fall asleep or you wake up.

You can cuddle in the spoon position or make love with your spouse, then go back to sleep. You can read or turn on the tube. You can get out of bed. Turn up the heat, turn down the heat, have a glass of wine, throw in a load of laundry, pay bills, and so on indefinitely into the wee hours of the morning. Perhaps you successfully address the issue and go back to sleep. Perhaps you don't.

What options does your child have?

If he's a little baby *all he can do is cry.*

If he's older he can cry. He can cry out—sometimes quite cheerily. He may be able to find a toy to amuse himself, unless it's pitch black. Maybe he can reach for a pacifier or his favorite blanket and go back to sleep. Maybe.

If he's old enough he can try to climb out of his crib or even successfully leave his room—to find you.

That's it. A child basically has *one option.*

He can want you and get you. Or he can want you and not get you. Period.

Notwithstanding his limited options, his fears, concerns, and reasons for having his sleep disrupted are varied. It may be physical. He may be teething, have a wet diaper, gas pains. He may be hungry. He may be hot or cold.

Sometimes, and more problematic, his reasons for waking are nebulous. He may be lonely. He may have had a bad dream. He may be going through separation anxiety. The older child may have social worries—day care, school, a baby-sitter he doesn't like.

Consider this one: There may be tension in your home. The happiest couples in the world sometimes get real mad at each other. Your empathetic child may have psychologically sound reasons for not wanting to be asleep. Your child may be afraid that you or your husband won't be there when he wakes up.

Often when you return to work, or sometimes out of the blue if you've always worked full-time and he's completely happy with his baby-sitter, he may wake up six times during the night *simply to know that you are there.*

These are just some of the reasons that a child's sleep may be disrupted.

The practical reasons are easily handled. You certainly wouldn't let your baby stay in a wet diaper. You change him and you all go back to sleep. Most parents can identify and respond appropriately to these needs, although hunger in the middle of the night sometimes throws us for a loop.

The more complex reasons, such as loneliness and fear, are often harder to know how to deal with. Like other aspects of parenting, we are required to be more mature emotionally than we sometimes feel. We must strive for an ideal: to recognize someone else's real needs in the moment and to meet them appropriately. Talk about a big lesson for parents.

I urge you to consider during the day so that you can remember during the night several ideas:

❖ Your child has limited options for dealing with sleep disruptions. You are his main comfort.
❖ *Your need* to get a good night's sleep may not always coincide with *his need* to be comforted in the middle of a particular night.
❖ Your instincts in the middle of the night are the best ones to follow.
❖ If you have to err, as we all do, I suggest erring on the side of softness. The child who is held and comforted too much is better off than the child who isn't comforted enough.

A. ESTABLISHING GOOD HABITS

Just as you have nightly rituals before bed, so should your child. Since every family has its own rhythm and style, the specifics are less important than consistency. I'll just mention the obvious.

Useful Rituals

❖ About an hour before bedtime, start winding down the day with quiet activities suited to your child's age. This doesn't mean he can't laugh. It means don't introduce a wild game of hide-and-seek. (Hello, daddies! Did you hear that?)
❖ If you include a bath, you may find that you need to time it a good hour before bedtime. Baths perk up many children.

Toddler Tip: If your child is at a struggle stage, consider getting him into his pjs well in advance of bedtime, even before dinner. This way you sidestep a free-for-all over pjs right before bed, when everyone gets all upset and has to spend even longer calming down.

❖ Some experts advise early suppers to induce better sleep; others advise giving a child good stick-to-the-ribs food close to bedtime to see him through the night. The reason for this discrepancy is that every child is different! Only you can determine the timing, kind, and amount of food toward the end of the day for your child; furthermore, you will have to readjust to suit his changing needs.

❖ Obvious bathroom rituals include brushing teeth, using the toilet, and washing.

❖ Once in his room, different families opt for pleasant closings to the day, such as saying prayers, spending quiet time going over the day, singing, saying a special word about all the people they love.

❖ As early as one for some children and usually by two, kids are ready for books. At whatever age your child finds them interesting and soothing, establish a limit: "We'll read three books before we turn out the light." This establishes a finite time for reading that can be used for the years to follow.

Toddler Tip from Our Editor: "Whenever Mary Kate won't have a book, song, or my usual cooing, I tell her the story of Mary Kate. It involves repeating her name a lot, as well as Mommy, Daddy, all her relatives and friends. She's always such a star in these stories that they make her feel good *and* tired."

❖ Choose whatever hugs, kisses, and phrases are appealing to you before you turn out the light. Then *turn out the light.*

❖ If your child needs to be reassured, go back in. Hug, kiss, say "night, night" again, pat his head, pull the covers up, *whatever* he needs to settle down. We're talking about young children here, not marine boot camp!

Less Useful Rituals

❖ Always allowing your baby to fall asleep on your breast or body. Music boxes, mobiles, lullabies, and back rubs help a baby fall asleep in a crib.

❖ Falling asleep in front of the tube. Although when he's a baby you may find yourself in exhaustion sinking down on the couch to space out and have him fall asleep on your body, this is not a great habit for a child to develop. After around six months make an effort, no matter how tired you may feel, to establish a bedtime ritual. Some families with toddlers find themselves, tired, winding down together in the parents' bed, TV on, till the child's eyes flutter closed and he nods off. N.G. (No good!) He has no sense of bedtime, establishing that the day has an ending as well as a beginning. Some families even put TVs and VCRs in their children's rooms as part of the child's nightly routine. But cuddling and reading are so much richer for a family than allowing your child to feel more connected to Barney than he does to Mom and Dad.

❖ Bedtime should not be carved in stone. Let's say bedtime is 7:30. At 7:30 on a particular night your child may be laughing. Interrupting with a firm bark of "Bedtime!" engenders a fight. But by 7:45, when the laughter has naturally run its course, he will be winding down himself. How much more pleasant suggesting we start getting ready for bed becomes when it's not an urgent matter.

Sure sounds nice to me. Personally, I lay eyes on the cover of *Good Night, Moon* and I'm out.

But what if you find yourself not having perfect evenings after the light goes *click* and you're—dare I say it—*free!* Free to talk on the phone, read a real book, fall in love again with your husband, free to *sleep!* Just what if it doesn't go quite like that?

B. "PROBLEMS"

Some babies and young children go into their cribs easily anywhere from 7:00 to 8:30 P.M. and stay there peacefully until 6:00 to 8:00 A.M. the next morning. If your child is one of these I suggest getting down on your hands and knees to praise the sleep gods!

Many more, however, don't go to bed easily. They wake frequently during the night or are ready to get out of bed at 5:00 A.M. With all due respect to Dr. Ferber, these children do not have sleep problems. Their *parents* have problems with the way their children sleep.

Neither I nor anyone else can tell you night by night how to deal with your child. I can, however, share with you some information that may make your life easier.

1. Predictable Times when Sleep Gets Out of Whack

❖ Sleep disruptions frequently occur around six to eight months, most likely due to teething and/or separation anxiety.

❖ Being sick. Colds, fevers, chicken pox, and all the usual childhood illnesses.

❖ Rocky moments during your marriage, due to conflict between you and your husband, external pressures such as job insecurity, illness, etc.

❖ The arrival of a new sibling.

❖ During any major developmental burst forward: a major acquisition of language skills, major mobility leaps such as learning to crawl or walk (although sometimes walking exhausts them so much they're dead to the world till morning), potty training, or social growth spurts, such as learning to share, not to hit, etc.

❖ During any major change in life, such as moving, beginning day care, nursery school, or kindergarten, or Mommy returning to work.

❖ Anytime a crib or bed is used as a place for punishment.

❖ Being in unfamiliar surroundings.

Baby Your Baby: When adults go through trying times or major changes, we often do nice things for ourselves. We see a friend, call our sisters, treat ourselves to manicures, massages, or a movie. Why? Because these little things comfort us and take our minds off whatever stressful event we're living through. Your kid obviously doesn't need a day at a health spa to get his head together. He needs a night with Mommy. Maybe two nights. Maybe three. Maybe a whole week when you are in his bed, or he is in yours. Be as nice to your child as you want somebody to be to you.

2. Once-in-a-while Wake-ups: Going to Your Child in the Middle of the Night
Babies

The longer your baby cries before you get there, the harder it will be to get him back to sleep. If he is really wound up he will be completely justified in not wanting you to leave. This is the most powerful argument for keeping your baby's crib either in your room or in a room close to yours until he's old enough to move down the hall.

❖ If your baby cries, go see what's the matter. Obviously, take care of any practical problems. A baby of a few months needs to eat. An older baby may need a change of diaper. Does the room feel hot or cold? Was there a loud noise? Often, a gentle pat on the back, a lullaby, and baby goes back to sleep.

❖ Consider washrags instead of pacifiers for babies who need to suck. They're soft, easy to wash and replace, and aren't unpleasant pieces of plastic rattling around in the crib.

❖ Some teething babies suffer more than others. If your baby is in pain from teething, hold him. All night long if that's what he needs. If he really suffers, your doctor can help with pain relievers. But there is no better comfort in the whole wide world than being held by your mommy.

❖ Some babies, sometimes, for unknown reasons, need to be picked up, held, and walked around. I know that doesn't sound modern, but they're babies. Most of them, when comforted, will settle down enough to be slipped back into their cribs. If they startle awake and cry, try putting them down and rubbing their backs and talking or singing till they drift off. (If you're having trouble with this, the Sears have a marvelous section on specific ways to help a baby stay asleep.)

❖ After enough of this has been unsuccessful, some families take their child into bed with them. I think it's a darn good idea.

❖ Often, the next night, when the baby feels more secure for who-knows-what reason, the episode will *not be repeated.* They will sleep all night long. Until the next round of teething, loneliness, or baby angst.

Toddlers

Toddlers don't have as many physical disruptions, such as teething, as babies do; their disturbances tend to be more developmental. When they call out to you, go. They need you.

❖ Some toddlers settle down once they know you're there adjusting the covers, stroking their heads, rubbing their backs.

❖ If it's not a physical discomfort, such as a dirty diaper, temperature control, or a slipped blanket, and none of your soothing has worked, your toddler might profit from slipping into your bed for the night. Most often, when your child feels secure tomorrow, he'll sleep all night long.

❖ A practical solution: Many families find that a couch or mattress in the *child's* room helps. Mommy lies down in child's room, talks to child, holds child's hand, child drifts off to sleep not feeling lonely, Mommy crawls back in her own bed—if she's still awake!

❖ *Night terrors* "wake" some children, or more precisely wake some parents. (The earliest I've heard of was an eight-month-old, but it's most frequent around the twos.) These are much more frightening for the parents than for the child, who usually doesn't remember them. They sit up in bed, often screaming. Their eyes are open, but they don't see you, recognize you, or respond to any of your soothing words or gestures. Then they flop down and go back to sleep. My advice is to comfort them as best as you can, since they don't seem to know you, and after you get back in bed, as your adrenaline stops pumping, look out at the stars and ponder the imponderable. You have just had your first taste of your child going places where you cannot follow and what you do doesn't matter. Talk about a terror!

Preschoolers

For the preschooler, just as for babies and toddlers, there are some nights when they simply wake up. For an occasional wake-up, what is bothering him, although interesting, is not necessarily as important as what response his waking gets. If you are awakened by a little prod in the tush and a whispered, "Mommy?":

❖ Some families pull the child into their bed and go back to sleep. Whatever was bothering the child that night won't bother him tomorrow.

❖ Another approach is to whisper, "Shh. Everybody's asleep. Let's go into your room." Take him by the hand and lie down in bed with him. Hold him. When he is fast asleep, tiptoe out.

Predictable Problem: "Easy for *you* to say. Every time I try and move, those arms reach out like an octopus and drag me back!"
Alternative 1: "Roll over, baby. Mommy has to go to the bathroom. I'll be right back." This is the only outright lie I have ever told my daughter. Half-asleep, she nods, rolls over, and is out.

Alternative 2: If you find yourself feeling "trapped" in bed by your needy preschooler, make a conscious effort to relax physically muscle by muscle. Your body relaxing will let your child relax enough to fall into a deep sleep.

❖ Many completely trained preschoolers find going to the bathroom in the middle of the night overwhelming. They need you to help them in their half-asleep state to get to the john, do it, get back in bed, and back to sleep.

Vacations: All Ages

Tell your child you're on vacation and that it feels funny to sleep in a different bed, but he'll get used to it. When you get home, say how nice it is to be home. Be prepared for wake-ups for several days to a week, depending on your child. Planning on having a fabulous vacation where you can catch up on all the sleep you've missed is a setup for disappointment.

3. Becoming a Pattern

Sometimes, whether from predictable disruptions such as change or growth or because of developmental issues such as fear—or reasons that may forever remain a mystery even to the child in question—a family will find itself confronting the odd demon of consistent trouble with sleeping. This may manifest either in trouble going to bed or trouble staying in bed.

For Babies All the Way Through Childhood

Including separation anxiety, bogeymen, and monsters in the closet, or any other fear that presents itself.

Talk to Your Child

This is a solution that many people ignore. With a baby as young as eight months, and certainly with an older child, explain *in a calm moment during the day* what's what.

❖ During the day, take a tour of his room. Show him the window, the curtains, the closet door, the lamp. Point out all the familiar things in the room. If he can look out his window from his crib or bed, remind him that his friends the moon and stars are right outside. Pull the blinds so that the room is darkened. Point out any shadows and explain what they are. Point out how things look different in the dark.

❖ Then tell him that at night Mommy needs to sleep. Daddy needs to sleep. And Daniel needs to sleep. If he wakes up he should look around his room and say to himself, "There's my window, my door, and my bookcase. This is my room. Mommy's asleep and Daddy's asleep and Daniel can go back to sleep too."

❖ Some children like night-lights, which you can remind him will always be on.

❖ Don't talk about all this in the middle of the night while he's afraid, or right at bedtime, which might make him nervous about waking up.

❖ This plain, simple explanation of what *should* be happening works, not with all children, but enough times to make it worth your while to try.

Lesson: *Mommy gave me words and advice that help me comfort myself. (Preschoolers will often even tell you proudly the next morning, blow by blow, how they woke up, looked around, reminded themselves of Mommy and Daddy sleeping, and laid back down!)*

For One Year to Eighteen Months

Let's say your child has been sleeping like . . . a baby. Bedtime comes, into the crib, "Night, night," and off we go. Then all of a sudden, around a year old or so, things change. Baby might even start pointing to your bed, even going so far as to say, "Mommy and Daddy bed." Before you run off half-cocked into the Ferber/Sears maelstrom, consider this: **You don't have a sleep problem. You have a linen problem!**

Take a look at your bed. It is cozy; the linens are enveloping. Now take a gander at your kid's crib. It has a small, hard mattress with a plastic protective covering that crinkles and makes him sweat. There are no pillows. If the kid's lucky he's got a little tiny baby blanket. If you saw his sleeping arrangements on a documentary about prison, your heart would bleed for the poor unfortunate having to sleep like that.

Your baby is making transitions faster than you! You no longer have to worry about SIDS or suffocation. You have to worry that his bed is like something straight out of a Dickens' orphanage.

❖ Go get him a little pillow and a cozy comforter.

❖ Shearling or rubber-backed flannel mattress covers soften the feel of the mattress.

This simple, practical solution very frequently does the trick. Your child happily settles back down into his crib, and all talk of ''Mommy and Daddy's bed'' becomes a faint echo of the past.

Lesson: *Oh, how comfortable my crib has become. Just like Mommy's and Daddy's bed, only my size.*

For Some Children as Early as Eighteen Months

Although for most it will take another year or two, some children around a year-and-a-half suddenly begin resisting going into their crib. As we saw earlier, they may point to your bed or talk about your bed. Consider this:

You don't have a sleep problem. You have a furniture problem!

For many children, particularly large kids or thrashers, the crib itself is too small. They bang into it as they sleep. For others, the very purpose of a crib—to keep the child confined—is enraging; they experience their cribs as jails. Others, who have older siblings or who just want to do what the grown-ups do, find a crib too babyish. *Many children are ready for this transition younger than most people think.* This readiness often manifests in what looks like a ''sleep problem.'' Once again, your child may be ready to move on before you are.

Bedtime for Baby

❖ Tell your child you realize he has outgrown his crib.
❖ Take him to the bed store. Select two or three mattresses in your price range that have the qualities you want. (If your child is particularly opinionated, go on a scouting expedition with your husband ahead of time to narrow down the possibilities.) Let your child choose one.
❖ Go to the linen store. Let your child choose sheets. (Yes, even with a very young child, who may do best if presented with a choice between two!) If budget or quality is an issue, direct your child to the sheets within the category that suits your needs. *Hint:* This is not a time for your taste to prevail; this is a time for your child to be actively engaged in growing up, which includes having the right to decide which sheets he wants to sleep on. Most children are drawn to bright colors and ''kid'' patterns. If you really hate them or find the quality not good enough, use a catalog so he

doesn't see the ones that will drive you wild. If you can afford it, get overnight delivery.

❖ Praise his choices. Mean it!

> **Lesson:** *Mommy knows when it's time for me to move on. I won't have to fight with her in order to grow up.*

COMMON QUESTIONS ABOUT BEDS

Question: What about a junior bed?

Answer: I don't know what the purpose is, except to fuel the economy. Save the money for your child's education.

Question: Won't my child fall out of bed?

Answer: Yes. Your child will fall out of bed. In the beginning. Here are a few tips to help you through this period:

❖ You don't need a bed frame. Use the mattress and box springs. This lower bed, at a child's height, will make getting in and out easier, which will imbue your child with a feeling of mastery rather than ineptitude at having to struggle up into it. If it's low enough, it won't be a big deal when he falls.

❖ If you can, position the bed along a wall, avoiding the problem of falling out on both sides.

❖ For the first few nights, put an extra top sheet on the bed. Place several pillows folded in half lengthwise all along the edges of the bed, under the sheet, and then tuck the sheet loosely over the pillows and under the mattress. This makes a soft barrier that teaches your child while he's asleep the physical parameters of the bed.

❖ If your child's room is not carpeted, spring for an area rug near the bed to cushion a tumble.

❖ After the first few nights most kids kinesthetically learn how big their bed is (just the way you know!) and you can dispense with the extra pillows.

Question: What about guard rails?

Answer: Guard rails are one more expense and something hard to bang into. That puts you right back where you started if part of your child's problem was being awakened uncomfortably by hard parts of the crib. If the bed is low enough, who needs them? (The exception to this is if your child has bunk beds.)

Question: My child seems to live to figure out more and more dangerous ways to get out of his crib. If he can get out of his bed easily, Lord only knows what trouble he'll get into early in the morning or in the middle of the night.

Answer: Often, crib-climbing monkeys settle down quite nicely when no longer presented with the challenge of a cage. During the first few nights of unmitigated freedom in a bed, if he gets up in the middle of the night, he will probably come into your room. Take him back into his own bed. If you have the kind of child who during the day shinnies up the stairs on the outside of the railing and hangs from his pinky over the two-story drop to the entrance hall, you would do best to confine him to his room. A gate may be the answer, although these Captains Courageous often scoff at gates as mere child's play. I knew one mother who installed a screen door for her son's bedroom. If you have a real fearless daredevil on your hands, you might do well to consider moving his bed into your room for a few months until the novelty of free-ranging has worn off.

HANDY TRANSITION TIMES

A first birthday is a good time to move your child from your room into his own. Big fanfare, big deal, big grown-up. As long as he doesn't feel that his room is a punitive banishment. *Tips:* Extra mattress or couch in his room for a parent to join him when he's feeling too lonely; teaching your pet to share his room, particularly if your dog or cat is allowed to sleep on the bed (you have to do tick checks anyway, if you have a pet); making sure that you are Johnny-on-the-spot when he needs you and, most importantly, that he is welcomed back into your room on a need basis.

Second birthdays or seasonal changes—such as after vacation, now that the flowers are out, now that it's snowy—are good times to introduce a bed for the child who sleeps contentedly in his crib but is physically getting too big.

Special Tip for Mothers who Nurse into Toddlerhood

Many mothers and children choose to nurse beyond the first year. If you are feeling it's time to give up nursing, but your child shows no signs of wanting to stop, connecting getting a big-kid's bed with giving up nursing is a very useful way to go about it. You've substituted the trauma of giving up a treasured—or at least habitual—custom with a new growth experience. At this age you can have a nice conversation. ''You're getting bigger. It's time to stop nursing. And a bigger kid gets to have a bigger bed.'' Follow the suggestions for acquiring a bed, and when the bed is delivered make the transition.

Food for Thought: If you've chosen to nurse this long, giving it up is often as emotionally charged for you as for your child, if not more so. Many moms experience waves of strong emotion about the passage of time in their own lives and how fast their baby is growing up. Life is a series of beginnings and ends. Lucky child: He has a mommy who feels things deeply. What a rich family.

C. SOME COMMON QUESTIONS ABOUT SLEEP IN GENERAL

Question: My child wakes up at 5:30 A.M., rarin' to go. What can I do?

Answer: Children don't always have convenient sleep schedules.

Until the age of three, if they're up, you're up. If both you and your husband work, rotate morning duty. Some families work it out that the dad who goes off to work has to get up anyway, so he gets up early with the baby. In exchange the mom who stays home covers middle-of-the-night crises. Whatever practical way your family works out early-morning coverage, no child under three should be roaming around without adult supervision.

By the time they're three-, four-, and five-year-olds, they can be asked to stay in their room until you wake up (as long as you're not thinking of sleeping till noon!). Have a box of special early-morning quiet toys, such as crayons, Legos, blocks, or special library books, that your child may play with while everyone else in the house is still asleep. Most fives and many fours can turn on the TV or put in a videotape. Some families limit a child's TV to only these early-morning hours; others ban TV, preferring specially selected videos. Some can turn on the computer and play games. Whatever activity you all agree on, one hour should be the maximum of this kind of unsupervised play. By six-thirty someone in the house should be able to drag him or herself out of bed in the morning. If you have a ''rooster'' living in your home, you may need to set the alarm to make sure somebody else can get up with the chickens!

Question: Every time I think I have his nap times down, he switches.

Answer: Particularly in the first year, nap times have a way of sliding fairly rapidly. You think they get up at six, go down for a nap at ten, get up, have lunch, take another nap at three, and are ready for bed at seven-thirty. Then, *wham-o!* they're sleeping until two and wanting to nap at six. You can't always plan. This is the point. Their sleeping habits cannot, or rather should not, be tailored to suit your needs. If you notice his nap times are shifting, be prepared to change your plans.

Question: My two-year-old hates his afternoon nap.

Answer: He may not need it any longer. No one can tell you at what time and for how long your child should nap or at what age he should give up napping. The best way to tell whether your child needs a nap or needs to give up a nap is by his behavior. If your child hates napping but seems in relatively good spirits most of the day, he may no longer need the same number of naps as your sister's boy who is the same age. On the other hand, if he hates taking a nap and is a basket case—either extremely grumpy, clumsy, or displays any other signs of a kid with not enough rest—he needs to rest.

Tip for a tired child resisting going to sleep either at night or at nap time (brought to you courtesy of my daughter's wonderful nursery school): "You don't have to go to sleep. You just have to rest your body. Close your eyes and your mouth so they can rest." Two minutes later, zzzzzz. . . . . .

Question: The 6:00 P.M. nap is a killer. After a day with one, he's up till 11:00 P.M.

Answer: Baths often give children a second wind. If you see your child getting cranky in the late afternoon/early evening, tub time will buy you a couple of hours of wakefulness so you can get him to bed for the night at a reasonable hour.

Question: My child takes two-hour naps twice a day and won't go to sleep until 11:00 P.M. We're all exhausted.

Answer: Shave both naps down in ten-minute increments, one week at a time. First week, wake him ten minutes before each two hours are up. Next week, ten minutes before that, and so on, until you've gotten two one-hour naps. Alternative for a preschooler: Shave one nap down in ten-minute increments until it disappears.

Question: My four-year-old still needs a two-hour afternoon nap. My day is shot.

Answer: That's right. He needs his nap, and your day is shot. He will only be a nap-needing four-year-old for one year. You will have many more days. That is what he needs. Give it to him.

Question: My husband and I don't get home until 8:00 P.M. If our child goes to bed at 7:30 P.M., we're working to pay our baby-sitter and we might as well be a childless couple for all the time we get to spend with our son.

Answer: If you, like many couples, both work long hours or if your husband can't get home every night until eight or so, let your baby have a sophisticated bedtime—if the baby can stand it. Some babies I know don't go to sleep until eleven o'clock. If this is the case in your house, however, I would make one recommendation: When your child is around two, enroll in a toddler class where you can practice getting up and being somewhere on time. His schedule eventually needs to be readjusted in tiny increments to conform with the rest of the world by the time he enters day care, nursery school, or kindergarten.

Question: Our baby-sitter has our child on a nice, regular schedule of meals and naps. But on the weekend we can't get our child down for a nap to save our souls.

Answer: Just as you have a schedule during the week that differs from your weekend schedule, so does your child. Your child's idea of a fabulous weekend, however, may not reflect your fantasy of lying around doing the crossword puzzle, having brunch, puttering in the yard, seeing friends, and catching up with chores. Your child's dream weekend is being with Mommy and Daddy all day long!!!! Yippie!!! Two whole days to test limits, act out, scream my head off, and know that these two will always love me no matter what. YAY!!!!! And they think I'm going to waste my time napping? Not a chance.

Question: My child wants more and more books read, and all I want to do is get him to sleep so I can collapse from a rough day at work.

Answer: If you find yourself chomping at the bit, chanting to yourself, "Go to sleep, go to sleep, go to *sleep!*" it's likely that your child can feel your urgency. No matter how exhausting your day has been, clear your head so that you can spend "quality time" at the end of the day with your child. What this means is that you're really, one hundred percent paying attention during the bedtime ritual. In most cases, if you pay attention to him and aren't distracted, he will be able to go to sleep more easily and more quickly than if you're halfway out of the room emotionally.

Question: My child just doesn't seem to sleep like others. He wakes easily, has a hard time going to sleep, and hasn't liked naps from the time he was two.

Answer: Have I got a happy little surprise for you. Wait till kindergarten! Those long days will exhaust him. He'll be out like a light at seven-thirty and stay there all night long. At least until the end of October! As hard as it may be on the parents, some people simply need less sleep than others. Your child is one of them.

A Message to You from the Future, Several Years from Now

When your elementary-school child wakes in the night—very rarely now—calls out for you, and you slip half-asleep into her bed, draw her to you. Feel her settle down, completely at peace and totally secure in your arms. Smell the cream rinse she puts in her own hair now that she's so big. In the darkness tempered by the light from the window, let your eyes make out her artwork plastered all over the walls and all her dolls, rocks, books, and delights. Thank God for the chance to do what you did when she was smaller. Treasure this infrequent moment to hold your sleeping child—secure in the middle of the night, whatever childhood fear that woke her rendered impotent because her mommy's there, keeping her safe.

SUMMARY:

❖ Sleep is a complicated affair.
❖ Striking a balance in all of parenting—and life, for that matter—is difficult. Because the needs of the parents and that of the child may well be in direct conflict, sleep is the most challenging area of child raising for most families.
❖ Most children learn to sleep over the course of a decade, not a few nights.
❖ No matter what any book says, including this one, the only right way to handle sleep in your family is the way that feels absolutely comfortable to *all* of you.

Our Bodies, Ourselves

The less a person is able to maintain herself, the harder to feel comfortable in her own skin.

The more a child achieves mastery over taking care of her body, the more independent she becomes.

Because dealing with cleanliness and getting dressed happen on such a routine basis, children often find these areas fabulous places to flex their emotional muscles. We parents find ourselves running up and down halls waving socks shamelessly, skipping our children's baths because we're exhausted ourselves at the end of the day, or feeling like drill sergeants marching in a relentless repetition of get dressed, get undressed, get washed, brush your hair.

A wise parent, however, views both these areas as fertile fields to help our children grow.

"Ten Fun Ways to Encourage Clean Teeth," "Bath Time for Baby," as well as serious articles on problematic topics such as bed-wetting are the kinds of useful articles most parenting magazines offer. They're usually very good and will offer you a rich variety of material to draw from.

Here I've tried to focus on ways to help your child build character. By necessity I've had to mention a lot of things I see that do the opposite.

CLEANLINESS IS NEXT TO GODLINESS

Kids get dirty. Parents need to clean them up. Not *keep* them clean. Besides actual hygiene, your child needs to learn positive ways of relating to her own body.

A. MOMMY NO-NOS
1. Messing Up Their Minds

Here are some common ways mothers have of inadvertently indicating that there is something dirty about the child herself, rather than just being dirty in the moment.

❖ Making faces of disgust, turning up your nose, calling her "stinky," or any other indication that her excrement is disgusting when you change her diaper.
❖ Constantly washing her hands and face.
❖ Saying how dirty she's gotten as if there's something wrong with her. Example: "Eeech. You're filthy again!"

Bad Lesson: *Mommy finds my dirt disgusting. Therefore, Mommy finds me* disgusting. *Therefore, I* must *be* disgusting.

A better way to handle these common occurrences is with laughter, love, and understanding. Children get dirty. Poop smells. But it's a child's right to have her mommy think that even her poop doesn't smell!

2. Intruding on Their Bodies

When you are handling your child, put yourself in her place. Imagine how you would feel if a giant were doing to you whatever you are doing to your child. Even a friendly giant.

Here are some common ways mothers have of unconsciously not respecting their children's bodies and feelings.

❖ Vigorously washing her entire face with a washcloth while holding her head firmly. If someone covered your whole face with a big, wet cloth, wouldn't you squirm and try to get away? And wouldn't it feel terrifying if you weren't strong enough?
❖ Coming at her from behind to wash her face or clean her nose.

Show her the tissue. Say you're going to wipe her nose. She may not like it, but at least you respect her enough to prepare her rather than making a surprise assault on her face from behind.

❖ Letting her scream while you change her diaper. Engage her interest in something else, such as a clean diaper, a tube of Balmex, a book. Sing songs or make silly faces. Some children hate to be flat on their backs. Prop her head on something soft. Some children hate lying on their backs so much that their mothers must change their diapers while the child stands. This is often hard on the mother. But the adult's inconvenience is not a good reason to make a child scream her head off at regular intervals during a day while a person who is monstrous in size physically overpowers her and is deaf to her screams.

❖ Making a child who is clearly uncomfortable about a dirty diaper wait until you're not quite so busy. No matter what you're in the middle of doing that's not a life-threatening emergency, shift gears and change her.

❖ Try to keep in mind that it is her body, not the kitchen floor, that must be cleaned up, lickety-split. The more tender and fun the experience of cleaning is for your small child, the more likely she will have good habits and a healthy self-image when she's older.

B. TOILET TRAINING

This is a very big step in a child's life. When she can control her excrement she is in command not only of her muscles, but also of her entire body. She no longer has to lie down and have somebody else clean her up.

Because of the developmental growth that it signifies, we should be very careful to follow her lead. This is a major area of your child's life that has nothing to do with your wishing the whole diaper ordeal with its paraphernalia was over, or with your wishing you could keep her a baby just a little bit longer.

Toilet training has to do with her. You are merely support staff.

If, however, you try and hold her back or push her forward, then it begins to have to do with you. You have added an emotional overlay that really shouldn't be there.

Best General Advice: Follow your child's lead *if you want it to go smoothly.*

With that concept in mind, let's take a look at some specifics.

The age range for potty training is anywhere from fourteen months to four years, depending on the child. Most of them come to it during their twos and threes. Boys are usually on the late end of things because they have less muscle control over urinating.

Recognizing Potty Readiness

Your child follows you into the bathroom and watches with inordinate fascination.

* ❖ This one can be particularly unnerving if you're a private person. But if you can stand it, let your child watch.
* ❖ Boys often get right up next to their dads. Be careful of the sprinkle factor if they get too close! And dads, could you please put the seat down when you're done as part of the procedure so they get used to it when they're small and don't have to fight with their brides when they're newlyweds? Thanks.

Your child says, ''Mommy, I just made a pooh.''

* ❖ This communication may also be nonverbal, but the message is clear: They know that they've done it.
* ❖ Others actually know when they are in the act of doing it. Some separate themselves from the action; others even go into the bathroom.
* ❖ This is encouraging. You can then, in increments, teach your child to notice the feeling that comes *before*.
* ❖ Your child starts pulling her diaper off, trying to climb onto the toilet, or in any other way shows that diapers aren't interesting anymore.

Useful Book and/or Video: There are many. One I find appealing for its simplicity and because there are versions for boys and girls: *Once Upon a Potty.*

Common Mommy No-Nos

Reproach

There is no difference between walking, talking, and using the toilet in terms of learning. When your toddler has an ''accident,'' however, there may be pee on the living room rug. No matter how crazed you may feel about having human waste in places it doesn't belong, try and remember: That's *your* problem, not your child's. Doo-doo happens. Avoid any permutation of this: ''Oh, no! Now look what you've done!''

Nagging

Learning to control these muscles takes time. Avoid any permutation of this: "Do you need to go? Do you need to go? Do you need to go? Don't forget to go. Do you need to go?"

Potty Seats

❖ Choose a plain miniature toilet. Why would you teach your kid to pee in a spaceship or poop in Mickey Mouse's shirt? Make sure that it's sturdy enough that your child feels independent. Some children need ones with arms in order to feel secure.

❖ Those that balance on top of the toilet are scary and cumbersome for most children.

❖ Most boys learn by sitting on their potty seats. When they're ready to stand on a stool at the big toilet, make sure it's sturdy.

C. THE BATH

Here are some ideas to establish early on that bathing is pleasure, not torture.

❖ Some babies seem to hate baths. But what they really hate are those little bathtubs that sit inside the big tub with a splash of water. As an experiment, run two inches of water into the tub. Get in. Is that fun? No. You're cold. You're naked, sitting on something hard with a little water lapping against your tush. Now fill the tub. Isn't that nice? Another comfort: Put a towel on the bottom of the tub.

❖ Some moms bathe their babies in the kitchen sink. It's a better height for the adult. The baby can feel the difference between arms that are comfortable and arms that are worried about having the baby slip. Plus you can fill the sink enough to give them buoyancy.

❖ Some families take their babies right into the tub with them. Most babies adore this and snuggle up against you very contentedly. You can glide them through the water, even when they're a couple of weeks old.

❖ Once they are past babyhood, many of us get gadget crazy. Have the confidence to give your child a bath without seats and faucet covers. A crawler cannot enjoy a bath confined to a circle seat. Instead of relying on gadgets for safety, supervise your crawler. You may even want to join her for safety and fun.

❖ On into toddlerhood, bathing is usually a joy. Every once in a while a child may suddenly have an aversion to a bath. Rather than start worrying that some hideous event has occurred to scare her, consider sponge baths until this stage goes away.

❖ Some toddlers enjoy showers; others find them terrifying. You will know the first time you try.

Paradox: The same child who does not want to get into the tub will not want to get out!

As with all other aspects of child raising, your child will take many cues from your own habits. If you are clean, she will be clean.

Now that your child is brushed, polished, clean as a whistle, and emotionally secure about the experience, let's peek into the closets, open the drawers, and take a look at clothes.

KIDS AND CLOTHES

What to wear is no small item.

How often have you ripped off your outfit in frustration fifteen times before settling on something to wear? How many times do we see a couple in the men's department, the scowling husband passively trying on whatever the wife and salesman pick out?

These are commonplace scenarios of adults who may still be involved with childhood dilemmas. The indecisive woman may well be hearing her mother's voice, backed up by a chorus of commercials. "You can't wear *that!* It makes you look like a [choose one from your own mother's lexicon of outrages!] floozy, loser, hooker, librarian; fat, elephant-legged, dumpy, bony." Many men truly are disinterested in clothes. They frequently zip through a catalog or department store, making choices in what to women seems lightning speed, whip out their credit card, take the stuff home, and don't give it a second thought until something needs replacing. Yet the ones who absolutely refuse to choose, thrusting the entire process into the hands of others, are still acting out a drama that may have played well in third grade, but gets wearing beyond the third decade.

In the area of clothing we have the opportunity to give our children a great deal of leeway that will help them learn how to choose and trust their own decision-making process. Perhaps someday our daughters will confidently dress for any occasion without agonizing; perhaps our sons will buy their own underwear before it turns into rags.

Goals

- ❖ To encourage your child to learn independence and choice.
- ❖ To allow her taste to develop and prevail.
- ❖ To make sure she's adequately protected from the elements.
- ❖ To make sure that she's comfortable.

Reminder

Parents are in charge of safety and health. Children are in charge of *all personal preferences, as long as they do not interfere with the areas above.*

Clothes are a wonderful area to make this distinction. An example of the difference:

- ❖ Do not insist your daughter wear only red shoes with a particular dress. Although her taste may not be your taste, color choice is a matter of preference.
- ❖ It *is* useful, on the other hand, to make sure she's wearing boots and not party shoes to go out walking during a cold, driving rainstorm. You may find, however, that for long-term learning you have to occasionally give your child enough leeway to discover on her own why we wear protective clothing.

Why Allowing a Child Freedom of Clothes Choice Is So Important

- ❖ She will learn through your example to respect other people's opinions and rights.
- ❖ If you and your taste always prevail, you run the risk of making a child nervous about her own decision-making process. Clothing choice is a benign area. The worst that can happen is she doesn't make the Best-Dressed Toddler list.
- ❖ Clothing is closely linked to self-expression. We see this dramatically in the teen years, when kids go wild trying to distance themselves from their families and make a statement in the world. If in these early years you can keep battles over taste down to a minimum, your teen years may be smoother. Maybe.
- ❖ Since recorded history clothing has been a primary form of decorative arts. Allow her artistic eye to flourish. It may be a great gift to the world.

Is My Child a Reflection of Me?

- ❖ If your child is so dirty that it's clear she's being neglected, that is an unpleasant reflection of your home. You need to take better care of her.
- ❖ If her hair is messy and hands and clothes dirty on the playground, that reflects your understanding of her needs.
- ❖ If your child shows up in nursery school in an extravagantly mismatched outfit, that shows she comes from a home where her self-confidence is being bolstered.
- ❖ If your child shows up at your sister's wedding in an extravagantly mismatched outfit, that shows that she is more in control of the family than is healthy for all the members.

How easy to make distinctions in the abstract. How hard it often is during a real-life day!

SECTION 1: THE FIRST THREE YEARS

There are three things to keep in mind when dressing a baby: comfort, comfort, and comfort.

A. NEWBORNS

- ❖ Many infants like to be swaddled, cozy and tight, reminiscent of the womb. Once they discover their hands, feet, and motion, however, loosen everything up.
- ❖ Consider cotton rather than synthetics. There are no long-term studies about how synthetics affect skin.

B. BABIES AND CRAWLERS
Don't Hurt or Annoy Her with Clothes

- ❖ Get rid of all dangling strings that can strangle her.
- ❖ Make sure there are no zippers pinching her under the folds of her neck.
- ❖ Sit her up straight in her stroller, please! While you were walking around looking in store windows, she slid down and is now crumpled up with a face full of fuzz.
- ❖ Get that hat out of her eyes, please!

Let Your Baby Go Naked
She will love it.

* As long as your home doesn't have old floors that will give a crawler splinters, concrete floors that will scrape her knees, or is drafty in the winter, strip her anytime you can.
* You'd obviously do yourself a favor by letting her go free right after you've changed a diaper, rather than letting her crawl on the carpet when you know she hasn't gone for three hours.
* In the summer, let her roam the backyard in the buff.
* The beach or an unshaded backyard, however, are not good choices. Don't expose a baby's skin to the full force of the sun.

Don't Impede Her Movement

* Long Onesies and overalls that flop down so that she's dragging her legs along like Sweet Pea are frustrating for a crawler.
* Dresses look cute, until your crawler is hanging herself on her skirt. No matter which grandmother or favorite aunt sent them as a gift, leave them in the drawer except for special dress-up.
* For play, put your crawler in a two-piece sweatsuit or anything else that allows freedom of movement.

C. NEW WALKERS

* Barefoot is best. Any place free from potential harm where they can go without shoes while they're learning to walk is a good place. Their toes can grip and lend them balance.
* Be careful, however, at the beach. Hot sand can burn.
* When buying shoes, choose soft shoes with flexible soles.
* Velcro is easier than laces. Laces are hard to tie securely on a squirming foot, and they frequently untie and trip her.

Exercise: The salesman at the shoe store, your mother, or both insist your baby should have good, sturdy shoes that go up the ankle for support and have hard soles for protection. Before you buy anything:

* Go to a store where they sell cowboy boots for grown-ups.
* Put on a brand-new pair.
* Take as many steps as you can before you're limping and want to cry.

❖ Go back to the children's shoe store and insist on soft shoes for your new walker.
❖ If someone sends you sturdy shoes for your child, bronze them. They make fabulous book ends.

D. TODDLERS

Once your child is past babyhood, your goal is to encourage autonomy and choice. Some of the following hints may be useful to you when your child is a year-and-a-half; some children at that young age, however, still need a lot of help getting dressed. Your child's development and ability with her fingers should dictate how you proceed.

Guide Them to Independence by Making Things Easy Physically

❖ Take advantage of Velcro.
❖ If your child loses things frequently, get mitten clips and a snow-suit with a hood attached.
❖ Buy pants with elastic waists instead of zippers or buttons.
❖ Buy dresses that slip over the head or close in the front instead of those with zippers or buttons in the back.
❖ Drawers with sliding hardware that can't fall out encourage a child to use them and prevent minor and major mishaps.
❖ Rig a clothes rack down low enough that they can hang up their clothes themselves.
❖ Put pegs near the door for coats and a shelf where they can put their mittens, etc.
❖ Keep a dirty-clothes hamper in their room or somewhere that they can get to easily.
❖ Teach them to put their pjs in the same place: either under their pillow, on a hook, or somewhere they can reach.
❖ Buy bathing suits for girls that don't have straps you have to be an engineer to step into.
❖ Suspenders and belts are adorable. Let your son buy them for himself when he's a Wall Street broker. They make little boys feel clumsy and inept.

> **Lesson:** I'm in charge of my clothes. I can get dressed by myself a lot. I'm getting to be real big!

Sidestepping Limit Testing

❖ Give your toddler a choice between two things. Say, "Do you want to wear the red shirt or the blue one?" rather than asking, "What shirt do you want to wear?"

❖ Put all inappropriate clothes away where they can't see them. This means in winter don't store their bathing suit in a drawer they can see, where it may become an object of passionate desire; in summer put away winter boots, unless you want to go to the playground in a heat wave with your toddler in fur-lined boots or red-faced from throwing a tantrum.

❖ Put any fancy dress clothes that you want to reserve for special occasions out of sight, up high, or in any other designated off-limits spot.

Confronting Limit Testing
Refuses to Get Dressed
Game 1: "I Bet . . ."

❖ Say with great drama, "I bet you can't get your pants on. I'm so sure of this that I bet you can't get *that* foot [point to left foot] into your pants leg."

❖ She can. She laughs. She is victorious!

❖ "Okay. You may be able to get your left leg into your pants, but I *know* you can't get your right leg in!"

❖ She can. She laughs.

❖ Continue with every single item of clothing.

Game 2: "Race."

❖ Set the kitchen timer and try to beat it.

❖ Race to see who can put her shirt on first, Kid or Mom.

Really Refuses to Get Dressed
She is not laughing. No game you can think of entices her to get dressed. You are late.
Strategy 1: "No Contest"

❖ Take her out in her pjs.

❖ What?! Yes! In her pjs.

❖ I promise after once, or maybe twice, of your refusing to fight about what she's wearing, the fight will no longer be fun for her.

Strategy 2: "No Game."
Now that there's no dressing game, she won't put on her pjs.

❖ Forget pjs.
❖ Dress her after her bath at night in sweatpants and a T-shirt.
❖ The next morning, *voilà!* She's dressed.
❖ Fooled you, my two-year-old!

> **Lesson:** *I'm not quite sure why, but fighting over getting dressed just isn't any fun.*

E. CLIMATE CONTROL
Snowsuit Blues

I am going to spend what seems like an inordinate amount of time on snowsuits, because I have seen an inordinate number of babies, toddlers, and preschoolers screaming their heads off, resisting getting bundled up. The basic approach that works is having fun, rather than urgent completion of an unpleasant task.

Infants

Whatever winter coat fit you when you were pregnant is big enough to cover the same baby now that she's on the outside. Put her, dressed, into her Snugli and put your coat over both of you. If you were dying from the heat during pregnancy and you had a coat that wasn't all that warm, put an extra sweater on her and you're all set!

Babies: Sack of Potatoes Game

Your baby hates her snowsuit. But does she really hate it, or does she hate being thrown on her back and shoved into it? Try this.

❖ Sit your baby up on your lap, rather than lying her flat on her back.
❖ Put her feet into the snowsuit, then shake her into the rest of it, singing, "And we shake the baby like a sack of potatoes."
❖ She will laugh, you will laugh, and the dreaded snowsuit will be on.

Toddlers

Toddlers often hate snowsuits, hats, and mittens because they are confining. They also dislike how inconsiderate we grown-ups can sometimes be. Here are some ways to prevent a fight:

❖ As with a baby, you will do better to dress her in an upright position rather than pinning her in a wrestling hold on the floor.

❖ Jackets and pants are often an easier choice than a one-piece snowsuit. Then you need the pants only when it's really cold and you're going to be outside a lot.

❖ Make sure the snowsuit in question is big enough. You're best off buying it at least one size too large. Two sizes up is even better.

❖ Make sure the zipper doesn't hit her under the chin.

❖ Don't dress your child and then get on your own coat, find your keys, make a last-minute call, run to the john, and put in your contacts. The kid is dying from the heat. No wonder she starts to struggle whenever she sees her snowsuit. Get yourself ready to walk out the door, then dress her at the last minute.

❖ Put on hats and mittens right at the door. If she really balks, take her out without them. Say, "This is cold." Soon she will want them.

Special Two-year-old Trick for Snowsuits

It's snowing. At the sight of her snowsuit your child has barricaded herself under the dining room table.

❖ Say in an agreeable voice, "You don't want to put on your snowsuit? Okay. But we have to go anyway." Hold out your hand. Your surprised toddler will come with you.

❖ As you leave the house say, "I have your snowsuit. If you want it, tell Mommy and we'll put it on."

❖ Don't worry what anyone says. If you live in the city, at least one old lady will cluck, tsk, and wither you with shameful glances. In the suburbs, pray that no one looks out the window and calls the cops about child abuse!

❖ Say, "Whenever you feel cold you let me know and we'll put your coat on."

❖ I guarantee that no more than five minutes will go by before your reinventor of the wheel relents and says, "I'm cold. I want my coat."

❖ Be generous. Don't gloat. Just help your child get warm as fast as possible.
❖ The next time you're both faced with the coat dilemma, you can remind her of what cold feels like.
❖ Say, "It's your choice, coat or no coat."
❖ She will wear her coat. I promise.

Tip: If you are going from your garage, into the car, out of the car, right into a store, back out, into the car, and home, consider not dressing your child for the tundra. A short jacket, a hat, and a blanket tucked around your child in the car seat will be a lot more comfortable and easier for both of you. Only enact the snowsuit drama if you need it!

Joggers

I see you out there in the park in the winter. You are running. You are very, very warm. But that little beezer all scrunched up sideways in the jogging cart, bouncing along, does not look very happy to this dog walker, who can see your child's face as I approach. I don't stop you. For one thing, those of you who are jogging in such cold weather are so intent on running that nothing *can* stop you. And I certainly don't want to be one of those know-it-all busybodies telling people in the park what to do with their children. But I'm telling you here, in case you're reading this: If the temperature is below freezing, and you are not an Eskimo who can get from place to place only by running through the snow, please leave your child at home when you run in the mornings. Take her out after the spring thaw. Thank you. *Whew.* Got that off my chest!

Heat Wave

She's a baby, not an orchid. Don't bundle her up, stick a woolly cap on her head, and tuck her in with a big, thick comforter if you're strolling around in a light jacket or less.

SECTION 2: PRESCHOOL

By preschool your child is still involved in learning how to choose and why we choose certain kinds of clothes when we do. Sometimes it is useful to allow them to make silly choices.

It's snowy. Your preschooler wants to wear her sneakers outside. If she doesn't want to wear her boots because they're too small, dig into her ankles, or some other physical discomfort, she needs different boots. *Tip:* If you discover that her boots really hurt, a temporary if inelegant solution is Baggies over her shoes until you can get new boots.

But if genuine discomfort is not the case, we're in a different territory.

After suggesting that she may be more comfortable, warmer, and drier if she wears boots in the snow, if she's still dead set against them, tell her to go ahead and see what it's like wearing sneakers in the snow. But people learn slowly and through experience. Whether it's the next time or only five minutes later when she sees the wisdom of boots instead of red, wet tootsies, and chooses to wear them herself, here's a tip. ''I told you so'' may be thought, but not said. ''That's a good idea'' is a more affirming response.

However, once she's outside playing in the snow in her boots instead of those darn sneakers, please feel free to jump up on the kitchen counter and do a wild victory dance!

A. GENDER PROBABILITIES

By the preschool years and sometimes earlier, clothes for the child take on a new dimension. Whereas before this point most children are interested predominantly in comfort, by the time they reach their threes and even toward the second half of their twos for some children, many of their preferences have to do with both comfort and taste.

Their preferences begin to reflect gender.

I. Boys

Here are some typical boy issues with clothes:

- ❖ Gets attached to a certain shirt or pants.
- ❖ Won't wear overalls.
- ❖ Won't wear anything but overalls.
- ❖ Won't put anything over his head.
- ❖ Won't wear turtlenecks.
- ❖ Will only wear T-shirts.
- ❖ Will only wear soft things.
- ❖ Will not wear tight clothes.
- ❖ Will not wear corduroy.
- ❖ Will only wear pants with elastic at the waist.
- ❖ Will only wear spaceman, fireman, cowboy, or cartoon action-hero clothes.

Please respect these preferences. If you do, you have helped your son begin to chart out his own territory on the face of the earth. If you do not, you may be infringing on his self-confidence, self-esteem, and daily pleasure.

2. Girls

Whether you "dress for success" or wear aerobics clothes all the time, the likelihood of your daughter exhibiting much of the following behavior during her formative years is high.

If you allow her to play out these various obsessions, they seem to go away. If, however, you come down hard on stylistic choices now, you may find that in later years—when what a girl wears really does convey heavy societal connotations—your daughter will still be dying to try out these various personae.

Do you remember the phrase "ontogeny recapitulates phylogeny?" It means that the human embryo, for example, goes through every evolutionary stage from single-celled life-form through fishies, froggies, I think we throw in some reptile and chicken stuff, until we emerge completely evolved as a human mammal. So, it would seem, do most little girls run through the various stages of womanhood in a kind of tryout version of what's ahead.

The Party Girl—Usually Around the Second Half of the Twos

Only wants to wear her party clothes.

* Reserve certain shoes. "These are your church shoes. You can't wear them to the playground."
* If you can afford it buy a cheap pair of fancy shoes reserved only for the playground. Many of them now have rubber soles, which is a good idea for children this small anyway.
* If she's in her party mode in the winter, suggest warm pants or leggings under her dress to keep her legs warm.
* If she insists on party tights, take her outside for a while. Ask her if she wouldn't rather go in and put on pants under her dress before you go out for the day.
* If she still refuses, pack pants. Nice Mommy. She'll be cold later, and grateful.

The Las Vegas Showgirl—During the Threes

Heads straight for glitz: glitter, sequins, and jewels.

* Cheap stores often have "jeweled" outfits. Let her have one.
* Stick-on earrings are an enormous pleasure.
* Dramatic hairdos are loved by many, the sillier (according to us), the better.

The Uniform—During the Fours

Around this age many children get into wanting to wear one thing and one thing only. Let her. Even if you have to wash and dry it every night so she can wear it again the next day.

The Emergence of Individual Taste—During the Fives

Most girls by this age have a burgeoning sense of their own taste.

One little girlfriend of my daughter's, on a shopping expedition for dresses, wanted a red dress with a white collar in the worst way. It resembled the one worn by Little Orphan Annie, a role she had played in a school play recently.

Her mother pointed out that it was badly cut. The little girl wanted the dress.

Her mother pointed out that for the price, the little girl could get two other dresses. The little girl wanted the dress.

Having introduced the ideas of quality and price, the wise mother allowed her daughter to have the dress she really wanted. For a whole year the girl wore the dress whenever she could. Wise Mommy. Good Mommy. Mommy who avoided a senseless fight and won her daughter's undying gratitude.

3. Marchers to the Beat of Their Own Drums

In many ways we are living in a more enlightened time, as sexual stereotypes become less useful and the manifestations of those stereotypes become less rigorous. We all wear unisex clothes for play, women wear suits, men wear earrings, and lots of styles that were simply unacceptable fifty years ago don't matter in the least. And yet I still see some moms who are uncomfortable with some of the choices their young children make.

A lot of little boys like pink! To them it is simply an appealing color. If your little boy says his favorite color is pink, you don't have to tell him that's a girl's color. Some preschool boys get into nail polish. To them it is exactly like face paint, Magic Markers on their hands, or ritualistic tribal paint, not feminine beauty and grooming. These kinds of lighthearted choices will be knocked out of them by the time they hit elementary school, where boy and girl issues get to be a big deal. In these early years, don't make a big fuss about these kinds of choices; their self-esteem is so much more valuable than learning the ins and outs of girl–boy stuff.

The same goes for the "tomboy." Some little girls despise frilly stuff. They don't like the feel. At this age clothes don't carry the same connotations they do for us. Clothes don't really "say" all the things that we infer from cut, color, and style. If your little girl happens to favor sneakers, pants, and baseball caps instead of lace and bows, please make sure that her preferences are honored. And also let her hear from time to time how great she looks.

As we parent our children through these early years, we are captains in the Army to Build Self-Esteem, not the Fashion Police!

B. ALL
I. Choice Through Buying

By the preschool years many children profit not only by the choice of what to wear, but also by choosing what to buy. Some boys will enjoy this experience more if they go with their dads. Others will find it boring. If they seem disinterested, there's no value in pushing them. They will probably get into it more than you like when they are teens. For the child who does find this an interesting activity, however, it can be a very useful thing to empower them.

Activity: Shopping Expedition

❖ Make it fun.
❖ You're trying to teach *how* to choose more than *what* to choose.
❖ Set limits. Even if you're rolling in dough, decide in advance on certain limitations. Stick to them.
❖ Examples: "You can choose three dresses." "You can have any-one from this rack." "You can choose one party dress." "You can choose three pairs of tights."
❖ Do not plan to spend your entire clothes budget for the season on this one expedition. If you do, the stakes are too high. If she happens to make a mistake and not choose wisely—which is quite likely since she's only a preschooler—you're both stuck with less than she needs.
❖ Confine the limitations even further for important single items, such as a winter coat. Let her choose among three, all of which you can afford and all of which are good, warm, and durable.
❖ As she begins her selection process you may wish to point out that this skirt has a matching top. If she doesn't like the top, let it go.
❖ You may wish to point out that she doesn't ever want to wear turtlenecks and suggest that she forgo this one, even though she loves the color. If she insists, let it go. If she never wears the turtleneck, the next time you go shopping remind her of the choice that wasn't so useful. We all learn through mistakes!
❖ If you have the money, tell her ahead of time that after she's chosen the things she needs, she can spend up to a predetermined amount that suits your budget on anything she wants. This will

take care of all those accessories they tempt little girls with: bows, baubles, beads, bags, etc.

Lesson: *I have a say in what I wear and in what we buy for me. I will treasure this skirt forever. Or, I didn't make such a good choice this time. Next time I'll know better. It's fun to go out with Mommy.*

---

2. Dress-up
Both boys and girls like to play dress-up.

- ❖ Since dress-up is acting grown-up as well as playing imaginary games, make their dress-up clothes available to them where they can reach them without always having to ask for help.
- ❖ Tip: Some slips and teddies from a ladies lingerie department make fabulous dress-up clothes. They're cheap, frilly, and washable.
- ❖ Girls usually like their own jewelry boxes. Even a shoe box will do; they just like to have their accessories someplace special.
- ❖ Boys are big on ''professional hats'': firemen's helmets, policemen's hats, etc. They also like big shirts, suitcases, capes, swords, and swashbuckling outfits. Some boys get into wearing their firemen's hats all the time. I think that's wonderful. A fireman, after all, is perhaps the only noble, selfless profession left in our country!

3. Parents' Choice—All Ages
Well, Then, When *Can* I Say What They Should Wear When?

Weddings, retirement dinners, christenings, naming ceremonies, any special occasion honoring someone else, as well as any religious service if your congregation pays attention to what people wear: these are times when your child should conform to the tastes of a larger community.

- ❖ Show your child what you are going to wear.
- ❖ Show what your husband is going to wear.
- ❖ Show pictures of your own wedding, pointing out how dressed up everybody is.
- ❖ If your child is part of the wedding ceremony, explain that the bride has chosen what she wants all her attendants to wear, and that your child has to conform just like the big girls are doing.

❖ Remind her that it is the bride's day, not hers.
❖ If she's not part of the ceremony, take her with you to pick out her dress, making sure you limit her choice to something you can afford and live with.
❖ Boys will usually accept the suit of your choice without having to be involved in the shopping process.
❖ Make sure the clothes are comfortable.
❖ Don't relent on silly shoes.
❖ For any dressy occasion, explain that this is someone else's special day and that we need to dress in a way that honors them.

Lesson: *I am not the center of the universe. There are times when I need to do what everyone else is doing.*

PURELY PARENTAL CONCERNS

SECTION 1: ACQUIRING CLOTHES

❖ Do not buy your child anything to wear that will break your heart if it gets messed up. Children make messes.
❖ Do not send your child to any class or playground in clothes that cannot be ruined. That forces your child to focus more on clothes than the experience.
❖ Don't overbuy. Keep quantities down. During these years children often become attached to favorites. If you buy a dozen pairs of play pants and all your daughter wants to wear are dresses, you have a fight on your hands—or waste. Furthermore, too many choices of the same kind of thing is too hard and may lead to frustration rather than independence.
❖ Don't buy terrific turtlenecks (or anything else) on sale dirt-cheap a year ahead. Tastes change. Your child may refuse to wear them.

RECEIVING HAND-ME-DOWNS

❖ Have your child write a thank-you note or draw a picture to send to the family.

❖ Don't force her to wear any of the things she doesn't like, any more than you would force her to buy things she doesn't like.

❖ Mention when she wears certain things how nice it was of cousin Karen to send you her sweater.

Lesson: *What goes around comes around. I send my clothes to Rachel, and Karen sends her clothes to me. We all take care of each other, and we don't throw anything out that someone else can use.*

A Mother's Dilemma: My sister's son, Drew, is two years older than my boy. My brother-in-law makes a fortune and she spends it all on Drew's clothes. She gives these gorgeous clothes to us, and here's my darn kid who'll wear only Ninja Turtle T-shirts from Kmart.

Advice: Put your nephew's beautiful, neatly ironed clothes in Baggies up in the attic. When your son is a teenager, drag them out. Show him. Say, "No, you can't have that pair of $147 ripped jeans from Armani! I spent that money when you were little! You could've worn these beautiful clothes from cousin Drew. But nooo, you had to have only Ninja Turtle T-shirts. So go get a job if you want to waste money on those jeans!"

Isn't that fantasy satisfying? Good. Now let your son wear what's comfortable, thank your sister, and pray that next year your boy will have passed his Ninja Turtle fixation.

SECTION 2: DISCARDING CLOTHES

Hand-me-downs are valuable for many reasons beyond the obvious savings to the recipient. They can serve to teach thrift, giving, and receiving.

GIVING AWAY YOUR OWN CHILD'S CLOTHES

❖ Engage her in the selection of what is still wearable and what is too worn to give away.

❖ Give some things to children who are "needier" and some to friends. Mention that cousin Rachel would like this, and the lady who cleans Daddy's office would like this. This kind of nondiscriminatory giving tends to keep hand-me-downs free from the "have/have-not" issue.

❖ Or select one child who receives all your old clothes.

❖ Keep some favorites tucked away in a box marked by year. Someday these will be heirlooms.

Lesson: *We don't simply discard what we're done with. We find a proper place.*

A special younger sibling note: Make sure that she gets something brand-new some of the time!

SECTION 3: CLOTHES ARE NOT A CONTROL ISSUE AMONG ADULTS

BABY-SITTERS

If you have a full-time baby-sitter, clothes can sometimes become a source of unspoken conflict. This is really, by the way, not about clothes, but about who does your child love more and who can care for the child best.

If there is a special event in your child's life that your baby-sitter will dress your child for, lay out the outfit of your choice.

But on a daily basis you would do everybody a favor, particularly your child, by leaving the dressing to your sitter. This is a way sitters have of connecting with the child. It's soft and tender. The same thing goes for hair grooming. Your sitter may give your child a hairstyle you never would. Leave them alone to forge a relationship. Ultimately, your child's taste will reflect yours. With a young child and a sitter, clothes are not about taste; they are about bonding.

If, on the other hand, you feel that your child is not being dressed properly (healthwise, not tastewise), this should be a red flag. A good sitter is a sitter who dresses a child comfortably for play.

DADDIES

Daddies' fingers are often too big for little buttons. Once you all realize this and point it out, it helps your husband to stop feeling as if he's all thumbs about dressing the child. Dads often put children's, particularly girls', clothes on backward. Be quiet. Be glad he's dressing the child, particularly if he's a man who's disinterested in clothes. As you would with a child, you may wish to show, rather than tell, how a particular outfit goes on. Is this belittling to men? Maybe. I have just seen too many fathers who are mildly uncomfortable about dressing a child get pushed out of the whole clothes arena by being made to feel incompetent. If you're lucky, sometimes daddies choose outrageous outfits you would never put together that are adorable.

SUMMARY:

❖ Treat your child's body with respect. This includes not overpowering them to "get something done."

❖ Inspire confidence, self-esteem, and learning how to choose by allowing your child as much autonomy as possible in daily clothes choices.

Whistle While You Work

*May our home be clean enough to be healthy
And dirty enough to be happy.*
—A grandmother's sampler

Whether you work full-time and have no household help or have a full-time housekeeper, nanny, and cook, your child needs to have household responsibilities.

THE BENEFITS OF CHORES FOR CHARACTER DEVELOPMENT
Early Years

- ❖ Chores foster a child's sense of competency.
- ❖ They help gauge time.
- ❖ They impart a sense of satisfaction at a job well-done.
- ❖ They make him feel part of the family.

Groundwork for a Satisfying School Experience

- ❖ By school age, children are expected to take care of books, supplies, and backpacks. The child who learns, young and at home, how to maintain his own things has more opportunity to learn academic and social skills in school, rather than spending most of his time searching for the right book, pencil, and lunch box.
- ❖ Chores teach how to approach a given task and follow it through to completion, a skill that will impact on every endeavor from school on into adulthood.

Carry-over into Adult Life

Work is an essential part of a productive life. If a child learns to cheerfully do whatever task is necessary, no matter how small, each aspect of his adult life—from home maintenance to whatever field he enters—will be more satisfying than if he resents what he has to do or feels exempt from responsibility.

GENERAL POINTS TO KEEP IN MIND

Choose chores that guarantee success.

❖ Never make the chore so difficult that he can't accomplish it.
❖ Never make it such drudgery that he detests doing it.
❖ Never make it something so important to you that if his way is inept you redo it yourself, thereby sending him the message that he failed.

Make your instructions clear.

❖ Saying "Clean up your room" is an exercise in defeat. Young children can't focus. They don't know where to begin.
❖ Choose a specific, discrete task that your child can focus on and finish. To a toddler: "Let's pick up all the books from the floor and put them on the shelf." To a preschooler: "Put all your books away [or on the shelf, for the child still mastering completion skills]."

Limit the number.

❖ An eighteen-month-old may be expected to help do one thing a day.
❖ By three a child can easily accomplish three or four simple tasks with regularity, independently.

Make cleanup fun! Music is a natural accompaniment to fun work.

❖ Sing "Whistle While You Work," "Just a Spoonful of Sugar," the Barney "Cleanup Song," or any other song your child knows.
❖ Put on fifties rock music, Latin music, country and western, polkas, or anything else with a good beat.
❖ Try melodramatic classical music, like Tchaikovsky's *Romeo and Juliet,* or lilting Viennese waltzes.

❖ For the younger child, the beat itself will encourage movement. For the older child, try dancing while you put things away.

Games make cleanup fun.

❖ At eighteen months and up, take turns putting books back on shelves.
❖ By three, children enjoy games of skill. Example: See who can get the *most* Legos in the plastic bin, the *first* one in, the *last* one in, *two at a time*. Try tossing all the *yellow* pieces, then the *blues*. Use your imagination, then encourage your child to come up with other variables. By the way, this kind of game encourages sorting and categorizing, a basic learning skill. By making it fun you have killed two birds with one stone. You're encouraging learning and teaching to focus on a fun way to do a chore.
❖ Have races. Example: ''I bet I can get all the puzzles piled up before you can get all the trucks in the box. On your mark, get set, go!'' Don't always let your child win. Don't always beat him.

Now that we know why our children should be doing chores and how we're going to orchestrate that, let's look at some specifics.

SECTION 1: CHORES

As you glance through these suggestions, please keep in mind that some children have better dexterity and attention spans than others. Adjust any of these ideas to your child. Take all age suggestions with a grain of salt; each child develops at his or her own rate. All children need their mommy to accept how they go about things and learn.

A. SUGGESTIONS FOR CHORES A KID SHOULD DO

Any child, no matter how young, should view some or all of the following simple tasks as expected:

❖ Bathtub toys cleared out of tub and put wherever you keep them before leaving the tub.
❖ Pjs put in the right spot, whether that's under the pillow, in a pj bag, on a hook, or wherever you designate.
❖ Dirty clothes put in the family hamper, a hamper in the child's room, or wherever you designate.

❖ Towels on rack or hook.
❖ Hats, coats, and boots or wet bathing suits and gear in a specific place, if they are part of your daily routine.

Verbally introduce these simple tasks to your baby. By six months a child should have at least heard the phrase, "Now Mommy is going to put your dirty nighty in the hamper. There it goes! When you're big enough you can put your dirty clothes there yourself."

Toddlers will need help, meaning your presence with as little physical intervention in their work as seems fair and useful. For example, after you help take your eighteen-month-old's shorts and T-shirt off, hand them to him, say, "Let's go to the dirty-clothes hamper," open the lid, and let him put them in.

By three most children should be able to carry out an instruction if you're nearby. You should be able to say, "Please go put your dirty clothes in the hamper [which is down the hall]. I'll wait here."

By four, give your child the opportunity to think of putting her dirty clothes in the hamper before you mention it. If she takes off her clothes and throws them on the floor, instead of saying, "Please put them where they belong," try, "That's a funny place to keep dirty clothes!" If this light touch doesn't work, revert to "Please put . . ."

By five these habits ought to be pretty much in place. But with these expected chores, even a much older child may need a friendly reminder from time to time.

If you have made these basic chores a relatively benign part of the day's activities, occasionally requiring reminders and help, and during any one of these stages your child suddenly begins to balk, the balking probably has to do with a developmental issue rather than a chore issue. For example, the two-year-old, once having mastered where the dirty-clothes hamper is, may very well refuse to use it. But your two-year-old is exercising "will clout." Your four- or five-year-old, who suddenly starts leaving dirty clothes all over the room may be integrating sophisticated stuff from nursery school or kindergarten and be on overload. Nevertheless, *don't do these basic chores for him!* It would probably help to say you notice he hasn't been putting his clothes in the hamper lately. Is it because the hamper's too far down the hall? A suggestion for a way to make the chore easier often will allow the child to save face enough to begin doing it again.

These simple chores are daily occurrences. Not only can you expect your child to be competent enough to do them, but if you help him consistently do these simple tasks, you will have given him a true gift: good habits!

B. SUGGESTIONS FOR CHORES A KID CAN DO

Try and keep in mind the idea of play. Your child's imagination can be sparked by finding fun ways to tackle any simple task. In many chores, sorting and categorizing come into play.

1. Eighteen Months and Up

Beginning with very young toddlers, the most natural place to introduce additional chores is with toys. It is a good principle to have him responsible for cleaning up at least some of the toys he's been playing with at the end of any play period.

Why do I say *some* and not *all*? Because it is quite likely during normal play for upward of one hundred tiny pieces of plastic to end up in a heap on the floor. Putting away every single toy piece may be so daunting to a young child that he will feel inept about not being able to do it, enraged because he's being pushed farther than he can go, or in the future unwilling to play with complete abandon.

I've heard the advice that a child should not pull out a new toy until the one he's finished playing with is put away. I feel that this may not be so useful. For one thing, a creative play period is one where several different kinds of toys may very well be used together in unconventional ways. Furthermore, children need uninterrupted time to play. If during any given half hour of play a child has to stop playing every five minutes to clean up before going on to the next tiny time increment, he hasn't really had any time to play!

The one exception, however, is art. Have your child help you clean up art supplies before moving on so that they don't dry out, spill, or get where they don't belong.

Toys

- ❖ Put all the books back on the shelf. (Try not to be obsessive about how the books get back on the shelf. You're trying to help him complete a task, not do more than he's able to do.)
- ❖ Put all the crayons in the box.
- ❖ Put all the doll clothes in their basket.

Lesson: I can take care of my toys.

Practical Storage Tips

Notice: There was a ''put in their place'' for these suggestions. If there is no place where things belong, it's impossible to clean up.

- ❖ Toy chests easily turn into garbage cans. Toys are jumbled; pieces get separated from their companions, rendering them useless. They are difficult to reach, to find, or to pull out. Most children ultimately dump them upside down or ignore whatever is not on the very top layer.
- ❖ Better choices for storage: open shelves or cabinets with doors a child can open easily.
- ❖ Plastic containers are useful, particularly if you get rid of the lids, which can frustrate a young child.

Predictable Parenting Trap: If you're such a neatnik that Golden books must go on one shelf, board books on another, etc., you have set up defeat for your child.

Other Household Activities

Here are some other ideas to play with. These are the kinds of things your child should actually be able to pull off—with some supervision in the beginning—all by his lonesome!

- ❖ Put all his clean socks in his drawer. (Don't be a fussbudget!)
- ❖ Help you sort dirty laundry.
- ❖ Help you sort clean laundry. (Hint: Don't let him help with permanent-press things if you're going to be in a panic over wrinkles.)
- ❖ Help unpack groceries. Find all the cans, diapers, or crackers, for example.
- ❖ Put all his plastic dishes in the dishwasher.

Lesson: Helping Mommy, and Daddy if your husband participates in household chores, is fun.

---

2. Three and Up

By three for most children and certainly by four, your child should be able to handle having certain chores that are his to do. Here are some ideas of the kinds of chores preschoolers can handle on a daily or weekly basis:

❖ Being in charge of emptying wastepaper baskets (small ones with small plastic bags that they can simply pull out).
❖ Putting the recyclable bottles into the right bin.
❖ Heaving the plastic bag of recyclables into the Dumpster, if you have one.
❖ Making his bed. (Please contain yourself. If your child manages to get the covers up over the bed, leave it alone, even if your fingers are twitching to smooth things out! It's more important that your child feel competent to carry out a task than it is that the bedspread be straight. If you're having company and you can't bear the mess, suggest that today you do it together. Show him how to sweep his arm across the bed to straighten it out.)
❖ Loading the dishwasher, except for knives and fragile glasses.
❖ Putting the groceries away—make him in charge of cans, for example.
❖ Putting dry food into the dog's or cat's bowl. (Please make sure that you're in charge of saying when it has to be done.)
❖ Putting the videotapes where they belong.
❖ Clearing the dishes from the table.

Lesson: *I am responsible for making sure certain necessary things get done around the house.*

When Not to Make Them Clean Up

As your child matures he may very well begin ambitious projects. A robot built of Tinkertoys or other mechanical parts or a fantasy land with created mountains and lakes are examples of the kinds of activities a preschooler may engage in. Any of these elaborate projects that very well may take days to complete should be left alone. They should be allowed to stay up until you notice that, rather than adding to, talking about, and showing off the project, your child has begun to step over it or not notice when a piece has become dislodged. Then it's time to suggest that we dismantle it so that there is room to build something new.

Predictable Parent Trap: Oscar and Felix

Some children are more orderly than others. By three you will know if your child likes things put a certain way. If your three- or four-year-old likes to have his Magic Markers arranged in color order, respect that wish. I have heard parents say, ''What difference does it make? You're such a nitpicker. Stop dawdling and put them away already. You're driving me crazy." They're his Magic Markers. You can help him by not rushing him. Give him enough notice at the end of a coloring period to clean up his way.

On the other hand, some mothers are fussy, but their children aren't. While you may take inordinate pleasure from having all the crayons lined up, sharpened, points up in the Crayola box, your child may prefer to toss them into a cigar box. Get him a cigar box. (Get yourself a nice new box of sixty-four Crayolas and you can play with them when he's asleep!)

SECTION 2: MOMMY'S MIDDLE NAME IS NOT "LOST AND FOUND"

"Mommy, where's my . . . ?"

This phrase resounds throughout our nation and the whole world.

Open your back window. Shh! Listen! "Mama, *donde esta* . . . ?" "Mamma, *où sont* . . . ?"

Since we've become so close, can I ask you something? Is there supposed to be a magnetic attraction to our womanhood that magically zaps Barbie shoes up from a pile of toys?

One reason children ask mommies where things are is that it's easier. I wouldn't mind having a personal assistant who followed me around all day and all I had to do was hold my hand out like a surgeon and get what I wanted firmly placed there. Another reason is that moms are usually the Caretakers of the Family Things. We make it our business to know where things are.

But another reason children ask where things are is that they *don't know how to keep track of them.*

A. SIMPLE WAYS TO TEACH HOW *NOT* TO LOSE THINGS

Here are some ideas that will help your child learn how to keep track of objects.

❖ Establish certain spots for certain things.
❖ Remind your child to put it back.
❖ If you find it out of place, hand it to your child and say, "Let's put this where we can find it again." Link finding something to where you put it. This is not necessarily a logical progression in a child's mind.
❖ Example: Put the remote control on top of the TV when you turn off the TV. Everyone in the house knows that that's its spot.

❖ In his room, let him choose certain places for certain things, *even if it doesn't seem logical to you.*

❖ Example: He wants to keep his car collection on the bookshelf. Let him. If he knows where he put it and where he can find it, that's the goal. Not necessarily having his room "look" right.

❖ He may discover that having his cars on the bookshelf is inconvenient and will find a better place on his own. He may also decide he loves having his cars on the shelf and would prefer to pile his books in the corner behind the door. Although awkward and unsightly in your eyes, if he always returns his books to that corner and he doesn't mind having to pull them all down in order to get one and then pile them all back up, there you go. He found his spot.

B. SIMPLE WAYS TO TEACH HOW TO FIND LOST THINGS

Even if you establish places for things around the house, point out that he should remember where he puts things, and allow him to determine where his own things should go, it's only a matter of time in the life of any child until something is lost. Your child needs looking-for-lost-things lessons.

1. Under Four

If you say, "I think I saw it in the living room. Go look," your child will go into the living room, stand in the middle of the room, perhaps physically turn his head, but not focus his eyes, walk out, and say, "I looked. It's not there."

❖ Go with him, saying, "Let's go look."

❖ Tour the room geographically.

❖ Say, "Let's start here, on the bookshelves. Let's look at the bottom shelf. Is it there? No. Let's try the next shelf. There? No," and so on all around the room.

❖ He needs to be shown many times how to look thoroughly around a room.

❖ After a couple of rounds of this kind of looking, move up a notch.

❖ The next time something's missing, say, "Go look on the bookshelf. You look first and see if you can find it. Remember, look at each shelf. If you do that and still can't find it, I'll help."

❖ If he finds it, praise him sky-high. "Good eyes!"

❖ If he can't and you find it on the shelf, say playfully, "You didn't have your looking eyes on!'' or some other silly thing. For some children this is a very advanced skill.

❖ The next time remind him to put his ''looking eyes'' on.

❖ Most children will find accomplishing the task more fun than simply waiting for you to do it, as long as you help them learn how to look step by step.

2. Four and Up

❖ Continue to use the above approach. But now you can also try the memory game.

❖ Say, ''Sit down, close your eyes, and picture your skates. When was the last time you played with them? Were you out skating with Sally? Did you come home through the back door? Did you leave them by the door?''

❖ Sometimes these questions will evoke a memory. You dash to the back door, and *voilà!* Skates!

❖ After that you can encourage your child to be a detective without your help.

The *I Spy* series is loads of fun. These beautiful books teach important skills: how to logically sift through lots of information, as well as visual memory and organization. Whether you look at the books or not, use the idea to help find things. ''I spy a pair of skates!'' It has become a game.

SECTION 3: REWARDS

Some families reward doing chores. For the younger child the reward may be toys; for the older child, an allowance. I'm not sure this is so useful.

The external reward becomes the goal, rather than the internal feeling of accomplishment.

You can make a very strong case that the reward system is good practice for learning good work habits. We work hard, we get paid. We slack off, we get fired. For a child older than our preschoolers, this may very well be an excellent lesson.

At the age we're involved with here, however, I would be very judicious in my reward choice. If you feel strongly that you want to link doing the job with external accomplishment, or if you find yourself with a four-year-old who refuses to do chores and you need leverage, I suggest charts and stickers. Make a chart including days and chores, and let him put a sticker on the chart when he's completed his task.

SUMMARY:

Chores help build self-esteem and teach a sense of accomplishment. In order to aid your child, ensure that he can successfully complete the chore and develop a sense of mastery.

PART III

Out in the World

All righty rooney. We're exhausted, but they're sleeping like babies. They're "helping" us around the house, and we're studying Zen meditation to be able to endure doing some things their way and to allow them to freely follow their tastes. Of course, we're a little embarrassed to be seen in public with them in some of those getups. But we'll cope.

Because that's exactly where we're about to go: out into the world.

Manners: The Golden Rule

With every generation we're starting from scratch. Left to their own devices, the darlings who share our homes would become Wild Men of Borneo, spitting, growling, and sinking their teeth into somebody just because they didn't like the cut of his jib. Occasionally, they'd make a flying tackle from the back and hug the heck out of somebody because they liked their looks.

Since physical aggression is common to all humans, we parents have to find ways to help our children temper their physical instincts and to provide them with acceptable ways to communicate displeasure. At the same time we want to help them acquire pleasant manners. Everything from resisting the urge to shove another kid because he's in our way to saying "please" and "thank you" are all types of behavior along the same continuum: treating others the way we would like to be treated.

INTRODUCTORY IDEAS

Definition
Manners include any behavior that makes human interactions pleasant. Good manners include:

- ❖ Expressing both negative and positive feelings in socially acceptable ways.
- ❖ Sharing and taking turns.
- ❖ Common social courtesies.

Bad manners include:

- ❖ Hurting people physically.
- ❖ Hurting people's feelings.
- ❖ Ignoring common courtesies.

General Advice

- ❖ This is a long, slow process. Don't expect to say something once and never have to say it again.
- ❖ Much teaching in this area is nonverbal and relies heavily on your modeling. So mind your Ps and Qs!
- ❖ The Golden Rule is very applicable here: Do unto others as you would have them do unto you. Love your neighbor as yourself. What is hateful to you do not unto your neighbor. Whenever you feel unsure how to get an idea across to your child, try rephrasing this ancient, profound idea: "How would you feel if someone did that to you?"
- ❖ Some children pick up the "please" and "thank you" aspects of manners more readily than others.
- ❖ Some children are more impulsive than others. Helping them curtail their aggressive tendencies requires a great deal of repetition and patience.

General Lessons Your Child Will Learn

- ❖ My actions affect other people. Theirs affect me.
- ❖ I cannot have good manners if I am selfish.
- ❖ I learn how to cooperate when I learn about manners.

Hardest Development Stages

- ❖ The entire toddler and preschool period of a child's life and well into adolescence are spent honing these skills. Toddlers and preschoolers, by definition, are self-centered human beings. Normal self-absorption makes it challenging for a parent to teach getting along in the world while encouraging the healthy development of the self.
- ❖ As in other areas, the so-called terrible twos may be a difficult, but important, time to teach how to control our tempers and our bodies.

Predictable Difficulties Parents Face

❖ Very mannerly or very noncombative parents are sometimes appalled by normal behavior. Often their tendency is to handle aggression inappropriately, apologizing profusely to the adult who's been wronged and then privately being furious with the "errant" child.

❖ Parents of a child with a "strong" personality will have to be more patient in this area than one whose child is amenable to direction.

Situations Ripe for Mistakes

❖ Only children, who by definition don't have to share in their own homes.

❖ Homes with more than one child where one child's personality is much stronger than the other's.

❖ Homes where parents think that aggressive behavior leads to success.

❖ Homes where money is dominant and where the adults mistakenly think you can buy your way into or out of anything. (As the Beatles so aptly put it, "Can't Buy Me Love." Without common courtesy combined with the tools for controlling aggression, a child may have a lonely life.)

❖ Homes where parents mistake affectation for manners and ignore the underlying kindness necessary to be mannerly.

❖ Homes where one or both parents have limited resources for controlling their tempers.

Let us begin with our raw, primitive creature and work on turning her into a more or less civilized human being.

TAMING THE BEAST

In order to teach our child the skills required to temper her instincts, we must first lay some ground rules for grown-ups.

Completely unsupervised play for children under the age of six is not a terrific idea. But different children at different ages require varying degrees of supervision. Here are some guidelines to consider when your child has a friend over.

Any children under two-and-a-half should never be so unsupervised that you can't get to them immediately to keep them from serious harm. If your toddler is playing with another one nearby in the yard or at the other end of the room, leave them alone. They don't need you hovering, but they need you in sight and close enough that you can reach them as soon as they get into a pickle they can't resolve.

Two mature almost-threes can be playing in the sandbox while you garden way at the other end of the yard. You should still all be able to see each other, and you should be able to get to them before a screaming or hitting event goes on for too long.

By three, letting them play out of sight—although not out of earshot—is useful, as long as they both know where you are and as long as you check in regularly to see if both children are happy.

By four and five they should be allowed to go off to their own room, the playroom, or the yard where an adult is within calling distance if needed, but far enough away to give them a sense of genuine autonomy. They still need regular checks.

Exceptions:

❖ The preschool-age child who has not been exposed much to other children might not fare as well as one with day-care, nursery-school, or neighborhood experience. If she is aggressive she needs to be taught the lessons some children begin earlier. If she is passive she may need someone in her corner helping her hold her own.

❖ If two children consistently fight and get hurt, they might need closer supervision to preempt injuries. But sometimes, "best friends" scrap happily all day long. Their adults need to tune their ears to hear if the scrapping has taken a turn for the worse that they might not be able to resolve; otherwise, they can be left alone.

Now that you are not hovering, but are nearby, let's take a look at the interesting maneuvers our little kids go through in their transformation from wild things and how moms might need to step in and redirect from time to time.

SECTION 1: IN THE CAGE: KIDS AND AGGRESSION

The most logical place to start is with two kids, one toy. Two preverbal toddlers will have an interaction that if they could talk would sound like this: "I want that. I'm going to take that."

"Hey, whadda ya think you're doing? Gimmie that back."

"No!"

"Oh, yeah? Well, how da ya like this?" *Slam.* And we're off and running . . .

Before we get to real fisticuffs there are skills to teach from the beginning of your child's life that oftentimes head disagreements off at the pass.

A. SHARING

Sharing is the basic foundation of all manners. It is a complicated, sophisticated skill. Unlike love, for example, or the desire to procreate, sharing doesn't seem to be a natural instinct. The ability to share implies understanding the ramifications of your behavior, being able to tolerate not having what you want when you want it, and at its highest form even taking pleasure from giving something that you want to someone else.

Sharing is hard. In the extreme, the adult version of the inability to share is war.

Useful Household Rules to Establish

❖ Keep some stationery supplies such as Scotch tape, scissors, and paper in the kitchen or family room for everyone to use. This shows a child that we can all make use of certain things. It also helps allay a child's fear that things will never be replaced once they're gone.

❖ Set aside some things as not for sharing, for example: supplies on Mommy's and Daddy's desk.

❖ By the same token, allow your preschooler to designate *certain* markers off-limits (I am not suggesting your child can refuse you the use of *all* markers).

❖ If you need a crayon or marker from your child's room, have the courtesy to ask first. Expect the same from her with your things.

❖ Make sibling rules for sharing fair. There needs to be a clear delineation of a few chosen objects that are off-limits and do not need to be shared. Everything else must be shared.

❖ This same fairness should apply to visitors.

Less Helpful Rules that Inadvertently Teach that Sharing Is Awful

❖ Parents making *all* of their own things off-limits to the children.

❖ Parents making *none* of their own things off-limits to the children.

Now we know our house rules. Bring on the babes!

In order to provide the foundation for sharing, a parent must be scrupulously fair. Otherwise, the child will learn that whoever is the most powerful gets whatever is in question.

I. Babies

With babies, the simplest rule applies: *Who had it first?*

Hannah and Jane are sitting face to face. Hannah has a rattle. Jane takes the rattle. If Hannah merely regards Jane with mild curiosity and then picks up another toy, everyone is home free. But if Hannah cries or reaches to take it back, you have entered the Sharing Zone, although your babies don't know this yet. An easy, fair rule for babies is: The one who had it first gets to keep it.

- ❖ Say, "Hannah had the rattle first, so Jane can have this key ring."
- ❖ Gently remove the rattle from Jane's fingers, giving her the key ring at the same time.

Lesson: Hannah: *That's nice. If I've got something I like, I get to keep it.* Jane: *If someone has something I want, I can't grab it. But I can have something else that's interesting.* Mommies: *Fair is fair. Being in my child's corner doesn't mean always letting her have her way or always backing off.*

- ❖ Do not insist, because you are polite and don't want the other child's mother to think your child is stingy, that your eight-month-old should be able to share. She can't. Nor should she have to.
- ❖ If a tussling match ensues, with both babies tugging on the rattle before you can get there, they may establish for themselves which child is dominant in this moment.
- ❖ Leave them alone if they work it out themselves. If the grabber ended up with the toy, but the first child found something else interesting, everybody's happy. There is no conflict.
- ❖ However, if either ends up crying, pick them both up and give each of them a *different* toy. Each mother should quietly explain to her own child that we don't fight over toys. Introducing the idea of sharing now will give your child a leg up on this complicated skill, as well as helping you think about how involved you need to

be in this long learning process. Both of you will get in the habit early on.

Food for Thought: Babies don't take toys from other babies because they're selfish, mean, or any other negative emotion. They take toys from other babies because when another baby is happily playing with something, the first baby notices it, thinks it looks like a jolly good time, and wants it.

Question: My baby always lets other children take things from her. Should I worry?

Answer: No. At first they often look bemused, as if to say, "Wait a second. Didn't I just have that rattle?" They show no negative emotion and find something else interesting. A few months later their faces crumple. They often look to you. Several months later the "giver" really cries. If she doesn't take the toy back herself, step in. Usually by eighteen months, sometimes much earlier, you see anger come over her face and she takes the toy back herself.

Mommy Issue: Toy-taking between babies is often a place where moms begin to compete silently. Don't worry about the baby who doesn't "stand up" for her rights. She's not a chump or a sissy. Don't be smug if your child generously offers a toy to another baby with obvious delight while the other baby seems to grab maliciously. Put yourself in the other mother's shoes. How does she feel? Could this be you next month? All kids will do many things that aren't pretty. The babies and toddlers who seem to be pushovers will eventually enter the fray. Sometimes, the longer it takes them to enter the fray, the more vengeful they are once they get there.

Question: My crawler will take any toy out of any other baby's hand, but not because she's interested in it. It seems that she only wants it because another child has it. The minute the other child picks up something else, my baby throws down the first toy and goes after the new one.

Answer: I've seen mothers have intense responses to this, I imagine because they think that it speaks unutterable volumes of selfishness about their child. They grab the toys back and utter angry, chiding "Nos." I've seen other mothers ignore it, presumably because they also think the worst of their child and seem to want to pretend it's not there in hopes that it will go away. They sometimes sit chatting agreeably with other adults as their baby leaves a path of crying babies in their wake. If you have a child who does this, work with her. Make sure when playing with another baby that you have several toys handy. When she takes a toy, give her a different one and return the first to the other baby. You will need to repeat this over and over. If she keeps showing no interest in the toys themselves and the other baby is crying, pick yours up and move her off to find something else interesting to do for a while. One problem you may encounter is the response other adults have. If you see disapproving scowls and hear tsks, I would suggest not getting together with that mom for a while, until your babies have matured some. Babies read nonverbal signals well. They don't need the reproof of others at such a tender age.

2. One Year and Up

Since sharing is an abstract concept, you will have more success introducing the activity of taking turns. While you're all busy having fun taking turns, throw in the word *sharing*. Let's say your walkers are both nudging each other out of the way trying to get on a sliding board at the same time.

Activity: "Taking Turns" as a Game

You need a minimum of two grown-ups and two children, but the more the merrier.

The Sliding Board Game:

- ❖ Each mother takes the hand of her child.
- ❖ Say, "Now it's Jamie's turn." Help Jamie up the ladder while Sam's mom helps him wait. Jamie will enjoy this more than Sam.
- ❖ Sam's mom encourages him to wait (which means holding him back!), pointing out that it's Jamie's turn.
- ❖ After Jamie goes down the slide her mom playfully runs her around to the steps again, saying, "Now it's Sam's turn," as Sam gets his chance.
- ❖ If the two moms enjoy themselves and laugh enough, the kids will catch on that it's a game! While you're all laughing, mention, "Isn't taking turns fun? We like sharing."
- ❖ Most kids take about four or five rounds before they notice that you're not just holding them back. Then they start to get in the spirit of things. If they catch on and manage to wait, please make sure you praise them! If they don't catch on, try it another day.

Other places where it's fun.

- ❖ On an escalator, at water fountains, or any other place where you have to wait. It's fun with balls too. Sit in a circle, roll the ball, and call out whose turn it is, helping your child when she can't quite roll the ball where she wants it and laughing as you all roll the ball back and forth by turns, sharing.

> *Lesson: Taking turns is fun. Mommy mentioned sharing. If this is what sharing means, it's not so bad.*

3. Eighteen Months and Up
Who Had It First?—A Useful Mom Option

In the playground or any other public place, if a child whose mother is not right on the spot "drops in" and begins eyeing a toy your child is playing with, try, "Lindsey's playing with this, and when she's done you can have a turn." After a short, reasonable wait (a couple of minutes) give your child a warning, such as, "In a minute we'll give this little girl a turn." Then announce that it's her turn. I would praise both children, yours for sharing and the other for waiting.

> *Lesson: We notice other people. We can have our turn but not make them wait forever. We have common consideration on both sides.*

Caution: If you make the other child wait too long, if you're wondering where the heck her own mom is and that comes out in your voice, or if you turn your back on the waiting child and don't include her by your smiles and comments, you may have unwittingly taught your child some bad lessons: Rudeness comes to mind!

While "who had it first?" remains a fair approach, at around a year-and-a-half many kids are ready to try their wings at more-sophisticated skills, such as playing with the same toy at the same time.

Here's a typical scene: One child is playing nicely with a cash register; another toddles over and yanks the cash register away. Mommy can step in with a nice game.

Activity: "Taking Turns" as a Game

- ❖ Don't yell, reproach, or talk about sharing.
- ❖ Make it positive. "What a good idea. You both want to play with the cash register."
- ❖ Give one child a red coin, another a yellow coin.

❖ "Okay, Reggie, put the red coin in. Doesn't this feel good? We're taking turns."

❖ "Okay, Jack, now it's your turn. Good! That was fun. You both took turns. Okay. Let's go again."

❖ If the kid who is waiting starts reaching out to the toy while the other one is sticking the coin in, *gently* put your arm on his to restrain him, whispering, "Ooooh, waiting is sooooo hard, and you're doing such a good job."

❖ Why whisper? Because kids love whispering. It's different, engaging, and a whisper's intimacy makes them feel grown-up and included. And in this moment it buys you time—get it?—while the other kid gets a chance. Well done, Mom.

Lesson: *I liked that we were all smiling and laughing and not shouting and frowning. Taking turns seems to be fun.*

Sharing Tips for Visits

❖ If you're going to someone else's house, take two or three of your child's toys with you. That way you have some bartering chips to offer when the going gets rough.

❖ Before another child comes over to play at your house, talk with your child. Remind her how she plays with Katie's toys at her house, and Katie can play with her toys here.

❖ A further help is to suggest that she choose three toys she doesn't want to share. We can take them out of your room. But we share everything else.

❖ When either child's sharing skills have been pushed to the limit, try marching, reading a story, starting an art project, or breaking out a snack. These are just a few of the neutral activities that do not focus on toys.

These kinds of fun strategies will help teach sharing during the toddler years. You will probably find yourself involved with some scenes that don't go so smoothly (Boy, is that an understatement!). If you have a toddler, you might be interested in skipping down to the next section, on "Hugging," and then ease your way into the rough stuff! Or you might want to look at preschoolers and sharing to get some ideas about where you and your child are heading sooner than you can imagine.

4. Preschoolers

While two preschoolers can often play nicely for long stretches, every once in a while we see flare-ups of difficulties with sharing that require a grown-up's intervention. Here are some fun games that deflect fights by enlisting a preschooler's knowledge.

Activity: Taking Turns

Situation: Playground. *Equipment:* One swing. *Typical dialogue:* "I was here first!" "No, I was!"

Mommy steps in with a fun game.

* Determine who goes first alphabetically, using the first letters of their names.
* If these two children play a lot together, you can alternate, letting the last initial alphabetically get to go first.
* Once you've worked out who goes first, let that one choose a number from one to ten (or as high as your kids can count).
* Then *both* children count out loud together until the chosen number while the first child swings.
* At the end of the counting, yell, "Switch!"
* The other child gets to do the same thing.

Lesson: *Mommy showed us how to have fun taking turns. We were counting together, which we love to do, and we forgot all about who got there first.*

Other Fun Sharing Tips

* If the children are small enough, put them both on one swing, sitting back to back.
* Use the alphabet instead of numbers. Example: "You can swing until we reach the letter *N.*" The next child gets to jump on the swing and finish the alphabet, while both of them say the letters out loud.
* Use the verses of a song they both know. One gets to swing during the first verse, then switch.
* Use your watch. Let them determine one, two, or three minutes. Let the one who is waiting watch the clock with you.
* Encourage them to make up their own system.

If you play these games right your children will end up laughing instead of screaming. Apply these kinds of games to any activity requiring taking turns.

Tip: If your child is happily swinging at the playground and another child is waiting, suggest after a reasonable time that your child give the other a turn. If your child wants to swing more after she gets off, stay with her as she waits for another turn. If the other child's mom is not nearby and the child needs a reminder, after a reasonable amount of time tell the other child that now it's time to give your child a turn, just as she did for him. They all need reminders from our world at large that we notice other people.

Verbal Refusals to Share

By three most children have acquired the rudiments of sharing, at least some of the time. Many preschoolers, however, are still not thrilled with the idea. They devise more sophisticated ways of hoarding.

A favorite ploy is, ''You can't play with that. It's special.''

There are very few toys that are actually special. The dolly or blanket your child carts around is special. The one you live in fear of losing, wash secretly, and pray for another one just like it to appear soon because you don't have a replacement if, God forbid, something happens to it. *Your child should not have to share that object.*

Tip: Try using other words, such as *favorite, beloved,* or *treasured,* since *special* gets misused so frequently among the preschool set.

No other toys are special. Do not let your child rope you into believing that she can't share on a play date because *everything* is special.

How to Handle "You Can't Play with That. It's Special"

❖ Don't embarrass your child by storming into her room and saying, ''That stupid stuffed parakeet? That's not special.''

❖ Take your child away from the room for a moment and reason with her. ''You seem to be having trouble sharing. How can I help?''

❖ If it's just free-form inability or unwillingness to share anything in the moment, tell your child that in the future if she wants she can remove the toy from her room, but right now she needs to make her guest welcome. Remind her how her friend lets her play with her toys.

❖ If she's got ''that look'' that tells you her heels are dug in too hard to be able to backtrack, shift gears into a neutral activity, away from toys. Stories, art, dress-up, snack, any pleasant activity that doesn't force the issue.

> **Lesson:** *Although I don't always like it, I am learning slowly to give and take, to take turns, and to share.*

B. HUGGING

Although we usually think of aggression in terms of hurting others, there's a behavior I see often enough to warrant mentioning it.

Many children, some as early as fifteen months and some continuing all the way through their preschool years, whether from overexuberant spirits, living in "touchy-feely" homes, or perhaps what psychologists might identify as "boundary" issues, consistently make *unwanted advances*.

The problem in dealing with a "hugger," unlike a hitter, for example, is that at first glance it appears so benign. Adorable even. But huggers are a bit like cats. You know how a cat will unerringly spot the person in the room who likes them the least and jump into that lap? So often a hugger is able to zero in on whomever will not return her affection.

Some choose a specific child as the recipient of continued embraces. Others will bear-hug any child they spot, even when the other child indicates that the hug is unpleasant. Because they do it in the face of what is sometimes an extreme negative response, such as a child crying or even hitting them, I consider it a form of aggression, or at least bad manners if aggression seems too strong a word for a hug.

However we analyze it, and even if you think your own child is lovely and there's something wrong with the other one for not wanting a hug, if you want to do right by your child, you need to look for ways to teach your hugger to back off.

In the early stages, when your toddler begins merrily chasing behind another toddler and wildly embracing him from behind while the huggee tries to shake her off, move in to deflect her. Find a toy to interest her. As you lead her away mention that the other child doesn't want a hug, and it's not nice to hug somebody when they don't want it. Since you are trying to teach not to make *unwanted* advances, you can say you'd like a hug if she feels like hugging.

Sometimes this kind of hugging is short-lived, lasting only a week or so. But if it continues, don't let your child hug until the other is upset. If you need to, remove your child from the other's immediate sphere. If you're in a playground, first try moving from the jungle gyms to the swing. Sometimes pulling out a book and sitting quietly together shifts the focus enough to change the pattern that day. But after repeated unsuccessful attempts to interest your child in some activity besides laughing, chasing a child, and hugging them till they cry, you might need to pack it in for the day.

Because with some children we can expect that hugging will go on for a while, here are some alternatives to help explain what they need to do.

Practical phrases work for children under three:

❖ Please keep your hands at your sides.
❖ Use words, not your arms.
❖ Smile instead of hug.
❖ You're too close. Back up.

These phrases continue to be helpful if needed for a preschooler, and you can also include some abstract ideas:

❖ You can like someone without hugging them.
❖ Jennifer asked you to stop. Please stop hugging.

Please make sure to praise your child when she shows restraint.

Lesson: *I am slowly learning that even if I smile, I can't do things that other people don't like.*

Although you have introduced taking turns and sharing games worthy of the Nobel peace prize, there will come a day when your toddler shows a side that is "not nice." Those little hands will get in there faster than you can. But even if you could always be faster than your child, that would not help. Your child needs your guidance in learning how to control his own little hands. Even when he wants something real bad.

C. GRABBING

For a child younger than eighteen months, grabbing isn't totally aggression. It's not having language skills to ask for something plus the inability to control the force in one's hands. A young toddler who wants something reaches and yanks.

But whether your child is thirteen months and the concept of wanting and taking are more or less the same, or your child is five and knows full well what she's doing, parents need to continually remind them that grabbing is not nice.

1. Under Eighteen Months

❖ Gently remove offending object.

❖ Be prepared to repeat, over and over in some cases until you want to scream, "Nicholas had it first. It's not nice to grab."

❖ Oftentimes a neutral adult can step in between two children who play together a lot with much better results than either of the mothers.

❖ During an extended play period in the playground with lots of grabbing, you can ask another mother you like to take the toy in question and hand it back to the kid who had it first.

2. Eighteen Months and Up

Some toddlers don't hear, screen you out, or in some other way manage to be off in a world of their own. If you notice that you have said, "It's not nice to grab," seventeen times in the last minute and your child has plunged on with the tenacity of a terrier taking toy after toy after toy, *get down in her face.* You don't have to frown and scold, but you do have to indicate by your firm tone of voice, serious expression, and direct eye contact that grabbing is not nice. She will grab again. We know that. You will have to get her attention again. And so on and so forth. Eventually, you will penetrate her cloud.

3. Twos

❖ "It's not nice to grab. Give it back, please."

❖ If your child does not give it back, hold out your hand. "Please give it to Mommy."

❖ If your child still does not relinquish it, take your child's wrist in one hand and gently pry her fingers off with the other.

❖ Give the offending toy to the child who had it first.

❖ Take your child away from the toy, explaining that if she grabs and can't give something back, she has to be moved away from that toy. (Telling her that she can't be with other children may not be the best threat. This may be exactly what she wants: to have that toy without the interference of all those annoying other tod-dlers!)

4. Threes

❖ Give her the option of giving it back herself.
❖ If your child still does not give it back, say, "I'm going to count to three. If you do not give it back by then, Mommy's going to take it from you. One, two . . ."
❖ Usually, it gets put in your hand.
❖ If your child *still* does not give it back, apologize. "I'm sorry, but now I'm going to have to take it."
❖ As gently as you can, pry it out of her hand and return it to the other child.

Common Response that May Backfire

Snatching, grabbing, yanking, or pulling things out of children's hands. It's a mixed message to grab a toy angrily from a child while at the same time saying, "It's not nice to grab."

Ideas to Help

❖ Praise your child whenever she manages to go for ten minutes or so without grabbing.
❖ Talk about grabbing before you go somewhere and get involved in a hot issue. Mention how grabbing is not nice and how proud she'll feel when she doesn't grab.

5. Four and Up

❖ If the grabbing has been going on for a while, tell your child that if she grabs once more you will take her out of the action.
❖ If she grabs again, remove her and sit down quietly. Ask why she's grabbing so much today.
❖ You may very well hear that cousin Brucie is a real stinker and won't share any of his toys. Believe your child. Agree, even. It's comforting to have a parent understand that someone else is being "bad." Explain that Brucie isn't behaving well and that the best thing to do is find something else to play with, or walk away, or tell Brucie outright that he's not being any fun. But point out that just because Brucie is a stinker doesn't mean your child can be a stinker back.

❖ Your child may be so grateful that you understand and are offering her some other way to behave that you may be surprised by how lovely the rest of the day goes.

❖ Please make sure to praise her when she shows restraint.

Lesson: *Mommy will have the patience to explain to me as many times as it takes me to catch on that grabbing is not nice.*

We've begun the slow process away from yanking. Now we're ready to move on to the nitty-gritty of physical aggression and take a look into the heart of the beast.

D. HITTING, PUSHING, SHOVING, KICKING, PINCHING: YOUR CHOICE

Five-year-old Allison has a Barbie doll in her hand.

Her best friend Jill very nicely asks, "May I see that Barbie?"

Allison gives Jill a look that could kill and turns her back.

Jill walks around in front of Allison and flashes an appealing smile. "May I please see that Barbie?"

Allison turns her head away so fast her ponytails flap.

That's it. Jill's had it. She grabs for the Barbie.

But Allison's quicker. She snatches it out of arm's reach.

Jill gets so darn mad that she gives Allison a push on the shoulder.

Allison gives a push back.

Jill takes stock of the situation for one second and then, *bam!* a two-handed push to the chest.

Barbie hits the wall as Allison goes for a return two-handed shove on Jill's chest.

It's Jill who comes up with a good ponytail grab. And Allison returns a one-two shove-and-pull move.

And Jill's got tears in her eyes, and her fingers are gearing up for a good, satisfying pinch, and there's just enough yelling right about now to bring on the mom.

Ah, yes. The peaceful, bucolic life, so enriched by children. . . .

Children fight. All children fight sometimes. Some children fight all the time. Some children fight with certain children and not others. Some children are more physical than others and their fighting manifests rather violently.

Hitting, pushing, kicking, shoving, and biting are all typical acts of aggression that children fall back on when angry, thwarted, or perturbed.

If your child hits, bites, or pushes, please do not feel that your child is bad. Negative emotions such as anger, in and of themselves, are not bad. Violent *behavior,* however, is bad.

One of our jobs is to teach how to express our anger or displeasure in acceptable ways. Before looking at specifics I want to offer you some things to keep in mind:

❖ Some people have shorter fuses than others.

❖ Some people can tolerate interruptions better than others.

❖ Some people care more than others about how things are done.

❖ Some people get on each other's nerves.

❖ Children take varying amounts of time to learn to control their physical aggression. Most do not completely master this during their preschool years.

❖ Some aggressive behavior is offensive; some defensive. They deserve different responses.

❖ "Overly aggressive" means that there is *never* any interaction between your child and another that does not include the other child crying within the first half hour, your child repeating the aggression over and over again, and the only way you can get it to stop is by removing her.

❖ Some overly aggressive children are being pushed too hard in too many directions. They need to have pressure taken off them. (We'll look at the last three ideas in Section 2, "In the Zoo: Aggression in Relation to the World.")

Mommy's Mantra: I must repeat, "We do not hit," a million times. I must repeat, "We do not hit," a million times. I must repeat, "We do not hit," a million times. I must repeat . . .

Let us now enter the world of "We do not hit." Please feel free to substitute push, shove, pinch, bite, kick, scratch, or whichever form of aggression your child prefers.

I. Thirteen to Eighteen Months

Hitting starts out kind of hit or miss (if you'll pardon the wordplay) a month or two past the one-year mark for some kids and by a year-and-a-half for most. I've seen hundreds of small-fry whose hands automatically fall hard on another toddler. What's interesting is the *variety* of their responses:

❖ Some seem shocked or distressed by the other child's cry.
❖ Some don't notice and go on about their business as if the other child weren't in the room.
❖ Some seem to watch with scientific curiosity.

This last group often become hitters. They know what they're doing. They may not be able to control it. But they know. Other children after an initial hit don't seem too interested in hitting. Stay tuned. They may very well turn into sluggers next month or next year!

Dealing with aggression is often very hard for first-time mothers, who've been living with an angel for the last year.

Remember when we talked about right and wrong in Chapter 2? Although the first time your child hits another you might feel waves of shock or horror, this isn't your child *being bad*. Your child is not feeling strong emotions of rage. The other kid took a ball she wanted. She was annoyed. She hit. This is bad *behavior*. We are now in the daily-grind part of teaching right from wrong.

The more upset you get in the beginning, including yelling "No!", grabbing her hand, swatting her hand, shrieking, or any other dramatic response, the more interesting the whole experience may become to your child. This is a continuum of learning. With a young toddler we start off correcting rather gently. "That's not nice" or any other gentle murmur as you distract your child from the scene is perfectly called for. If the other child is crying, which means it was a fairly hard hit, apologize to the mother, who will be comforting her own child, and everyone moves on. For many toddlers, they take our cues and pull back themselves. We do not pull out the big guns until they are warranted.

Useful Ideas for Beginning Hitters

❖ Apologize to the other mother.
❖ Gently lower your child's hand to her side, telling her it's not nice to hit.
❖ Make eye contact so that she knows something of import is being said.
❖ Make your tone one of correction—not anger, and not support.

Useful Ideas for Occasional Hitters

❖ Stay vigilant and close. Try and get in there before a blow falls for two reasons: to protect the other child, and to not let your child enjoy the habit of clunking someone.
❖ Remind her that we don't hit.

Useful Phrases besides "We don't hit"

❖ It's not nice to hit.
❖ Watch your hands.
❖ Keep your hands to yourself.
❖ Hands are for making things, not hurting.
❖ You wouldn't like it if someone hit you, would you?

Lesson: *Although it is interesting to watch that other child's face get red and wet, Mommy seems to be saying something to me that I don't quite get. . . . But wait, she seems to be repeating it and she looks very serious and it seems to have to do with this feeling in my arm of raising it up and bringing it down. . . . Now that's interesting . . .*

Less Useful Responses I've Seen

❖ Pretending it didn't happen (Sorry, Mom. We can't wish our problems away).
❖ Huffing, puffing, gasping, grabbing her hand, yelling, or in any other way reacting angrily.
❖ Hitting her or smacking her hand while saying, "We don't hit."
❖ Snatching her up off the floor and running her, legs dangling, away from the other child.
❖ Laughing nervously.
❖ Smiling and saying, "Oh, no, Hillary, we don't hit."
❖ Saying in earshot of your child, "Oh, he's such a boy!" or "Oh, she's got such a temper! Just like her dad."
❖ Walking away, sighing, "I just don't know what to do about Hillary's hitting."
❖ Listening to your friend over there telling you to ignore it because "they all do it."

There is nothing wrong with a fifteen-month-old who hits another kid. There is everything wrong with the mother of a fifteen-month-old sitting around and gabbing with her friends while her child is busily smacking the others with impunity—or with her hand, whichever comes first.

If your child is an occasional hitter she will catch on and the hitting will die down. For the chronic hitter, however, we have to up the ante.

What is a hitter? A child whom you know will hit during the course of *any* interaction with another child.

2. Eighteen Months and Up

By this age a child is old enough to be removed from the action after repeated hits. But try these things first.

❖ Make sure you stay close.
❖ Move in before the blow falls.
❖ Get down in her face, look her in the eye, and say, "No hitting. If you want something, tell your friend, or tell me. But no hitting."
❖ When the next hit comes, tell her, "If you hit, you can't play with other children."
❖ When the next hit comes, separate her from the other children. Away from everybody, tell her again that we do not hit.

Useful Alternatives

❖ You can hit this table, but you can't hit a person.
❖ If you feel like hitting, here's a pillow.
❖ If you feel like hitting, try clapping. (This sometimes makes them laugh and the problem is circumvented!)
❖ Give her another shot at playing. If you see that little hand getting ready to let fly again, move in with a more-supervised game to get her attention away from hitting.

An Idea to Consider if Your Child's Only Interactions Involve Hitting

Sometimes, between the ages of about one-and-a-half to two-and-a-half depending on the child, hitting, pushing, biting, or whatever aggression your child prefers gets really out of hand for a couple of months.

It has a way of escalating into an unpleasant pattern. Kid hits. Mom moves in swiftly. Other kid cries. Other mom comforts crying kid. Kid hits again. Mommy's patience is wearing thin; her remonstrances are harsh rather than firm. Other kid wailing his head off. Other mom glaring, making disapproving noises. And we all go round and round in the same rut, digging deeper and deeper, unable to get out.

Think about limiting the amount of time your child spends with other children during this brief period. This may take the pressure off both of you. It is very hard on a mom, as well as a child, when her kid behaves aggressively a lot. By cutting down on the amount of time both of you are engaged in this difficult lesson, you may allow time—that wonderful healer—and natural maturity to work in your favor.

This, by the way, is not a punitive measure. Your child doesn't need to be told, ''You hit so much that from now on I can't take you to your gym class!'' Just try not going to that class for a week or so. Often, when you return, the pattern has been broken. Everybody's able to move on.

> *Please make sure that when your child does control herself that you praise her. I promise it will happen.*

3. Two and Up

Once a child begins to have some command of language, meaning she can string a couple of words together, you can introduce a popular parenting technique: ''We use words, not our hands.'' For a verbal child, this may begin as early as eighteen months.

Scene: One two-year-old happily digging. Along comes another toddler and grabs the shovel out of her hand. First toddler frowns, possibly screams, and grabs it back. Second toddler grabs it again. First toddler—your toddler—lets one fly.

You zip in and suggest, ''We use words, not our hands.'' By doing this you are offering her a socially acceptable way to express her feelings.

Useful Phrases

After ''We use words, not our hands,'' descriptions of what happened are useful suggestions to your child.

❖ I was playing with that shovel.
❖ I had that shovel first.
❖ Please wait your turn. I'm playing with this shovel now.
❖ There's another shovel over there if you want a shovel.
❖ Please don't grab.

A word of caution: I have heard many mothers tell their children to say "I'm angry that you took that shovel."

Well. Harrumph. The mother is definitely angry that the other child took that shovel. *Possibly* her child is angry too. But her child may also be upset at having been startled, annoyed that she was interrupted while digging, or hurt because the shovel scratched her hand as it got yanked away.

By suggesting that her child is feeling the same anger she is, the mother has in fact managed to distance her child from the very thing— using words to express our feelings—that she was trying to teach.

If you restrict your supplied responses to statements of fact, you will enable your child as she matures to express what she is really feeling rather than teaching her to respond the way you do.

Less Useful Methods of Dealing with a Toddler's Physical Aggression

A. NOT PAYING ATTENTION UNTIL YOUR KID HITS

When I see a mom chatting with her friends at the other side of the room, but then, eyes flashing, she dashes across the room, yanks her toddler away from the others, and says, real mad, "Don't you do that again!" and *the kid smiles,* I know that kid is going to do that again.

You know what's appealing to our young aggressor? The fabulous way she's managed to get Mommy completely focused on her. Every single fiber of Mommy's being is pulsating in her direction and boy, oh boy, is that fun!

True Tale from the Trenches: I had a mother recently tell me that her sixteen-month-old son, a kid I happen to adore, had begun biting. Questions elicited that both parents went on the warpath whenever he did it. Further questions revealed that Dad in particular hit the ceiling. And when was this little cutie pie biting? When his dad had all his tools out and was extremely engaged in a project. You can almost hear those little wheels turning. "You think that toolbox and that wood and that tape measure and that paper and pencil are interesting? More interesting than me? Well, I'll show you something that'll get your face up out of those complicated plans. Try this on for size, if you want interesting." *Chomp.* And then there was Daddy, full-faced, paying complete attention! This particular kid is a very clever little boy and an apt pupil. I look forward to seeing him grow up. He is one resourceful child!

B. NO VALUE JUDGMENT EXPRESSED BY MOM

Don't say in the same flat tone, "We don't hit," "Put on your boots," "Pick up that book," "Here's Daddy," and "There's Big Bird." How the heck can this poor kid know what's what?

C. SAY "I'M SORRY" SYNDROME

"Say you're sorry" should not be the first words out of your mouth after your two-year-old hits another child. Your first instruction should be "It's not nice to hit," as you remove your hitter from the hittee. *You* should certainly apologize to the child who's been hit, and also to the mother, as you move your hitter away. Your apology is appropriate and called for.

"What's wrong with I'm sorry?" any mannerly mother might ask. "Shouldn't my child be sorry if she hurts someone?"

Yes. We certainly want to instill in our child a feeling of remorse when she does something wrong. But too often the phrase "I'm sorry" gets perverted into permission to do anything.

Let's put ourselves in our toddler's position for a moment and imagine how she thinks: "Okay, I get it. We hit. Then we say 'I'm sorry.' Then we go on about our business. Piece of cake."

Well into an aggressive child's threes, "I'm sorry" begins to be appropriate. Even then it should never be the very first thing you offer them. It should come after "We use words." When everybody's simmered down it is then an appropriate time to ask your preschooler to go over to the child she hit and say she's sorry.

By the time some children reach five they have perfected the skill of using "I'm sorry" to get them off the hook. They toss the phrase off with perfunctory nonchalance.

If you know of such a kid, understand that some of it is developmental, and they get some from each other in nursery school, kindergarten, and wherever kids hang out together. Nevertheless, if it's *your* kid try this:

"Every time you're going to say, 'I'm sorry,' substitute 'Would you like to do that to me?' If you grab the crayon out of Mindy's hand, say to her, 'Would you like to grab it back?' "

If you're lucky this may make both kids laugh so hard they go back to an amicable game in short order.

True Tale from the Trenches: I overheard a kindergarten mother say this beautiful phrase: "You said 'I'm sorry' with your lips. Now try it with your heart."

When is "I'm sorry" appropriate?

❖ "I'm sorry" is appropriate for mundane accidents. Model for your child and also encourage her to say, "I'm sorry," during the course of a day. Examples: We bang into someone on the street, we let go of a door too quickly and someone's almost hit, we stop short, making someone bang into us.

❖ "I'm sorry" is also appropriate for things you've had time to reflect on. Examples: Mommy's sorry she lost her temper yesterday. I'm sorry I forgot that you asked for peanut butter and jelly and I packed turkey.

D. "GIVE CHELSEA A HUG, AND SAY YOU'RE SORRY"

The nicest, most well-meaning moms often suggest this one. But what they're forgetting is that Chelsea just got smacked in the head. Chelsea really doesn't want a hug from Alexandra. Chelsea wants her mommy to hold her or Alexandra to disappear off the face of the earth. Chelsea quite possibly even wants to hit Alexandra back. A hug from Alexandra is not high on Chelsea's wish list.

E. HITTING YOU

Occasionally, I see a toddler in a mother's arms haul off and slug her mom. Since the mom's carrying the child, the blows fall on her head or face.

If this should happen to you, your small child has just stepped over an absolutely unacceptable line. Put her down. Reprimand her soundly. "You never, ever hit your mother!"

Unfortunately, I have seen too many moms respond very inappropriately. Most have looked around in embarrassment, still holding their flailing child, deflecting blows and muttering, "Oh, she's really tired."

There is no reason—tired, hungry, or any other unfulfilled need—that excuses hitting your mother. Don't be concerned with what other people think or be too polite or acquiescing for anyone's good.

If your child hits you in the face in this way more than once and you realize that you did not have a firm negative response the first time, use it productively as a wake-up call. Your child may be telling you that you've ceded your power to her and she's mad at you for doing it. This is a case where you are doing her a real disservice if you let her get away with it. You've taught lack of respect for her elders and that she is in charge emotionally. This is not a useful lesson for a child.

4. Preschoolers

Since learning to control both our tempers and our physical responses is such a long haul, you will probably still be using a lot of the methods we've already talked about once your child passes toddlerhood.

"Use words, not your hands"—upgraded now into age-appropriate concepts such as "You need to ask for something if you want it," "If you don't like what someone is doing, tell them," and words suited to particular situations—continues to be a helpful piece of guidance.

We still have to remove them from the action if they're having too much trouble. Although we talked about "time-out" in Chapter 2, I just want to put in a reminder. They're still too young for a real time-out, in terms of thinking about what they did and collecting themselves. They are old enough, however, to understand that if they continue to hit you'll take them away from the swings, and if they still continue you'll take them home. They are also old enough to recognize an idle threat. If you warn them and they continue, make sure you carry out whatever threat you offered.

If you can muster it up genuinely, a touch of *disappointment* often helps a preschooler understand that this is unacceptable.

Shifting gears to a more neutral activity continues to remain a terrific way to deflect two kids who've turned into Velcro and can't peel themselves off one another.

But since they're more sophisticated now in many ways, we can introduce a more mature way of handling physical aggression, an alternative that many adults find useful.

Walking Away

For mature threes, fours, and fives who occasionally lose physical control, say in a quiet moment, "I notice that you and Jacqueline sometimes get so angry with one another that you end up hitting." (Avoid blame, such as, "I notice that brat Jacqueline pushes your buttons until you lose it and then gloats when you get punished!") "Would you like to know what I do when I'm angry with someone?" Your child will be all ears. This is the real stuff, the grown-up stuff. "First I try to tell them what's bothering me. And if they can't stop, I go away." Let your child think about that.

"Here's my suggestion. If Jacqueline does something that annoys you, first try and stop her with your words. 'Jacqueline, I am using this part of the table now. Please find another spot.'

"If she's still leaning on you in your spot, tell her, 'I'm not going to play with you if you keep this up.'

"If she keeps it up, walk away. You're too big to be hitting now, even when somebody's annoying you."

5. Five-year-olds

By this age most of them are so big on rules and who's who and what's what that you'll get a lot of "It was her fault; she started it."

A time-honored mom response that remains viable is: "I'm not interested in who started it. Any more fighting and we'll put the game away."

Lesson: *Although I still lose my temper sometimes, I am getting better and better at not hitting. Mommy doesn't like it when I do it sometimes. She really doesn't like it if I do it a lot. But she really notices when I control it. That makes her smile and sometimes even hug me. I like that.*

E. BITING
Playful Bites

A young toddler sometimes experiments with a playful puppy nip. Like a puppy, she needs to be taught that human flesh never goes between the teeth. Look her in the eye, close her mouth gently with your hands. "We don't bite people. We bite food." That is usually the end of that. Usually.

But I've seen quite a number of biters. Some experiment with it. Some find it the method of choice.

Nursery-school teachers, day-care workers, and psychologists all assure us that biting, from a child's point of view, is the same basic instinct as hitting, scratching, and pushing. But biting puts people's teeth on edge. Ha-ha. Adults cringe in horror when a child bites, and the parents of biters are always more ashamed of their aggressors than the parents of hitters or pushers.

> **True Tale from the Trenches:** Here is one mother's adroit way of handling biting that may work for your family.
>
> Harry is in his mid-twos. Betsy, his mom, arrives at nursery school. His teachers report that he bit a girl.
>
> Situation: Harry had a chair. Girl wanted chair. Harry preferred to keep said chair, thank you very much. Girl grabbed for chair. Girl's arm went right in front of Harry's mouth. Harry bit.
>
> Teachers (I'm telling you, they *all* say the same thing!) assured Betsy that biting is a normal act of aggression. She shouldn't worry. She should monitor.

Contrary to the notion that toddlers, like puppies, cannot remember beyond the moment and that if you don't reprimand them when it happens you might as well not, many toddlers have memories like elephants.

Harry is one such child. Extremely verbal and exuberant, he is not prone to inordinate amounts of physical aggression.

Betsy is an easygoing mom. When she does get angry it is a moment to remember.

And this was a moment in young Harry's life to remember.

She knelt in front of him, looking straight into his eyes, and said very sternly, "You bit Charlotte. That was bad. Teeth are for food only. Now I will have to call Charlotte's mother and see if you hurt Charlotte so much that she had to go to the hospital." (Please notice, the hospital, not the doctor. Hospitals are serious. Doctors should never be used as a scare tactic.)

Betsy pretended a call in Harry's presence and then reported that he was lucky. Everything was okay. But biting is very, very bad.

Later she did call the mother. Everything was okay.

Harry never bit again.

I am the mother of a reformed biter (sounds like a "Biters' Anonymous" codependency admission, doesn't it?).

If you are the mother of a biter, or hitter, or pusher, a pincher, scratcher, or kicker, please take heart. Notice that I said a "reformed" biter. I promise you will live through this one. Our family is here as proof that you can survive an extended bout of aggression, learn from it, and come out at the other end in one piece. I know that when you're in it, however, you feel as if there's light way at the end of the tunnel. It's the headlights of a Mack truck, barreling your way.

Annie's biting went on for what felt like a lifetime. It began at around eighteen months, when another child bit her until she bled. Enraged, she bit back. We were off and running. Her biting peaked during her twos and did not completely sputter to a stop until she was past three. Though no different from a child learning not to hit, because it was biting it felt awful.

While I was thinking about writing this section I asked Annie if she remembered biting.

Oh, yes, she certainly did. I asked her if she could remember why she bit.

"I only bit Jacqueline [the child who first bit her], Kathleen, and Sarah." This was true.

"Why those three girls?" I asked.

"Their cheeks were so fat, I just wanted to go chomp, chomp, chomp." She chuckled rather affectionately.

Only two of them were chubbettes when they were little, I pointed out. One was downright skinny.

She thought for a moment. "They were all annoying," she announced. In fact, of all the children we know, these three girls from a very early age delighted in getting Annie's goat—which is a pretty easy goat to get, I might add.

I pressed on. "Yes, but why did you *bite?*"

She said as if it were obvious, "I thought it wouldn't hurt as much as slapping."

It's hard to gauge how accurate the interpretation and memory is of an about-to-be-seven-year-old. I can, however, tell you that this same child just recently reminded me of a time when she was two. She was playing with gravel in my friend's driveway. We have not been there since she was three. She described many details that I was amazed she could remember, such as how we were standing right near the car. She also reported being excited that I allowed her to toss the pebbles and watch them bounce down a big hill. She has consistently amazed me with her memory. Therefore, although unscientific and only the thoughts of one child, her statements about biting are at least worth passing along. Attractive flesh and thinking it won't hurt . . .

It's possible that you might not think I can give such hot advice about biting. I mean, you can say, Jeez, Louise, it took them two years to get rid of biting? I mean, what did they do—or not do?

We did all the things I've mentioned to you about the long process of helping your child control aggression. Talking, removing, praising self-control, reminding, talking, removing, and so forth.

But if I had to do it again, there is one major difference in how I would deal with the situation.

I overlooked an essential piece of information. I made a big mistake.

But parenting, after all, is not an academic exercise. It is real life. Mothers, fathers, and children all grow. We adults sometimes ignore what ought to be as plain as the noses on our faces.

In the case of "Annie the Biter," I *didn't pay attention.*

When she reminded me recently that there were only three girls whom she bit and that they all annoyed her, it was true. Each of them found that it was easy and pleasurable to get Annie riled beyond control.

Flashback. Chatting with the other mom on the sidewalk. Annie holding Blazer's leash. Vaguely notice Kathleen ask to hold Blazer's leash. Hear two-year-old Annie say, "No." Remember being absorbed in talking, noticing only peripherally that below us Annie is backing up. Kathleen is moving forward, repeating, "Hold leash? Hold leash?" Annie taking several sidesteps. "No!" "Hold leash?" It becomes a laughing game for Kathleen, little running steps, reaching to take the leash. "Hold leash? Hold leash?" Blazer being dragged patiently back and forth. Annie moving next to me. Loud "No!" My complete attention *finally* caught. I look down. Kathleen grabs leash. My reflexes too slow. Annie bites. All hell breaks loose. Biggest focus: "We do not bite!"

My ineptitude makes me want to cry.

She wasn't biting as a first response. Nor even as a second or third. She was biting only after she'd been pushed beyond her endurance. She wasn't biting anything that moved. She was only biting certain children. And only after they pushed her hard.

What I should've done was move quicker in the moment. Pay attention sooner. Bail her out after the first or second "No."

But also, lying in bed late at night thinking about what to do, I realized I should've stopped focusing on the biting itself. I should've thought about how she was biting only some kids, how with other kids she wasn't losing her temper so much. I should've thought about how the other mothers weren't helping their children; there was no mention of how Kathleen needed to accept the answer "no." I should've stopped constantly putting her together with certain kids in situations where it was predictable that she would be pushed beyond her limits; I shouldn't have come down on her hard when she did exactly what I should've known she would do.

Shoulda, coulda, woulda.

Hopefully this confession will help you not make the same mistake we made.

Listen to your child. What might those hands, or teeth, be telling you?

That leads me to the next section.

SECTION 2: IN THE ZOO: AGGRESSION IN RELATION TO THE WORLD

I want to explore a topic that I haven't seen enough of in general parenting literature. Although we do find specialty books that address the "difficult" kid, in my experience there are a slew of kids behaving in difficult ways who aren't "difficult" kids. They are kids like any other kid, responding to the world around them.

I know from my own family's experience and from other mothers I've since had in class that on the issue of biting, for example, advice is pretty scarce. We find references to nursing and biting, as well as scattered mentions of young toddlers biting. We are offered vague advice such as telling our child, "If you need help, I'll help you"—whatever that means. It is even suggested by an eminent child expert that a biter past two may need psychiatric care. And if a line in a book saying your toddler needs a shrink doesn't make you hyperventilate, nothing ever will. Yet what it does hint at, which can be productive, is that there is something going on that is bigger than the aggression itself.

Scads of kids I've seen who are well past two and who show forms of aggression that are more than a hit here and there have not seemed to me in need of *professional* intervention. Intervention of their parents on their behalf, however, might be called for.

I have seen many mothers in class and in our neighborhood struggling to work out their own relationships, and I have seen the impact of those relationships on their children. I've been lucky enough to get to really talk to a lot of moms. Often, when they're describing a situation outside of class, it's easier as an observer rather than as a participant to think of reasons why their child might be acting out in a given moment or for an extended period of time. I've seen their kids in action and have noticed patterns in their lives that don't always present themselves to the mothers, because they are so involved in them. Just like what happened to me.

Sometimes we get tunnel vision. We see only what's in front of us, unable to lift our heads to get perspective. We see our kid hit someone else. We move to stop the individual blow. And in fact, as mothers we need to stop the individual blow. Our child needs us to correct him in the moment. But sometimes we also might do everybody a favor by stepping back and thinking about what's going on around that individual blow.

Here are some ideas that may help you think about what's happening in your own family and in your child's world at large.

A. PROBLEMS WITH SOME KIDS

If your child has the capacity and skills to share, but refuses to use those skills with a particular child or behaves particularly aggressively with a certain child, then it may be a problem in the relationship with that child.

Ask yourself some questions about why these children get together.

❖ Are they forced to be in each other's company because they are in day care or nursery school?

❖ Do I get together with these people for reasons other than my child's friendship? Is this the child of a business associate whom I feel obliged to see socially or whose friendship I think will further my or my husband's career?

❖ Do we mothers like each other so much that we keep making our children get together, hoping they'll become friends even though it's clear they don't get along?

❖ Do I throw my child together with the other one for my own convenience (such as with a nearby neighbor)?

If they are together all day in school, there are steps you can take to help. Such small children don't yet have the social skills we can expect from an elementary-school child—where it may be very profitable to learn how to get along with someone we're forced to be with—yet they are in the same situation. Ask for the teacher's help. Most teachers, whether you bring it up or not, will take active steps in the classroom or day-care center to separate two children who are like fingernails on a chalkboard with one another. They usually can help you by telling you about specific events that set your child off. You can then talk at home about ways for your child to disengage with the other during the day. If you can arrange it, try to arrive and leave at different times from the child in question, cutting down on walking in and out of the door together, which is often a very social time for little ones. Should one of the children "like" the other, which interestingly enough usually happens, discourage play dates outside of school. Arrange for playtime with children your child does get along with, and make sure you spend as much time, if not more, telling your child how you noticed what a good time she had with Janie and how nicely they played together.

Any business relationship is no business of your kid's. Baby-sitters work magic for the times when you just "have" to go to a business/social function.

Those first two are on the easier side of things. We see it and take steps to shift. The other two are sometimes more problematic.

During the toddler and preschool years your child's social life is controlled by you. And often vice versa. The social fabric between mothers sometimes gets sticky. Since we're in a chapter on manners it is not remiss to talk about how to handle rebuffing and being rebuffed.

With a mother in the neighborhood, cut down the time you spend together or the time you spend trading child duty. No matter how much you may like her or how convenient it may feel to be able to drop your child off so you can dash to the store, the convenience is not worth it in the long run. Stop initiating times to get together and gracefully decline invitations until you've faded a bit from each other's lives. Sometimes, if the kids aren't thrown together constantly, they have enough distance to enjoy occasionally spending time together.

From the mother's point of view, the hardest kind of relationship to get your child out of is one where you are genuinely friends with the other mom. Do you call your friend and 'fess up? Isn't real friendship all about honesty? Isn't one of the reasons that you like your friend so much that you can really talk about anything? This may be one of those times in life where truth for truth's sake is not so thoughtful. Very few mothers, even your best friends, have the emotional bedrock to accept the fact that your child is rejecting their child. Probably you would do best to skirt the issue.

Even with the dearest friend, rather than saying, "I've been thinking about it, and I notice that Jacqueline gets Annie so angry that she ends up losing control. In fact, Annie has said to me the last few times that she doesn't like Jacqueline, she doesn't want to play with her, but I've insisted," it might be more graceful to say, "When we're with the kids I feel like we can't get a sentence out. So why don't we get together, just us, without the kids?" She will probably be as relieved as you.

Am I advocating running from difficult situations? Yes. During these early years there is no productive purpose for putting your child in a situation where she is in over her head. Some children don't like other children. They bring out the worst in each other. Ultimately, your child has to come first, not your feelings or the feelings of a friend. Pulling your child out of *all* relationships will not help teach her how to get along with other people. But pulling her out of really hard ones will give her the opportunity to learn how to get along in smaller bits that she can handle.

If you should be on the receiving end of a velvet door shutting—or an iron door slamming—remember that not everyone will like your child. Don't take it personally. It is, after all, your child's social life, not yours.

B. PROBLEMS WITH SOME SITUATIONS

Like problems with some kids, sometimes we put our children in situations that they may not be able to handle and where they might profit from our intervention.

❖ If your child seems to loathe a particular class—or all organized groups—consider waiting until later to try it. It's possible that they'll enjoy a group experience even six months later and worth retrying if you feel you'd like to. Many very sociable people have grown up without early group settings. Because toddler classes are so fashionable, we sometimes forget just how young these children really are and want them to be doing what everybody else is doing. But if they are unhappy and acting out, they will not be gaining the enriching experience that you had hoped for. What they really need is to be doing what they enjoy, can handle, and will garner self-esteem from.

❖ If your child is not generally angry, but is very aggressive in day care, consider finding a different center. If the same behavior ensues in another day-care center, consider getting a full-time baby-sitter or relative to provide one-on-one care.

❖ The same applies for baby-sitters. A normally pleasant child who turns into a pit bull around a particular sitter is telling you something. Find her a sitter better suited to her personality. I've seen some truly lovely sitters with justifiably glowing references who didn't hit it off with a particular child. No matter how reliable, intelligent, and trustworthy a lady may be, if she and your child don't like each other, it's not good for either of them.

❖ Siblings often disagree. This is normal and even healthy. But sometimes the fighting reaches hideous proportions. Consider keeping them apart for a while as a means of allowing each of them some peace at home. Naturally, siblings are part of a complicated family structure. It's glib to say "separate them" out of context. But if both of your children get along well with other children, but go after each other with a real vengeance, the sad reality might be that their personalities clash. Usually, one of them takes a lot more beating than the other. For the sake of family harmony and for the sake of helping them build a better relationship later in life, you might want to help them not rub the same wounds raw constantly. Don't write it off. There are phases in family life. But when the going gets really rough they might be grateful to be relieved of having to keep trying—and failing—at being constantly together and being expected to get along during a particularly difficult period.

C. PROBLEMS WITH ALL KIDS

By the time your child is three she ought to be able to get along *sometimes* with *some* other children.

"Ought to" is one of those phrases that make mothers nervous if their child "isn't." But let's say that almost every interaction your child has with other kids is a disaster of crying, screaming, bossing, and hitting.

Take a look at some of the following ideas. If one of these rather unpleasant possibilities hits home, don't get bent out of shape. Just take a deep breath and try to make things better. Even the most serious problem can be corrected only by going step by step.

- ❖ If your child always gets her own way, always gets to go first, and always wins at home—in other words, if she's spoiled—she will probably find that getting along with other kids is way beyond her scope.
- ❖ If her needs are being met through things rather than other forms of love, she may cling to the objects given to her by her parents as substitutes, and therefore experience kids wanting to play with her toys—or any toys—as wanting to take her parents.
- ❖ If she is not spending enough "kid" time with her parents, she may find spending time with other kids enraging because that isn't what she wants to be doing.
- ❖ Sometimes a younger sibling who's always the underdog at home, who always has to go second, wait, and get smacked around, will turn the tables once out in the world and get downright obstreperous.

If the word *spoiled* made you think, "Spoiled! *My* child? She may be willful, and she certainly knows her own mind, but I wouldn't say she's spoiled. It's those *other* children," consider these ideas.

- ❖ Get her to play with older children. Most seven and eights, if they can tolerate a smaller child around, will clue her in quickly to how things work in kid land. She won't be able to pull her monster stuff on the older ones, and the battle won't be with you. She will learn the ropes of taking turns, sometimes losing, and not always getting to go first in the school of hard knocks. It's a harsh but realistic school where the lessons are valuable. Your older stepchild's friends are not good candidates for this teaching experience. Try to find some neutral children, such as neighborhood kids, ones from your church or synagogue, or second- and third-graders from your kindergartner's school.
- ❖ Practice cooperating together without bringing up the word *sharing*. Try a simple art project, for example. A collage is a good

one. Have one bottle of glue and one pair of scissors. Don't automatically hand them to her the second she demands them. She needs to learn how to wait and not get angry when she has to. After you've each successfully made a collage, tell her how much fun it was to sit at the table together.

❖ Anytime you notice that she is managing to get along with another child, tell her you noticed and you're glad she's learning.

If the possibilities of *too many things* or *not enough kid time* made you sit back and go, "Hmm . . ." you might need to rearrange your lifestyle a bit. Since these two things often go hand in hand, some of the same ideas will help.

❖ Think about glancing again at Chapter 3, "Materialism and Greed," which has some hints about cutting back on things.

❖ If you live in the fast lane or high society, it is unrealistic to assume that you will suddenly enjoy trips to the playground or to an amusement park. None of us should be expected to be who we aren't or to do things that we dislike intensely. By the same token, neither should we expect that of our children. If all of your preferred social events are formal or very adult, and your child is expected to handle herself well all the time when she is with you or else kiss you quickly as you run out the door, consider dropping out a bit so you can add some time to be with your child. Choose child-centered activities that both of you can enjoy, such as story time at the library, a children's festival in your town, or a visit to a children's museum.

❖ If both you and your husband work long hours, figure out ways to steal more time from work to spend together with your child.

If your youngest child gets pushed around at home, but is a bully with her peers, glance back to the section in this chapter called "Problems with Some Situations," and provide your children with more autonomy from one another in the home.

If any of these things ring bells of recognition with you, you might also glance at the list of suggestions in the section titled "Real Life," page 280.

If you notice that whenever your child is playing with others, she is consistently on the receiving end of unpleasantness, no matter *who* the other child is, you might think hard about what's going on.

Here are some signs to watch for:

❖ Other children are *always* hitting her.
❖ Other children are *always* screaming, "No!"
❖ She messes up what other children are doing rather than joining in.
❖ She crowds other children and doesn't back off when they ask her to, either verbally or nonverbally.

If this sounds familiar it might be useful to ask yourself some questions:

❖ Do you show your love by physically overpowering her—scooping her up from behind, kissing her, and plunking her down again, and then going on about your business without so much as a how-do-you-do?
❖ Do you love her so much that you don't mind that she's always pulling on your clothes, interrupting you when you speak to other people, grabbing food from your plate, or taking things out of your hand without asking?
❖ Do you let her intrude on whatever you're doing without pointing out that you were doing something? If you're addressing an envelope and she comes over, takes the pen, and scribbles on the envelope, do you say, "Nice picture," get another envelope, and readdress it without mentioning what she's done?
❖ Do you grab things from her without explaining why you're taking them?
❖ Do you hit her?

These are some types of interactions that may be going on in your family. If you recognize any of these patterns in your family, make moves to alter them.

If you have a child whom *all* other children respond to negatively, who cannot get along with any other children, and you can't think of anything your family does at home that would in any way cause this kind of response, it might be helpful to talk to somebody else who has a lot of experience with children. It sounds as if you need an objective observer to help you help your child.

Is that just a kinder, gentler way of saying seek professional help? Yes and no. If it were me, I'd start with another mom who seems to handle her children well and see what she might do that's different from what I do. I'd talk to a teacher if you have the ear of a good one. I'd suggest family therapy, or counseling just for you, if you think that might improve your mothering skills. In terms of therapy for your child, however, I personally do not think any child who has not suffered a serious trauma but cannot get along with any other children under the age of six is in need of her own therapy, unless there are absolutely no alternative measures that anyone is able to take in her behalf.

D. PROBLEMS WITH ALL KIDS AND/OR ALL SITUATIONS

If your child is having problems with all kids or in all situations, we have to step back even farther.

A child throwing major tantrums on a daily basis, hitting all kids all the time, or hitting you more than once or twice, requiring your baby-sitter, day-care workers, or nursery-school teachers to talk with you, is telling you through behavior that something is not right. There are several general categories that you should think about.

Physical Causes

A child who's extremely difficult to handle may have a hearing problem, a processing problem, may need glasses, or is suffering from physical discomfort or pain either from normal childhood diseases or more serious illness.

❖ Call your pediatrician in advance, explain that your child is throwing more tantrums than you think is normal, and say you want to rule out any physical cause.

❖ Do not tell your child she's going to the doctor because she's been throwing so many tantrums. You do not inadvertently want to link ''bad'' behavior with the ''punishment'' of a visit to the doctor.

❖ A toddler with hair in her eyes can be a terror. This sounds so silly, but I have seen it in several children. It's a problem that sneaks up on both the parent and child and is obviously very easily remedied.

Real Life

If there are any of the kinds of stress that many families are under such as divorce, predivorce, major illness, major economic insecurity, or the terminal illness of a grandparent, these stresses bear down on the youngest members of our families and often come out in the form of their not being able to get along with anybody.

During stressful times that are out of her control, your child desperately needs to know that she is important enough to you that no matter what kind of stress you're under, you're still paying attention to her and her behavior.

If your family is going through a really rough spot, some of the things that help a young child are:

- ❖ Keep her routines as regular as is humanly possible. These include food, clothes, providing fun things for her to do every day, making sure that she gets her bath, and that her bedtime rituals are consistent. Sometimes when under stress adults couldn't care less about food, for example. But whatever you're going through and however you're reacting, these normal everyday routines are places where your child will feel better if her own routines are kept in order.
- ❖ No matter how upset you are about something else, make sure that you pay attention to the parenting issues that all children need: She needs to have limits set, consistency in those limits, and consistency in how you deal with her going beyond those limits.
- ❖ Try to find something that she did each day that is good. Don't fabricate some praise just because you feel she needs strokes. A kid will see right through that in a minute, and it'll make her feel even worse.
- ❖ Make sure that if she is in day care or nursery school it is a nurturing environment, rather than a more rigorously organized situation where the adults get angry if kids don't do what everybody else is doing.
- ❖ See if there's an extended-family member who adores your child and who can spend time with her on a regular basis.
- ❖ If you're in one of those messy things where your child has to spend a lot of time with another family, if you can humanly arrange it choose a family where she's not going to be either an inconvenience, the straw that breaks the other mother's back, or with a bunch of kids who'll pick on her.
- ❖ She needs, every single day if you possibly can, to spend some kid time with you. Either snuggling, reading a book, playing a game, singing a song, walking down the street holding hands and not being in a hurry to get somewhere else, or whatever small moment you can find where both of you can forget about everything difficult going on around you and simply enjoy one another's company. One of the hardest things about this may be that just because you have the time or you have cleared your own

emotional distractions out of your head and are really ready to ''be'' with your child, your child's mood may not be exactly the same as yours. She may very well use that time to let you know in no uncertain terms just how upset she is. If she acts out with you, correct the behavior, and if you can, move on. If you had reading a book in mind and she knocks the book clear across the room or tears it up, let her know that that's unacceptable. Then try doing something else, going for a walk, or something that takes both of you away from the place where you just had an unpleasant scene. If at all possible it would be best for both of you to feel good together before hustling off to the next obligation.

If there are big problems at home, these suggestions won't wave a magic wand in your child's life where suddenly she will be skipping through her days merrily, cooperatively, and agreeably. But they will help. And that is all a parent can do: Help your child to the best of your ability, no matter what hand life has dealt you at the moment.

Problems Beyond the Scope of This Book

If you suspect serious problems with child care, your spouse, a neighbor, or a relative, please seek professional help. Don't, however, just turn to *Psychologists* in the Yellow Pages. Perhaps the best source is a neighbor or friend whom you know has gotten help, such as marriage counseling, and you can see positive changes in their life that you approve of. Their therapist will either help your family or be connected to a reputable group of others who can help you. If you don't know anyone like that, ask for a referral from you pediatrician or clergyman.

E. THE DUKE-IT-OUT SCHOOL OF THOUGHT

I have suggested vigilance if your child is aggressive and altering any family patterns that may be getting in the way of her learning how to control herself. Yet there are moments when adult intervention is uncalled for.

I. Appropriate Parental Choice

You may remember that in Chapter 1 we talked about Jed and Colin. Jed made a big mistake. He pushed Colin off the sliding board. He got a good what-for and he will never, as long as he lives, poor kid, make that mistake again.

But before that terrible incident, when Colin had simply annoyed him and Jed had shoved Colin, I mentioned that one reasonable parenting alternative was to leave it alone.

There are times when hitting isn't so terrible. What are those times?

For children under three there is never really a time. They are still learning the basics. No matter what happens between them, they should not feel that if they show physical aggression the adults condone it.

For preschoolers, however, a physical response sometimes is appropriate.

❖ Let's say that one child is annoying, intrusive, or aggressive all the time. Another three-year-old has been the recipient of this behavior once too often. She has used methods available to her. She has told the child to leave her alone. She has walked away. Yet the child continues to be intrusive. If the second child hits or pushes, this is a moment where many decent, sensitive people would not intervene. The child has had enough. She has communicated appropriately: "You keep acting like a jerk, I'm going to get you out of my face."

❖ If two children play together all the time, and once or twice during every play session they have a pushing match that they resolve themselves after a few minutes, leave them alone. They are doing great!

❖ If an unknown child walks up to your child in the playground and for no apparent reason slams your kid, and your kid slams back, more power to her. If her response works to get the bully away, good. If, however, it escalates beyond that, step in. These are still small children.

> **Lesson:** I am not allowed to hit whenever I feel like it. But if somebody is being really horrible I can defend myself. If my friends and I lose our tempers every once in a while, it's okay, as long as we make up.

2. Inappropriate Institutional Stance

Many respected day-care centers, nursery schools, and centers for child development encourage children to find their own balance during the course of the day. They have a hands-off approach. If children get into tussles over toys the adults step back and see what happens, letting the children establish a miniature society with some personalities more dominant than others. They feel that children should be encouraged to meet their own needs, to articulate their own desires, and to act on their own wants.

While appealing in theory, on a practical note, what about the poor little sucker getting the crap smacked out of him day in and day out? What are we teaching him? And for the stronger, more self-reliant child, we should be wary of allowing him to think that society condones "might makes right."

Some people are stronger than others. Some are leaders and some followers. Siblings and neighborhood children who play together always establish hierarchies. In those lovely twilight hours during the summer, as they run through the backyards playing, they definitely know who's the top dog. They know which kid comes up with the most fun ideas, which kid comes up with the ideas that are this side of naughty, and which comes up with the ideas that the rest of them reject as too far beyond the pale. These healthy pecking orders are based not only on personality types, but on age and experience.

In a day-care center or nursery school, where the children are closer in age, a different approach seems warranted to me. Day-care centers and nursery schools are institutions. They represent our common beliefs as a society. Each child should be treated evenhandedly. All the children should know that the same behavior is expected of them *no matter what kind of personality they have.*

If you are investigating child care for your child, and you hear those in charge say that they try not to intervene much, I would view that as a red flag. I suggest you watch them in operation. If you see a lot of tussling, or some children never in the thick of things and no adult offering them suggestions of how to enter the play, or one child who seems to be hitting a lot without an adult stopping him, or one child getting hit a lot and no one trying to readjust these imbalances, I would look for a different place for my child. Children need to feel safe. Security can make them blossom. They deserve a chance to be welcomed into the world by taking baby steps toward holding their own, until each child regardless of his temperament has the resources to stand up for himself.

F. DEALING WITH "HER" KID
Or Hey! I'm Busy Busting My Kid's Chops. What about Her?

Sometimes you read, "Don't interfere with another child's misbehavior." If a mother is disciplining a child in a way different from yours, it is none of your business. But I feel very strongly that it is all of our business if a child is getting no guidance whatsoever. The withdrawal of common expectations for children and the accompanying lack of adult correction toward other children is one of the factors that I believe is contributing to the disintegration of our community fabric.

If a child litters, for example, and her parents don't have the good sense to teach her not to, then she should know that other people in the community find littering unacceptable. Otherwise, how is the child expected to behave properly? If you see a child throw wrappers on the ground in the playground, I think it is within your rights to pleasantly point out that the garbage can is over there and that we don't litter. You can even try a game. "I bet you can't get that wrapper in the garbage can." She may or may not pick up on your cue. But you have allowed her the opportunity of hearing something she might not be hearing at home.

Likewise, if a child in the playground is not being supervised by her own mother and is behaving badly with your child, it is in everybody's interest to introduce the idea to her that certain kinds of behavior are unacceptable in the world at large.

I'm going to use the example of grabbing, but you can substitute hitting, biting, pushing, or whatever aggression comes your way.

Here's a typical toddler scenario: In the sandbox an unsupervised toddler comes over and grabs your toddler's shovel.

❖ Try to find something likable about the other child.

❖ Remember that, like your child, she's still young.

❖ Put another toy in the grabber's hand. "Here, this one's for you."

❖ If the grabbing continues, say, "Grabbing is not nice." Gently stop her hand.

❖ If the grabbing continues, move to another part of the sandbox.

❖ If the grabber follows you, say, "You can play with us, but only if you don't grab."

❖ If the grabbing continues, ask the child where her mommy is. Take the child to her and say, "Your child was asking for you."

❖ Try your best to say this without a reproachful tone.

❖ If, by some fluke she asks nicely what happened, tell her both of your children were grabbing from one another—in other words, don't say, "Your little monster kept grabbing my kid's toys, and you were over here yakking it up." It's possible you may have made a friend.

❖ More likely she won't thank you, and she might even be annoyed. Why would a woman who doesn't know enough to teach her child not to grab suddenly turn into the Martha Stewart of the playground and exhibit gracious manners?

❖ If this happens, do not engage. Say, "bye, bye," nicely to the child and move on.

Lesson: *Unacceptable behavior is unacceptable behavior. Mommy doesn't let other children do things that aren't nice any more than she lets me do things that aren't nice. We are all part of the same playground and follow the same rules.*

Here's another predictable playground scene. A kid of ten or twelve is standing on a swing, swinging fast and high while a lot of younger children are wandering dangerously close by.

You can point out to him that there are a lot of little kids around and the way he's swinging might hurt one of them. Most children will slow down. Just like your child, they still need a grown-up's guidance from time to time, even though by that age their parents shouldn't be breathing down their necks in the playground.

But if your suggestion is met by his ignoring you or defiantly swinging harder, he is not playing by the same rules that you're requiring of your preschooler. Move your child away. Tell your child point-blank: "That child is not playing nicely. We don't have to be around him."

Lesson: *If somebody bigger and angrier than me doesn't listen to reason, then I take myself away from him because he might hurt me.*

Is that a chicken response? Perhaps if you're raising Arnold Schwarzenegger, Mike Tyson, and Sylvester Stallone, all wrapped up in one powerful package. But for the rest of us, that happens to be a very prudent lesson to teach your child, who will be in high school before you know it. It is not useful to prepare a child to live in a world where everybody's sometimes disagreeable, but usually peachy keen. Unless you know where that world is and can take our family with you.

With that in mind, if your child sees another mother hit her child, don't pretend it didn't happen. A little swat will draw curiosity from a child who's never been hit. A serious hit will distress your child. Whether she asks with words or with nonverbal signals, tell her the truth: Some people are not nice.

POLISHING THE DIAMOND

I don't know about you, but since we've just been through such a hard part of things, I am ready to relax and have as much fun as possible with some of the finer things in life. As your child matures she will acquire enormous amounts of refinement at your knee. But here I'd like to suggest the essentials that you can expect from a person of such a tender age. Care to join me?

SECTION I: ELOCUTION

It is the rare child who does not need to be advised to lower her voice when she's excited. Try not to shout, "Lower your voice!" It's counterproductive. A popular phrase that works is, "That's your outside voice. Please use your inside voice."

Often the same child who shouts in your ear until you want to cry when you are at home becomes a tiny mouse out in public. Say in the same nice tone, "It's hard to hear you."

Whining is another "attractive" habit that many toddlers and preschoolers come by naturally or eagerly embrace once they hear it from a friend. One mother I know pretends it's bagpipes.

Perhaps you might find either of these options more to your liking: "I can't hear you when you talk like that." When your child is not whining, praise her. "I love that regular voice."

Screaming is another. Some children scream when thwarted. A verbal two-year-old loses all language. An older child cries histrionically. Here are two that often work: "When you scream like that it makes me want to say 'No.' Find a better way to ask for what you want." "If you scream I can't help you. Try to talk."

SECTION 2: POLITE PHRASES

PLEASE AND THANK YOU

It may very well take five or six years, if not longer, before your child uses these phrases automatically, but you must keep at it if she's to learn these words at all.

The more often your child hears *please* and *thank you,* the more likely she will use them when she's older. So please use these phrases at home. Thank you.

During her twos, try reminders. "I didn't hear 'please.' " "Did you forget to thank Grandma?" Praise her when she uses the words.

By two-and-a-half for verbal children and by three for all, try, "What's the magic word?" Do not give her what she asked for until you hear "Please." If you find yourself saying, "What's the magic word?" to someone else's child, you're on automatic pilot. Teaching should be more conscious.

If you find yourself saying, "What's the magic word?" to an adult *in any situation,* please get a baby-sitter and go to an R-rated movie.

Make sure you model *please* and *thank you* as you go about your day, and make sure that whenever your child interacts with someone in a store or on the street that she uses *please* and *thank you.* At this time you will also need to add, "It's hard to hear you."

EXCUSE ME AND I'M SORRY

We looked at *I'm sorry* while talking about aggression.

Excuse me is another phrase that is useful to model as you glide gracefully through the world.

Children often adore this phrase, although many threes may need gentle reminders for two things: Repeating "Excuse me" louder and louder while tugging on her mother's arm until she is bent over sideways as a means of successfully interrupting a conversation or screaming "Excuse me" at the top of her lungs while riding her bike through a group of children are not how we use this pleasant phrase.

SWEARING

I've been playing with these other ideas. This one doesn't make me smile. Try and watch your language around your child. There is something offensive about hearing even "hell" and "damn" come out of the mouth of a child. Should you hear these words or stronger language, you can point out that nice children don't use language like that. If you overreact you may find your child saying really "bad" words just to get a rise out of you.

SECTION 3: DINING

Some of us eat at long, polished dining tables with candles, crystal, silver, and linen. Some of us think taking the pizza out of the box is big time.

Your child will learn the style that fits your family. There are, however, two social graces that every child has the right to be introduced to so that she can move through the world without making people gag.

CHEWING WITH THE MOUTH OPEN

"Please close your mouth when you chew" should be repeated at regular five-minute intervals in any home with children three and over. Even when you're not eating. (Just joking.)

Make sure you chew with your own mouth closed. Don't mention that your child is spitting and slobbering if she is in the middle of telling you something. But after you've responded to what she's said, mention that it's easier to hear when she doesn't have a mouthful. If she's not talking, point out that she is chewing with her mouth open.

NAPKINS

Most children will wipe their hands and faces on whatever is available. Usually their clothes. Often yours. Nevertheless, "Please use your napkin" is one of those Mom things that if repeated often enough, will sink in by the time they are on a dinner date in college.

SECTION 4: THE PERSONAL HABITS OF LADIES AND GENTLEMEN

NOSE PICKING

Around two, many children find that their noses are a darn good place to stick their fingers. By nursery school, some children—and we've all seen them—eat it.

With children who take direction easily, gently removing their fingers from their nose works. With most children who are willful by nature or who are in a limit-testing phase, which often coincides with the beginning of nose picking, this may backfire, causing them to want to do it even more. The habit is only encouraged when moms make a big deal and either scream, swat their two-year-old's hand, or laugh out loud.

Most two-year-olds need to be discouraged gently. If a gentle removal hasn't worked, try simply ignoring it. If it lasts more than a week or so, try, "I'll give you a Kleenex." Have them handy.

If it still persists, try, "This is one of those things we don't do in public. If you want to pick your nose, tell me and I can take you to a bathroom." After being taken into the bathroom often enough and missing enough fun, most kids will find nose picking not worth the hassle.

The preschooler who develops a real habit is a bit harder to handle.

The child may not know that she's doing it. Whenever you see her say, "Your fingers are in your nose." Ask her teacher to help out.

If you can't stop it your child has a habit, like nail biting and thumb sucking. These problems eventually go away with maturity if you don't make too big a deal of them.

PUT YOUR DRESS DOWN

Little girls need to be taught to keep their dresses down. Oh, yes, I know it's not fair, and I know it's Victorian, and I know they're just little.

Now I'm going to use a word I bet you haven't heard in decades. *Modesty.*

What purpose does modesty serve? It serves to keep your girl safe. It serves to help her understand that her body is her private business to be shared with whom she chooses to share it when she chooses and that it is not public property.

❖ When she lifts her skirt up over her head, say, "We keep our skirt down in public," and gently put it down.

❖ If she sits with her legs up and she's wearing a dress, tuck her skirt down, reminding her that we keep our skirt down in public.

❖ If she's in the playground, however, and her skirt is flying, leave her alone. That's a time when she should be focusing on play. You might, however, suggest that she wear pants to the playground so she doesn't have to be bothered with her skirt.

If you put ruffled pants on your toddler and say, "Show Grandma your new panties," you might as well throw in the towel on the "put your dress down" issue.

TAKE YOUR HAND OUT OF YOUR PANTS

Although we talked about this in Chapter 4, I want to mention it again briefly here in terms of manners, which is slightly different from helping your child acquire healthy sexual attitudes.

Sometimes a preschooler's hands slip into his or her pants to give a good scratch. Sometimes those hands go in there because it feels good.

Remind your child that we don't put our hands in our pants in public. You can go to the bathroom or into your room if you want to do that.

SECTION 5: THE TELEPHONE

The phone is a major part of our lives and a source of contention in homes across our nation.

It might be useful to take a look at the phone from the child's point of view in order to understand why this particular object evokes such frequent family conflict.

Consider how fascinating an object it must be to a baby. It is inert. It does not differ dramatically from a videocassette or a box of wipes. It makes an interesting beeping noise, but so do the microwave and dryer.

Yet Mommy has an intense emotional relationship with it. She listens hard. She smiles. She says, "How nice to hear from you." She throws back her head and laughs. Or she frowns and says, "No! We do not want any! And please do not call us again!"

Whoa! What a rush!

Sometime during the first or second year of life, the voices of favorite people such as Daddy, Grandma, Grandpa, and sometimes Mommy herself come through the little holes in the piece of plastic.

Eventually the child catches on that Daddy is not inside the box. Somehow he is able to talk through it. *Voilà!* Your child has understood the power of the phone.

Contact with the outside world. When you are on the phone you are not completely available to your child. Many children find this disconcerting.

There is another element: the amount of emotional mileage a child can get from a phone interruption.

This favorite pastime of interrupting on the telephone begins early on and is an attractive way to kill time for children *way* beyond their preschool years.

If I had a buck for every time I've heard "Please don't interrupt me while I'm on the phone" and another for every time I've said it, I'd be able to donate my teaching time. Better yet, I'd be sittin' pretty on some hot little island drinking carrot juice, having somebody else make the beds and do the dishes, and gabbing on the phone all day to my girlfriends—uninterrupted!

But back here in the real world . . .

Here are several typical Mom responses that are not particularly effective.

❖ *The English Method:* Murmur, "Excuse me," put your hand over the mouthpiece, and say in beautifully modulated tones,

"Darling, please don't interrupt Mummy while she's on the phone."

❖ *The Fraidy-Cat Method:* Hunker down in a closet and whisper so your children won't know you're on the phone.
❖ *The Wisecracking Method:* "Does this piece of plastic attached to the side of my head have any meaning to you whatsoever?"

One mom suggested this: Bind and gag your children for one hour a day while you make calls. Although I'm told it's effective, it doesn't go along with my child-raising philosophy.

In order to keep peace and have a life of your own, I suggest a couple of skirting tactics:

❖ Understand that you simply do not have as much phone time as you did prechild.
❖ Don't make long social calls during peak neediness times, such as bedtime, right before dinner, when your child has just come home from nursery school or day care, or if your child has just had a play date that was fun, stimulating, or upsetting.
❖ Make as many important phone calls as you can while your child is being looked after by someone else, is napping, or is already in bed for the night.
❖ When she begins to make her own calls, such as talking to Grandma, *do not interrupt* and feed her lines to say. A very small child can be told, "Speak up, Grandma doesn't hear so well," or, "You have to say 'Hello.' Otherwise, Grandma doesn't know you're on the phone." But anything beyond helpful "how to use the phone" hints constitutes an interruption. And what's good for the goose is good for the gosling.
❖ Once your child reaches the age of three or so you can assume that there will be times—not constantly, by the way—when you can speak on the phone uninterrupted. If you restrict the length of most of your calls, you are justified in explaining to your child that you have to make a very important call and that you don't want to be interrupted. Ask her what activity she would like to do for the next ten or fifteen minutes. Make sure that you set her up with everything she needs. This is a technique that works only with a child who has a decent attention span and in a home where the mother is not on the phone all day.
❖ If your five-year-old consistently interrupts, a good way to punish the interruption is this: Make a call to find out information about

something fun to do with your child. When she interrupts, say, "I asked you not to interrupt me. Because you interrupted I couldn't hear the information I needed for us to go to the movie [go ice skating, etc.]. We will not be able to go." She will carry on, and you can tell her to remember this the next time you ask her not to interrupt. Remind her when she interrupts the next time.

❖ A cordless phone is a double-edged sword. While it allows you to talk and still be able to pour her a glass of juice, it is tempting because it's so easy to overuse. Restrict its use to times when your child is busily engaged and you're trying to straighten up and still be available to her. Don't use it during tub time, meals, or any other moment when you really should focus on your child.

CHILDREN'S MANNERS ON THE PHONE

Your child should learn phone manners as early as you permit her to make calls and answer the phone. Each family has their own time-frame for both activities.

Making Calls

By three she should be taught to identify herself when she calls someone. "Hi, Grandma, this is Sarah" is a polite, simple phrase that most young children catch on to.

By four and five many children enjoy calling their own friends. Make sure they identify themselves when someone else answers and ask if they may please speak to their friend. Also monitor their calls for time. Several minutes is plenty for several squawks, a couple of giggles, and a few feigned baby noises. Then remind your preschooler that both families may now want to use their phones.

Taking Calls

Whenever you are ready to have your child answer your phone, teach her to say "Hello." (They often think that if you stand there with the phone to your ear, things will start happening!)

If someone says, "Who is this?" or "What's your name?" she should answer, "Who are you?" And she should never, ever tell her name, unless it's Daddy or someone she knows well.

You don't have to launch into a discussion of possible hideous things that happen to little children when crank callers know their names. But make it absolutely clear that they never tell their name over the phone to anyone they don't know.

SUMMARY:

❖ Teaching children how to handle physical aggression is a long, slow process. Don't get discouraged. Keep at it.

❖ Help your child as much as you can by providing the best environment you can.

❖ If you see your child having too much trouble in the moment or over a long period of time, shift gears. Try to change whatever is going on that is exacerbating the aggression.

❖ The rudiments of good manners lie in controlling aggression. During these early years you can teach several basic forms of politeness that will pave the way for more refinement as your child matures.

Public Places: Where a Child Can Be Seen and Heard

Inconsiderate behavior in public places is perhaps the only area where people of all races, colors, creeds, sexual preferences, socioeconomic classes, and cultures unite splendidly: We share a common disregard for the feelings of others.

Public bathrooms are treasure troves of examples of inconsiderateness for one another. People sprinkle tinkle on toilet seats, drop toilet paper on floors, and leave sinks hairy. Even more disgusting, some don't flush.

A major exception are the bathrooms at Disneyland and Disney World, which are so clean you'd think you died and went to heaven.

But when you stop to think about it, Disney's clean bathrooms are humiliating.

Disney doesn't rely on you and me, the way airports and Amtrak do. The clever Disney people said, ''Americans are slobs who can't be trusted to flush a toilet or turn off a sink. But we'll rig it so everything is done automatically by electric eye. That way people aren't personally responsible. But we'll give them the famous Disney illusion: without having had to do one darn thing besides pay, they will leave here emotionally satisfied and feeling good about themselves.''

I wish I were joking.

Although much of what I cover in this chapter seems self-evident, once you glance through it, go out and do some fieldwork. See if you don't notice how frequently we find rude behavior. I'd love to know if your observations gel with mine.

Dirt in public is part of the low-key stress we live with. Rudeness between strangers erodes our sense of well-being. We become selfish, self-protective, and suspicious. Sometimes, unfortunately, our suspicions are warranted.

Often, being out and about with our child isn't fun. Running a maze between keeping our child from knocking all the soup cans down in the supermarket and making sure he doesn't get snatched while we're not looking can be wearing.

But however complicated and sometimes trying being out can be, out we must go.

I'd like to divide this material into two parts: how we are when we're out and about (with some of the things we might wish we did better if we thought about it), and how to evaluate those people around us who might not be as nice as we are.

SECTION 1: PUBLIC PLACES

Many suggestions in this section are modeling. Your young child doesn't behave any differently at home or abroad. You, however, probably do. While ideally, we would all be models of politeness, especially to our families, the likelihood is that we are looser at home about some things.

I'd like to run through some of the most common places we go, and point out some of the behavior I've seen where moms maybe haven't thought out what it is they're teaching their children.

A. BATHROOMS

Here are some things to teach your child either through example or by telling.

- ❖ Keeping your voice calm, make sure your child doesn't touch anything. Introduce the idea of germs in public places.
- ❖ If you are a squatter, *pick up the toilet seat!* Then the seat won't be damp for the next sitter or the toddler who puts paper down.
- ❖ If you find sprinkle tell your child, "Someone wasn't considerate. We would never leave such a mess."
- ❖ Make sure your child flushes. Point out that just as we don't enjoy finding someone else's mess, we don't want to leave a mess for the next person.
- ❖ Use your foot in a gross bathroom or a piece of toilet paper in your hand in a bathroom that looks fairly clean. Flushers are places where germs exist.

❖ If your child misses the garbage, make sure he picks his paper towel off the floor and tries again.

❖ Air blowers are often difficult for children. They're mounted high, so when a child reaches toward them water drips into his sleeves. Pick him up so he can dry well.

❖ If you're in a really disgusting bathroom, use a piece of toilet paper to pull the door open.

❖ If your son is at least four, there's no man with you, and you need to change in a locker room, change in a corner. This is for the privacy of the people using the locker room as well as for your son, since he doesn't need to see so many bodies of grown-up women.

❖ By five he can go in a bathroom by himself if it's not in a raunchy, crowded place. Tell him you'll be right outside and if anybody offers to help him, he should come right out and tell you.

B. STORES

Whether a sprawling department store or a tiny shop, stores can be useful for teaching a young child consideration. Here are some suggestions of ways to model decent behavior and some expectations for your child while in a store:

❖ Anything we take off a shelf or rack should be put back exactly where we found it.

❖ If you happen to discover something in your child's hands and you have no idea where it came from, rather than shoving it on the nearest shelf, give it to an employee, explaining that you don't know where your child got it.

❖ Take anything you or your child inadvertently breaks or opens to an employee and say, making sure your child hears you, "We're sorry. We broke this."

❖ Be prepared to pay for it. If it's a small item most reputable shops will thank you for telling them and wave you away. If it's a larger item, ask to speak to the manager. Explain that it was an accident and that you prefer to teach your child respect for other people's property rather than lying and stealing. You'd be grateful if she could either not charge you or give you a discount. Most reputable stores will do this. Nevertheless, be prepared to pay.

❖ Be prepared for some employees to look at you as if you're nuts. These people do not understand right and wrong, ownership, responsibility, or ethics. If your child is four or older and notices that the employee is acting as if you've done something strange, tell your child that person was never taught right from wrong. Suggest how sad that is.

❖ Don't take a rambunctious child to a store with many things you cannot afford to pay for.

> **Lessons:** *Merchandise in a store is not ours. We have no right to mess up other people's property. I respect other people's property.*

Touching Things

Whether at a store, street fair, carnival, or anywhere else things are displayed, little fingers often tingle with desire. They want to handle tantalizing jewelry on velvet, try on hats, touch, feel, hold. With particularly delicate objects here is a handy phrase: *Look with your eyes, not your hands.*

❖ When he succeeds, praise him. He will feel proud and competent.

❖ Practice what you preach. If you pick up and put down every bauble, your child will follow suit. If you are a toucher yourself, please make sure you put things back where you found them in order to model for your child.

❖ If your child is foaming at the mouth to touch and is old enough to be trusted not to fling something, ask the salesperson if it would be all right to hand him one thing.

❖ If so, kneel, hand him one thing, and carefully monitor his examination. Make sure you put it back where you got it.

❖ Thank the merchant when you're done.

❖ If the seller *does* mind, move your child away. Explain that the lady doesn't want you touching her things. Suggest that you go somewhere where it's a better place for children to be.

> **Lesson:** *We take care of other people's things, therefore showing respect. We ask other people permission before grabbing.*

C. RESTAURANTS

This may seem obvious, but children should be under control in a restaurant. Too often, however, we let down our guard a bit or assume that everybody else will make space for our developing child.

Waiters and waitresses move quickly, carrying trays of dishes, silverware, and hot food. If a toddler or running child suddenly gets underfoot, the accident probability is high. Hot coffee can scald the child. A glass can shatter and really hurt someone. An old lady can get knocked down and break her hip.

Besides these safety elements there is the matter of consideration for others. Not everybody has children. Even people who do have children may prefer a quiet meal.

Whether you are in McDonald's or the Four Seasons, here are some basics to keep in mind.

Unacceptable Children's Behavior

- ❖ Crawling anywhere except under your own table—regardless of the child's age.
- ❖ *Any* form of unescorted locomotion. This includes walking, running, crawling, skipping, moving from table to table, leaving the table to look out the window, leaving the table to look at the aquarium, or any other movement in the restaurant without a grown-up either carrying the child or holding the child's hand.
- ❖ A composed five-year-old, however, can go to the bathroom alone in a local, uncrowded restaurant as long as the child understands that there is no running. However, in a crowded restaurant off a turnpike or any other situation where he can come to harm, he still needs a grown-up to go with him.
- ❖ Screaming, squealing, loud singing, protracted Bronx cheers, or any other loud vocalization that is not an occasional laugh or the pleasant murmur of quiet voices pitched to be heard only by the people at your table. This includes crying babies. Nobody thinks a baby shouldn't cry. But patrons in restaurants should not be asked to listen to them.
- ❖ Loud banging of silverware, dishes, banging on the table, banging feet against a high chair, banging a spoon against an unmuffled high-chair tray, banging the back of a chair against a wall, and any other form of spontaneous sound experimentation is unacceptable. If you have a nine-month-old banger, put a napkin under his spoon so that he can bang without making a racket.

Thoughtful Adult Behavior that Teaches Through Modeling

- ❖ Respect our neighbor's personal space. If your child keeps banging into the person at the next table, move your child. Do not continue to say ineffectually, "I'm sorry," or even worse to pretend it's not happening.

❖ If you have a young baby who needs to be walked around between courses, walk the baby out into the lobby or somewhere other than back and forth through the diners, which may interrupt their meals.

❖ If your child has made a real mess—dropping bread all over the floor, for example—either pick it up or at least apologize.

❖ If your child spills liquid, let someone know so that no one falls.

❖ When a waitress has been particularly helpful and efficient, you can use her job well done to teach that we respect and acknowledge hard workers. "Mommy's going to leave an extra big tip because this waitress did a good job. I appreciated that she brought your food quickly when I asked her to. She helped us clean up the spilled milk and brought us more right away, saying that she knew accidents happen. This is my way of thanking her for being nice and for working hard."

Methods to Avoid Predictable Disruptive Behavior

❖ Children don't have the sense of time necessary for unoccupied waiting. Bring crayons, a book, or other quiet toys. Make up guessing games. Occupy your child.

❖ Choose your restaurants wisely. Obviously, you can loosen up on noise in a fast-food place, pizzeria, or child-geared restaurant.

❖ If you child is particularly hungry, let the waiter know so that you can get some food for your kid pronto.

❖ Just because a place is cheap doesn't mean it's a free-for-all.

❖ If you see a childless couple or group, keep your children under tighter reins than you might, especially if your table is right next to theirs. Explain that our loud voices are annoying those people and we need to be courteous.

❖ Don't go to restaurants that discourage children.

❖ Some fancy restaurants can handle children at off-hours. But senior citizens may be there. Be considerate.

Lesson: When we eat out in public, we respect and pay attention to the people around us.

D. PUBLIC SEATING

This includes transportation, movie theaters, waiting rooms, any public chair or bench.

* Although you find your child's feet to be the cutest appendages known to heaven and earth, the lady next to you does not. Teach your children to keep their feet to themselves. This means constant reminders and vigilance. "Don't put your feet there. Other people need to sit there."
* Kicking the back of the seat in the row ahead of you is a pain in the tush. Do not allow your child to do it.
* A bouncy child who catches the hair of the person in the row ahead more than once is a child who is not being properly supervised.

> **Lesson:** We keep to our own seat when we're sharing places with other people.

E. LITTER

Every time somebody drops trash on the ground, on the floor, on the sidewalk, or by the side of the road, the world dies another small death.

* Never litter.
* Don't let your child litter.
* If either of you throws something in the trash and it misses or blows away, go get it. Trying doesn't count. Not littering counts.
* Your pockets offer handy receptacles for sticky gunk—at least from your child's point of view.

F. TRAFFIC FLOW

We drive on the right side of the road. This commonly accepted practice saves our lives. If you follow basic driving concepts even while walking, you end up being considerate.

* Point out to your child, from the time he can climb stairs, that we go up and down the stairs on the right so that we don't get into other people's way.
* When we walk down a sidewalk, a mall, a hallway, or any other

public place where people are going in different directions, we pay attention to other people. We walk on the right.

❖ When we are walking where there are other people, we don't wobble, wiggle, shift lanes, come to a dead halt, or not move aside a bit so that someone else can pass. This is rude.

❖ We let older people go ahead of us into elevators, onto escalators, through doorways.

❖ We do not shout at our friend across the mall at the top of our lungs, not noticing that our mouth happens to be close to the ear of a stranger.

❖ This one's for moms: When we are pushing a stroller we don't go into a semitrance in the narrow doorway of a store while we think about what to have for supper.

Lesson: *It is not nice to get in other people's way.*

G. GROWN-UP PLACES

There are child-focused places, such as playgrounds, puppet shows, children's religious services, and animated movies. There are child-friendly places, such as malls, some stores and restaurants, crafts fairs, and county fairs. In these places children can "be children."

But there are still a few places where, in fact, children should be seen but not heard any louder than adults may be heard: libraries, high-scale stores and restaurants, weddings, hospitals, and standard religious services.

❖ Point out to your child how quiet everyone is.

❖ Mention that they are not squirming and banging.

❖ See if you can make it fun to whisper.

❖ Make a game: How long can you fold your hands in your lap?

❖ How long can you keep your feet still?

Lesson: *I can behave like a grown-up in a grown-up place.*

Tip for the child who can no longer control himself: There is nothing wrong with him. He is a child. However, you need to remove him. You are not in a place where childlike behavior is appropriate. This also applies to you and your husband if you should get the giggles.

Now, I know that you're real considerate. You just skimmed through that last section, flipping pages, thinking, "I know that, don't do that . . . why, I'd never . . . I don't need this." But in this world we live in not everyone is as considerate as you and me.

Let's stop focusing on nice us and our kids and take a look at who else we're sharing public space with.

SECTION 2: PUBLIC PEOPLE

There are some nasty people, nasty situations, and both real and potential threats to you and your child out there in the real world.

Although "street smarts" originated as a term for urban dwellers, the sad truth is that in any mall or idyllic town in our nation, there is not one of us who can afford to go through our days as if we were living in a mythical past. We must be aware when we are out that it is possible that harm may come our way. This awareness allows us to assess how vigilant we must be and in what way. It protects us. Furthermore, we must teach our children some simple rules that will protect them.

As you glance through the following ideas, don't snort and say, "How ridiculous. The likelihood of any of this happening isn't worth the paranoia." You're right. Probably none of these things will happen.

Your house probably won't burn down either. But I bet you have insurance.

The problem with having true street smarts is that you have to be able to think like a crazy person who wishes to harm you.

I have taken the liberty of suggesting the kinds of crazy things people may do. They will sound paranoid. Hopefully, they will make you giggle with their absurdity. Hopefully, they will also drive home why I've suggested the precautions I think are sensible.

A. PRECAUTIONS FOR MOMS

There is one cardinal rule to follow, without fail, whenever you are in public: *Never leave your child unattended.*

I. Cars

❖ Don't leave your child alone, sleeping or awake, in the car seat. Whether in the safety of your own driveway, parked in front of a store while you dash in to pick something up, or in front of somebody else's house where you have to run in for even the briefest second—no matter how badly she needs a nap and you need a break. Your sleeping child may wake up and panic to find no one there. The car brakes can slip and your car can roll into the path of a teenager speeding down a quiet street. A car thief, a kidnapper, or both can take your child or your car with the child in it.

❖ Lock your car doors. The moment you get into your car, habitually lock the doors in the same way that you habitually put the key in the ignition and your seat belt on. If you do not have automatic child locks, teach your child to lock his own door, starting from eighteen months old. He should know that we are safer when the doors are locked. This is a safety precaution in terms of a child falling out. It also precludes being part of any "weirdness."

2. Planes and Trains

❖ If your child is asleep and you are dying to pee, find a friendly-looking person and ask if she'd keep an eye out. *Ask loudly enough that other people hear.* Having several people hear your request is insurance against that smiling lady in the next seat on the train being stark, raving mad.

❖ Don't go to the dining car of a train without your young child if the car is halfway down the train and it's lunchtime. If your five-year-old wants to stay in his seat, ask that a nearby passenger keep an eye on him, again loudly enough that several people hear.

❖ Other mommies with kids are always the best bets.

3. Strollers

❖ In a store don't leave your child strapped into his stroller while you wander into the next aisle shopping.

❖ Don't leave your child strapped into his stroller while you lock yourself in a bathroom stall in a public place to pee.

❖ Don't take your hands off his stroller in busy places, such as airports, train stations, or crowded malls, while you turn your attention to something else.

This habit precludes some lunatic coming along and snatching your child.

B. TEACHING KIDS
1. On Foot

Whether in the mall or walking down the street of a town or bustling city, your child will be protected from the more likely potential traffic incident as well as the unlikely "lunatic" dimension if you teach him this simple rule: *"We have to see each other."*

By the time a child is eighteen months you can begin teaching this rule. On the sidewalks in small towns you can probably start to loosen up by four. In big cities or busy malls, this is a useful rule well into elementary school.

❖ Explain that he may go only where you can see each other. If he can't see you, he can't be there. If you can't see him, he can't be there. This includes turning corners, going into doorways, or disappearing behind seating arrangements.

❖ If you live in a city teach your preschooler who is skipping ahead of you to stop at the end of the buildings, not at the curb. This prevents them from tripping right into the street. It also prevents some lunatic coming down the street from whisking your kid away before you can get there.

Movie: For late threes and up, rent the movie *Pete's Dragon.* Shelley Winters and cohorts play a horrible family that tries to snatch a cute kid. Their name is Gogan. After you see the movie, explain that there are Gogan people. Reassure your child that as long as you know about them and watch out for them, they can't get you. As long as we follow the "We have to see each other" rule, no Gogan can ever, ever get us.

Are we scaring our children and putting the onus of their own safety on their small shoulders? I don't think so. The adult has to be vigilant and constantly aware of who's around them at all times. But if you let your child know that there are real dangers, they will be more likely to obey the rules than if they think it's a rule like "soda only at parties."

2. Who Can Pick You Up

While fear of strangers may not be a pleasant feeling out in the world, a healthy respect for strangers is prudent.

A child under three shouldn't be far enough away from a responsible adult to have to deal with strangers on their own. But by the mid-threes and certainly four we need to start giving them guidance about how to handle situations that may arise.

Without alarming them, tell them never to get in any car without you unless you tell them to.

Most nursery schools and kindergartens have systems of knowing who is supposed to pick up your child and who isn't. Nevertheless, make sure you tell your child:

❖ Pick-up at school: "Mommy [or whoever the designated person is] will pick you up today. If I can't, only your teacher can tell you who else can pick you up. If someone you know or do not know tells you that I sent them, tell him *or* her, 'Thank you, but I go home with my mommy.' Then go find your teacher and tell her."

❖ On the way outside to play in a neighbor's yard: "When you're on your way to Molly's house, if someone says I need you and I sent him or her to pick you up, you say, 'Thank you, but my mommy told me to go straight to Molly's.' Go inside and tell Molly's mommy."

❖ Play date out of the neighborhood: "If I can't pick you up I will send word to Molly's mom. If she tells you to go home with someone else, you can. Otherwise, if somebody comes into the yard and says to go home with them, you tell the person—even if you know them—that you're going inside now. And go inside and tell Molly's mom."

❖ In stores: "I will *never* leave a store without you, so don't leave without me. If someone says I'm waiting outside, I'm not. You stay put. You can even call out 'Mom,' if you don't know where I am. I'll be right there."

Movie: *Chitty Chitty Bang Bang* is appropriate for late threes and up. There is a perfect example of the kind of stranger you want to teach your child to avoid. He is aptly named the "Child Catcher." He entices Jeremy and Jemima into a cage by the age-old perfect strategy: candy. Sometime after you have watched the movie, mention that if any stranger ever offers your child anything—candy or any other attractive thing—your child should immediately remember the Child Catcher. This person is not someone whose gifts we accept.

3. Homeless People

Homeless people present an enormous challenge to parents today. On the one hand you don't want to teach your child to be cold and heartless, able to pass another human being lying in a heap on the street like a piece of garbage. On the other hand you can't be naive and risk putting your child into potential danger.

In fact, homeless people are like any other group: Some are good and some are bad. Some are down on their luck but still have their dignity and habits intact. Others are mentally ill or on drugs and have left the conventions of civilization far behind. As with any group, it is better to judge an individual by his behavior rather than by lumping him into an unsavory category. In terms of parenting, it's prudent to have a sense of who may be dangerous to your child and who is probably not. In terms of a moral lesson for your child, it's important to teach how to judge.

Here are some various types of behavior for you to think about and the kinds of simple words you might find useful when trying to help your child learn to judge behavior rather than outward trappings.

❖ If someone is going through the garbage carefully gathering cans and bottles, point out "He is working." Many families save their cans and bottles for a person they see regularly. Others put them out where collectors can easily find them. Involving our children in setting out cans for the collector teaches a valuable lesson.

❖ If someone is ripping up the garbage and throwing it around, "he is not nice." If you judge by his motions that his behavior is potentially dangerous, it's often prudent to cross the street.

❖ If you see someone lying on a park bench or a protected stairwell, covered with newspapers or blankets with his cart of things nearby, "He is sleeping. He has no home. Let's not disturb him."

❖ If someone in rags falls down in front of you, find a policeman or dial 911. "He is sick and needs help."

❖ If someone is shouting, waving his arms, or punching the air, "He is having an argument with an imaginary person. We walk away from him." Give someone like this wide berth. Their behavior is unpredictable and potentially violent.

❖ If someone sitting propped against a building calls a greeting, nod and walk on.

Food for Thought: The face of a child in a stroller is at the same level as someone sitting on the sidewalk. A person wasted by life and dealt a dirty hand still has the capacity to wave, smile, or call out a friendly greeting to your child. Acknowledging their humanity by not completely ignoring them seems a small act of kindness to return to someone who has so much less than we do.

Acknowledge with a nod, *not* a great big forced, "Hey! How ya doin'?" Don't insult them with familiarity you don't feel.

You also won't run the risk of opening a door of friendliness that may encourage him to get up and want to engage with you further as you walk down the street.

If that should happen, go into a store or other public place off the street.

Special Tip for Five-year-olds

If you have taught them from a young age some of these ways to determine the difference between homeless people, they will have a fairly sophisticated street sense for their protection without having lost compassion and respect for different kinds of people. By five it might be useful to pave the way for their ever-widening exposure to the rest of the world. This is a good age to begin to show them what drugs do.

Let's say you see a heap of flesh drugged out on the street. First, how do you determine that what you are seeing is probably from drugs? Drug users themselves have coined a very apt phrase: "Wasted." If a person is sprawled out, often on his back, not tucked into a corner for his own protection or comfort, with no belongings that he cares for any longer, he is "wasted," either by drugs or drink. He has made choices, notwithstanding how difficult his life may be, that you may wish to point out to your child are harmful life choices.

- ❖ Come right out and say, "See that over there? Drugs. He stuck a lot of bad drugs in his body. That's what drugs do. The rest of his life is going to be like that. What a crummy choice he made, wasn't it?"
- ❖ Maybe a year later you can repeat this. This is not one of those lessons you want to say over and over like "Use a napkin." This is just an idea that you want to plant in the back of your child's head. It is an image that you hope will be sufficiently striking to reverberate in later years when the actual choices will be presented to your child.

C. OFFSETTING FEAR OF STRANGERS

Since we have focused in this section on all the bad possibilities, they may feel rather overwhelming. Yet you will not be advising your children to watch out for the Gogans and be careful of the Child Catcher every day. However, whenever you are out you will have to remind him to stay where you can see him and to be careful of streets, corners, and numerous other safety precautions that you have to introduce.

There is a good way to counteract all the negative information. The easiest way to model behavior that will help your child *not* be phobic of all strangers is this: *Make small talk with strangers.*

❖ Chat with strangers in elevators about the weather.
❖ Chat with the person sitting next to you on the plane, train, or bus.
❖ Make a little joke to the person in front of you in line at the supermarket.
❖ Say something to the person getting into their car next to yours in the parking lot.
❖ Make small talk with another mother and child waiting in line near you.
❖ Don't chat only with people who look exactly like you. Chat with people of all kinds who have a nice mood about them.
❖ While in waiting rooms, chat with other people waiting and with the receptionist.
❖ Exchange pleasantries with cashiers.
❖ Move through the world with friendliness and the world will be friendly back.
❖ Move through the world with a chip on your shoulder and the world will be a nasty place.

SUMMARY:

❖ We must teach our children consideration for others in public places.
❖ We must be aware of potential danger.
❖ We must give our children simple rules to protect them from people who aren't as nice as we are.

This was nice. We've gone to the bathroom together, done a little shopping, eaten out, hung out at the mall, and looked into the depths of some of the most depraved souls in town.

It's all in a normal day of being a mother with a preschooler.

Perhaps those lunatics lurking in corners wanting to snatch your child made you feel a little leery about going out.

Perhaps all that talk made you feel like staying home, where it's safe and you can control what your child is exposed to.

Guess again.

Let's tackle the media.

✗ 13 ✗

The Media

It's easy to see how the predominant imagery of any civilization comes into being. The big guys hire artists to create what they are paid to create.

During the Renaissance, for example, the church and nobility combined their wealth and power to erect cathedrals and castles, still awe-inspiring in their majesty and intentionally humbling to man. They commissioned great painters: Michelangelo, da Vinci, Botticelli. The work of these geniuses, as well as that of lesser artists and artisans, both reflected and shaped the predominant beliefs of their civilization: a rigorous hierarchy with God at the top, the church and kings nuzzling each other right up there, and all the picayune nobodies at the bottom.

Picture a medieval jousting match, or a Roman spectacle in the Colosseum. The banners of famous houses wave. The athletes represent noblemen, regions, political entities.

Picture a European soccer match of today, an American football game, the Olympics. The great banners strung around the arena pronounce in bold imagery who is in power: Marlboro, Nike, Reebok, and Bud.

In our culture our greatest resources are dedicated to commerce. Procter & Gamble foots the bill for artists. They are commissioned to use the entire weight of their artistic skills to do one thing and one thing only: Sell.

Creatively, each artist strives to push boundaries, to boldly go where no one has ever gone before, to move people emotionally, to enlighten and capture the human experience. Practically, artists need to eat. Other than the ''starving artist,'' a romantic path that few choose, if an artist wants to pay the rent, he must sell. If the journalist wants to keep her job, she must sell papers. If the TV producer wants to create a new show, it must appeal to a wide enough audience that advertisers will buy time during that show so they can sell. If the rap group from the mean streets of Newark wants to get paid, their songs must sell.

In order to sell, the artist must get our attention.

And they are brilliant at getting our attention.

In some ways, advertising is the highest art form in our culture. It reflects and shapes who we are. The copywriter is our poet, the photographer our prodigy, the jingle and theme composer our virtuoso. They are able to capture an entire emotional experience, to sum up an entire life, with a few well-chosen images.

They ply a more subtle craft that affects all of us, grown-ups and children alike. They create a longing in us to be just like the people they show us.

Admit it. Don't you wish *your* family would merrily toss their laundry into the washer on their happy way in from a glorious day through the sunlit sunroom of *your* house? Don't you drool for hair like the girls have in Pantene commercials? Don't you stand for a long time in the hair-care-products aisle, wondering if this one will make your hair rich, shining, and luxuriant? Like theirs.

Don't you wish you could throw out all the bottles that you spent good money on that didn't make your hair look like that?

Although insidious in creating a longing, these false images of unattainable beauty and happiness are relatively benign.

But what about the darker images?

What about the pervasive jeans and underwear ads that are soft-core—and sometimes not-so-soft-core—porn?

What about teens with guns, spouting violence and vitriolic hate messages in MTV videos?

What about cartoons where a character gets smashed over and over again, only to rise each time, as if we can repair a giant hammer's violent blow with a silly, oversize Band-Aid?

From the unrealistic emotional fulfillment connected with a single laundry product to the vilest of vile, these images flash by every moment of every day. On TV. On billboards. On magazine covers that we pass on our way to buy diapers.

For better or worse, this is the imagery of our age. If we are to continue to live in a free society, we cannot be completely free from these images. Nor can we keep them from our children.

Therefore, it seems to me we parents have several routes to take. We can take steps to limit our children's exposure to unpleasant imagery and, perhaps more important, give them guidance about evaluating what they see. If we are inclined, we can take an active part in trying to change what is acceptable imagery in public.

SECTION 1: TV

Every hour that your child is not sitting in front of the tube watching moving pictures of either broadcast TV or a videotape, she is doing something else. Probably more constructive and educational. Almost always more physical.

In Chapter 7, "Food: The Staff of Life," I mentioned that most of our bad health, besides our genetic makeups and environmental factors beyond our control, was due to unhealthy eating habits and lifestyle. Although "lifestyle" includes driving instead of walking or biking as a means of transportation, pushing a button instead of washing dishes and clothes by hand, pushing a pedal instead of a lawn mower, just to name a few, the major lifestyle choice most Americans make which negatively impacts on our health is that of watching television.

In terms of TV watching and weight, which we know affects health, studies have shown that regular exercise is the strongest predictor for which people will keep their weight off. The more TV people watch, the more likely they are to regain whatever weight they have lost.

There are all kinds of studies about the physiological changes that take place in the body during TV watching, from blood pressure to brain activity. Everything slows down. But most moms who have older children don't need million-dollar studies to tell them what TV watching does. Just try and talk to a child who is watching TV. They are zonked. They are zoned out. They are on planet "D." Most moms end up shouting whatever innocuous question they asked. Even then they frequently get no response. Moms across America know all too well that the only way to bring most children "back" from a TV trance is to stand in front of the child and wave a hand in front of her face three or four times before the hypnotic trance has been broken enough to get her attention. Oh, how I wish I were joking or exaggerating.

Television is junk food for the mind. And just like junk food, there is some nutrition to be gained, but it is swimming in a sea of detritus. A steady diet of it will harm you.

There are many families who choose not to watch TV at all. Their children spend those precious hours in their rooms reading or engaged in imaginative play. If it is a choice that the adults in your family are comfortable with, it may be a good choice.

However, as with any other blanket limitation, it's usually only a matter of time before your child catches on to the rest of the world—and wants to join it. In the same way that completely forbidding sweets may result in a junk-food freak, so may a TV-pure preschooler turn into a tube-aton the minute he leaves your house.

True Tale from the Trenches: I am still haunted by the image of one child who came to our house. Had I known his home was TV-free, I never would've okayed the kids' watching a sing-along tape at the end of a long day. When the child's mother arrived in a hurry to get home to make dinner, she literally carried her child out the front door. The child's arms were outstretched toward the TV screen, sobbing, "Oh, please let me watch the rest, oh, please!" It felt like a deportation camp where a child was being dragged from his mother. I feel the child wouldn't have been harmed nearly as much by a controlled hour of TV as he was by the unyielding ban.

A. HOW MUCH?

It seems to me that a sensible course for most families is to decide *how much* TV your child can watch and *what kind*.

Babies

Although I have mothers in my classes who say their eight- and nine-month-olds like TV, I see no productive purpose for any child under one ever being offered the opportunity to watch moving pictures on a screen. They should be busy exploring the world around them. The passive aspect of watching is not in their best interests, even if they seem to enjoy it.

Fourteen Months

A half hour of downtime for a young toddler, although not great, is the most I would ever recommend.

A reasonable time and place to plunk a toddler in front of the tube is in the late afternoon, after a particularly full day, while you are preparing dinner. What is the child doing? He is doing what we all do in front of the tube: spacing out. This form of TV as baby-sitter doesn't seem out of line. After a long day many children are cranky. It's hard to get dinner ready and amuse an irritated child. *Sesame Street* to the rescue. For both of you.

I am *not* fond, however, of hearing from my moms that they use the tube to baby-sit while they do their morning chores. This is an active time of the day. Your child would be better served by providing engaging books and toys. If she's not interested in playing alone, take her with you and let her "help" you do your chores. It will slow you down. But which would you prefer to slow down, your daily grind or your child's developing mind?

Two and Up

One half hour a day, tops, of TV and tapes is enough for a child of this age. TV is best used to bridge meltdown times rather than during lively learning hours.

By two many kids are TV addicts, running to turn it on, begging to watch.

❖ Set limits. For example, "We watch only when Mommy's making dinner."

❖ Give them a choice. "Would you rather watch a tape or *Sesame Street*?"

❖ After the half hour is up, tell your child the TV naps until tomorrow.

Preschoolers

For preschoolers, you may wish to allow one hour of TV, which lets them see an entire *Sesame Street,* where they do, in fact, learn something useful.

Depending on the particular child's attention span and interests, anytime from three and often not till five we begin to see a different approach to watching.

Feature films, with their extended characters and plots, begin to absorb some children. They often want to watch the same movie, day in and day out, over and over, until you want to tear your hair out. Remember, repetition is a major learning tool.

They are learning sophisticated language patterns and are often eager to repeat entire segments of dialogue, sometimes whole films. They dance with the characters. Some of them perfect the dance steps. Some of them learn all the songs.

There is nothing wrong with a preschooler dancing in front of the screen singing, moving around, shouting out the lines. They are actively engaged—physically and intellectually.

Feature films are usually good weekend choices. Family viewing is a good idea. Treat the whole family to a movie together on a weekend. During the week two hours of a movie means watching it during dinner and then immediately getting ready for bed. One alternative is to let her watch half this afternoon and half tomorrow.

Rather than always using the tube to baby-sit, watch *Sesame Street* with your child. You will have shared experiences. You will be able to joke about the show and know what your child finds funny.

Some children, however, turn into couch potatoes. They lie down and glaze over no matter what is on the screen. For these children I would suggest cutting out viewing time completely. Any child who is comatose the moment the tube goes on is a child who should be engaged in more active areas of life.

B. WHAT TO WATCH

Here are some selections to keep her safely and happily entertained.

PBS and local education stations have the best children's programming. They also show ballets kids like to dance with and symphonies. Don't be surprised or disapproving, however, if your child prefers to have it on as background music. Some nature shows are often frightening for the young child, particularly ones with graphic hunting scenes.

Most *network* fare is inappropriate, with some exceptions:

❖ The Thanksgiving Day parade, almost all the shows they run at Christmastime, the Olympics.
❖ Occasional programming geared for children.
❖ Sports shows such as ice skating and swimming. Watching major sports along with their parents is fun for children. There is one major drawback to watching network shows: the ads. I'll talk about them in a minute.

Any of the feature-length Disney films that are rated *G* are good choices.

Crafts shows on cable are fun to watch, particularly for five-year-olds.

C. WHAT TO CONSIDER NOT LETTING YOUR CHILD WATCH

Boxing, wrestling, hockey, or any other show where a child is introduced to people hurting each other, making nasty faces and violent gestures, and fighting in between the game as a normal, acceptable way for grown-ups to behave is a poor choice.

Although I know they're popular, the *America's Funniest* shows often glamorize people getting hurt. If you and your child enjoy them, so be it. But if your child asks, ''What's funny?'' after seeing a child her size go headfirst into a swimming pool and come up crying, maybe it wouldn't hurt to respect her opinion. What *is* so funny about that? (Although I usually laugh out loud when the adult dancers fall off stage.)

On the plus side of cartoons, children like to watch them because they're animated and usually drawn well. Many people feel they are an essential part of childhood, an icon of American culture, and may help instill a sense of humor. But coupled with their appeal is, of course, the amount of violence and how matter-of-fact the violence is. Personally, I don't think they're a good idea for any child under three, and even for preschoolers I have my doubts. If you decide to let your child watch them, I would suggest limiting the amount of time. I would also stick to the ''classics,'' like Bugs and Tweetie.

Most nursery schools I come into contact with ban Ninja Turtle and other action figures from school. Why? Because they inspire the kids to act out too much.

> **True Tale from the Trenches:** We had a two-and-a-half-year-old boy in class who had several older brothers. "Unruly" is a kind way to describe his behavior. During circle time he began to execute a series of sophisticated karate moves, kicking and chopping. He was a coordinated boy, and in fact, it was impressive. Unfortunately, it was also scary. I asked his baby-sitter if he'd been watching Ninja Turtles. Yes. I called his mom, whom I'd been in touch with anyway, since she was concerned about his behavior. I asked if they could cut Ninja Turtles out for a couple of weeks to see what would happen. She could. She did. He settled down—not completely—but his rough edges mellowed and the kicks stopped flying. She said her older boys' teachers noticed a difference too.

D. HANDLING WHAT YOU WISH THEY WOULDN'T SEE

So you're all having a grand ol' time. Your whole family's watching the Rose Bowl. Your two-year-old is hollering, ''Touchdown!'' He's not sure what touchdown means, but the hollering is fun. And he likes to hang out on the couch and eat and shout as much as you do. The halftime spectacle knocked his socks off.

But what about the moments in between the game? The ads are geared toward a beer-drinking, gas-guzzling, kissy-faced bunch of sports fans. There are a lot of big muscles, grimacing faces, sweat, and sneakers. Toward the end of the game the station is gearing up for the Sunday night movie and the eleven o'clock news. Steamy kisses, naked shoulders, and couples slowly lowering themselves onto beds are intermixed with screaming women, terrorized children, and shooting men.

Are these healthy images for a little kid? Call me fussy, but I don't think so. You probably tune it out. But don't assume your child does. He is taking everything in nonjudgmentally. Everything.

Therefore, if you think some of those images may not be so good for your child's developing mind and morals, here are some ideas:

❖ Hit the OFF button on the remote control. You've got about three minutes before the game comes back on, and they'll only be standing around talking when they come back anyway!

❖ Make "pit stops." As soon as the ads come on, take your child to the bathroom, the kitchen, out onto the deck, up and down the stairs to "stretch," or in some way get him away from the screen.

❖ If you're desperate not to miss a moment, at least mute the sound. Express your disapproval. "Feh. We don't like stuff like that." Keep a book or crayons handy. Throw popcorn into the air and catch it in your mouth. Stand on your head or your hands. In other words, distract your child. When it's over, turn the sound back on. "Ah, here's what *we* like!"

Some Suggestions for the TV-Watching Family

❖ If your child should wake up and walk into the room during a particularly lurid scene, say hello without getting flustered, but with enough animation to distract him. Use the remote, and change the picture.

❖ If you watch late-night movies that have lots of shooting guns, screeching cars, and people screaming, keep the sound low. A child shouldn't have to sleep with scary noises in his subconscious.

❖ If your quarters are so small that you can't hear without your child hearing, get a pair of earphones.

❖ Try not to channel surf when your child is in the room. Are you listening, Dad? I don't even know why I'm bothering to say this. I know you're all out there doing it. But just because you're not seeing anything as you flick by lookin' for the big one doesn't mean your child isn't. Besides being disturbing in the moment, images of violence and violent sex become the accepted norm with the passage of time.

❖ Turning the TV on the minute you wake up and not turning it off until bedtime may be the way you lived prebaby. But it's not a great way for a kid to spend the day, with canned laughter, screaming talk-show hosts, sobbing soap opera queens, and ads for perfect abs flickering in the background.

❖ If you absolutely must watch the early news, PBS is usually better than network stuff, unless there's a bombing, airplane crash, or other major news event, and then there you are watching sad faces and twisted limbs at dinnertime. But at least PBS has the decency not to repeatedly run pictures of hidden cameras catching baby-sitters hitting kids. If it were me, I'd restrict news-watching to the eleven o'clock show and make a house rule: no adult TV at all till the kids are in bed.

❖ That goes for you working parents too, no matter how zonked you feel at the end of a long hard day, and no matter how soft that sofa looks!

E. TV ADS CAN BE YOUR FRIEND!

Nowhere do modern artists show their flair more brilliantly than in TV advertising geared to children. They create magical worlds perfectly crafted to capture the imagination of a young child. They are geniuses at market research and finding what will work. They know how to construct ads that make boys beg for toys and render girls shameless. "Oh, Mommy! I want that! Can I have it? Pleeeease?"

Under Three

Most children under three don't know the difference between a commercial and the show. They see pretty pictures, happy children, and toys. They see flying birds and talking tigers. Maybe they know something we don't know: Sometimes there isn't really a difference. Point out that it's an ad. "The people are trying to get us to buy something." Even if you feel silly saying that to a two-year-old, they are old enough to be introduced to the concept of selling. Forewarned is forearmed.

Preschoolers

By this age your child is old enough to learn how ads work. Take an ad, any ad, for the toy of your child's choice. What worked in our home was a campaign for Care Bears. A magical kingdom of bears appeared on the screen, pink and pale green, darling, dancing in air, circling a pretty little girl's head. A three-and-a-half-year-old's vision of perfection. My daughter wanted to *be* that little girl. "Mommy, oh, please, can I have one of them?"

The time had come!

Activity: Teaching Your Child How to Evaluate an Ad

❖ Take your child to the toy store. "Let's look for the toy we saw on TV."

❖ If you are as lucky as we were—and maybe you shouldn't rely on luck, but check it out in advance—you will find what we found: a rack with tiny, unappetizing, stiff bears hung in vacuum packs. The bears had looked so soft, cuddly, and alive on TV. In contrast, these looked like what they were: pieces of plastic junk.

Your conversation will probably go something like ours.

"They're so little!" Although I felt her disappointment, I wasn't disappointed in the least. "You know, sweetheart, things in real life aren't what they seem in commercials."

"They're not very pretty."

"No. They're not nearly as pretty as the cartoons of them were."

She made a couple of desultory reaches toward the rack.

"Do I have to have one?" came the small voice.

"Of course not. Now you see that ads and real life are never the same."

"Can I pick out something else?"

"Absolutely. Let's go find something that looks interesting when we see it in person."

Lesson: *Ads do not always accurately reflect the product they're pitching.*

No child catches on to this truth immediately. Why should children be less susceptible than we? But with your help it eventually hits home.

❖ Remind them when they're watching an ad how they were deceived by the last one.

❖ When you look at packaging, remind them that what's on the picture and what's inside may be very different.

❖ When you see an elaborate Barbie commercial, point out that real Barbie dolls don't move and do all the things they do in the ads.

❖ Likewise for GI Joes, trucks, and any other moving toy.

❖ As you watch an elaborate commercial say, "Boy, that looks like fun. But we don't have a jungle in your room. Remember, when you buy the truck you don't get the jungle along with it!"

❖ If you're in the kitchen and your child comes running, saying, "Mommy! Come and look at this! I want it," point out how successful the ad was. It made her want the toy enough to ask for it. Remind her how different ads and real life are.

❖ When you see a commercial for some heavily colored and sugared breakfast cereal, point out how the ad works. "See how happy those kids look? The ad people want you to think you'll be happy, too, if you eat that cereal. But buying that cereal won't make you happy. Having fun with people you love makes you happy."

❖ If they ask for a cereal while in the store, ask them if they saw an ad for it. If they say yes, laugh. "See? Those ad people are good. They got you to want it! Let's look and see if it's something we really want to buy." Check the ingredients along with your child. If it's an acceptable cereal say, "Okay, we'll try that." If not, point out with your finger: "Look at all those chemicals. It has sixteen grams of sugar. Oh, no, we don't eat that for breakfast. They didn't fool us this time!"

❖ Anytime you try a product that is disappointing, remind them that they wanted it because they saw an ad. Suggest that they remember this the next time.

Lesson: *To be repeated over and over and over: Everything we see in ads does not necessarily reflect real life. We have to pick and choose for ourselves what we like. We should not automatically buy something because we see an ad anymore than we should automatically reject it because we see an ad for it. We remain aware that we are in control of what we buy, rather than having commercials be in control of what we buy.*

SECTION 2: PRINT: WHAT YOU CAN'T PREVENT YOUR CHILD FROM SEEING AND HOW TO HANDLE IT

TV mixes images of clean-cut laundry products with rape. Print ads cut out the clean part. *Sexy* blares from every pore of our culture. Not just sex. Rough sex. Wild sex. Leather and pierced-body sex. Lots of nipples. Lots of knowing sideways eyes and lots of tongues reaching around red, wet lips. Lots of big, slick, sweating muscles and grins. And that's just *Glamour* and *Vogue*.

Before you think, "Get out the Thorazine. Lois just went over the edge," check out your local mall. Zip around the newsstand, the bookstore. Take a gander at the windows of the video or music store. Get yourself down where your child's face is, either in the stroller or at five-year-old level. Don't be surprised when you see a woman chained, clothes ripped, and a man standing over her with a whip.

How do you think these images translate to your child?

I'll tell you what I think: that degradation and sex go hand and hand, that sex is rough, and that it is a commonplace event.

I'm sorry. I am not a prude. But these are not healthy images for a growing mind.

Since we cannot avoid this imagery it becomes important to transmit a value judgment to your child about what she sees around her.

Here are some suggestions of ways to handle this imagery.

❖ If you see your child looking at a magazine cover that's raunchy, say, "Isn't that ugly?" Point to another nearby that's not offensive. "But this one's nice, isn't it?" Anytime you notice she's looking at an unpleasant image, use any words that make sense to you. Dumb. Ugly. Nasty. Cheap.

❖ Don't direct your child's eyes for the purpose of instruction.

❖ When you're looking at a magazine with your daughter (girls tend to like fashion mags better than boys do), say, "This girl looks cheap. This one doesn't. That's not my taste. Is it yours? That's ugly. This is pretty." Train her eye to see a difference between sexy and smutty, between pretty and shocking, between degradation of women and respect.

❖ If you see a muscle mag and your four-year-old boy's eyes are glued to the bikini crotch, try, "Good muscles. But he's showing off more of his privates than Daddy or any other nice man would."

Do we have the right to make these value judgments? Ab-so-positively.

Lesson: *Rough, mean-looking people smiling and not wearing many clothes are not our taste. They are not nice.*

SECTION 3: MOMS IN ACTION

There is another option available to us, which most of us won't have time for. But if I mention it maybe it'll give you some ideas for some things you might be able to do.

Every race, color, and creed is represented in all forms of the media. Why? Because it reflects the glorious melting pot that is America? Because it is more honorable and just? Because it is better for the self-esteem of each individual? Get real! We see diversity because every race, color, and creed in America has *buying power.*

American business, supported by democracy and capitalism, is the most egalitarian, nonjudgmental institution in the history of mankind. My dollar is as good as your dollar is as good as his dollar is as good as hers. American business wants them all.

We may be tiny. We may be just a bunch of moms. But we can wave our dollars, one at a time. And if we all wave enough of them, just as we've seen the representation of races and types shift in the media, so we can effect a change to clean it up.

If you don't want to see so much violence and pornographic sex, and you feel like doing something in the public sector, let your dollars do the talking.

Write one letter about one image that offended you. Here is a sample:

Dear President of Tri-County Olds,

We bought our car from you and have no complaints about your service or the car itself. In fact, we are very pleased with both. I am writing to you about something different.

I saw your ad last night on the five o'clock Channel 3 news. During the same ad break and the next one, Channel 3 repeatedly ran pictures of a baby-sitter hitting a baby. This did not even happen locally. They kept running the picture, over and over again, saying to "stay tuned for more on this shocking story."

My four-year-old was in the room. She got upset and asked me why the mean lady was beating the baby. I had to explain that there are some terrible people in the world.

I turned off the news before it was over.

The reason I am writing to you is to tell you that if you continue to advertise on a station that brings that kind of violence into my living room, I will not buy my next car from you.

Maybe you could suggest to the station master that violence like this is offensive, particularly during the dinner hour when families are watching. If you explain that your customers are complaining, maybe he will come to his senses. Maybe he doesn't realize that it doesn't make people watch, it makes people turn off the TV.

Since you advertise on that station, I'm sure they'll listen to you a lot faster than they'll listen to a letter-writing mother!

I believe in freedom. I would not like to see the government say what we can and what we cannot watch. On the other hand, I would like to be free from such violence, particularly before ten o'clock at night when my children are likely to be influenced by it.

Thank you for your time.

Your name

Proud owner of a 1995 Olds—we're almost due for a new car!
P.S. My husband agrees, he just doesn't have time to write to you.

If one out of every ten of you reading this writes one letter about one offensive thing you have seen to one individual businessman who is footing the bill for that image, we will begin to see a shift in the number of offensive images that come our way relentlessly.

Why write to the advertisers and not call the station? The station looks at ratings. If you turn off your set it doesn't matter. Millions of other people are watching. But the owner of Tri-State Olds takes every customer seriously. He cannot afford to lose their business.

Wave those dollars!

They'll clean it up faster than you can say, "We're sensual, not cheap! We're lusty, not easy! You can't push us around, knock us down, or tie us up! We're moms with a mission: Clean up your act or go bankrupt!"

SUMMARY:

❖ Limit the amount of time your child watches TV to make sure it's a learning experience rather than a spaced-out freebie baby-sitter.

❖ Give your child a moral framework, and make value judgments about the seamier images that permeate our daily lives.

14

In Sickness and in Health, Till Death Do Us Part

In a world created by parents, days would be sunny and funny. My dazzler would forever stay as enchanting and high-spirited as she is today. Your beezer would shriek, "Mamma! Look!" with perpetual trust in his eyes. Our beloved children would throw back their heads and laugh for the sheer joy of being alive. Eternally.

Yet the only constant in life is change.

The only thing we all do is die.

The unyielding final truth makes each moment with our children rich. Poignant. Important and sublime.

If you think too much about death, you might as well not bother being alive.

But there's a thought way back in all of our minds.

I, too, will go someday.

My child will have to say good-bye.

Just as we pave their way toward adulthood and the joy of life, we need to smooth a path toward an inevitability that is as unknown to us as to them.

Your child will be examined routinely by doctors, unless your religion precludes it. He will have fevers, catch colds, and suffer the discomforts of common childhood diseases. He may have accidents that require medical attention.

The mood we create around routine medical events, including the birth of a sibling, will have a profound effect on our child's present and future. If we are considerate we will make the minor events easier to go through. Furthermore, creating trust rather than fear in medical procedures will give him inner calm to face whatever is in store for him later.

How we introduce him to the natural progression of life, including varying degrees of illness as well as the fact that each life must end, will stay with him as he grows up and realizes that he, too, shall have to go.

That he, too, will have to stretch his hand across time to the child he loves.

Who will in turn have to say good-bye.

SECTION 1: CHILDREN'S RX

We have two goals in handling routine medical events:

1. Getting through them as painlessly—both emotionally and physically—as possible.
2. Creating a trusting mood that will help our child during any more serious events he may be confronted with.

With these goals in mind, first let's look at who's taking care of our kid.

A. YOUR PEDIATRICIAN

Pediatricians have become a very patient-conscious group of doctors. Your child has every right to expect kid-friendly treatment.

The practice:

❖ The office should be clean, cheerful, and stocked with decent toys.
❖ The nurses, receptionists, and all physicians in a group practice should know how to engage a child of any age.
❖ The receptionist and staff should not frown if your child cries.
❖ You should be able to call in—*a lot* if you need to in the first year—without feeling as if you're imposing.

The examination:

❖ The doctor should engage the child before beginning the physical exam.
❖ Both you and your child, in age-appropriate language, should be told what's coming.
❖ This does not entitle you to a medical education. He should not have to explain in detail *what* he's looking for in her ears, but he should tell both of you *that he's going to* look in her ears.

❖ A good doctor will certainly tell you before giving your baby a shot. I suggest that you, in turn, tell your baby, ''The doctor is going to give you a shot. It won't feel good. Mommy will hold you.''

❖ For all procedures on kids over one year old, they should hear amusing or informative kid things. ''I see Big Bird in this ear!'' ''This shot is going to feel like a nasty bug bite. It won't feel good, but we need to do it to keep you healthy.''

❖ The doctor should warm the stethoscope, or have cute *Sesame Street* figures on it, or in some way introduce the object into your child's sphere so she does not experience it as an assault.

❖ The visit should be a pleasant experience with a couple of unpleasant moments inserted into the fun.

The medical approach:

❖ It is not useful for you and the doctor to be in conflict about the kinds or amounts of treatments prescribed.

❖ There is a great deal of controversy about *antibiotics*. Read up on this issue. If after having done your homework your pediatrician is giving what you consider too many antibiotics, you should be able to discuss this. If the physician is unwilling or unable to explain the course of treatment and waves your questions away, this is not a good physician for your child.

❖ The *ear infection* issue is up for discussion. Just as in deliveries, where it has been documented that too many cesareans are taking place, so many highly respected pediatricians are questioning the number of ear-tube insertions. If your child is prone to ear infections, inform yourself about recent findings. You should be in agreement with your doctor's method of handling the problem.

If the entire practice does not meet the needs of you and your child, find another doctor.

Nonmedical issues:

❖ A person who went to medical school was obviously interested in and had a talent for correctly interpreting measurable, physical symptoms and finding the right medical cure. This quantitative approach, so very valuable and mandatory for good medicine, is less useful in other areas.

❖ ''I see here on your chart that your baby is one. Get rid of that bottle.'' This is the kind of advice an informed mother may need to take with a grain of salt.

❖ Sleeping, eating, emotional and intellectual development, and behavior are paced *individually*. While there is a mathematical formula for successfully prescribing antibiotics based on weight, advancement of the infection, and other quantitative information, with a known dosage and course of treatment, there are no right and wrong answers or prescriptions for behavioral and developmental issues. There are only suggestions that may or may not work for you and your child.

❖ If you find a doctor who is nice to you and your child, whose medicine is up-to-date and impeccable, but whose advice on behavior doesn't always sit well with you, follow his or her *medical* prescriptions to the *T*. This is what you want your doctor for.

❖ If you find a medically reliable pediatrician who offers *individual advice that suits your child,* you have won the pediatrician jackpot. Don't bank on winning this jackpot any more than you base your financial future on winning the lottery!

B. GOING TO THE DOCTOR
Child's Rights

Starting from your infant's very first pediatrician's appointment, *tell your child that you're going to the doctor.*

❖ If you spring a doctor's visit on children, it makes them afraid. Ask yourself this: Do you spring a visit to the playground on them? A visit to Grandma's? To pick up Daddy at the train station? Of course not. You pave the way for pleasant experiences by allowing them anticipation. By the same token, allow them preparation for an experience that may not be so pleasant.

❖ Most one- and two-year-olds recognize the waiting room, if not the parking lot. The fact that you didn't prepare them will engender concern, fear, terror, or betrayal, depending on your child's temperament.

> **Lesson:** Mommy helps me prepare for something I might not love by arming me with information, even when I don't really like the information.

Parents' Choice

❖ If you become so tense around doctors that you feel your child may pick up your fears, let your husband take her.

❖ If you have a mildly neurotic aversion to doctors, understand that this current experience is not the historical one that messed you up. Let go of your fear. This is an instance where being a mother can help you grow up!

❖ Although time and working schedules are tight for many of us, I think it's best for a parent rather than a care giver to take a child to the doctor, even for a routine checkup. Some children become frightened. For some it's the only time, besides falling down, when they hurt. In terms of building long-term comfort in the face of medicine, a parent's presence during the early years is important. It is also medically sound to hear what your doctor has to say firsthand, rather than having your care giver report or even speaking on the phone to the doctor later after he's spent an entire day examining children. *Your* child is fresh in his mind, including all the little things, when he is in the room with her.

C. HELPING YOUR SICK KID
I. Is He Sick?

Many general parenting books give you excellent rundowns on symptoms, how to recognize childhood diseases, when to call the doctor, and the treatments of choice to help you evaluate the medical care your child is receiving.

They are by far the best sources to consult for specifics. But I sometimes find them, like doctors, to be a little bit more "by the rule and by the book" than might always be warranted, particularly with insignificant instances of "being sick."

I've also noticed that firsttime moms in particular have a tendency to worry. Sometimes we pull out the atom bomb when all we really need is a flyswatter.

There are a couple of steps you can take before turning your child upside down, grimacing, and inserting a rectal thermometer. These are not always hospital-accurate methods. They don't need to be. You need to know whether your child needs medical or mom treatment.

Temperatures

With an eye toward keeping medical procedures kid-friendly, you can determine by the comforting feel of Mommy's touch if your child has a fever.

You can feel a fever. Both your hands and your lips are excellent tools! Children's foreheads and cheeks are often warm simply from being overheated or from the ambient room temperature. But ears are a dead giveaway. If you feel hot little ears you can use several benign ways of taking his temperature.

If, however, his whole body is pulsating with feverish heat—which, I promise, you can really feel—call your doctor immediately, who will advise you from there. He will either require a rectal reading or let you know which method below is acceptable.

Ear thermometers are quick, easy, and not experienced as invasive by most children. If you can afford one, figure it's about ten bucks a year for the first six years.

If you can't afford one, hold either a rectal or oral thermometer under your baby's arm for at least five minutes. Many moms find this easiest and least upsetting to a baby while nursing or giving a bottle. For toddlers, cuddling and reading a book together works to keep your child's arm close to his body.

Under 100 or 101 or 102 degrees, depending on the doctor you ask, your child is yucky-sick. If you feel you need to, a phone call to your doctor will suffice. Over that, your doctor will advise you. Point of information: a baby or young child with a fever of 105 is definitely sick, but not necessarily scary-sick like you and I would be with a temperature that high. If you should get a reading this high, or your child's temperature rises fast, you should call your doctor immediately.

Band thermometers that change color when placed on the forehead are fun and good enough to weather your toddler or preschooler through a normal cold. Put it on you own forehead. Have your child watch the colors change. Then put it on your child's forehead while he stands in front of the mirror. They do not give a hospital-accurate reading, but put you in the ballpark enough to know where you stand. If they shoot way up suddenly, call the doctor immediately.

Digital thermometers are fun as soon as your child reaches an age where you know he won't bite (some mature threes through fives). Let him push the button to turn the thermometer on. Let him watch until the flashing stops. Let him put it in his own mouth. Let him hold it and watch until the numbers stop rising. As soon as he can read numbers, let him tell you what it says. Again, should you get a very high reading, call the doctor.

All of these noninvasive, fun ways of gauging temperature are perfectly safe for monitoring low fevers. You really only need to use a rectal thermometer for a very sick child, under a doctor's explicit request.

Treating Symptoms with Over-the-Counter Remedies

Although I am not medically trained, I would like to suggest that we use our good common sense by dispensing symptom-relieving, over-the-counter drugs very judiciously.

We have consistently found over time that most drugs have side effects and/or long-term effects. Your child's cells are growing rapidly. I would think twice about loading up a child with symptom-relieving concoctions at the drop of a Kleenex, even if your pediatrician says you can.

If your child is unable to sleep at night and the whole household has been up for several nights in a row, that would seem to me a reasonable time. During the day, however, if your toddler has a runny nose . . . he has a runny nose. Although uncomfortable, your kid is just plain sick. He doesn't need drugs.

However, there are ways besides over-the-counter medicines to make a kid who feels crummy feel better.

2. Mommy's the Best Medicine

What can you do when he doesn't feel well? *Shift gears and stay home!*

Babies and Toddlers

- ❖ Keep your child away from other children, both for the other children, naturally, and for the sake of your own. His resistance is down. He doesn't need to be exposed to something that may make him really sick, as opposed to just crummy-sick. This may mean missing toddler classes, birthday parties, and other wonderful planned activities.
- ❖ If he's all stuffed up, prop him up. A couple of pillows underneath a crib mattress or some extras if he's already using a bed will do the trick.
- ❖ Take him into the bathroom, shut the door, blast a hot shower, and make a nice steam room.
- ❖ Take a bath with him.
- ❖ Many babies and toddlers, when they're sick, like to lie on their mommies like limp dishrags until they feel better. For the twenty-four-hour period of the worst of a cold, chicken pox, and other childhood diseases, *hold him.* If you work, call in sick yourself if possible. Life is short. You may never again have the opportunity to provide such complete, utter comfort to another living creature.

Lesson: *Mommy makes me feel better when I don't feel well.*

Preschoolers

Once you cancel all regularly scheduled activities, here are a few suggestions to get you through the day.

* ❖ Books, videos, and CDs. There are many good "rainy day" crafts books on the market.
* ❖ Quiet play.
* ❖ Chicken soup.

The night is another story. Many children like to be held when they're sick. This is a personal decision, but I think a sick kid who wants to be held at night and gets to be held is a kid who feels emotionally secure when he's well.

At The Parenting Center, all of us who teach have two family rules for our sick kids:

* ❖ Don't send them back into the world of children until their fever has been gone for twenty-four hours. If you do, don't be surprised if you're in for another week of being sick.
* ❖ When they're sick, forget bed rules. Two days after a fever is gone—back to business. Period.

Question: Does all this holding promote whiny, hypochondriacal crybabies who pretend they're sick when they want to be held?

Answer: If the only time you hold your child or pay attention to him is when he's sick, you may be encouraging him to act sick, feel sick, and possibly even *get* sick in order to feel loved. But if your child is getting plenty of love and attention every day, then getting his needs met when he's feeling down will only strengthen his emotional foundation in the world.

Special Tip for Kindergartners: "Mommy, I Don't Feel Well . . ."

Around five kids start catching on that human beings actually feign being sick. The movie *E.T.* introduces this idea quite artistically!

* ❖ For the child trying out his baby wings on cutting kindergarten, let the thermometer be your friend. (By the way, tuck this in the back of your hat for elementary school!)

❖ Say as sympathetically or as neutrally as suits your personality, "You don't feel well? Let's take your temperature."

❖ When it's normal, say matter-of-fact, "No fever. Let's get ready." Let the thermometer be the bully, not you.

❖ If your child actually does have a fever, make sure you affirm what he's said. "No wonder you don't feel well. You're sick."

If your child pulls this once or twice during kindergarten, he is exploring an interesting phenomenon. If on the other hand your child says this every day for a week, or at regular intervals such as every Wednesday, you've got a different circumstance. Either something is not going well at school, on the way to school, or in the playground, or there is an activity that is throwing him for a loop on a certain day. These kinds of maneuvers deserve a different treatment, including careful talking with your child and maybe the teacher, not simply the thermometer.

3. Giving Prescribed Medicine

It is quite likely that a few times during the first five years of your child's life you will be shaking that bottle of pink, bubble-gum-flavored antibiotics, and you and your sick offspring will have those dreaded face-offs four times a day.

Although there are some children who never seem to mind, there are others who hate taking medicine their entire lives. Others suddenly hit rough patches during one or more developmental stages.

Remember, the bottom line is that, if prescribed, they have to take their medicine.

Caution: Do not stop giving antibiotics the moment your child feels better. If a person takes just some, all he does is kill off the weak bacteria, allowing the stronger ones to grow even stronger and develop their own immunity to the antibiotic. Even though it's tempting not to have to face the last several days of this sometimes-unpleasant experience, you are risking your child's life in the future when he may really need a potent antibiotic to cure a life-threatening infection.

A syringe applicator is the best bet in my experience. Measuring spoons tend to spill. As the child grows older, the syringe gives the child more control over the experience.

Here are a group of pleasantries by age that might help you avoid a forceful dosing.

Under Two

The general idea is to make it as small a deal as possible.

❖ Have some pleasurable toy ready to distract your child immediately after giving the medicine. Some children also like a bottle ready with something they prefer the taste of.
❖ Even for a very young baby, explain ahead of time that you have to give them medicine, rather than suddenly making a surprise attack.
❖ Try not to look hideously upset yourself.
❖ Syringe it into their mouths.
❖ Do it fast, get it over with, and move on.

Lesson: *I don't exactly understand why Mommy shoves that thing into my mouth, but it's bearable and afterward she shows me the most fascinating picture books.*

Two- to Three-year-olds

From now on the idea is to have the child involved in *taking* the medicine, rather than *getting* the medicine. Remember that some kids like to drink something to clear their palates.

Here are several approaches that usually work.

❖ Let them put the syringe into their own mouths and push the plunger.
❖ Play a "give the medicine to dolly first" game. Your child can hold the syringe, "give" it to a doll, then put it in her own mouth and push the plunger for real.
❖ If they're back in nursery school or day care after a few days at home and have a week of dosages left, get the teacher to help: Let them show off to the other kids by taking their afternoon dose by themselves, like a big kid, in front of everybody.
❖ Remind them on the second or third day how awful they felt just yesterday and how fast this medicine works.

Lesson: *Mommy lets me take my own medicine. She must think I'm pretty grown-up!*

Four and Up

Give him as much power over the experience as you can. You can also add his increased interest in art and letters.

- ❖ Make a chart of the ten days, four times a day.
- ❖ Let your child mark off each time he takes his medicine. Magic Marker, crayons, stickers, a computer-generated chart, or one that stays on the screen—any method that's fun.
- ❖ Let him continue to push the plunger himself.
- ❖ If he's really having trouble, let him decide how many counts before it goes down (try and keep the number under one hundred!). Some children like to count themselves; some like to choose the number and have the grown-up do the counting. If we're still in resistance land, incorporate, "I'm counting to three and then down it goes."

Lesson: *I am in charge of taking my own medicine. I better keep that chart going. What color shall I choose today?*

For a Particularly Resistant Child

If your child enjoys "absurdity" you can play a silly game that sometimes deflects the bad mood.

- ❖ "I'll give you one minute to carry on about taking your medicine. After that, down it goes. Okay, on your mark, get set, go! You're not screaming enough! That's not quite loud enough!"
- ❖ Clock the minute by your watch, then say, "Stop!"
- ❖ Usually by then you're both laughing. Hand the child the plunger, and down it goes.

If you use common sense, common consideration, and are an informed consumer of medical services, the chances of your child developing a positive attitude about medical procedures are high.

Remember, the goal is twofold. First, you and your child's normal, everyday experiences will be more enjoyable. Secondly, you will create a comfort around medical procedures and being sick so that in the unfortunate event that something nonroutine should occur, your child won't be paralyzed with fear by something as benign as a thermometer.

SECTION 2: ADULT'S RX

A. WHEN YOU'RE NOT UP TO SNUFF

Every once in a while you—yes, you, Mom, that supercharged, non-stop driving force behind the family—are allowed a moment, a day, or even a couple of days when—dare I say it?—you are sick.

❖ Some people advise you to take over-the-counter symptom relievers, put on a little blusher, and go on about your business. I say nuts to that. Schlepp around the house in your robe and slippers. It will give you the illusion that you have a life of your own left!

❖ Pray that your husband will at least open up a can of Campbell's. This is a good time to teach through example that adults take care of each other.

❖ If your husband should get felled, be nice to him. This is a good time to show small children that adults are vulnerable and also need to be taken care of sometimes—and that they come through on the other end.

Food for Thought: "I don't need some book telling me to be nice to my husband when he's sick!" If you and your husband are nice to one another when you're sick and you have a small child in the house, you are in the minority. We are under many pressures: time, work, money, responsibilities. In addition, many of us weren't handled as well when we were children as you are handling your little one now. Therefore, many men become grumpy; many women martyr themselves. Many partners get mad if the other one breaks down. You're not alone if you and your husband have not worked out a nice, postbaby way of handling each other when one of you isn't feeling well. You would do your whole family a world of good by simply being nice to each other. It's not always as simple as it sounds.

B. "WOMEN'S" ISSUES

Moms, I want to talk about *menstruation*. Most of us have our periods; they crop up like clockwork. But I suppose because of the intimate nature of the topic it's as if our periods simply do not exist in most parenting literature. Yet so many women in my classes have been curious about how to handle the whole subject that I'm going to talk here, in print, as straight as if you and I knew each other well.

Although different families have different degrees of openness, I would advise even in the most open homes that you keep your period to yourself during the toddler years. This may mean closing bathroom doors in homes where this is not a habit.

If you succeed in keeping your period out of your toddler's awareness, it gives you the chance to address it when he's older, which might make the topic easier to explain.

However, as often happens because of either stains on the sheets, toddlers bursting into the bathroom, or any other normal part of a day with a child, your child may see some signs of your period. Please explain that mommies bleed once a month, it's not a boo-boo, it doesn't hurt, and all women do the same thing when they're grown-up. If you say the blood she sees is "nothing," you will be lying. She cannot help but wonder what horrible injury you are covering up.

If they find any pads or tampons (or diaphragms and condoms, while we're at it), feel free to make up anything you want! Stuff mommy uses, bathroom things, any innocuous answer will do. Caveat: If you look shocked, guilty, secretly amused, or any other expression that indicates that your toddler has stumbled onto a special treasure trove of emotional riches, you are in for more and more questioning!

If they come in on you when you're changing your pad, "a special diaper for mommy" is a way to explain what the thing itself is. At that point they need a simple explanation such as the one above so they don't connect it with Mommy not being toilet trained.

I do not think it is useful for a small child to see a tampon being inserted. It prematurely introduces the idea that we stick things in our bodies.

Many small children come up with the idea of how much fun it would be to shove a raisin in their nose, for example. I would advise letting them discover any "insertion game" on their own, rather than leading the way. Even if your family routinely leaves bathroom doors open, I would make a serious attempt to be sure that your child is busily engaged and/or supervised by another grown-up to limit the possibility of your being walked in on.

However, should your child happen to see you either putting one in or taking one out, don't freak, scream, or any other kind of response that would indicate that something is "wrong." Please explain that it is a special thing that only grown-up women do. Men don't and children don't. If you have a daughter, now might be a good time to say, "Someday you will do this too."

Your mood around the introduction and further handling of this topic will profoundly affect your daughter's own feelings about being a woman when she is older. It will also profoundly influence how your boy feels about "women's stuff" when he matures.

If you have a normally "closed" home, you can continue to keep the topic out of your child's realm for quite some time. If your child is used to never seeing you in the bathroom, you might not want to have the very first image, for either a boy or a girl, be one of blood.

But if you have an "open" home, in which your child routinely sees you in the bathroom, you might consider consciously allowing your three-year-old to see you change a pad.

Without a lot of fanfare or special invitations, loosen up on the closed-door policy when you are changing your pad. I still think a tampon is not such a hot idea. I would also suggest that if you are doing this for educational purposes, time it so that your flow is light. You're teaching your child, but at the same time stacking the deck a bit so she doesn't see so much blood that it's hard for her to comprehend that this isn't an injury and doesn't hurt.

Girls are getting their periods earlier than they ever have. Some as early as nine, many begin at ten. If your daughter is comfortably, securely, unself-consciously introduced to menstruation by her own mom when she is quite young, you will have laid the foundation for her to mature without any of the discomfort and secrecy about such a normal occurrence that many of us still feel. This is why I think most parenting literature pretends this area of womanhood doesn't exist.

Furthermore, although there is a great deal of advice out there about how to introduce your elementary-school *girl* to menstruation, many *boys* are still kept from all knowledge of it. This sets up an uncomfortable illicitness or secrecy that I don't think is healthy for either gender or for their subsequent relationships. I feel that if the topic is handled without nervousness when they're small, before sex becomes a topic of overriding interest, they might have a healthier attitude than the generally prevailing one today.

While we're on "unmentionable" parenting topics, I'd like to kick out the jams completely and include another topic that many of the moms in my classes ask about: *PMS.*

PMS is real. I have seen too many women going through it to ignore it. I have seen moms come into my classes extremely distressed about how they lost it yesterday with their kids.

If you, like many, suffer from this once-a-month meltdown, there are many mainstream and alternative methods that work for some women. They include vitamins, dietary limitations and supplements, and meditation, to name a few. But just in case you don't have time to do a thorough investigation of PMS, meditate, and deal with your two-year-old at the same time, here are some tips:

❖ See if you can arrange to be off-duty, either with your husband's help, with a baby-sitter, or with somebody who can pinch-hit for you, particularly if your child is in the twos. A mom with PMS and a toddler throwing a tantrum are not the most salubrious couple.

❖ You can accuse your husband of having forgotten the toothpaste on purpose on the camping trip you took in 1989. You can call your sister and leave a spiteful little message saying you'd really appreciate her returning that lilac cashmere sweater that she insists you gave her even though you merely lent it to her last Christmas. In short, you can say off-the-wall things *to grown-ups,* who are able to not take high-strung assaults personally. But try as hard as you know how *not to seriously overreact to your child.* It's not fair.

❖ Counting to ten, counting to one hundred, taking five deep breaths, or leaving the room are all useful tricks when you feel your pressure cooker about to explode.

❖ Also, try a variation on this theme: ''Mommy's feeling prickly today. I would really appreciate your not being difficult, because my patience is very thin.'' You'd be surprised how responsive a little child can be. Even if your child's behavior doesn't ''improve,'' meaning he doesn't become a different child, you have acknowledged that *you* are in a bad mood. This is very important in helping even the youngest child understand that *he* has not done anything wrong.

SECTION 3: BIRTH OF A NEW BABY

The entire sibling issue is complex and filled with both large and small nuances. There is a whole school of psychology founded simply on a person's position in the family. There are popular books about how to stop rivalry.

It is beyond the scope of this book to try to cover all the specifics of what may occur in your family, since the variations are endless. You may already have twins, a two-year-old, a four-year-old, an adopted first child with a biological second on the way, or vice versa. Each of these situations will present its own interesting dimensions.

Rather than attempt, and fail, to address the myriad individual moments that your family will face, I would like to give some generalizations that will set the mood. They try to address the most-common concerns that moms share about the introduction of a sibling.

I'd like to suggest two concepts to hold on to during your pregnancy, delivery, and expansion of your family to include its newest member. Although these ideas may seem self-evident, I find that often we get so balled up in specific complications of a new situation that we sometimes forget the heart of the matter.

Whenever you find yourself wondering if you're handling something in the best way, see if one of these generalizations helps you out.

A new child is an addition, not a subtraction.

We are sharing our family time, not dividing it.

In Chapter 4 I gave you what I consider some helpful philosophical ideas to offer your child when the question "Where do babies come from?" arises, as well as some general guidelines on walking your young child through the process of gestation.

Here I'd like to cover the most-common concerns about siblings the mothers in our classes voice.

A. BEFORE YOUR CHILD KNOWS
I. Useful Choices

❖ The time has come to tell when your belly is too big to ignore (from the child's point of view), when your child can no longer sit on your lap easily, or when your child says, "Mommy, are you getting fat?"

❖ Past your first trimester, but still not showing, you might want to mention in passing how cute babies are. "Maybe we'll have a little baby in the house one of these days." In this way you plant an idea that your child has time to integrate.

2. Avoid Telling Too Soon

Although you may be ecstatic the moment you know for sure, I suggest you hold your horses on sharing the good news.

Let me remind you of a sobering statistic. One out of every four pregnancies ends in miscarriage. Getting past the first trimester is the hardest. If you introduce the pregnancy too early, you run the risk of having to explain that it didn't make it, an issue that might be better avoided if possible. That's the grim reason for holding off.

From your child's point of view nine months is an eternity. It makes him focus unduly on a far-off future event, rather than paying attention to the present, a much more productive way for a young child to spend time.

If you discover that your child has found out earlier than you would've liked, through overhearing or the "well-meaning" person who has mentioned it to him, tell him how happy you are and how you *hope* you will have a new baby sometime. It is not fair to raise a child's expectations about something that you cannot guarantee. Furthermore, you have put it far enough in the future that it's not something he has to dwell on now.

B. AFTER YOUR CHILD KNOWS
1. Useful Choices

❖ Open your heart and your child's heart. Talk about all the people we love. We love Grandma, Grandpa, Aunt So-and-So, baby-sitter, etc. This reinforces the idea that we can love many. It is not necessary to introduce the idea that your child may be afraid you won't continue to love him when the baby comes. Some children never even think that. Talk about how much love you have, not how little.

❖ Tell your child ahead of time, "Babies cry a lot. They can't play with you right away." Don't set up a fantasy land of pure delight that is contrary to what we know the reality to be. Prepare your child.

❖ *Games:* Talk, sing, and read stories with your child to the baby *in utero.* Toward the end of pregnancy many children enjoy games like, "Come on out! We're ready for you!"

2. Things to Avoid

❖ Don't introduce a "talk" about how he feels about the impending birth. Often during "talks" a mother's own anxieties come up. Avoid suggesting that he may feel put out or jealous. Do not try in advance to soothe feelings that for all you know may never come! The very fact that you're talking about them may introduce the feelings you were trying to avoid. If, however, your child should express any thoughts, don't try and shut him up. Listen and respond to what he says, don't use it as an opening to introduce your own projections.

❖ If you know the gender of the baby, don't share it with your child. Don't talk about "your new baby sister [or brother]." Make up a fun *in utero* gender-free name if you want to call it something besides ''the baby.'' In the unfortunate event that something goes wrong, your child will have to deal with a more tangible and therefore more difficult loss. Losing a hoped-for baby will be hard enough. Losing the baby sister that she had already begun to love is extremely difficult.

❖ Choose books for your child about the arrival of a new sibling very carefully. Most of them on the market now introduce crummy ideas. ''Mommy's going to have a baby.'' Drawing of a pregnant mommy with child. ''Grandma will come.'' Picture of the smiling grandma and child. ''You will feel sad and miss Mommy.'' Picture of miserable kid. ''But then Mommy will come home with new baby!'' Picture of the mommy holding new baby and kid standing next to them. Who needs it? Choose books only if they do not take it upon themselves to introduce misery.

C. PREPARATION FOR BIRTH

❖ Arrange who's going to be with your child when it's delivery time.

❖ If whoever you choose—for example, your mother—lives farther than fifteen minutes away, make a backup plan. A nearby neighbor who your child is comfortable with is best.

❖ Make sure to tell your child all the arrangements if your child is older than one.

❖ If your plan is to drop your child off at a neighbor or nearby relative's house, help your child pack a bag—including his favorite bunny—at the same time that you pack your bag.

❖ If your arrangements are for your child to stay home and have someone come over, you might like to establish trust by the following: ''Before I leave I'll tell you.'' Wake your child and say, ''Mommy's going to go have the baby now. I'll be back soon.'' Some children go right back to sleep (since it's usually in the middle of the night); others are up for a while. If this is a plan you like, make sure whoever is taking care of your child understands that your child may be up for a while and is prepared to play or read to them.

❖ Other families prepare this way: ''If you wake up in the morning and find Gerrie sleeping on the couch, it means Mommy went to have the baby. I'll be home soon.''

❖ If you are using a midwife in a birthing center or at home, make sure that you provide coverage for your child other than your husband, who you may need. Not all deliveries go smoothly; not all children go along with sharing the birth as planned.

❖ Make it clear ahead of time with whoever is taking care of your child that they *not* tell your child whether you had a boy or girl. This is special family news for you, your husband, and your child to share.

❖ Some families like to take their child to a toy store a week or so before delivery day and buy a dolly so that you can take care of babies together.

D. HOSPITALIZATION
Routine Birth

Although hospitals usually allow siblings to visit the maternity ward, if you have a normal delivery and will be released after one, two, or even three days, you might consider *not* having your young child visit the hospital.

A visit usually sounds so ''Kodak Moment'' in fantasy. Everything in soft focus: you smiling beatifically, wearing a little light-pink lip gloss; the new baby nestled comfortably at your breast; your husband protectively over you; your firstborn, combed, smiling, cuddled comfortably next to you. The reality is often different. Although smiling beatifically, we often look wan and haggard. We are often hooked up to this and that, making cuddling for your firstborn difficult if not impossible. The new baby is often red-faced, squash-eared, and squalling. Your husband is yawning and making faces of disgust, drinking dreadful hospital coffee, perched on a hard chair because nobody can get near that hospital bed.

But even if you chose a beautiful birthing center, free from unpleasant ''hospital paraphernalia,'' there still exists one real, overriding probability that might be better if avoided: *Many young children, once reunited with Mommy, do not want to leave.* Then you're involved in a family drama. Grandma, or Daddy, dragging a screaming toddler from his mommy. Who is choosing to stay with the new baby.

As I say, your choice. But on a routine delivery I would seriously consider nixing a visit.

❖ Don't force your child to talk on the phone to you. Sometimes they don't want to.

❖ Don't be surprised if when they do get on the phone, they want to rush off because Grandma is about to take them to the zoo!

❖ Your toddler or preschooler does not need to be privy to how long or how difficult labor was or any of the other unpleasant aspects of birth. There is time to learn about these things later.

Nonroutine

If there is a medical reason that you will be in the hospital for an extended stay, then your firstborn needs to come see you. In that event the hospital will have visiting hours, etc., and a social worker who will have many useful ideas beyond the expected. Make sure someone packs toys, books, etc., for a visit with Mommy. If you can avoid it medically, don't make the visits so short that they are more of a tease than a visit.

E. COMING HOME

❖ Let someone else carry the baby—and everything else—so that your arms are free for the big hug your child might want. (This applies also if you decide to have your child visit in the hospital.)

❖ Don't be surprised if your child doesn't want a hug. Be prepared for possible anger that you were gone. Keep your hands free for as long as you can. Usually after a few minutes your firstborn will decide that a hug sounds like a good idea after all.

❖ Bring a present home for the firstborn "from the baby." Choose a toy that will keep the older one busy, which after the initial greeting will give you time to get yourself and the baby organized.

❖ Sometime during the first few days, if not the very first day, have your older child choose one of his toys for the baby. Make sure he knows it has to be soft. No matter how many presents your second child gets, keep the older one's gift as the only one in the baby's bassinet or crib (or in your bed, if that's where the new one will sleep).

F. VISITORS

❖ When they call to ask when they can come, ask them not to ignore your first one! They'll all say, "I'd never!" Most need the reminder anyway.

❖ If your friends and family will all come bearing gifts, have a stack of little "big brother" presents wrapped and tucked away, just in case they didn't bring something for both of your kids.

❖ When they make a big fuss over the baby, make sure the elder is not excluded.

G. BECOMING A FAMILY
I. How You Can Help

❖ Rule number 1: Relax. The individual temperaments of your children will dictate what goes on as much, if not more, than anything you do or do not do.

❖ During the first week or so, if your older one has to miss a planned activity, so be it. You are involved in something new.

❖ If the new baby is colicky, make sure your older one gets a break. This includes a visit to a neighbor's, a walk outside, or something other than simply being in the house with a crying baby.

❖ When you nurse or feed the baby, try "Time to read!" rather than "Time to feed the baby." Have a slew of new books tucked away for this special time. This way, feeding the baby becomes cozy cuddle time with Mommy for the elder rather than banishment. Try to pick books your newborn will like. (Only half-kidding!)

❖ If your firstborn is clumsy or heavy-handed, don't leave them alone.

❖ Plan time—even if it's ten minutes a day—where it's just you and the older child. Plan the same amount of time, and announce it to the older one, that you spend only with the baby (even if the older one is in nursery school all day).

❖ Think twice before you run out, frantic to provide both kids with exactly the same things. We see parents eager to give them each their own room, own toys, and in extreme cases even their own TVs and baby-sitters! Being a family is giving and taking. Sharing is part of what we do with people we love.

❖ Step back if you find yourself feeling nervous and guilty when your children have to share, wait, or even do without. Learning these skills is essential. Remember, you have given them a gift: being part of a family.

2. Predictable Adjustments to Expect

The first child has been the center of the universe. It is only natural that there should be some response to another child entering the constellation.

Regressive Behavior

We see "accidents" for the toilet trained, wanting a bottle for the child who already gave it up, temper tantrums, clinging.

Here are some hints:

❖ Let them have the bottle; don't make a big deal about the "accidents."
❖ Be careful not to say, "Bottle? Oh, no! You're the big sister." Some children don't want to grow up. The label is threatening. Try to link the "big sister" idea to something they're handling well; don't use it as chastisement for something that's understandably slipping.
❖ Don't link the regression to the advent of the new arrival unless they do.

Physical Aggression toward the Baby

We talked about serious physical aggression in Chapter 2. But more typical is inadvertently hurting the baby or experimental pokes and jabs. With both we should have one goal: to teach our children that they are brothers and sisters who share the same space.

Inability to Control Hands

Toddlers are uncoordinated and not always aware of how hard they're touching. We want to teach both children that family activities are fun and cozy. Games like the following set the mood and teach the elder how to control his hands.

"This Little Piggy":

❖ Sit the baby in a baby seat.
❖ You sit next to the toddler.
❖ Let your toddler gently play This Little Piggy.
❖ If the toddler is rough, either by design or through his inability to control how hard he touches, you do the "Wee-wee-wee" part all the way home to the tummy.
❖ Tell your toddler he may be able to try that part tomorrow.
❖ Praise him when he improves.

Other supervised, fun suggestions: "Want to wiggle the baby's toes?" "Let's play Ten Little Indians"; using fingers or toes. Hold off on any face game until little hands are very, very careful and little baby is several months older!

Experimental Pokes, Jabs, Thrusts that Are Not so Intense They Need "Lay Down the Law" Responses

❖ "I'd never let anyone do that to you."

❖ Ignore the aggressor. Scoop the baby up into your arms without looking at the older one. Say, "Alexia hasn't learned yet how to control her hands. We'll play with her when she can." Walk away, ignoring the older child.

Less Useful Techniques I've Heard Of

❖ Coming down hard, with lots of shouting. Sometimes toddlers and older children feel so left out that they'll take any kind of response they can get from you. Having your face turned fully toward them, even if it's in anger, is better than you always looking down with that sickeningly sweet smile (the way they see it) at that little goo-goo! Some of them poke the baby just to get attention; that's the reason for the above suggestion to ignore the aggressor.

❖ Always keeping them separate, using gates if you have to. This creates a division and an expectation that you will tolerate their not getting along.

❖ After a hit, holding your child and telling him, "Don't worry. Mommy's not going to let you lose control." Hugging your child after he has hit a baby sends the wrong message. The words are meaningless; the hug says you condone the behavior.

H. COMMON WORRIES
Confessions Whispered by Many Mothers

"I feel guilty about the arrival of the second one, as if I'm betraying my first." Most of us are so deeply in love with our first child that we cannot imagine loving a second in the same way. The truth is, you never love two children in the same way. They are two different people. You will love the second as deeply as the first. Only different.

"I feel like I'm going to get 'paid back' for how easy my first is." Or, *"I'm scared to death I'm going to have to go through what I went through with my first."* Nature is funny. Often, in homes where the first child is "a handful," the second will be "mellow," or vice versa. But temperament is temperament. Who they are is not your "fault," neither is it a judgment, punishment, or reward for you. It is who they are.

"I'm having trouble dividing my time between my children. My older

one is used to being with me all the time, and now I don't have the same kind of time.'' You're having trouble because you're trying to achieve the impossible. You can try—and fail—at dividing your time, or you can succeed at sharing your time. If you view most time as family time, your older one will catch on. If you try and divvy up the whole day into separate components, you'll all lose.

I. DIFFICULTIES
Laid Up

If you're laid up for any reason during pregnancy, your child, of course, will have to know that you can't get out of bed.

❖ Tell your child that the doctor said Mommy has to lie down for a while. When you can get up you will be all better.
❖ This reassures your child that there's not something so serious it will never get better. Leave out that it's because you're pregnant. Linking your physical unavailability to pregnancy may set up resentment before the new baby even arrives.
❖ Expect regressive behavior from your toddler.
❖ Find as many pleasant activities as possible to do in your bed with your child.

Miscarriage

Should this happen to you, my deepest condolences.
For the early miscarriage:

❖ When it's clear you're grieving, tell him there was something that you were looking forward to that won't happen. It makes you feel sad.
❖ Do not try and pretend you're not sad.
❖ Do not burden him with having lost a baby.
❖ Hug him (this is for you, not him).

For the late miscarriage:

❖ When your child knows you were expecting a baby who doesn't make it, tell him something comforting: ''The baby wasn't ready to be born into the world. We would've loved him. We will love the next one. We can pray that he's happy wherever he is.''
❖ If you don't provide a comforting note, your child will use his

imagination to come up with more frightening things than the reality.

SECTION 4: HOSPITALIZATION

If you, your spouse, or your child has to be hospitalized for minor or major disease, here are some practical guidelines:

- ❖ Tell your child in simple language what is going on.
- ❖ Get your own small circle of friends together to help you out with child care.
- ❖ Make use of the social worker in the hospital.
- ❖ Become a member of a support group.

These last two suggestions will offer many specific ideas of how to treat a serious illness and how to help your child. But please, for your sake as well as the sake of your child, do not try to go through any hospitalization or serious illness alone.

On a less practical, but perhaps as important, note I'd like to offer these thoughts. In the last decade or so, modern western medicine has begun gathering promising data and even incorporating some of the ideas maintained by Christian Scientists in recent history and many eastern religions and philosophies for centuries. A person's state of mind affects his physical well-being.

Imaging, where a person concentrates and is able to increase his white-blood-cell count, for example, is successfully incorporated now on a fairly routine basis in many major, highly respected teaching hospitals for cancer patients requiring chemotherapy. People who live in isolation have been documented to have a higher incidence of death from heart disease than those who have any connection with other people. Although still inconclusive, there is fascinating data being gathered on the effects of group prayer on people who are ill. These are just a few areas where scientists and laymen are beginning to shift in our attitudes toward sickness and health.

If I or any of my loved ones were to become seriously ill, I offer for your consideration the course of action I would take. I would go after whatever illness it was with all the force of modern medicine behind me. I would be very wary of treating a serious disease with only what are called alternative methods. However, I would be equally as wary of relying only on medical cures. I would do everything in my power to remain hopeful. And I would try to bring to bear the power of my mind by using imagery, and the power of something unexplainable by using prayer and the love of my family and friends, to try and heal me or mine.

Only by incorporating the best of both approaches would I feel that I had done the most I could.

If a grandparent is seriously or terminally ill, the hospital may not let young children visit. Should you have the option, consider the effect of what the medical equipment as well as the physical appearance of a beloved grandparent who is ill might have.

SECTION 5: DEATH

Because of the steadily climbing age of a large proportion of first-time parents, many young children will face losing a grandparent or even a parent within the first five years of their lives.

Unfortunately, our culture doesn't give adults much help in dealing with death, let alone providing commonly accepted answers for children.

The constant barrage of movie, cartoon, and TV-news imagery anesthetizes our sensibilities, callously implying that death is not real, permanent, or particularly significant. Modern medicine seems to be in denial, acting as if death is an enemy whom we can ultimately vanquish.

But whether we pretend it's not real or manage to delay it, we cannot keep death permanently at bay. It is a natural, albeit sad, part of life.

Whether your child has to confront death at close quarters now or not until adulthood, face it he must. Your guidance will not alter the inevitability of death. It will, however, profoundly affect how your child feels about death throughout his entire lifetime.

A. QUESTIONS ABOUT DEATH

Pets die. Neighbors die. Family members die. Most children ask a variable of a time-honored question.

I. Where Do We Go when We Die?

Before we can offer an age-appropriate answer, however, it might be useful to think about the question from an adult point of view.

Some of us believe in life after death, in souls, in reincarnation, in heaven and hell. Others believe that this is it. Some of us are not sure what we believe.

But the operative word in all of this is *believe*.

The question about death is exactly like the one about birth.

We do not know where we go when we die.

This lack of knowledge makes some of us edgy, for we often feel that to be good parents we must be omniscient. Perhaps a valuable lesson for us, then, as well as for our children, might be to acknowledge the unknown.

At the same time, however, we need to provide our children with answers that comfort, just as we seek ways to comfort ourselves in the face of death.

There are many different kinds of responses we can offer our children that include what we believe to be the truth while at the same time accommodating their young minds.

Here I'd like to offer you some answers you might feel comfortable with.

Some Possible Responses

❖ For a child under two-and-a-half, a good answer to "Where did Grandpa go?" might be "Somewhere safe." Such a young child will be satisfied with a simple, comforting answer.

❖ If you have firm religious beliefs, you have ready-made answers. "When we die, we go to heaven." This is a nice, concrete answer for a young child, who may as an adult question it. Personally, I would add, "We *believe* that when we die," which acknowledges the unknown. If you offer heaven as an answer, be prepared for further concrete questions. "Can I go visit Grandpa in heaven?" "Not now" or "Someday" are answers that satisfy in the moment. If pressed, or if it comes up again later when your child begins to really miss Grandpa, you might try, "It's not your time to go to heaven."

❖ "Although our bodies no longer live, we believe that whatever is special about us goes on."

❖ "We believe that we go back where we came from before we were born."

If you cannot bear the unknown, here are some answers that we can be sure of:

❖ "Grandpa lives on in our memories now." Whether this is the answer you choose or not, I recommend mentioning Grandpa. Tell stories of things he did, taught you, or how he made you laugh. This *is* one way we live on.

❖ "We become part of nature, the grass, the trees, flowers, and the sky."

Less Useful Ideas

❖ If you believe that we don't "go" anywhere, I'd like to suggest that you think your answer out carefully. Answers such as, "We just stop living and don't go anywhere," are hard for a young child to digest. See if there's not some kind of idea in the preceding lists that you can stand saying.

❖ A point-blank "I don't know," without the addition of, "but what I think is . . ." is a tricky answer. One mother I know confided that although honest, in retrospect she felt it was not a helpful answer. Her child, who was five at the time and developmentally interested in death, became obsessed with the idea of death instead of being comforted.

❖ "We go to sleep and don't wake up." This sets up potential fears about going to sleep.

❖ Should you have your pet euthanized, rather than saying "We [or the vet] had to put Fritter to sleep," try, "Fritter died at the vet's."

❖ "He took a long trip." "He went away and can't come back." These kinds of answers might backfire when anyone needs to travel or even go on a simple family vacation.

Where do we go when we die? is a profound question that challenges philosophers and theologians. Find an answer that you can live with. But more important, find an answer that your *child* can live with. Give them an answer that acknowledges the unknown, comforts, and does not instill needless fear.

Most children, either at the time of a death or later, will ask you another predictable question.

2. Why Did Grandpa Die?

Some Possible Responses

❖ "Every life has a beginning, a middle, and an end. This was the end of Grandpa's life."

❖ "It was Grandpa's time to go."

❖ "Grandpa was ready to go." This might be particularly useful if your child knows Grandpa was very sick for a very long time.

Less Useful Ideas

- ❖ "He was old." This will cause him to worry if you say you're getting old or when you appear old to him.
- ❖ "He was sick." This makes some children afraid if they catch a cold shortly after Grandpa died.
- ❖ If someone else says to your child, "Grandpa died because he was sick," try to ameliorate. Try, "Grandpa was too sick to get better. But that doesn't happen all the time."
- ❖ If your child should catch a cold right around the time of Grandpa's death, make sure you point out that he is just "a little sick and will be feeling better soon."
- ❖ If "Grandpa" was your own dad, it is likely that you may catch a cold or get a flu. Often, when we lose someone we love, our resistance goes down. In this event you might want to tell your child, "I'm sad. I'm so sad that I don't feel well because I miss Grandpa. But I'll feel better soon." This is particularly useful if everybody's walking around saying how much better off Grandpa is now and what a blessing it is, because he's out of his misery and not so sick anymore. The minute you feel better, make sure you tell your child, "See? I'm much better now."
- ❖ "God took him." Even if you believe this devoutly, you might want to wait until your child is older to introduce this idea. This answer will worry most young children. God will take them. More upsetting, God will take you. If you feel strongly that you want your child to associate God and death, you might be laying a stronger, more positive foundation by saying, "He's with God now."

3. Will You Die Too?

- ❖ Answer truthfully. "Yes, me too. But not now. A long, long time from now."
- ❖ If he asks, "Me too?" answer truthfully. "Yes, you too. But not now. A long, long, long time from now."
- ❖ If he doesn't ask, don't introduce the idea.

Good Book: *Lifetimes* (Bryan Mellonie and Robert Ingpen, Bantam Books, 1983). This book should be required for any child *over two*. If you can, try reading it before you are confronted with having to explain death. It is the most beautiful book I have seen for small children about death.

Useful Video: *Charlotte's Web.* For the mature three-year-old and most four- and five-year-olds. Death is treated as a natural, sad, yet accepted and expected part of life.

B. GRIEVING

Children grieve for family members and pets in as many ways as adults. Any regressive behavior can be expected. Anger sometimes shows up. Carelessness, forgetfulness, and physical illness are all the kinds of things to be expected. Some children, however, will neither display nor feel sadness. They are not callous. They are young.

If you are mourning the loss of someone you love, you will grieve in your own way. As a mother, however, there is one piece of advice I'd suggest: Don't pretend that you are not sad.

C. CEREMONIES
Appropriate Places for Young Children

Any ceremony where a group of people come together to grieve and say good-bye is appropriate for a young child. These include funerals held in churches or funeral homes, as well as home gatherings such as wakes and sitting *shiva.*

For any gathering where there are many people, I would include my young child in the event. There will be many people who will be able to take turns being with the child. It might be interesting, and lingering, for even the youngest toddler to see how many people loved Grandpa and came together to honor him.

Furthermore, in any gathering there are often stories told about that person that make people smile, if not laugh. This can be a very valuable thing for a young child to witness.

Times and Places that Many People Think Are Inappropriate for Young Children

Although in some cultures and religions it is done as a matter of course, personally, I would not have such a young child as those discussed in this book actually view the body in an open coffin.

Burials, also highly personal and cultural, are another exception I would make for a child under six. I feel that might be too young to see a burial. They haven't quite integrated what *dead* means, notwithstanding all of your lovely explanations. Seeing a closed box that has Grandpa in it put into the ground and covered with earth might set up many fears that will not be easily laid to rest.

There is one other instance where I would advise that it might be best if your young child is not with you, depending on how you feel.

Throughout this book I have implicitly and explicitly suggested that during the course of your child's early years his needs take precedence over yours.

Death is an area where the opposite is true. Your need to grieve is strong and must be addressed.

Mothers want to protect their children. If you are grieving at a funeral and your little one is there, you may instinctively want to hold on to emotional control in front of your child. But it's not fair to you to have to hold back. Furthermore, other adults have the same right. Your mother or father, at the loss of their spouse, may not want their grandchild to see them lose it. Yet a funeral or burial is an appropriate place in our society where one can lose it.

Should you, your mother, or your father feel that either for the funeral or the burial, or both, they would be more comfortable if your toddler was not present, leave your child at home with a close family member.

Life, Death, Laughter, and Love: When my daughter was four I lost my dear grandmother. My husband stayed with Annie during the graveside funeral and burial. As we were getting ready to leave my mother's house, Annie sobbed, "*I* want to go to the carnival too!" It took a moment to realize she had heard *carnival* instead of *funeral*. My grandmother would have laughed her head off at that one!

SUMMARY:

❖ Help your child develop a comfortable ease with routine medical procedures. This will help in the present, as well as the future.
❖ When you add a new member to your family, increase the love for everybody rather than taking it away from anybody.
❖ Treat death honestly, and comfortably, as an unknown inevitability.

May the last part of this chapter be simply reading material for you. May all your days and nights be filled with love, joy, and happiness.

May your child never suffer from hunger: physically, intellectually, or spiritually.

May your child test your limits in ways that you can endure. When your child finds your breaking point, may you have the resources and heart to back up, fix things, and move on.

May you use every ounce of your ability to parent your child through the rough-and-tumble roads of babyhood, toddlerhood, preschool, and beyond.

May you love your child with all your heart and all your soul.

May the Lord, or whatever name you call the spirit in the universe that gives us life and takes it away, smile on you and yours.

Index